alpha time™

PROFESSIONAL GUIDE

CONTENTS

alpha™
time

COMPONENTS

These items work with the AlphaTime curriculum and can also be found on places like Amazon

Letter People CD

- Each of the twenty-six Letter People has his own theme song by which he introduces himself. Children have the opportunity to hear and repeat the letter sounds in words (oral/aural discrimination) and to move and dance to the various kinds of music (listening and motor responses).

Letter People Chatter Album CD

- Each of the five vowels arrives and explains how she gets her sound. In each skit, children have the opportunity to discuss motivations, develop a sense of humor, make evaluations and judgments. (listening, social living)

- Four dramatic readings of the Alpha Time Storybooks. Children may turn pages of a book as they hear the words they see. (relating the written and oral word)

READ TO ME Storybook Set

- These are entertaining, vividly illustrated stories about four of the Letter People, which the teacher reads to the children, or which may be looked at while listening to the "read along" recording of the story. The children develop good listening habits. (purposeful listening for detail, information, recall) The full-page illustrations lend themselves individually to picture-reading skills. Activities and discussions of the stories include all the major comprehension skills.

FABLES FROM Storybook Set

- These are entertaining, vividly illustrated stories about four of the Letter People, which the teacher reads to the children, or which may be looked at while listening to the "read along" recording of the story. The children develop good listening habits. (purposeful listening for detail, information, recall) The full-page illustrations lend themselves individually to picture-reading skills. Activities and discussions of the stories include all the major comprehension skills.

ALPHA TIME Worksheets

- These whimsically illustrated activity sheets serve as reinforcement and evaluation of each day's learning experience which the children may take home. Each has a note to the parent, thus serving as a liaison between school and home. Included are letters to parents describing the Alpha Time process.

Letter People DVD

- Contains all episodes from the Letter people PBS television show on two discs

ABOUT THE LETTER PEOPLE

There are 21 consonants called Letter Boys and 5 vowels called Letter Girls.
The Letter People are introduced in classifcations as follows:

Group I—Since all children come to school with their bodies, we introduce the first five Letter Boys as exaggerated body parts. (Their letters are made of straight lines.)

Mr. M   Mr. T   Mr. F   Mr. H   Mr. N

Munching Mouth   Tall Teeth   Funny Feet   Horrible Hair   Noisy Nose

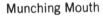

Next Miss A, the first vowel, is introduced. She has a special sneeze, a´choo, from which she gets her short sound, the sound which is used in most words in the language of the children.

 Miss A   Ă´choo

Group II—Our second group of Letter People is also related to children's experiences—this time as articles of clothing.

Mr. B   Mr. Z   Mr. P   Mr. S   Mr. V

Beautiful Buttons   Zipping Zippers   Pointy Patches   Super Socks   Velvet Vest

The next Letter Person is Miss E, who does exercises with the children.

 Miss E   Exercise

Group III—Children eat a wide variety of foods, but the four Letter Boys who are foods are all made of sweets.

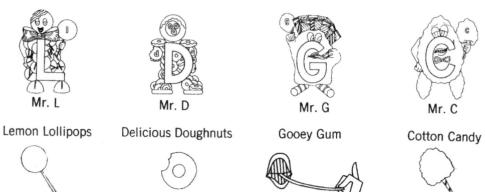

Mr. L — Lemon Lollipops

Mr. D — Delicious Doughnuts

Mr. G — Gooey Gum

Mr. C — Cotton Candy

Miss I's itch is a familiar phenomenon to children who know about poison ivy, allergies, measles or chicken pox. Is there a child who has not at times been as obstinate as Miss O?

Miss I — Itching

Miss O — Obstinate

Group IV—Next come the action boys all of whom do things every child has done.

Mr. K — Kicking

Mr. W — Winking

Mr. Y — Yawning

Group V—Then there are three Letter People who carry with them, as many children do, ripping rubberbands, jumbled junk and an umbrella.

Mr. J — Jumbled Junk

Mr. R — Ripping Rubberbands

Miss U — Umbrella

Group VI—Last come two Letter People who for the moment cannot make a sound. One of them is too quiet, the other is too mixed up.

Mr. X — All Wrong

Mr. Q — Quiet

1M₁

PLANNING AND PREPARATION: Huggable, Mr. M; Record #1; Alpha Time Masters #1 and #2.

If possible, place Mr. M outside the classroom door. Be sure there is enough clear floor space so that the children can reach the door, carry Mr. M into the room, and move around him freely.

NOTE: To make Alpha Time a successful experience it is important that each Letter Person become a real personality to the children. Maintaining an on-going conversation with the Letter People will help the children enter easily into the fun and fantasy of Alpha Time.

MEETING MR. M

Gather the children around you. Let them know that something exciting is going to happen.

He's here! He's really here! Wait until you see him. Let's go to the door to meet him.

(John), (Elayne) and (Mary), please help our visitor into our room.

Give the children plenty of time to greet the new Letter Person and to talk to him and ask him questions.

Come in! Come in! We are so glad you came.

Did you have trouble finding our school?

Did you have to ask where our classroom was?

Would you like a cooky?

This Letter Person says that he wants you to know his name and what he does. Let's listen to his music.

Hearing Mr. M's Name

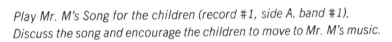

Interpretation of music

Play Mr. M's Song for the children (record #1, side A, band #1). Discuss the song and encourage the children to move to Mr. M's music.

What is this Letter Person's name? (Mr. M)

What does Mr. M tell us about himself? (He has a Munching Mouth. He likes to munch.)

How does the music make you want to move?

Show Mr. M how the music makes you move.

Let's all move to Mr. M's music.

Mr. M would like to meet everyone in the room.

We'll sing our names to him—a few of us at a time.

Singing to Mr. M

How do you do, Mr. M?
How do you do?

1

(Susan), (Barbara) and (Alan)
Want to say hello to you!

How do you do, Mr. M?
How do you do?

Following directions

The children who are named in each round of the song may go up to Mr. M and greet him with a hug, a kiss, or a handshake.

If possible, include Mr. M in the children's activities. This will make Mr. M live for them. At snacktime, Mr. M might be given a cooky. He might also be invited to join the children during art, gym or library.

TYING IT TOGETHER

Give each child a copy of Alpha Time Master #2 to look at, talk about and take home.

Look at your picture. Who is in it? (Mr. M)

What is Mr. M doing? (coming in the door)

Show Mr. M his Munching Mouth.

What does Mr. M like to do? (munch)

Where was Mr. M before we opened the door? (outside)

Alpha Time master #1 is a letter to parents introducing them to Alpha Time. It is suggested that the children take this letter home today.

ON THEIR OWN

Children may choose from the following activities:

Color Discrimination

Coloring or decorating the picture of Mr. M. (Alpha Time Master #2)

Talking about Mr. M's colors while pointing to them on Mr. M (e.g., Mr. M has red hair; he is wearing a green suit; his tie has polka dots).

Naming Body Parts

Using the pictures of Mr. M, the children may show one another parts of Mr. M's body. (e.g., Here are Mr. M's eyes; here is his hair; this is his mouth.)

Using Descriptive Words

Describing Mr. M to one another. (e.g., Mr. M has small eyes, a big mouth, a fat belly.)

Music

Moving to Mr. M's music. (record #1)

1M₂

PLANNING AND PREPARATION: Huggable, Mr. M; Records #1 and #4; the storybook, "Meet Me At The Market"; Alpha Time Master #3; paper circles or squares; a variety of art materials for making munching medals including pieces of string.

REMEMBERING MR. M

Play Mr. M's song (record #1, side #A, band #1) and encourage the children to join in.

(Tony), (Alice), (Charles) please give Mr. M a hug. Tell him that you remember his name.

Mr. M would like to whisper in your ears to show that he remembers your names too.

Singing to Mr. M

Have the children sing "How Do You Do" to Mr. M again.

(Johnny), ask Mr. M if he liked the way we sang. *(Johnny may say no. Accept any answer—since the objective is to encourage him to talk freely.)*

INTRODUCING MR. M'S MUNCHING MOUTH

Listening to Mr. M's Story

Gather the children around you so that they may easily see the pictures as you read them Mr. M's storybook, "Meet Me At The Market." The recording of this story may be played as you or a child turn the pages of the book (record #4, side A). Encourage the children to discuss Mr. M's story.

Where does Mr. M shop? (at the market)

On what day of the week does Mr. M love to shop? (Monday)

What are some of the things Mr. M munched at in the market? (marshmallows, macaroni)

Comprehension skills:
  remembering
  drawing inferences
  drawing conclusions

Why was the manager happy when Mr. M first came to his market? (He wanted Mr. M to buy many things.)

Why did he change his mind?

How did the manager feel about Mr. M at the end of the story? (He liked him.)

What would you do if you met Mr. M in the supermarket?

Show Mr. M which picture in the book you liked best, and tell him about it.

Singing A Song

Sing the Munching Mouth Song with the children to the tune of Old MacDonald. Have the children form a circle around Mr. M. Let them skip and dance around him while they sing.

> Mr. M has a Munching Mouth—
> Munch, munch, munch, munch, munch!

In his mouth he puts some foods—
Foods he likes to munch.

With a munch, munch here,
And a munch, munch there. . .

Here a munch, there a munch—
Everywhere a munch, munch!

Mr. M has a Munching Mouth—
Munch, munch, munch, munch, munch!

Repeat the song, each time naming a different food for Mr. M to munch. Discuss with the children which things are safe and unsafe to put in their mouth.

Talking About Things That May Or May Not Be Put In The Mouth

What are some things you like to put in your mouth?

What are some things you don't like to put in your mouth?

Why aren't all things that taste good, safe to put in your mouth?

Point out that many medicines taste like candy, but are not candy.

Why aren't sharp things good to put in your mouth?

What is the best thing to do when you are not sure whether or not something is safe to put in your mouth?

Making Munching Medals
Visual discrimination: color and shape

Let the children make Munching Medals. Using small construction paper squares or circles as bases, they may look for pictures of food which may be cut out and pasted on them; or, they may draw pictures of Mr. M's Munching Mouth on their medals and decorate them with pipe cleaners, bits of foil, or pieces of uncooked macaroni.

When the Munching Medals are finished, the children may punch holes in them and attach them with pieces of string so that they may wear the medals around their necks.

TYING IT TOGETHER

Give each child a copy of Alpha Time Master #3. Tell the children that Mr. M is still not sure about which things are safe for him to put in his mouth. They are going to help Mr. M by telling him which things are safe for him to eat and which things are not.

If one of the local druggists would supply poison labels for the class, the children might paste these on the items in the picture that are not safe to be eaten.

4

ON THEIR OWN

Children may choose from the following activities:

Reading Along

Hearing the recorded story, Meet Me At The Market (record #4, side A) as they "read along" in the book.

Story Telling

Looking at the pictures in the storybook, *Meet Me At The Market,* and retelling the story to each other. (If a tape recorder is available, the children may tape the story that goes with each picture as they turn the pages.)

Health And Safety

Using Alpha Time Master #3, the children may check all the foods that may be munched and cross out all those that may not be munched.

Classifying

Making charts or scrapbooks of different foods. Separate pages may be reserved for special categories (e.g., breakfast foods, dinner foods, vegetables, meats, cereals, desserts).

1M₃

PLANNING AND PREPARATION: Huggable, Mr. M; Filmstrip, *Meet Me At The Market;* Alpha Time Master #4.

There should be plenty of floor space cleared before playing the *Munch And Move* game.

INTRODUCING ACTION WORDS

Following Directions

Gather the children around Mr. M and play the Munch And Move game.

Mr. M says he wants all of us to munch along with him.

Let's show Mr. M how we munch!

Mr. M would like us all to munch and move at the same time.

Understanding related vocabulary

How can we move? (e.g., running, jumping, hopping, skipping, crawling, galloping)

(Bobby) will stand next to Mr. M.

Mr. M will whisper to (Bobby) and (Bobby) will tell us how he wants us to move while we munch.

We will do what Mr. M says, and then (Bobby) will tell us when Mr. M wants us to stop. We will all keep saying, "Munch, munch, munch!" while we are moving.

REMEMBERING SEQUENCE

Mr. M has watched *us* move. Now *he* wants to move from place to place.

He wants to be with us in the block corner. He wants to be at the painting easel. He wants to go to the book corner, and he wants to visit the housekeeping corner.

Why can't Mr. M be in all these places at the same time?

Lead the children to the conclusion that Mr. M can visit only one area at a time.

Sequence:
  first
  second
  third
  fourth

Help them to decide where Mr. M will go first, second, third and fourth. Have them repeat the sequence several times so that Mr. M will remember.

When it is time for Mr. M to move to the next area, have the children repeat the sequence so that he will know where to go.

Where is Mr. M supposed to move? (e.g., first the block corner; second the painting easel; third the book corner; fourth the housekeeping corner)

Where is Mr. M now? (e.g., the block corner)

Where does he go after the block corner? (e.g., the painting easel) (Ellen), you may take Mr. M to the painting easel.

PICTURE READING

Frame 1

Locating details

Show the children Mr. M's filmstrip "Meet Me At the Market" and discuss each frame.

Who is in this story? (Mr. M)

What is Mr. M doing? (munching marshmallows)

Where do you think Mr. M is going? (to the market)

Frame 2

What is this? (a clock)

What does a clock tell us? (the time)

This is a special kind of clock that wakes people. What is this kind of clock called? (an alarm clock)

Frame 3

Whom is this alarm clock waking? (Mr. M)

Who woke up? (Mr. M)

To what is Mr. M pointing? (calendar)

What does a calendar tell us? (the date)

Frame 4

Drawing conclusions

Where is Mr. M? (in the market)

What kind of food is on the counter? (fruit)

How does Mr. M feel? (happy)

Who is with Mr. M? (the manager)

Frame 5

What do you think Mr. M is saying?

Frame 6

Talking about details

Why is the manager surprised? (Mr. M is standing on a mountain of marshmallows.)

Who else is in the picture? (a little boy)

How many marshmallows does the boy have? (four)

Frame 7

Identifying colors

What are the people doing? (munching marshmallows)

What are some colors in this picture? (blue, orange etc.)

Frame 8

Drawing inferences

What does the manager have in his mouth? (marshmallows)

How do you think the marshmallows got into the manager's mouth?

Frame 9

Estimating

Why are the people following Mr. M?

How do they feel? (happy)

How can you tell how they feel? (their faces)

About how many people do you think are following Mr. M?

Frame 10

How does Mr. M look? (upset)

What is in the boxes? (macaroni)

Why do you think the boxes are tumbling down?

Frame 11

What are the people doing? (tasting the macaroni)

How do they look? (upset)

Why don't they like the macaroni? (it doesn't taste good; it is not cooked)

Frame 12

Predicting

What do you think Mr. M is saying?

What do you think the manager is telling him?

What has to be done to the macaroni? (it has to be cooked)

Frame 13

Making a judgment

Tell us some things that the people are holding?

What jobs do some of the people have?

Frame 14

Why do you think Mr. M is looking at his clock? (e.g., it is getting late; time to go)

When else did we see a clock in this story? (at the beginning)

Frame 15

What is Mr. M giving the lady at the check-out counter? (money)

For what is he paying? (the things he munched)

Why are his shopping carts empty? (he munched all the things)

How does the manager feel?

What is the little boy thinking?

Frame 16

What did the people bring with them? (forks, knives, napkins)

Why did they bring these things? (they will munch with Mr. M)

Frame 17

What does the sign painter have in his hand? (paint brushes)

What is he painting? (a new sign)

What do you think the sign says? (Munching Monday Market)

TYING IT TOGETHER

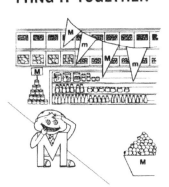

Give each child a copy of Alpha Time Master #4.

Where is Mr. M? (at the market)

What things do you see on the shelves behind Mr. M?

What things could go on the empty part of the shelves?

What are some things that are packed in cans?

What are some things that are packed in boxes?

What would happen if you put grape soda in a cardboard box?

ON THEIR OWN

Children may choose from the following activities:

Classifying

Coloring all the bottles on Alpha Time Master #4 red, the boxes blue, and the cans green.

Marking all the objects on Alpha Time Master #4 that have the shapes of circles, triangles and squares—each in a different color.

Science

Playing *Store*. A mini-market may be set up on a table—with a variety of items which the children may box, bottle or wrap. Empty milk containers, plastic jars, cans and bottles should be available for the liquids. A variety of wrapping paper, plastic and paper bags, and aluminum foil —plus a variety of empty cardboard boxes—should be available for the dry items. Such things as dry lima beans, split peas, nuts, soup, juice, milk (in pitchers), canned corn, jelly beans, dry macaroni, peanut butter, soap powder, cakes of soap, cookies and pretzels make good groceries. If a scale is available, the children may weigh the groceries they buy and sell.

1T₁

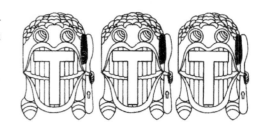

PLANNING AND PREPARATION: Huggables, Mr. M and Mr. T; Record #1; Alpha Time Master #5.

Display Mr. M. Keep Mr. T out of sight, but placed where he is readily accessible.

MEETING MR. T

Tell the children that Mr. M is unhappy.

Mr. M says that he is lonely. When we are not in school, there is no one to play with Mr. M.

What can we do to make Mr. M happy?

Lead the children to the conclusion that Mr. M would like another Letter Person to keep him company.

Mr. M says, "Close your eyes and munch five times very slowly. My munching magic will make a new Letter Person appear."

While the children have their eyes closed, bring out Mr. T.

Here's the new Letter Person!

Who can he be? Let's find out.

Have the children talk to Mr. M and the new Letter Person. Have them think of what his name might be. (If some of the children identify Mr. T correctly, ask them to check with Mr. M. This is fun for them and allows you to keep the lesson going.)

Mr. M wants to introduce his new friend.

Mr. M says, "This is Mr. T, and he has a song he wants to sing for you."

Listening To Mr. T's Song and Moving To The Music

Play Mr. T's Song (record #1, side A, band #2).

Replay Mr. T's music several times, giving the children the opportunity to move to the rhythm.

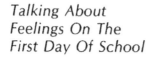

What are some of the things Mr. T told us in his song?

How does Mr. T's music make you feel?

What is special about Mr. T? (Tall Teeth)

Mr. T likes meeting all of us, but he still feels a little strange. This is Mr. T's first day of school. Ask Mr. T how he feels.

Talking About Feelings On The First Day Of School

Do you remember how you felt the first day you came to school? Tell Mr. T about it.

Some children may want to whisper to Mr. T. Others may be willing to talk aloud. Encourage them to share their thoughts by saying that Mr. M would like to hear about it, too.

Have the children show Mr. T around the room in order to make him more comfortable.

Mr. T doesn't know where we keep our things or where we play. Let's take him around the room and show him. Mr. M may come, too.

Singing How Do You Do

After Mr. T has visited around the room, the children may sing the How Do You Do? song to him.

How do you do, Mr. T?
How do you do?
(Susan), (Jean) and (Joe)
Have come to say hello to you!
How do you do, Mr. T?
How do you do?

TYING IT TOGETHER

Interpreting emotions

Give each child a copy of Alpha Time Master #5. Encourage discussion.

Whom do you see in the picture? (Mr. T and Mr. M)

What is Mr. T doing? (coming in the door)

How do we know how Mr. M feels? (His face has a happy expression.)

What makes him feel that way? (Mr. T will be his friend.)

Without talking, use your face to show us how you feel about Mr. T.

Put a mark on Mr. T so that your family will know which Letter Person he is.

ON THEIR OWN

Children may choose from the following activities:

Color Discrimination   Coloring Mr. T on Alpha Time Master #5.

Music   Playing Mr. T's song (record #1) and dancing with Mr. T.

Singing along with Mr. T.

Role Playing   Helping the Huggables, Mr. T and Mr. M, to make friends.

1T₂

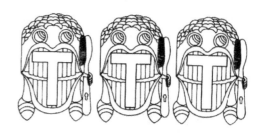

PLANNING AND PREPARATION: Huggables, Mr. M and Mr. T; Record #1; Alpha Time Master #6; child's toothbrush; paper, long cardboard strip, scissors and crayons, slip of paper for each child.

INTRODUCING MR. T'S TALL TEETH

Listening To Mr. T's Song

Play Mr. T's song (record #1, side A, band #2).

Let the children reacquaint themselves with Mr. T by talking to him and by asking him questions.

Tell the children that Mr. M is complaining about Mr. T.

Mr. M is glad that Mr. T came. There is just one thing wrong. Mr. T is so busy taking care of his teeth that he has no time to play with Mr. M.

Why do you think Mr. T is so busy with his teeth?

What is different about Mr. T's teeth? (they are very tall)

Let's ask Mr. T about his teeth.

Illustrating Tall With Hands

Tell the children: "Mr. T says that he has tall teeth!" Demonstrate the word "tall" with your hands. Encourage the children to do the same as they repeat the following Tall Teeth rhyme.

When we look at Mr. T,
Tall, tall teeth are what we see!
Tall, tall teeth are what we see,
When we look at Mr. T!

Listening To Mr. T's Story

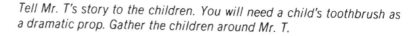

Tell Mr. T's story to the children. You will need a child's toothbrush as a dramatic prop. Gather the children around Mr. T.

Mr. T knows that Mr. M is unhappy because he has no time to play. Mr. T wants to have more time to play with Mr. M. Let's listen to his story and see if we can help him.

"I was so happy when I came to this class. I loved meeting each of you. When you left school. Mr. M and I were going to play and play and play — with the blocks, with the dolls, with the crayons, and with the puzzles!

"Guess what? I had no time to play! I had to brush my Tall Teeth. I took a tiny toothbrush (show it to the class) and started to brush just one of my Tall Teeth. Tall Teeth take a terribly long time to brush. I used up a lot of toothpaste.

"I brushed and brushed with my tiny toothbrush all through the night. Tall Teeth take a terribly long time to brush. I brushed and brushed with my tiny toothbrush all through the morning. Tall Teeth take a terribly long time to brush. . . such a long time that I had no time to play.

"I don't know what to do! What would you do if you had Tall Teeth?"

12

Making a Tall, Tall Toothbrush And Comparing Sizes

Poor Mr. T! Tall Teeth can be a problem. How can he brush them and not take so much time?

Let the children discuss Mr. T's problem. Then lead them to the conclusion that he needs a tall, tall toothbrush.

Help the children to make a tall, tall toothbrush out of a long strip of cardboard. Cut enough slits in the brush end to accommodate one slip of paper for each child. Let each slip of paper represent a bristle. Print one child's name on each bristle.

When the tall toothbrush is finished, have the children stand next to it. Decide which is taller—the children or the toothbrush.

TYING IT TOGETHER

Distribute copies of Alpha Time Master #6 to each child.

Let's look at Mr. T. Show us how tall his teeth are.

What is the size of his toothbrush? (small)

How does Mr. M feel? (unhappy)

How can we tell that Mr. M is unhappy? (the look on his face)

What is in the tall pile of things next to Mr. T? (empty toothpaste tubes)

Why do you think there are so many empty toothpaste tubes in this tall pile?

Estimating and comparing

Which is taller—Mr. T or the tall pile of toothpaste tubes?

How many tubes do you think there are in the pile?

ON THEIR OWN

Children may choose from the following activities:

Measuring

Using a ruler to measure the tall pile of toothpaste on Alpha Time Master #6. Measuring Mr. T and comparing sizes.

Using a yardstick or marks on the wall to measure how tall they are.

Counting

Counting Mr. T's Tall Teeth.

Drawing happy and unhappy faces (with turned up smile and turned down mouth) to show how Mr. M felt when Mr. T came and then how he felt when Mr. T was too busy to play.

Art

Making scrapbook of advertisements for toothpaste and toothbrushes.

PLANNING AND PREPARATION: Huggable, Mr. T; Picture Card 1; Alpha Time Master #7.

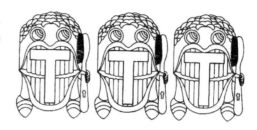

PICTURE READING

Talking About Dental Care

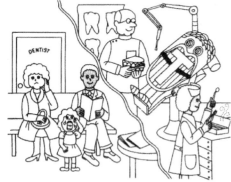

Comprehension skills

Mr. T is worried. He doesn't know the right way to brush Tall Teeth—or any other teeth.

Mr. T needs help. Whom can he ask how to brush his teeth? Who knows a lot about teeth and how to care for them? (dentist)

Display Picture Card 1. Distribute matching Alpha Time Master #7. After the children have had a chance to look at the picture, encourage discussion with questions such as the following:

Where is Mr. T? (in the dentist's office)

Who are the people in the picture? (patients, nurse, dentist)

What is the dentist doing? (showing Mr. T how to brush his teeth)

What do you think the dentist will tell Mr. T about brushing teeth?

Explain that it is especially important to scrub the teeth near the gum line where most germs (plaque) collect.

Talking about details

What is the nurse doing? (sterilizing instruments)

Drawing conclusions

Why must the instruments be kept very clean? (to keep the germs away)

Remembering and relating

Exchanging ideas

Tell Mr. T about some instruments the dentist used when you visited his office.

Exchanging experiences

Look at the faces of the people in the waiting room. Tell Mr. T how one of them feels.

Encourage the class to share their experiences at the dentist's office with Mr. T. Some children may want to dictate stories or draw pictures about their experiences.

Playing A Toothbrushing Game

Mr. T wants us to play a *Toothbrushing Game*. He wants to watch us brush our teeth. He wants us to brush his teeth for him.

Directions: Children form a circle around Mr. T. One child stands alongside Mr. T. Mr. T tells the children whether he wants to watch them brush their upper or lower teeth.

The following words may be sung to the tune of Here We Go Round The Mulberry Bush.

This is the way we brush our teeth. . .
Brush our teeth. . .
Brush our teeth. . .
This is the way we brush our teeth. . .
So early in the morning.

TYING IT TOGETHER

Give the children the following clues and ask them to point to the figure you are describing on Picture Card 1.

As each figure is identified, the children may mark it on their own Alpha Time Master picture.

Look at the people in the picture. One of them is the person who helps the dentist keep his instruments clean. Which person helps the dentist? Yes, it is the nurse. Where is she standing? (Billy), you may point to the nurse in the dentist's office.

Another person in this picture is waiting to be examined by the dentist. It is a man. Where is he? (Alice), point to the man in the waiting room.

Another person in this picture wants to know how to brush his teeth. Who is he? Where is he sitting? (Mark), point to Mr. T in the dentist's chair.

ON THEIR OWN

Children may choose from the following activities:

Role Playing

Dramatizing the story of *Mr. T Visits The Dentist.*

Art

Making an *At The Dentist* diorama. Alpha Time Master #7 mounted on construction paper makes a good backdrop.

Health

Making posters for Mr. T to help him remember which foods are good for his teeth.
Mr. T may be used to stimulate a discussion about foods that are good for teeth and foods that cause tooth decay.

Science

Conducting the following experiment which demonstrates the effect of concentrated sugar on teeth.

Materials: 1 cup of water
1 cup of *non* diet cola drink
2 teeth
2 pieces of string or thread

Method: Tie a piece of string around each tooth. Suspend one in the cup of cola, the other in the cup of water. Leave both submerged for two or three weeks, checking weekly for any change in their appearance.

Expected Result: The tooth suspended in cola shows signs of decay. The one suspended in water remains unaffected.

NOTE: Every scientist performing this experiment should keep notes (dictated or drawn) on his experiment's progress. He should be encouraged to draw his own conclusions. He should also be made aware of the importance of the control—the tooth suspended in water—which helps him in his conclusion.

Rhythms And Dancing

Playing Mr. T's music and doing rhythms and dances to the music. Mr. T makes a good dancing partner.

Counting

Using Alpha Time Master #7, to count the number of (a) people in the waiting room, (b) people in the dentist's office, (c) feet and hands in the entire picture.

PLANNING AND PREPARATION: Huggables, Mr. M, Mr. T, Mr. F; Record #1; Alpha Time Master #8.

Arrange the three Letter People so that they look as if they are talking to one another.

MEETING MR. F

Let the children discover that a new Letter Person has come to class. Give them a chance to question the other Letter People about him.

Who is the new Letter Person?

From where did he come?

Ask Mr. M and Mr. T to tell us.

Even if some of the children are able to identify Mr. F, they will enjoy asking Mr. M and Mr. T if the new Letter Person's name is really Mr. F.

Gather the children around you to hear how Mr. F came to class.

Yesterday, Mr. T and Mr. M were sitting on some blocks in the block corner. Mr. M was munching and munching. Mr. T was brushing his Tall Teeth.

Suddenly, Mr. T heard a new sound. He turned around and—guess what he saw? He saw this funny fellow flipping and flopping and falling through the door!

That's a funny way to come into a room!

"Who are you?" asked Mr. T. And this funny fellow sang a song. Listen to what he sang.

Listening To Mr. F's Song

Play Mr. F's Song (record #1, side A, band #3).

What is the new Letter Person's name? (Mr. F)

What are some of the things Mr. F tells us in his song?

Replay Mr. M's Song and Mr. T's Song. Encourage comparisons.

Is Mr. F's music different from Mr. M's? Mr. T's? How is it different?

Use your body, and show us the different ways each Letter Person's music makes you want to move.

REMEMBERING MR. M, Mr. T AND MR. F

Tell the children that instead of singing the How Do You Do? song for Mr. F, he would like them to play a How Do You Do? game. Mr. M and Mr. T will play, too.

Pick a child to stand behind one of the Letter People and have him hold it up in the air. The rest of the children sing the How Do You Do? song to that Letter Person.

Then a second child stands behind a different Letter Person, and the game continues until several children have had a chance to hold up Mr. M, Mr. T or Mr. F.

TYING IT TOGETHER

Determining main idea
Interpreting emotions
Talking about details

Give each child a copy of Alpha Time Master #8. Questions such as the following will stimulate discussion:

Whom do you see in the picture? (Mr. F)

What is Mr. F doing? (coming through the door)

How does Mr. F feel? (happy)

How can we tell how he feels? (his face)

What do you think Mr. F is saying?

ON THEIR OWN

Children may choose from the following activities:

Music

Playing Mr. F's Song (record #1, side A, band #3).

Dancing to Mr. F's Music and using Mr. F as a dancing partner.

Learning the words to Mr. F's Song. (If a tape recorder is available, the singing may be recorded.)

Art

Painting Mr. F flipping and flopping and falling through the door.

Guessing Game

Playing *Guess Who?* Two or more players may take part in this game. One child is blindfolded, and a second child gives him one of the Letter People to hold. The first child must then guess which Letter Person he is holding—only by feeling his shape. Each child may have two guesses. (This makes a good team game. Scores may be kept.)

1F₂

PLANNING AND PREPARATION: Huggables, Mr. M, Mr. T, Mr. F; Picture Card 2 ; Alpha Time Master #9; pieces of red, yellow, blue, white, and black construction paper mounted on a color chart; matching pieces of construction paper for the children; optional: drum or tone blocks.

Arrange the Letter People so that they are lying down and appear to be resting. If small blankets, pillows or mats are available, they will add to the fun.

INTRODUCING MR. F'S FUNNY FEET

Tell the children that all the Letter People feel very tired.

What are the Letter People doing? (resting, lying down)

Mr. F says that his feet hurt.

Mr. M keeps rubbing his eyes.

Mr. T keeps yawning.

What could have made the Letter People so tired?

What makes you tired?

Mr. F says that all the Letter People are tired because they had a lot of trouble helping him shop for shoes.

Hold up Mr. F.

Why do you think Mr. F had trouble finding shoes for his feet?

Lead the children to the conclusion that Mr. F would have trouble finding shoes because he has Funny Feet that are hard to fit.

Mr. F tried on shoes of many different colors. He wants us to show him each color as he names it in the story.

Discriminating Among Colors

Distribute the strips of construction paper, one strip of each color to each child. As you mention a color in the story below, point to the appropriate strip of paper on the chart you have prepared and have the children hold up the same color paper.

Mr. F says: "I have Funny Feet. Look at my Funny Feet.

"I wanted to buy shoes for my Funny Feet. Funny Feet are not easy to fit. I asked Mr. M and Mr. T to help me look for shoes to fit my Funny Feet.

"Funny Feet! Funny Feet! That's what I have!

"We all went to the shoe store. First I tried on *red* shoes. (Let's show Mr. F what color shoes he tried on.) Then I tried on *yellow* shoes. (Let's hold up the yellow). Then I tried *blue* shoes. *(Hold up the blue.)* Next I tried on white shoes. (Hold up white), and then I tried on *black* shoes. (Hold up black.)

"My Funny Feet did not fit into *red* shoes. My Funny Feet did not fit into *yellow* shoes. My Funny Feet did not fit into *blue* shoes. They did not fit into *white* shoes, and they did not fit into *black* shoes."

18

Continue the story as above, naming different kinds of footwear instead of shoes: slippers, sandals, ice skates, socks, flippers. (e.g., "I tried on boots. First I tried on red boots. Then I tried on yellow boots.")

"Finally, my Funny Feet felt so tired that we all went home."

Funny Feet, Funny Feet,
What can I do?
How would you like to have
Funny Feet too?

Let the children discuss and demonstrate what it must feel like to have Mr. F's Funny Feet.

How would you feel if you had Mr. F's Funny Feet?

Dramatizing Having Funny Feet

Show us how you would walk if you had Mr. F's Funny Feet. Show us how you would run, skip, hop, jump.

Play the Funny Feet Game with the children. (If possible, a drum or tone blocks should be available.)

One child stands behind Mr. F. He must tell the rest of the class what Funny Feet should do, and beat the rhythm — fast or slow.

Following Directions By Playing A Game

(John), you will tell us what Mr. F says our Funny Feet should do — and we will all do it. You may beat the drum (tone blocks) for Mr. F so that we will know how fast to go.

Mr. F says: "Funny Feet — run, run, run!"

All right, let's all run!

Mr. F says: "Funny Feet — hop, hop, hop!"

Several children should have a chance to be Mr. F.

Display Picture Card 2. Give each child a copy of matching Alpha Time Master #9. Some of the following questions will stimulate discussion.

Discussing The Picture Card

What kind of store is this? (shoe store)

Whom do you see in the picture? (man, woman, child, salesman, Mr. F)

Why are they there? (to buy shoes)

What is Mr. F doing? (looking at a pair of shoes)

The picture shows different kinds of things to put on feet. Tell us what some of them are. (e.g., boots, slippers, galoshes)

What is the salesman holding? (tiny shoes)

Talking About Details
Drawing Conclusions

Who do you think will try on the tiny shoes the salesman is holding? (baby)

Looking For Detail

Point to the man who is wearing glasses.

Point to (or mark) the shoes that he might want to try on.

Which shoes are for ladies?

What do you think is in the boxes on the shelves?

Are any of the shoes the same shape as Mr. F's feet? (no)

Making Comparisons

Look at the size of the boots in the picture. Now look at the size of Mr. F's Funny Feet. Will the boots fit Mr. F? (no)

Who has the biggest feet in the picture? (Mr. F)

Who has the smallest feet? (baby)

Refer to other types of footwear, encouraging the children to compare sizes by using phrases such as "bigger than," "smaller than," and "same as."

TYING IT TOGETHER

Call on children to identify (or mark on their copies) some figures in the picture. They must listen to the rhyme clues to know which figure it is. Clues are as follows:

In this picture you can tell,
I have many shoes to sell.
(salesman)

Me, oh my, what can I do?
My feet won't fit in any shoe.
(Mr. F)

My baby and I are here for shoes
Which of these can my baby use?
(mother)

Rhyming Riddles

Other clues may be given. (e.g., Point to the person in the shoe store who is a lady or mother. The next person is a man wearing a suit. The last person is someone who cannot find shoes to fit his feet.)

ON THEIR OWN

Children may choose from the following activities:

Color Discrimination

Coloring their copies of Alpha Time Master #9, using colors named in the story or any other colors.

Classification

Using Alpha Time Master #9 for any of the following activities:

Drawing lines, connecting the shoppers to shoes they might like.

Marking all the ladies' shoes red.

Marking all the men's shoes blue.

Making a scrapbook, with pages reserved for special kinds of shoes (e.g., baby shoes, sport shoes, overshoes).

Dramatic Play

Using Picture Card 2 as a background for playing *Shoe Store*.

Art

Using clay or other construction material, to make different kinds of shoes—perhaps a pair that would fit Mr. F's Funny Feet.

20

1F₃

PLANNING AND PREPARATION: Huggable, Mr. F; crayoned outline of your (teacher's) feet on piece of construction paper; drawing paper, scissors, crayons; Alpha Time Master #10.

REMEMBERING FUNNY FEET

Hold up the crayoned outline of your feet.

Guess whose feet these are?

They are not Mr. F's Funny Feet!

Maybe these feet belong to one of us.

Let's take off our shoes. Then we will put our feet on these paper feet so that we can see to whom they belong.

Comparing Sizes

Mr. F, are these (Billy's) feet? Are they as large as (Billy's) feet? Are they smaller? Are they the same size?

Mr. F, are these (Helen's) feet? Are they as large as (Helen's) feet? Are they smaller? Are they the same size?

After the children have tried, place your feet on the outline. Let Mr. F discover that they are the same size.

Mr. F is right! They are *my* feet!

Using Visual Memory

Give each child two pieces of drawing paper so that he can trace his own feet. The children can then decorate the tracings to make them look like Funny Feet. Then they may show them to Mr. F. They can compare Mr. F's Funny Feet with their own.

REVIEWING DIRECTIONAL WORDS

Mr. F is so excited and so happy with all these paper feet that he wants us to play a *Follow Funny Feet* game.

Mr. F wants us to stand up holding the Funny Feet we made. Let's listen carefully. Mr. F will tell us what he wants us to do with our Funny Feet.

Following Directions By Playing A Game

The children may play the Follow Funny Feet game. The children follow Mr. F's directions by moving their Funny Feet according to his instructions.

Mr. F says:

Developing directional concepts:
    up
    down
    around

"Follow Funny Feet.
Follow Funny Feet wherever they go.
They climb up.
They climb down.
They turn round and round.
Follow Funny Feet wherever they go."

Repeat the refrain, including directions such as climb up, climb down, skip round and round. Include the directional words practiced in the M lessons in the Munch And Move game.

TYING IT TOGETHER

Making comparisons

Give each child a copy of Alpha Time Master #10 to take home. Explain how it may be used.

You may trace one of your feet on this paper. You may trace one of your mother's feet on it too. Then you can see if your foot is bigger than your mother's—or smaller, or the same size.

You may trace your father's foot on another piece of paper. Then you can see who has the biggest foot of all, and who has the smallest!

ON THEIR OWN

Children may choose from the following activities:

Measuring

Using a ruler or tape measure, some children may measure their own and their friend's feet. They may keep a record of each person's foot measurements.

Art

Drawing or painting a mural of *Funny Feet Land.* Everything in the picture must be shaped like a shoe or a footprint.

Map Making

Making a *Funny Feet Map* which shows the road to school. Footprints should start at the child's home and lead to the school.

Game

Playing Follow the Funny Feet Road board game. (Directions are in the *Games* section of manual.)

 **PLANNING AND PREPARATION:** Huggables, Mr. M, Mr. T, Mr. F; an envelope containing a note; Alpha Time Master #11; Mr. M, Mr. T, Mr. F playing cards from Alpha Time Decks 1 and 2.

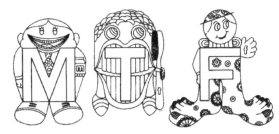

Stand the three Letter People so that their backs are turned toward the children.

REVIEWING THE IDENTITIES OF MR. M, MR. T AND MR. F

Let the children discover that the Letter People have their backs turned.

Why are the Letter People turned around?

Here is a note! Let's read it. Maybe we can figure out what is happening.

Here is what the first part of the note says.

Applying Reasoning Skills To Solving Riddles

Riddle #1

I love my snacks, my breakfast and lunch.
My mouth must always munch and munch.

Turn me around if you know my name.
That's how we play the guessing game.

Which Letter Person do you think wrote that? (Mr. M)

Which Letter Person may we turn around? (Mr. M)

Now listen to the next part of the note.

Riddle #2

I don't have any time to play.
I brush my Tall Teeth night and day.

Turn me around if you know my name.
That's how we play the guessing game. (Mr. T)

Riddle #3

Drawing conclusions

My Funny Feet leave footprints on the ground.
Follow them up and down and all around.

Turn me around if you know my name.
That's how we play the guessing game. (Mr. F)

After the last Letter Person has been turned to face the class, all three Letter People may be turned around again — and the game continues.

Riddle #4

When I go to market, the manager smiles
As I munch my way around the aisles.

Turn me around if you know my name.
That's how we play the guessing game. (Mr. M)

23

I go to the dentist and sit in his chair.
I give my teeth the best of care.

Turn me around if you know my name.
That's how we play the guessing game. (Mr.T)

Riddle #6

I went to the shoe store, but could not find,
Shoes or boots of any kind.

Turn me around if you know my name.
That's how we play the guessing game. (Mr. F)

You might make up additional riddles. They need not rhyme, but might include things that happened in class with the Letter People—e.g., (John) used my tall toothbrush to measure how tall he was; (Ellen) made macaroni for me.

Show the children Mr. M, T and F's playing cards from Alpha Time Decks 1 and 2 and explain that they belong to the Letter People. The children will help each Letter Person in turn find the two cards that belong to him.

One of these cards is a picture of Mr. M. (Barbara), help Mr. M find his picture. One of these cards is Mr. M's Munching Mouth. (James), help Mr. M pick the card that shows his Munching Mouth.

Repeat procedure for Mr. T and for Mr. F.

TYING IT TOGETHER

Give each child a copy of Alpha Time Master #11. Help the children match each set of pictures: Mr. M and his Munching Mouth; Mr. T and his Tall Teeth; Mr. F and his Funny Feet.

Mr. M wants his Munching Mouth to touch him. How can we help him?

Mr. T would like to touch his Tall Teeth.

Mr. F would like to touch his Funny Feet.

Some of the children may want to draw connecting lines between each set of pictures. Others may want to cut out the pictures and place one above the other (e.g. Mr. M's Munching Mouth over Mr. M). Other materials such as string, straws or pipe cleaners may be used to connect the Letter Person with his characteristic.

ON THEIR OWN

Children may choose from the following activities:

Music

Playing a guessing game: All three Letter People must be nearby. Use the music for Mr. M, Mr. T and Mr. F (record #1, side A, band # 1, 2 and 3). The children work in pairs. One child puts the phonograph needle on any one of the three songs, as soon as the other child recognizes the music he runs to the Letter Person whose song it is. Then the roles are reversed.

Matching Picture And Symbol

Using the M, T, and F playing cards from Alpha Time Decks1 and 2 to play one of the following games.

Game 1: The cards must be shuffled and then arranged in three groups of two matching cards each—i.e., *Mr. M* (Deck 1) and *Munching Mouth* (Deck 2); *Mr. T* (Deck 1) and *Tall Teeth* (Deck 2); *Mr. F* (Deck 1) and *Funny Feet* (Deck 2). For more challenge, a time limit may be set using an electric timer or hour glass.

Game 2: Two children each pick one Letter Person card from Deck 1. The other four cards are put into a bag. The children take turns picking a card out of the bag. The first person who picks the characteristic to match his Letter Person wins. (NOTE: As more Letter People are introduced, their corresponding cards may be added to the deck. Thus, the game becomes more interesting. Eventually, each child may start with two or more Letter Person Cards, and the winner of the game is the player who has all his cards matched, or, if there are no more cards left, the player who has the most pairs.)

Art

Making a collage of mouths, teeth and feet that have been cut out of periodicals. The cut-outs may be arranged any way the children like before they paste them down. This could be a class mural project if a large piece of paper is pinned along a wall or on a floor area where many children have room to work together.

1H₁

PLANNING AND PREPARATION: Huggables, Mr. H, Mr. M, Mr. T, Mr. F; paper strips and clear plastic tape put together to simulate adhesive bandages, several for each child (real adhesive strips would be ideal); Alpha Time Master #12; Record #1.

Place Mr. M, Mr. T and Mr. F in separate areas of the classroom. Hide Mr. H where he will be readily accessible.

MEETING MR. H

There is a new Letter Person hiding somewhere in this room.

Hunting For The New Letter Person

(Judy), is he hiding behind you?

Encourage the children to look behind each other to see where the Letter Person is hiding.

Is the new Letter Person hiding behind Mr. T?

Is he hiding behind Mr. M?

Behind whom could he be hiding?

Close your eyes and guess!

While the children have their eyes closed, place Mr. H behind Mr. F. Then tell them to open their eyes and look again.

Give the children a chance to talk to the new Letter Person and to guess his name.

Listening To Mr. H's Song

Play Mr. H's Song. (record #1, side A, band #4)

Discuss the song with the children.

What is the new Letter Person's name? (Mr. H)

What is special about him? (Horrible Hair)

What are some things Mr. H told us in his song?

How does his music make you feel?

Show us how Mr. H's music makes you want to move.

INTRODUCING MR. H'S HORRIBLE HAIR

Let's look at Mr. H.

Why do you think his hair is so long?

Mr. H says he is afraid to have his hair cut.

Why do you think he is afraid?

Mr. H has never had a haircut! Mr. H has Horrible Hair.

Following Directions

Ask Mr. H why he has never had a haircut.

Mr. H is always worried about cuts.

Give each child three paper bandage strips to use as you tell the following story:

When Mr. H was little, he was riding along on his bicycle. All of a sudden, the wheel hit a rock and—PLOP!—Mr. H fell down and cut his knee! He started to cry.

His mother said, "You cut your knee. That cut hurts!"
Quickly, Mr. H washed his cut and put a bandage on his knee.

Tell Mr. H about a time you cut your knee. Put the bandage Mr. H gave you on your knee.

Mr. H didn't want to ride his bicycle anymore that day! He decided to cut out some pictures of horses instead.

Mr. H took his scissors and started to cut. . . and guess what? Poor Mr. H cut his finger! He started to cry because that cut hurt.

Quickly, Mr. H washed his cut and put a bandage on his finger.

Tell Mr. H about a time you cut your finger. Put the bandage Mr. H gave you on your finger.

Mr. H did not want to use his scissors anymore! He kept walking up and down, trying to decide what to do next.

He wasn't watching where he was going and—THUMP!—he bumped into a piece of furniture that had a sharp edge. Guess what happened? That's right! Another cut for Mr. H!

Where do you think Mr. H got his cut this time?

Let each child decide for himself where Mr. H got his last cut. Then he may place his bandage on it.

The next day, Mr. H's mother told him that he would have to have his hair cut! Mr. H cried and cried. He kept thinking òf all the bandage strips he would need if his hair got cut. He thought he would need a bandage strip for each hair!

His mother said, "Haircuts don't hurt! Just try it!"
Mr. H said: "Cuts always hurt! I know they do! I cut my knee and my finger—and other parts of me too. And all those cuts hurt!"

His mother said, "Mr. H, if you don't get a haircut, you'll always have Horrible Hair!"

And Mr. H said:

"No haircuts for me—
No sirrreee!
My Horrible Hair can stay horrible—
That's fine with me!"

TYING IT TOGETHER

Give each child a copy of Alpha Time Master #12.

Which Letter Person do you see in the picture? (Mr. H)

What is Mr. H doing?

What might he be thinking?

ON THEIR OWN

Children may choose from the following activities:

Picture Reading

Using their copies of Alpha Time Master #12 children tell each other about Mr. H.

Art

Decorating or coloring their pictures of Mr. H.

Music And Dance

Listening to Mr. H's song and learning the words. If a tape recorder is available, they might record their singing.

Dancing to the music with Mr. H.

Dramatic Play

Using Mr. H and the other Letter People, the children may introduce Mr. H to Mr. M, Mr. T and to Mr. F. Mr. M may tell Mr. H about his Munching Mouth; Mr. T may tell him about his Tall Teeth; and Mr. F may tell about his Funny Feet.

1H₂

PLANNING AND PREPARATION: Huggable, Mr. H; Picture Card 3; Alpha Time Master #13.

REMEMBERING MR. H

Teach the children the Hair Song, Tune: Do Your Ears Hang Low? encouraging them to dramatize it as they sing to Mr. H.

Singing A Song

Does your hair hang low?
Does it grow and grow and grow?
Can you tie it in a knot?
Can you tie it in a bow?
Can you throw it over your shoulder —
Like a continental soldier?
Does your hair hang low?

Have the children sing the answer, dramatizing it as they sing.

Yes, my hair hangs low.
It can grow and grow and grow.
I can tie it in a knot.
I can tie it in a bow.
I can throw it over my shoulder —
Like a continental soldier.
Yes, my hair hangs low!

PICTURE READING

Finding details
Drawing conclusions

Display Picture Card 3. Give each child a matching copy of Alpha Time Master #13.

What kind of place is this? (barbershop)

Whom do you see in the picture? (e.g. Mr. H, barbers)

Who is having his hair cut? (a man)

What is the barber using to cut hair? (scissors)

What is the lady in the picture doing? (filing nails)

What does she use to cut the man's nails? (nail file)

What does the barber use to cut (shave) the man's beard? (razor)

Where is Mr. H? (outside the shop)

Why do you think the boy is crying?

Drawing Conclusions From Given Facts

Give the children clues to help them identify some of the figures in the picture. As the figures are identified the children may mark them on their Alpha Time Master pictures. Clues may include the following:

Someone works in the barber shop. He is cutting hair. (Ellen), please show Mr. H the barber in the picture who is cutting hair.

Someone else works here. It is the manicurist. (Richard), please show Mr. H the manicurist in the picture.

Locating information

Someone is a customer in the barber shop. It is the man having a shave. (Sharon), please show him to Mr. H.

29

Clues may be phrased in a more abstract way for children who need more challenge:

Show us the person whose job it is to cut people's hair; to cut people's nails.

Show us the man who wants a hair cut. Show us the man who wants a shave.

TYING IT TOGETHER

Have the children complete the following rhymes:

Mr. H started to write some rhymes. He wants you to finish them.

You may look most anywhere.
Nothing is as horrible as my _____(Horrible Hair).

My hair is long and shaggy, but
I will never have it _____ (cut).

ON THEIR OWN

Children may choose from the following activities:

Dramatic Play

Using Picture Card 3 for dramatizing "At The Barber Shop."

Classifying

Marking the things that have sharp edges on Alpha Time Master #13.

Counting

Looking at Alpha Time Master #13 and counting various objects, e.g., how many people there are; how many chairs.

Matching

Mr. H's playing cards from Alpha Time Decks 1 and 2 may be included in any of the games suggested in the *Games* section of the manual.

Art

Making a Mr. H collage; Draw a circle for Mr. H's head and paste pieces of string, wool, or cord along the top and sides of the head.

Sculpture

Making a Mr. H sculpture: Stick pipe cleaners and wires into a ball of clay and shape the wires so that they will look like Mr. H's head of Horrible Hair.

1H₃

PLANNING AND PREPARATION: Huggables, Mr. H, Mr. M, Mr. F, Mr. T; Alpha Time Master #14; a selection of pictures showing different hair styles.

REMEMBERING MR. H'S HORRIBLE HAIR

Display pictures of hair styles. Have the children decide which hair styles would look best on Mr. H. Let one child select a picture of one of the hair-styles and pretend to be a barber who tries to persuade Mr. H to have a haircut.

Make believe you are a barber and try to tell Mr. H that he should have a haircut. If you give Mr. H good reasons, maybe he will forget about being afraid.

Remind the children that Mr. H keeps refusing. He keeps saying:

"No haircuts for me—
No sirree!
My Horrible Hair can stay horrible—
That's fine with me!"

REVIEWING MR. M, Mr. T, Mr. F AND MR. H

Explain the Hiding Game to the children:

Mr. H wants all the Letter People to play a *Hiding Game* with him.

We will all close our eyes.

(Harry), you take *one* Letter Person out of the room with you. The rest of us will try to guess which Letter Person is hiding.

Encourage the children to think of which Letter Person is hiding by identifying the Letter People who are left in the room. Have the children think aloud as they figure out who is missing—e.g., I see Mr. M and his Munching Mouth. I see Mr. F with his Funny Feet. I see Mr. H with his Horrible Hair. It must be Mr. T who is hiding.

The child who did the guessing may open the door to see which Letter Person is hiding.

INTERPRETING A POEM

Mr. H liked the way you played his *Hiding Game*. Now, he wants all of us to ride his own special horse! What do you think Mr. H's horse looks like?

Let's ask Mr. H questions about his horse.

Have the children include questions about the horse's name, his color, his size and where he lives.

(Before reading the poem to the children, discuss the words "reins" and "saddle," explaining their purpose in riding. If possible, show the children a picture of a horse with a saddle and reins.)

Mr. H says one day someone was riding his horse. Something strange happened to the person riding the horse. Listen to the poem and see if you can discover what happened.

I am Mr. H's horse, as you can see.
Come to the farm and ride with me.
Put on my saddle, don't be slow.
Hop on my back, I'm ready to go.
Pick up my reins and hold them tight.
Turn me to the left, then to the right.
Now kick your foot and make me run.
Let's run and run and have some fun.

I'm galloping faster than before.
Why don't I feel you upon me any more?
I wonder what the trouble can be.
Whoops—where's that rider who was riding me?

Who is telling this story? (Mr. H's horse)

What do you think happened to the person riding the horse?

Reread the poem slowly, having the children dramatize it as you read.

TYING IT TOGETHER

*Positional terms:
on, under, in, behind*

Give each child a copy of Alpha Time Master #14. Questions such as the following will help the discussion:

Where are the Letter People? (on a farm)

Who is sitting on the horse? (Mr. H)

What animals do you see? (e.g., horse, pigs, chicken)

What animal is under the horse? (chicken)

What animals are in the pen? (pigs)

What building is behind Mr. F? (barn)

ON THEIR OWN

Children may choose from the following activities:

Crafts

Making wigs out of partly shredded crepe paper or cotton wadding.

Using copies of Alpha Time Master #14 as a background for a barnyard diorama.

Sorting

Cutting a variety of pictures of hair styles out of magazines and sorting them according to color, hair length, or texture. (e.g., wavy, straight, curly)

Classifying

Making a scrap book or chart of pictures of horses or of farm animals.

1N₁

PLANNING AND PREPARATION: Huggables, Mr. N, Mr. M, T, F, H; assorted noisemakers; Record #1, Alpha Time Master #15.

Collect a group of noisemakers (e.g. horn, drumsticks, bell), and place them in a large box or under a table so that you can produce them one at a time. Put Mr. N someplace where he will be hidden—but easily accessible.

MEETING MR. N

Experimenting With Noisemakers

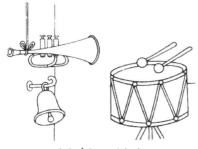

Making Noises With Body Parts

Gather the children around you. Show them the first noisemaker (e.g. bell) and give them a chance to identify and discuss it.

How does the (bell) make noise?

Let several children use the (bell), and ask each one: "What are you going to let the (bell) make?" Then introduce the other noisemakers and have the children make noises with them.

Now we are going to make some more noises. This time, we will make noises by using parts of our bodies.

What kind of noise can we make with our hands? (clap)

Let's clap hands!

Have the children make noises with their hands, fingers, tongue, teeth and feet. Then have them stop at a signal from you.

Can you stop clapping whenever you like? (yes)

Following Directions

When I hold up my hand, stop clapping.

Yes, you can stop!

Repeat, substituting clapping with snapping, stamping, emphasizing the fact that the children can stop when they want to. Tell the children about the new Letter Person they are about to meet. He makes a noise that he can not control.

Now we will meet a new Letter Person. One part of his body makes noise all the time. Noise, noise and more noise! He wants the noise to stop, but he cannot make it stop. Close your eyes, and the other Letter Boys will bring him in. When you look at him, see if you can tell which part of his body makes noise all the time.

Have the children gather around Mr. N. Lead them to the discovery that Mr. N's nose looks like a horn.

Play Mr. N's Song (record #1, side A, band #5) for the children. After they listen to the words, they may move to the music.

What is special about Mr. N? (He has a Noisy Nose.)

Let's make noises for Mr. N's Noisy Nose. Take any of the noisemakers we used, and make noises for Mr. N and his Noisy Nose.

Be sure you ask Mr. N how he liked the noise you made for his Noisy Nose.

Now, make noises for Mr. N by using a part of you body. (e.g., hands, feet)

Mr. N is not sure you know his name, and he doesn't know any of your names.

Developing Social Amenities: Introductions

Give each child a chance to say: "Hello, Mr. N. I'm (John)." Make sure each child repeats Mr. N's name as he introduces himself.

REINFORCING THE CONCEPT OF NOISE

Mr. N would like us to sing and play a game about noises. Listen to the song first, and then we'll all sing it and make noises.

Singing The Noisy Song

Play or sing the Noisy Song to the tune of "Join In The Game." Then, the children may participate.

The Noisy Song
Let everyone make noise with me (noise, noise).
It's easy—as easy as can be (noise, noise).
Let everyone join in the game (noise, noise).
You'll find that it's always the same (noise, noise).

Before we sing, someone will ask Mr. N what kind of noises he wants us to make. He may want us to make noises with our bodies (e.g. clap or stamp) or with a noisemaker.

TYING IT TOGETHER

Distribute copies of Alpha Time Master #15.

Who is in the picture? (Mr. N, a boy and a girl)

What are the children doing? (holding their ears)

Why do you think they are holding their ears?

How can we know how the children feel? (expression on their faces)

ON THEIR OWN

Children may choose from the following activities:

Crafts

Making noise makers of their own, using such materials as marbles in tin cans, bells, beans in boxes.

Classifying

Marking Alpha Time Master #15 with a different color for designated things such as hands, noses, legs, heads.

Art

Painting "noisy" and "quiet" paintings. Children would use sharp colors such as reds, yellows and bright violets for the noisy paintings, and pastels (greys, blues, and pale greens) for the quiet paintings.

Music And Dance

Listening to Mr. N's song (record #1, side A, band #5).

Dancing with Mr. N.

1N₂

PLANNING AND PREPARATION: Huggables, Mr. M, Mr. T, Mr. F, Mr. H and Mr. N; Record #1; Picture Card 4; Alpha Time Master #16; five small squares of blank paper.

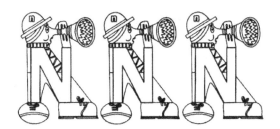

REMEMBERING MR. N AND HIS NOISY NOSE

Playing A Noise-Guessing Game

Play Mr. N's Song. (record #1, side A, band #5) Let the children reacquaint themselves with Mr. N.

Tell the children that Mr. N wants to play a Noise-Guessing Game with them.

Mr. N is a noise specialist. He says he knows every noise in the world.

He can tell the sound a pencil makes when you tap it.

He can tell the sound a ball makes when you bounce it.

Using context clues

Use anything you like and make a noise with it. Mr. N will listen and listen. He will not peek. Then he will whisper the name of whatever is making the noise to someone in the class.

Let's play with Mr. N.

(John), you and Mr. N will close your eyes. You may put your hands over Mr. N's eyes so he can't peek.

(Mary), you pick something in the room and make a noise with it. Mr. N will whisper to (John) what he thinks made the noise. Then (John) will tell us.

Continue the game until several children have had a turn at closing their eyes and guessing for Mr. N.

PICTURE READING

Hold up Picture Card 4 and give each child a corresponding copy of Alpha Time Master #16.

Where is Mr. N? (in a music store)

What kind of things are for sale here? (instruments)

What other things in this picture make a sound? (e.g. clock, cash register, radio, phonograph)

Show Mr. N one of the things and tell him about it. Tell him what kind of noise it makes. He loves different noises!

Call on children to point to objects in the picture by listening to descriptions of them. Clues such as the following may be used:

One of the noisemakers makes a ringing noise. (alarm, cash register)

Talking about details
Locating information
Pictorial comprehension

Find the noisemaker that has money in it. (cash register)

Find the noisemaker that makes noise when you beat it with a stick. (drum, triangle)

Find the noisemaker who is a Letter Person. (Mr. N)

DISTINGUISHING BETWEEN FIRST AND LAST

Tell the children that they are going to help the Letter People get on line.

Each of the Letter People wants to be first on line.

Everytime they try to line up, there is trouble.

Taking Turns

Let's show them what happens when everyone tries to be first.

Ask five children to demonstrate what happens when each wants to be first on line.

Tell the Letter People why everyone can't be first at the same time.

What can the Letter People do so that it will be fair for each of them?

Lead the children to the conclusion that the Letter People should take turns being first. They may arrange the Letter People in line, giving each one a chance to be first. Each time, let them call out the name of the Letter Person who is first and the Letter Person who comes next.

Mr. T says that if he can't always be first on line, he wants to be last.

Let the children arrange the Letter People in line, putting Mr. T last.

Oh dear! There's trouble again. Now all the Letter People want to be last on line.

Once again, have five children demonstrate what happens when each wants to be last.

Why can't they all be last at the same time?

What can the Letter People do so that it will be fair for each of them?

TYING IT TOGETHER

Mr. N has thought of a game that we can help the Letter People play. In this game, each will have a chance to be both first and last on line.

Show the children how Mr. N's First and Last Game is played.

Use five small squares of paper. Let some children draw a simple outline of one of the Letter People on each square. Place the squares in a container.

One of us will pick a piece of paper from the container. The Letter Person whose picture is on that piece of paper will have a turn at being first. We will place him *first* on line.

Then one of us will pick another piece of paper. The Letter Person whose picture is on that piece of paper will have a turn being *last* on the same line.

We know who is both *first* and *last* on line. Where will the other Letter People go?

Continue the game so that other Letter People have a chance to be first and last.

ON THEIR OWN

Children may choose from the following activities:

Classifying

Using Alpha Time Master #16 to mark all the objects that ring; make noise when you blow in them, when you strike them, when you shake them; have strings; are made of metal; are made of wood.

Dramatic Play

Using Picture Card 4 and Mr. N in playing *"Music Store."*

Number Sequence

Playing a variation of the *First and Last* Game by writing numerals 1-5 on five squares of paper and then picking them one by one out of a box and lining up in order.

Matching

Mr. N's playing cards from Alpha Time Decks 1 and 2 may be included in the games described in the *Games* section of the manual.

1N₃

PLANNING AND PREPARATION: Huggable, Mr. N; Alpha Time Master #17; crayons, colored paper, string, and other decorations.

TALKING ABOUT MR. N'S MAKE-BELIEVE FRIEND, NEEDLEDEENOOP

Gather the children around you and the Letter People to talk about make-believe friends and Needledeenoop.

Mr. N has a friend whom the other Letter Boys have never seen. Only Mr. N sees him.

Tell Mr. N about a make-believe friend you have.

Tell Mr. N about make-believe people on television, in the movies, or in storybooks.

Mr. N's make-believe friend is Needledeenoop.

Here is how Mr. N first met his friend Needledeenoop:

Listening To
The Needledeenoop
Rhyme

"What is that?" Mr. N said.
"What is hanging from my head?
Crash! Bang! Zowee! Oop!
It's my friend Needledeenoop!"

Mr. N picked up a broom,
And chased Needledeenoop around the room.
In and out and all about—
They turned the whole place inside out!

"What is that?" Mr. N cried.
"What is hanging from my side?
Clang! Buzz! Clatter! Oop!
It's my friend Needledeenoop!"

Listening
Drawing conclusions

Mr. N picked up a broom,
And chased Needledeenoop around the room.
In and out and all about—
They turned the whole place inside out!

Needledeenoop nooped through the air.
Mr. N collapsed in a needlepoint chair.
"I give up!" Mr. N panted.
"Needledeenoop must be enchanted!"

Have the children ask Mr. N questions about Needledeenoop. They will enjoy repeating the name.

Reread the rhyme and have the children dramatize it. One child at a time might be Mr. N and chase Needledeenoop around the room.

Making
Needledeenoops

Mr. N would like to see *your* Needledeenoops. After we make them, he will tell us if our Needledeenoops look like his.

Using a variety of materials, the children may make their versions of Needledeenoop.

TYING IT TOGETHER

Distribute Alpha Time Master #17.

Who is in this picture? (Mr. N)

What is Mr. N doing? (chasing Needledeenoop)

What trouble is Needledeenoop making?

How did the lamp tip over?

ON THEIR OWN

Dramatic Play

*Inferring Cause
And Effect
Relationships*

Art

Children may choose from the following activities:

Creating a Needledeenoop play in which an invisible Needledeenoop plays pranks on an unsuspecting person.

Marking on Alpha Time Master #17 all the evidence of mischief Needledeenoop has caused.

Drawing Needledeenoop on Alpha Time Master #17.

 **PLANNING AND PREPARATION:** Huggables, Mr. M, Mr. T, Mr. F, Mr. H, Mr. N and their playing cards from Alpha Time Decks 1 and 2; Alpha Time Master #18.

REMEMBERING MR. M, MR. T, MR. MR. F, MR. H AND MR. N

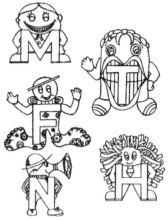

Remembering a sequence.

Group all five Letter People together in an easily accessible part of the room.

All the Letter People are talking to one another. They are all glad to be here.

Which of the Letter People arrived first? (Mr. M)

(Jimmy), ask Mr. M why he is glad to be here.

Who came next? (Mr. T)

(Ann), ask Mr. T why he is glad to be with us.

Continue questioning Mr. F, Mr. H and, finally, Mr. N.

Have the children sing The Letter Song to the tune of "Bingo."

*Singing A
Letter Song*

Following directions

We are a class that has some friends;
And these are their names, sir:
M, T, F, H, N!
M, T, F, H, N!
M, T, F, H, N!
And these are their names, sir.

Repeat substituting one clap for the letter M—i.e., "(clap), T, F, H, N!"

Repeat again, substituting two claps for the letters M and T—i.e., "(clap), (clap), F, H, N!"

Repeat again, substituting three claps for M, T and F—i.e., "(clap), (clap), (clap), H, N!"

*Continue until all the letters have been replaced by claps—i.e., "(clap), (clap), (clap), (clap), (clap)!
And these are their names, sir."*

Tell the children that Mr. N would like to listen to riddles about himself and all the other Letter People.

*Identifying The
Letter Boys
Through Riddles*

Listen to each of these riddles and decide if it is about Mr. N, or if it is about one of the other Letter People. When you think you know which Letter Person the riddle is about, you may come up and hug him.

My Munching Mouth munches fast and slow.
I munch and munch wherever I go.
(Mr. M)

When you look at me,
Tall, tall, Tall Teeth are what you see.
(Mr. T)

My Funny Feet run and hop.
My Funny Feet flip and flop.
(Mr. F)

No haircutting for me.
With Horrible Hair I'd rather be.
(Mr. H)

It's never quiet when I'm around.
My nose makes the noisiest sound.
(Mr. N)

The dentist is the one I went to see.
He showed me how to brush teeth properly.
(Mr. T)

Shoes, sandals and sneakers are fine;
But none fit feet that are like mine.
(Mr. F)

A barber is someone I'll never see.
Razors and scissors are not for me.
(Mr. H)

On Mondays, I shop for quite awhile.
I must munch up and down every aisle.
(Mr. M)

You played a Noise-Guessing Game with me.
I guessed your noises easily.
(Mr. N)

Matching Characteristics With The Letter People

Show the children the playing cards for M, T, F, H, N Alpha Time Decks 1 and 2. Have them identify the pictures on each. Then, they may sort them and give to each Letter Person the playing cards that belong to him.

These cards belong to the Letter People, but they are all mixed up.

What pictures are here? (i.e., Mr. M, Mr. T, Mr. F, Mr. H, Mr. N, Munching Mouth, Funny Feet, Horrible Hair, Noisy Nose, Tall Teeth)

(Joey), give one of the pictures to the Letter Person to whom it belongs and tell him why it belongs to him. Then, you may call on someone else to pick a card.

TYING IT TOGETHER

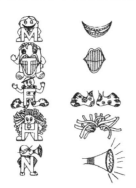

Give each child a copy of Alpha Time Master #18.

Tell the children that the Letter People want to touch their special features. Some children may want to cut out the characteristic and paste it next to the Letter Person. Others may want to draw lines connecting the two. Still others may want to use pipe cleaners or tape to "touch" one to the other.

ON THEIR OWN

Children may choose from the following activities:

Matching

Using the playing cards for M, T, F, H, and N from Alpha Time Decks 1 and 2 for playing any of the card games suggested in the *Games* section of the manual.

Music

Using bands 1-5 on record #1, side A, the phonograph needle may be put on any spot on the record; the object is to see how quickly the music can be identified.

Crafts

Making stick puppets by cutting out the Letter People on Alpha Time Master #18 mounting them on construction paper or oak tag, and stapling them to an ice cream stick.

1A₁

PLANNING AND PREPARATION: Huggables, Mr. M; Mr. T; Mr. F; Mr. H; Mr. N; Miss A; Alpha Time Master #19. Records #1 and #3.

Display all the Letter People except Miss A. Conceal Miss A behind a closet door or outside the classroom. Record #3 (Meet Miss A, Side A—Band 1) should be in place, ready to be played.

MEETING MISS A

Gather the children around you to talk about what the Letter People have been doing:

After you left school yesterday, those Letter Boys were just impossible! They wouldn't play. They kept saying, "We have nothing to do. We have nothing to do."

Talking About How It Feels To Have Nothing To Do

Tell one of the Letter People about a time when *you* had nothing to do.

Let several children discuss their experiences with the Letter People and with each other.

Listening To A Recorded Story

Let's listen to what happened when the Letter Boys had nothing to do. The Letter Boys will sit with us so they may listen too.

Play Meet Miss A (record #3, side A, band #1) up to the break in the story. When the story breaks (Mr. H sees the new Letter Person) reveal Miss A. Let the children examine the new Letter Person. Lead them to the conclusion that this is not a Letter Boy but a Letter Girl.

Discovering That Miss A Is A Girl Who Has A Special Sneeze

What can you tell us about the new Letter Person?

How is this Letter Person different from the others? (She's a girl.)

Why do you think the boys will be surprised to see her? (They are expecting a boy.)

What do you think her name is?

Let's listen to the rest of the story and find out what happens.

Play the record to the end of the story.

The children may want to join in the ă'choo game at the end.

ESTABLISHING MISS A'S SPECIAL FEATURE, A'CHOO

Who is the new Letter Person? (Miss A)

Imitating Miss A's Sneeze

Remember to say Miss A's name when you talk to her. She wants to make sure everyone knows her name.

What is special about Miss A? (her sneeze)

Stand behind Miss A, and sneeze for her the way she sneezes.

TYING IT TOGETHER

Give each child a copy of Alpha Time Master #19.

Which Letter People are in the picture? (Miss A, Mr. M, T, H, F and N)

Look at the Letter Boys' faces. Their faces are telling us something without words. What are the faces trying to tell us? (how they feel)

How do the Letter People feel? (surprised)

Show us how you look when you are surprised.

ON THEIR OWN

Children may choose from the following activities:

Dramatic Play

Dramatizing the story of Miss A's arrival. The children may use the Huggables as actors.

Identifying Letter Characteristics

Circling or marking each Letter Person's characteristic on Alpha Time Master #19. (e.g., Miss A's sneeze (finger under nose), Mr. M's Munching Mouth)

Sequencing (1 to 6)

Writing the numerals 1-6 on each Letter Person on the Alpha Time Master according to the order of their arrival (e.g., Mr. M—1, Mr. T—2, Mr. F—3).

Listening

Listening to the recording of Miss A's story (record #3).

Story Telling

Retelling the story of Miss A. If a tape recorder is available, the stories may be recorded and shared with the rest of the class later.

Classifying

Finding pictures of groups of people and checking or circling the girls (or women).

1A₂

PLANNING AND PREPARATION: Huggable, Miss A; Alpha Time Master #20; The M, T, F, H, N, A Alpha Playing Cards from deck 1 and deck 2; Alpha Match board.

DISCUSSING MISS A'S SNEEZE

Gather the children around Miss A and you. Wiggle your nose as though you are about to sneeze.

My nose keeps wiggling and wiggling. It feels as though I have to sneeze, but no sneeze comes.

Demonstrating Wiggling And Tickling Noses

How does a wiggly nose look?

Let's see noses wiggle!

Now my nose is tickling and tickling. It feels as though I have to sneeze, but again—no sneeze!

How does a tickling nose look?

Let's see tickly noses!

Pretend Miss A is telling you the reason for the wiggling and the tickling.

Miss A says she knows who is making noses wiggle and tickle.

She says it is her sneeze. Her sneeze loves to tease. Her sneeze wants to talk to us.

Read the poem "Miss A's Sneeze" to the children.

I am Miss A's sneeze.
I love to tease and tease.
I am Miss A's sneeze.
I love to tease and tease.
I make Miss A say ă, ă, ă for a start.
And sometimes I stop before the 'choo part!
I am Miss A's sneeze.
I love to tease and tease.
Here I come to tease you too.
Ready now—sneeze!—ă, ă, ă'choo!

Discuss how Miss A's sneeze teases. Be sure the children say ă, ă, ă before the 'choo.

Playing A Sneezing Game

Let the children dramatize the game The Teasing Sneeze.

Directions: Several children play the part of Miss A's sneeze. They run around the room, gently wiggling the other children's noses. These other children (the sneezers) pretend to start sneezing and keep saying "ă, ă, ă." Before they can say "'choo," the sneezes hold up their hands and say "Stop!" Any sneezers who forget and say "choo" are out.

EMPHASIZING THE SHORT "A" SOUND

Help the children sing Happy Miss A Has A Sneeze to the tune of Old MacDonald.

**Singing A
Song In Parts**

Happy Miss A has a sneeze—
Ă, ă, ă, ă'choo!
And with that sneeze she has a wiggle—
Ă, ă, ă, ă'choo!
With an ă, ă here—and an ă, ă there.
Here an ă—there an ă.
Everywhere an ă, ă!
Happy Miss A has a sneeze—
Ă, ă, ă, ă'choo!

We'll all sing together until we get to "With an ă, ă here." Then we'll sing it this way:

Group 1:   "With an ă, ă here—"
Group 2:   "and an ă, ă there."
Group 3:   "Here an ă—"
Group 4:   "there an ă,"
All Groups: "Everywhere an ă, ă!"

Repeat the song substituting words for "wiggle." (e.g., tickle, cold)

Note: A natural opportunity to reinforce the ă'choo presents itself any-time a child sneezes—by saying: "Miss A's sneeze is at it again! Let's hear a Miss A sneeze."

TYING IT TOGETHER

*Using Context Clues
Locating Information
Picture Reading*

Distribute copies of Alpha Time Master #20.

Whom do you see in this picture?

What are all the people doing? (sneezing)

Pick one person in the picture and tell Miss A what is making him (her) sneeze. (feathers, flowers, a cold, dust, pepper)

Sneeze the way the person in the picture sneezes.

Have the children identify the figures in the picture by listening to clues such as the following:

Show Miss A the person in this picture who is in bed; who is gardening; who is having dinner.

Show Miss A the person in the picture who is holding the pillow.

Show Miss A someone who is using a feather duster.

ON THEIR OWN

Children may choose from the following activities:

Cause And Effect

Using their copies of Alpha Time Master #20, some children may mark all the things that caused the sneeze. (i.e., the feathers, flowers, pepper)

Alpha Board Game

Using the *Alpha Match* game board and the M, T, F, H, N, A playing cards from Alpha Time Decks 1 and 2, the appropriate cards are laid on the corresponding pictures on one side of the board.

Matching

Playing any of the card games in the *Games* section of the manual, using the M, T, F, H, N, A playing cards from Alpha Time Decks 1 and 2.

1A₃

PLANNING AND PREPARATION: The Huggables, Mr. T and Miss A; blocks; Record #1; Alpha Time Masters #21 and #22; scissors; a variety of collage materials.

Stand Mr. T and Miss A near one another. Clear the block corner so that the children have room to build a tall block tower. Since they will be playing a running game, provide enough clear floor space for this activity.

REMEMBERING MISS A AND HER A'CHOO

Tell the children that the Letter People complained to you about Miss A and her ă'choo.

They say Miss A's ă'choo causes trouble. What kind of trouble do you think an ă'choo can cause?

Mr. T says he will tell us how Miss A's ă'choo makes trouble. Let's listen and see if we think Mr. T is right.

Gather the children in the block corner with Mr. T. Tell the children the following story:

Listening To A Story

Mr. T was building a tall, tall tower. He put one block down. Then he put another one on top of it, then another one, and another and another and another.

Miss A said, "Mr. T, don't put any more blocks on top of your tall, tall tower. All the blocks will tumble down."

Mr. T said, "Don't worry, Miss A. I always build tall, tall towers. This will be the tallest tower I ever built."

Mr. T added another block and another one. The top of the tower started to shake. Just as the tall tower came tumbling down, Miss A suddenly sneezed. . . Ă—Ă—Ă'CHOO!

Mr. T was very angry with Miss A. He said, "Your sneeze made the tall tower tumble!"

Miss A looked upset. She said, "The tall tower tumbled because you made it too tall!"

Giving Reasons (Inferences) For The Tumbling Blocks

Why do *you* think the tall tower tumbled? Tell Mr. T and Miss A.

How can we find out whether Mr. T was right—or whether Miss A was right?

Have the children build tall towers to discover whether the towers tumble because of the sneeze, or because they are too tall.

Experimenting: What Makes The Block Towers Tumble?

(Barbara), (Jimmy) and (Joseph)—you may all be Mr. T. *You* start building a tall, tall tower.

(Anne), (Charlotte) and (Nicky)—you may all be Miss A. As your Mr. T builds his tall tower, *you* keep sneezing—ă,ă,ă'choo, ă,ă,ă'choo, ă, ă,ă'choo.

The rest of us will keep watching and see whether it is your ă'choo that makes the tower tumble—or whether it tumbles because there are just too many blocks.

Have the children tell Miss A and Mr. T what their conclusion is.

REINFORCING THE "Ă" SOUND IN A'CHOO

Listening To Miss A's Song

Playing The A'Choo Game

Let the children listen to Miss A's Song (record #1, side A, band #6) several times. Encourage them to sing and move along with the music.

Adapt the game Duck-Duck-Goose and make it the Ă—Ă—Ă'Choo Game. Have the children sit in a circle. Choose a child to be the Ă'choo. Explain the game to the children.

(Tommy) will be the Ă'choo. As Tommy walks around the outside of the circle, he will tap each child on the head as he passes.

As he taps, Tommy (the Ă'choo) will keep saying, "ă,ă,ă." Then the ă'choo will tap one child on the head and say, "choo!"

The child who is tapped will leave his place and chase the Ă'choo all around the circle to see who will get back into the empty place first.

Continue the game, giving several children turns at being the Ă'choo.

TYING IT TOGETHER

Give each child a copy of Alpha Time Master #21.

Who is in the picture? *(Miss A and Mr. T)*

What is Miss A doing? *(sneezing)*

How do you think Mr. T feels?

What happened when we built tall, tall towers?

Have each child use paper and other art materials to make his own version of Miss A's Ă'choo. Distribute paper, scissors, paste and collage materials.

You know how Miss A's sneeze sounds. Now how do you think her sneeze looks?

We can use some paper and other materials to make an Ă'choo. Make it the way *you* think an Ă'choo looks.

Understanding Positional Terms (High, Low, Under).

You may cut it out if you like, or you may use the whole paper. You may paste on as many things as you like.

When the Ă'choos are finished the children may fly them around the room.

Sometimes the Ă'choo wants to fly very high. Fly your Ă'choo very high. Show us where an Ă'choo is when it is up *high*.

Follow this same procedure for other positional terms (below, on top of, underneath, inside, next to).

NOTE: *Alpha Time Master #22 is a letter to parents explaining the progress the children have made thus far with ALPHA TIME. This letter may be sent home with the children at this time.*

ON THEIR OWN

Children may choose from the following activities:

Music And Dance

Listening to (or dancing to) Miss A's music (record #1, side A, band #6).

Learning Miss A's song and recording it if a tape recorder is available.

Counting

Building a tall block tower and counting how many blocks it has before it tumbles. Counting the blocks in the tumbling tower on Alpha Time Master #21.

2M₁

PLANNING AND PREPARATION: Huggable, Mr. M; Record #5; stamped air mail envelope containing a piece of letter paper and addressed to Mr. M at your school (to be used again in the next lesson); Mr. M's Picture Squares; a bag for Mr. M (a shopping bag is ideal, but any bag, paper or plastic, will do); Alpha Time Master #23.

Before the lesson starts, perhaps as the children come in—or during rest period, play Mr. M's music (record #1 side A band 1) to set the mood for a discussion about Mr. M.

MR. M GETS A SOUND

Hold up Mr. M's air mail letter—so that all children can see it and begin to talk about it.

Discussing Mr. M's Air Mail Message

Something is written on this envelope. It says AIR MAIL! What does that mean?

How can we tell who is supposed to get this message? (address)

Tell the children that the message is for Mr. M. Encourage them to talk to him about it.

Ask Mr. M if he was expecting a message.

Ask him if he knows who sent the message.

Remove the letter from the envelope and show it to Mr. M, and read it to the children:

Listening To Mr. M's Message

Dear Mr. M,
   This is a message from Letter People Land where all the Letter People are born. I hope you are having fun in the classroom. You were sent to this class to do a job. You have to make a sound. You will have your own special sound to say. None of the other Letter People may use your sound.
   Mr. M, do not worry. We will always help you to remember your own special sound. Just remember what is special about you. It is your Munching Mouth. You will never forget about your Munching Mouth. You get your own special sound from the words Munching Mouth.

What does Mr. M like to do best? (munch)

What is special about Mr. M? (his Munching Mouth)

Have the children say "Munching Mouth" for Mr. M several times. Show them how to press their lips together, emphasizing the M sound.

Emphasizing The Initial Sound In Munching Mouth

We will all say Munching Mouth for Mr. M. We are going to say it in a special way.

Tell Mr. M that his sound is the first thing he hears when he says *munching,* and the first thing he hears when he says *mouth.* We will have to find lots of things that start with the same sound that starts *Mmmunching Mmmouth.*

NAMING OBJECTS THAT START WITH THE INITIAL M SOUND

*Discovering That
Mr. M's Picture
Squares Start With
The Same Sound
As Munching Mouth*

Show the children Mr. M's Picture Squares (i.e., monkey, milk, man, moon, mouse).

Pick any one of these pictures and tell us what it is.

Show your picture to Mr. M and tell him what it is.

Repeat this procedure for all the pictures.

Have a child point to each of Mr. M's Picture Squares as the class repeats its name for Mr. M. Encourage them to emphasize the initial M sound.

Why does Mr. M especially like these words? (They begin with the same sound as Munching Mouth.)

Show the children the bag you have prepared for Mr. M, and explain that Mr. M would like to keep in it all the things that begin with his sound.

*Listening To
"Prove It"*

Play the Prove It sequence on record #5, side A bands 1 and 2. Band 1 describes the Prove It procedure, and band 2 introduces the Prove It Song. Note: The Prove It process is a very important part of the learning experience. The children should "Prove It" throughout the program.

What helps Mr. M remember his sound? (Munching Mouth)

How can Mr. M be sure that *monkey* starts with his sound? *(Children may refer to the record if they are not sure.)*

We'll have to prove this word to Mr. M by saying *Munching Mouth* and then *monkey*. Tell Mr. M to watch how our lips are pressed together as we start the words.

Let's prove another word that starts with Mr. M's sound.

Follow the same procedure for the remaining Picture Squares. When the children are comfortable with the procedure play band 3 of the record letting the children participate in the Prove It Song.

TYING IT TOGETHER

Give each child a copy of Alpha Time Master #23.

Name all the things you see in this picture (matches, money, mittens, mountains, macaroni, mushrooms). Prove to Mr. M that they each start with his sound.

Why is Mr. M's Munching Mouth here?

Mr. M would like his Munching Mouth to touch something that begins with his sound. How can you make his mouth touch something? (Draw a line; cut and paste; attach a string.)

ON THEIR OWN

Children may choose from the following activities:

*Sound
Discrimination*

Looking at Mr. M's filmstrip, *Meet Me At The Market,* and naming some things that begin the same way as Munching Mouth.

Doing the same while looking at the storybook, *Meet Me At The Market.*

Music

Playing Mr. M's Song (record #1, side A, band #1) and listening for words that begin with Mr. M's sound.

Playing and participating in the Prove It Song (record #5, side A).

*Visual Memory
Game*

Playing Mr. M's Song (record #1, side A, band #1) and listening for words that begin with Mr. M's sound.

Playing a remembering game with Mr. M's Picture Squares: the object of the game is to remember the position of the Picture Square.

    1. All five Picture Squares are placed face up.

    2. Players look at the Picture Squares and try to remember the position of each picture.

    3. Turn Picture Squares face down.

    4. One player at a time points to one square at a time calling out the picture he thinks it is.

    5. As each picture is called it is turned face up. If the picture was named correctly the player may take it and continue guessing until he misses. If the picture is not named correctly, it is turned face down again and the player loses his turn.

    6. The player who holds the most squares at the end of the game is the winner.

2M₂

PLANNING AND PREPARATION: Huggable, Mr. M, Record #5; Mr. M's bag; Mr. M's Picture Squares; magazines; drawing paper; scissors; crayons; clay; paint; paste; pipe cleaners; Alpha Time Master #24.

REMEMBERING OBJECTS THAT BEGIN WITH MR. M'S SOUND

Show the children Mr. M's bag.

Mr. M wants us to fill his bag. He says, "Please fill it with things that start with my Munching Mouth sound."

Talking About What Belongs In Mr. M's Bag

What things can we use to fill Mr. M's bag?

Tell the children to take one of Mr. M's Picture Squares (e.g., monkey) and prove that it belongs in Mr. M's bag.

All the things that start with the same sound as Munching Mouth may go into Mr. M's bag.

(Jane), Mr. M likes the picture of the (monkey). How can you prove that it may go into his bag? You say *Munching Mouth — monkey.*

Where can we find *other* things that belong in Mr. M's bag?

What things can we make?

Making Things For Mr. M's Bag; And Proving Each One

Let the children decide for themselves whether they want to look through magazines and cut out pictures of things that start with the same sound as Munching Mouth — or whether they want to draw, paint, or make things out of clay, pipe cleaners and other art materials. They must prove that each thing may go into Mr. M's bag.

Before you tear or cut a picture from a magazine, show the picture to Mr. M. Then Prove It by saying *Munching Mouth* and the name of the picture.

Together, the child and Mr. M decide if the picture may go into the bag. Follow the same procedure for the children who are making or painting objects for Mr. M's bag. When the children have finished cutting or making the objects, they are ready to put them into Mr. M's bag.

Participating In The Prove It Song

Before we put things into Mr. M's bag, let's Prove It to him with the Prove It Song (record #5, side A, band #3).

Whenever possible, help the children to rename objects so that they may go into Mr. M's bag. Anything that a child can prove may go into the bag (e.g., if he says a dime is "money").

TYING IT TOGETHER

Give each child a copy of Alpha Time Master #24. Have the children name each item shown in the picture (i.e., moon, mouse, marshmallows, man, mailbox, milk, monkey). Make sure they realize that Mr. M is shown holding his bag. Let them decide whether or not each item shown may go into Mr. M's bag and Prove It.

Look at the pictures.

Name a picture that may go into Mr. M's bag.

ON THEIR OWN

Children may choose any of the following activities:

Auditory Discrimination

Playing the Prove It Song and proving more words or objects for Mr. M.

Art

Making a gigantic Munching Mouth by drawing the outline of a mouth on the side of a carton and painting it. An opening may be cut in the middle for the children. Objects or pictures that start the same way as Munching Mouth may then be "fed" into the Munching Mouth.

Logical Thinking

Using Mr. M's playing cards from Alpha Time Decks 1, 2, and 3, children may tell Mr. M why these cards belong to him. (i.e., They show his picture, his Munching Mouth, and something that starts with the same sound as Munching Mouth.)

2M₃

PLANNING AND PREPARATION: Huggable, Mr. M; Mr. M's bag with contents; Mr. M's Picture Squares; Mr. M's air mail letter (from previous lesson); Alpha Time Master #25; one red crayon and one green crayon for each child; Mr. M's playing cards (one from each of the four Alpha Time Decks); Mr. M's Alpha Time Puzzle.

IDENTIFYING THE UPPER AND LOWER CASE LETTER M

Put your arm around Mr. M. Tell the children that Mr. M is sad. Explain that Mr. M doesn't understand how he can be in so many different words at the same time.

Mr. M says he understands about his sound, but he doesn't understand how he can be in this word and that word, and in so many other words, all at the same time.

Pretend to reread Mr. M's air mail letter from Letter People Land.

Let me see. Hmmm, hmmm, hmmm. Let's listen and see if we understand. It might be hard to make Mr. M understand.

The note says, "Mr. M, *you* are not going to be in the words. Just your *letter* M will be in words. When we see your letter M we will know it belongs to you. The M must make the sound that starts Munching and Mouth. Mr. M, your letter is easy to see. The letter M is part of your body."

Gather the children around Mr. M.

Mr. M still does not understand where his letter M is.

We'd better show Mr. M's letter to him.

Discovering The Capital Letter M On Mr. M's Body

Have the children point to the capital letter M and trace it with their fingers.

Write the letter M on the board. Write two or three words using capital M (e.g., man, mug, milk) below it to show how the letter M can be in many words at the same time.

Introduce the lower case m by telling the children that Mr. M has another kind of letter.

Discovering The Lower Case M On Mr. M's Milk Container

This is one way the letter M looks. This is the way it looks when it is capital M. Sometimes Mr. M's letter looks another way. Do you see another letter for Mr. M? Ask Mr. M where the other letter is.

Have several children trace the lower case letter m on Mr. M's milk carton.

Write the same three words on the chalkboard as before, this time using the lower case m.

Forming The Letter M

Mr. M has a good idea. He says that we can make his capital letter M by using our bodies. Each of us can be a different part of his letter.

Let's look at and touch his letter M and see how many parts we will need.

Help the children to discover that the letter M is made up of four straight lines. Have four children demonstrate for the class how to make the capital letter by lying on the floor.

(Mary), (John), (Barbara) and (Jim), you make the capital letter M for us. First, decide which part of the capital letter M each of you is going to be.

When you lie on the floor, you must keep your bodies very straight and stiff—just like the lines in Mr. M's capital letter.

The rest of us will look at Mr. M's letter and make sure your M looks like his.

If the letter was incorrectly made, ask a child to help the others.

Have the rest of the children form groups of four. Each group may form a capital letter M.

Working With Mr. M's Puzzle

Show Mr. M's Alpha Time Puzzle to the children. Have them remove one piece at a time and tell what it is. (i.e., Mr. M's capital letter; Mr. M's Munching Mouth; Mr. M's pictures that begin with Mr. M's sound) Before the children replace the pieces they may give reasons why each piece belongs with Mr. M (e.g., Mr. M has a Munching Mouth; it belongs to him. The pictures on the puzzle start with Mr. M's Munching Mouth sound. . . monkey—Munching Mouth; moon—Munching Mouth).

Use Mr. M's playing cards from Alpha Time Decks 1, 2, 3, and 4, and have the children match the pictures on the cards with the puzzle pieces.

TYING IT TOGETHER

Pictorial comprehension:
details
locating capital and lower case M

Give each child a copy of Alpha Time Master #25 and a red and green crayon for marking his picture. Discuss the picture.

What room is this? (a classroom)

What are some things you see in the room? (e.g., child, easel, ball)

Mr. M's capital letter M can be seen in many places in your picture.

When you find the capital letter M, put a mark on it. Use the red crayon.

Now look for a lower case letter m and put a green mark on it.

Find as many M's as you like and put marks on them. Then show your picture to Mr. M.

ON THEIR OWN

Children may choose from the following activities:

Motor Coordination   Using Mr. M's Alpha Time Puzzle.

Letter Tracing   Using copies of Alpha Time Master #67 to trace the upper and lower case M.

Painting the letter M on paper, or drawing it on the chalkboard.

Matching   Matching puzzle pieces with Mr. M's four playing cards.

2M₄

PLANNING AND PREPARATION: Huggable, Mr. M; box of uncooked macaroni, salt, water, cooking pot, pot holder, measuring cup and spoon; art materials; Alpha Time Master #26; blue crayons for each child; Record #4.

COOKING MACARONI FOR MR. M

Recalling Story Of The Munching Monday Market

Hold up the box of macaroni, and tell the children that it was sent by the manager of the Munching Monday Market.

Today, boxes and boxes of macaroni came to our school. They were sent by the manager of the Munching Monday Market. He cannot sell the macaroni.

Help the children to recall details of Mr. M's adventures in "Meet Me At The Market" by playing record #4, side A, band #1.

What happened to Mr. M at the Munching Monday Market?

What did Mr. M say about the macaroni? (It tasted awful.)

Drawing Conclusions From Given Facts

Why do you think the manager is having trouble selling the macaroni? (Mr. M told all the people that the macaroni in that market tasted awful. Since then, no one will buy macaroni there.)

The manager put up signs that said "Free Macaroni." Even so, no one would take his macaroni. The manager said it was Mr. M's fault.

Why did Mr. M think the macaroni tasted bad? (It was not cooked.)

The manager asked if we would please cook some of his macaroni and tell everyone how it tastes.

Following Cooking Directions

Let the children do as much of the planning and preparation as practicable. If possible, help the children cook some macaroni in the classroom for them to taste.

Read the instructions on the macaroni box aloud. Let the children decide how they will measure the macaroni, water and salt. Have them decide what equipment they will need. (measuring cup and spoon, pot, etc.)

Using Descriptive Language:
hard — soft
rough — smooth
cold — warm

Let the children look at and touch the uncooked macaroni. Have them use words to describe how it feels (e.g., hard, crumbly, rough, cool). They may then compare it with the cooked macaroni. Have them use words to describe how it feels (soft, slippery, warm).

Let each child taste some of the macaroni after it is cooked. Help the children to think of words that describe how it tastes. List their words.

Distribute paper and art materials. Let each child make his own sign.

What can the signs say? (e.g., MACARONI IS MIGHTY TASTY. . . . . YUM, YUM, YUM)

TYING IT TOGETHER

Distribute copies of Alpha Time Master #26. Discuss the picture with the children. Questions such as the following might stimulate a discussion of safety in the kitchen:

What room is this? (kitchen)

What is cooking on the stove? (a pot of water, macaroni)

What would happen if you touched the pot while it was hot? (hands would burn)

What should the woman use when she wants to take the hot pot off the stove? (pot holder)

Pictorial comprehension: talking about details drawing conclusions visual discrimination for size

Why must she be careful to keep clothing, paper and her hair away from the flame? (A fire could start.)

How else can a fire start in the kitchen?

Talking About Safety

What should the woman tell her baby about touching the handle of a pot on the stove?

What should she tell the baby about matches? About sharp knives? About putting cleaning fluids in his mouth?

Today Mr. M likes blue. Let's mark a lower case letter m with a blue crayon. Find some more lower case m's and mark them with a blue crayon.

ON THEIR OWN

Children may choose from the following activities:

Sound Discrimination

Finding, saying and marking items that begin with Mr. M's sound on Alpha Time Master #26.

Location

Using Alpha Time Master #26 to find items that are (a) on the table, on the chair and on the stove; (b) inside the glass, inside the box and inside the pot.

Shape Discrimination

Marking all the things on Alpha Time Master #26 that have the shape of circles and squares.

Mathematics
Counting
Estimating
Weighing

Filling a small jar with macaroni and guessing the number of pieces of macaroni it contains. Then counting the pieces to see how close the estimate was.

Weighing macaroni and putting it into boxes.

Following Directions

Preparing other foods by following recipes. Some foods that don't require cooking are powdered soft drinks, lemonade, vegetables, salad dressing, fruit salad, butter, whipped cream, and instant puddings.

"Reading" Along
(Audio Visual
Coordination)

Listening to "Meet Me At The Market" (record #4, side A, band #1) while looking at the storybook or the filmstrip.

2M₅

TEACHER OBJECTIVES:

To reinforce the characteristic and sound of Mr. M.

To introduce the children to the months of the year.

To familiarize the children with the calendar.

PERFORMANCE OBJECTIVES:

The child will demonstrate an awarenes of the calendar.

The child will demonstrate an awarenes of the names of some of the months.

The child will say words with the *m* in initial position.

DEVELOPMENT

Mr. M made special booklets for us.

Distribute the Mr. M *All About Us* booklets to the children.

Look at the front of the booklet.
Find the words at the top.
Mr. M wants us to listen to them.

Point to the words, "All About Us."
Read them to the children.

Which Letter Person's picture do you see? (Mr. M)
Whose picture do you think is next to Mr. M?
Mr. M says that the words under the pictures will tell us.

Read aloud, "Mr. M has a friend."

Let's ask Mr. M who his friend is.

Have several children ask him.
Pretend he wants to talk to you.

Mr. M says he wanted to draw a picture of each of us, but it was too hard.
He wants you to help him make the picture look like someone you know.
If you want the picture to look like you, color the hair the same color as your hair.
Color the eyes the same color as your eyes.
Make the shirt look like a shirt you have.

What did Mr. M forget to draw on the face? (a mouth)
You can make the mouth look like your mouth.
Remember, you do not have to make the picture look like you.
It can look like anyone you wish.

Give the children the opportunity to complete the picture.

Have them open their booklets.
Point to the first sentence on the left-hand side.
Read it to the children: "Mr. M has a munching mouth."

Mr. M put a picture in the sentence to help him remember what it says.

59A

Point to the rebus of the munching mouth in the sentence.
You may want the children to pretend to reread the sentence with you.
Explain that Mr. M wrote something important in the next sentence.
Read aloud, "Mr. M's favorite month is March."
Discuss with the children the months of the year. Introduce the word *calendar*. Talk about months as they relate to the seasons of the year.

What is Mr. M holding? (a calendar)
What month do you think he is looking at? (March)
What did Mr. M tell us? (His favorite month is March.)
Why do you think Mr. M likes to talk about months?
Why do you think his favorite month is March? (*Months* and *March* start with the same sound that starts *munching mouth*. Stress the *m* in *months*, *March* and *munching mouth*.)

Mr. M took this whole page to tell us about himself.
He told us he has a munching mouth.
He told us his favorite month is March.
Mr. M says the next page is for us to tell him about ourselves.

Look at the next page.
Put your finger on the dotted line.
Write your name on the dotted line for Mr. M to see.

Select a child's booklet and read his/her sentence. (*e.g.*, Patsy has a mouth.)
Read several other children's sentences.
Have them turn to the back of the booklet.

Let's listen to what Mr. M wrote at the top.

Read aloud, "Let's talk about months."

Where did Mr. M put all the months? (on the clothesline)
Find the clothesline closest to the little bird.
Put your finger on the first month.

Its name is January.
Let's say it for Mr. M to hear.

Continue this procedure with the remaining eleven months.

Mr. M has listened to us say the name of each month.
He heard two names that start with the same sound that starts "munching mouth."
What are they? (March and May)
He wants each of us to choose a favorite month.

Give the children the opportunity to discuss reasons for preferring one month rather than another (*e.g.*, birthday, holiday).

Have the children open their booklets.
Refer them to the second sentence on the right-hand page.
Explain that Mr. M wants them to use this sentence to write their names and favorite months.

Have them write their names on the dotted line.
You may want to mention the apostrophe s. It is not necessary to go into anything more than a superficial explanation.

Explain that the sentence is not finished. To prove this, select a child's booklet and read the sentence aloud. (*e.g.*, Carol's favorite month is   .)

Mr. M says he knows why the sentence isn't finished.
It doesn't tell what Carol's favorite month is.

Read several other sentences, following the same procedure.
Explain that some children may finish the sentence by dictating the name of their favorite month for you to write.
Others may be able to copy the name of their favorite month.
Some may wish to draw a picture of something they associate with their favorite month.
When the sentences have been completed, read several aloud.
You may wish to prepare a timeline depicting the months of the year.
Encourage the children to take booklets home.
Have them ask members of their family to tell Mr. M their favorite months.

2T₁

PLANNING AND PREPARATION: Huggable, Mr. T; Mr. T's Picture Squares; a bag for Mr. T; scarf; ruler, yardstick or other stick; Record #5; paper plate with Tall Teeth drawn on it; Alpha Time Master #27.

Wrap Mr. T's Picture Squares in the scarf. Tie the scarf to a ruler, yardstick or other kind of stick so that it looks like a hobo stick. Rest this hobo stick against Mr. T. Play Mr. T's song (record #1, side A, band #2) to set the mood for Mr. T.

HEARING THE T SOUND IN TALL TEETH

Let the children discover Mr. T and his hobo stick.

Mr. T has packed his things. He is leaving. He says he won't stay unless he may have the same thing that Mr. M has.

What could Mr. T mean? (Mr. T would like a sound.)

From what did Mr. M get his sound? (Munching Mouth)

Why won't Mr. M ever forget his sound? (Mr. M's Munching Mouth is his special feature.)

Drawing Conclusions: How Mr. T Can Get A Sound

How can Mr. T find a sound that he will never forget?

Lead the children to the conclusion that Mr. T can get his sound from his Tall Teeth.

Say Tall Teeth for Mr. T so that he can hear the first sound when you say *tall*, and when you say *teeth*.

Where is your tongue when you say tall, and when you say teeth?

Help the children discover that when they make the T sound in Tall Teeth, their tongues are behind their upper teeth.

Call attention to Mr. T's scarf.

Mr. T says he doesn't remember what he put in the scarf. He wants you to open his scarf and show him each thing that is in it. This will help him to remember.

Using Related Vocabulary

Have the children take out each of Mr. T's Picture Squares, show it to the class, and name it for Mr. T (i.e., tiger, toothbrush, tent, telephone, table).

After each picture is named, repeat the name—emphasizing the initial T sound. Let the children discover that each object starts the same way as Mr. T's Tall Teeth.

Mr. T says that you always prove everything for Mr. M. *Prove It* is so much fun, he wants you to play *Prove It* with him.

Descriptive Language:
Loud—Soft
Fast—Slow

Mr. T remembers that sometimes when you sang the Prove It song, he was far away—but he could still hear you. What kind of voice did you use then? (loud)

Other times, Mr. T could not hear us when we sang the Prove It song. What kind of voice did you use then? (soft)

How else can we sing the Prove It song for Mr. T? (fast and slow)

Singing The Prove It Song

Distribute Mr. T's Picture Squares to five children. Play record #5, side A, band #3. As the Prove It song is sung, a child holding a Picture Square will name it and prove it for Mr. T. Then he may place the Picture Square in Mr. T's bag.

Replay the song, giving another child the chance to prove one of Mr. T's Picture Squares.

Tell the children that Mr. T has a game he would like to play with them. Show them the paper plate with Tall Teeth drawn on it.

Mr. T likes the sound he has from Tall Teeth. He also likes the way we sing the Prove It song. He gave us this special plate we may use for a game. Mr. T wants to tell us how we can play the game.

Playing A Tossing Game To Reinforce T Sound In Initial Position

Directions: Distribute Mr. T's Picture Squares. One child is Mr. T. The children holding the Picture Squares show them to Mr. T. He calls out the name of one of the pictures (e.g., tiger). The child holding the tiger picture calls "Tall Teeth—tiger." Mr. T turns, tosses, spins or twirls the paper plate to the child holding the tiger picture. That child catches it and then becomes Mr. T. He gives his Picture Square to a child who did not get one. The game continues as long as interest is sustained.

TYING IT TOGETHER

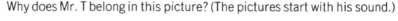

Give each child a copy of Alpha Time Master #27 to look at and discuss.

Which Letter Person do you see in the picture? (Mr. T)

Tell Mr. T the names of the things in the picture (tiger, toothbrush, tent, telephone, table and a top).

Prove each thing for Mr. T.

Why does Mr. T belong in this picture? (The pictures start with his sound.)

Let Mr. T touch something that starts with his sound.

The children may connect Mr. T to one or more objects that begin with his sound by using lines, straws, strings, pipe cleaners, ribbon, and tape.

ON THEIR OWN

Children may choose from the following activities:

Sorting And Classifying

Using Mr. T's and Mr. M's Picture Squares in a sorting game:
Begin with only 4 Picture Squares—3 for Mr. T, 1 for Mr. M. The child has to pick the one picture out of four which does not belong. For example, if the four pictures are of a tiger, a telephone, a table and a mouse, the child should take out the picture of the mouse—because mouse begins the same way as Munching Mouth, while tiger, telephone and table begin the same way as Tall Teeth. (Two or more children can work together, changing the card combinations and listening to each other Prove It.)

61

**Sound
Discrimination**

As the children become more proficient, more Picture Squares may be added and finally, all ten squares may be sorted into two groups of five. As more squares are added in later lessons, the sorting becomes more and more complex.

Continuing the Mr. T game, using the paper plate with Tall Teeth drawn on it.

**Visual Memory
Game**

Naming and proving all the things that begin with T on Picture Card 1.

Using Mr. T's Picture Squares in the Memory Game. (See *Games* section of the manual.)

2T₂

PLANNING AND PREPARATION: Huggable, Mr. T; Mr. T's bag; magazines; paste; paper; crayons; art materials; Alpha Time Master #28.

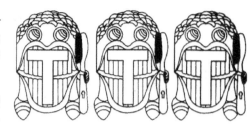

Place a magazine, a jar of paste, a pair of scissors and some assorted art materials in Mr. T's bag. Set up several work areas around the room with old magazines and a variety of other art materials.

RECOGNIZING OBJECTS THAT START WITH MR. T'S SOUND

Call the children's attention to Mr. T's bag.

Mr. T didn't wait for us to fill his bag. He filled it all by himself!

(Jack), take something out of Mr. T's bag (e.g., pair of scissors) and show it to us.

As each item is taken out of Mr. T's bag, ask the children why they think Mr. T put it there.

Why would Mr. T put a pair of scissors into his bag?

Ask Mr. T why he put a pair of scissors into his bag.

Mr. T says he saw you using the scissors when you were making things for Mr. M's bag. Tell him how you used the scissors.

(Jane), what else did Mr. T put into his bag? (e.g., jar of paste)

Ask Mr. T why he put a jar of paste into his bag.

Mr. T says he saw you using the paste when you were making things for Mr. M's bag. Tell him how you used the paste.

How can we use the things Mr. T has in his bag?

Making Things For Mr. T's Bag

Help the children to conclude that they can use the art materials to make things for Mr. T's bag.

Discuss some things the children can make or find that start with the same sound as Tall Teeth. Have the children work in different areas of the room. They may cut pictures from magazines or make things to put into Mr. T's bag. Before they put an object into the bag, the children should show each of their things to Mr. T and Prove It for him.

PRACTICING PROVE IT

Playing A Circle Game

The children may play another Prove It game with Mr. T. Each child reaches into Mr. T's bag without looking, and takes out the first thing he touches. They then all form a circle around Mr. T.

(Jane) may stand in the center with Mr. T.

We will walk around and around to the music until Mr. T tells Jane that he wants us to stop.

When we stop, Jane will ask one of us to prove something for Mr. T and put it into Mr. T's bag.

The child who proves it may then take (Jane's) place in the center with Mr. T.

As the children circle around Mr. T, they sing the following words to the tune of Here We Go Round The Mulberry Bush.

Here we go round and round Mr. T,
Around Mr. T,
Around Mr. T.
Here we go round and round Mr. T,
So we all can fill his bag.

TYING IT TOGETHER

Give each child a copy of Alpha Time Master #28.

The children may draw or paste more pictures that start the same way as Tall Teeth in the empty spaces. They may connect the pictures to Mr. T's Tall Teeth.

ON THEIR OWN

Children may choose from the following activities:

Music
Aural Sound
Discrimination

Playing Mr. T's song (record #1, side A, band #2) and listening for words that begin with the same sound as Tall Teeth.

Tug And Tumble
Game

Having a tug of war with Mr. T:

Tie a cord around Mr. T, leaving a five or six foot end.
Before tugging Mr. T's rope, the player must tell Mr. T something that starts the same way as Tall Teeth and *prove it*. Then another player, speaking for Mr. T will say *Tug!* Then the rope is tugged until Mr. T tumbles.

NOTE: If a child cannot think of a word, he may look in Mr. T's bag for help.

Crafts

Making Tug of War pictures. Cut a variety of lengths of cord or wool (from 2-7 inches), and put them into a box. The child may pick three pieces of cord and arrange them on a large piece of construction paper in order of length—the longest piece on top. These may be taped or stapled down. Then he may draw a picture of Mr. T at one end of the rope, and a picture of himself at the other end.

2T₃

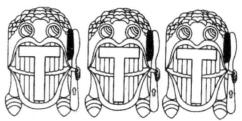

REINFORCING THE T SOUND

Help the children recite Jack And Jill for Mr. T.

Jack and Jill went up the hill,
To fetch a pail of water.
Jack fell down and broke his crown,
And Jill came tumbling after.

Mr. T says he wants to do what Jill did in the poem.

What did she do? (tumbling)

Mr. T says he loves the word *tumbling.*

Have the children discuss tumbling to make sure that they understand what it means.

Do you like tumbling?

Show Mr. T how you tumble.

Playing A Tumbling Game

Mr. T wants us all to tumble toward him. He thinks tumbling is terrific!

Have each child start some distance from Mr. T and tumble toward him.

We are going to tumble for Mr. T and land near him. Mr. T will stand there to help catch us.

Mr. T wants us to tumble with something that starts the same way as his Tall Teeth. You may use anything from his bag. As you tumble, we will tell Mr. T what you are holding.

As a child tumbles with an object, the class tells Mr. T: "(Billy) is tumbling with a (tiger)."

IDENTIFYING THE CAPITAL AND LOWER CASE LETTER T

Look at Mr. T. Show us the part of Mr. T's body that will work in words.

Forming The Capital Letter T With Bodies

Give several children a chance to touch the capital letter T on Mr. T's body. Then they may identify and touch the lower case letter t on his toothbrush.

How many straight lines make the capital T? (two)

Let us make Mr. T's capital letter. How many children will we need? (two)

Let the children experiment in making the capital letter T with their bodies. Have them form small groups so that each child is involved in being part of the capital letter T.

USING ACTION WORDS

Mr. T says he knows how to tell time in a new way. He will tell us what time it is.

Mr. T says it is time to *tap*; it is time to *tiptoe*; it is time to *turn*; it is time to *type*; it is time to *tickle*.

Why did Mr. T pick all these times?

Help the children discover that Mr. T has picked times that start with the same sound as Tall Teeth. Help them to think of other action words by giving clues.

Mr. T is thinking of a *time to*. He says, "Jill did it when she came down the hill."

What did Jill do? (Jill tumbled.)

Other words for which you might give clues would be telephone, talk, tie, tag, tug and touch.

Playing The Time To Game

Play the "Time To" game with the children and Mr. T.

This is how we will play the game:

Mr. T will whisper a *time to* to (Billy).

Maybe Mr. T will say, "It is time to *tap*." Then we will all tap.

Sometimes Mr. T won't talk. If Mr. T doesn't tell (Billy), we will. (*This will avoid embarrassing any child who cannot think of an action word.*)

Take the children visiting around the school.

We are going to take a walk around the school. Mr. T is too tired to go with us. Let's try to remember what we see in the halls, on the walls, and on the bulletin boards. We will tell Mr. T about it when we get back.

TALKING ON THE TELEPHONE

While the children are out of the room, remove Mr. T from view. When the class returns to the room, tell them that Mr. T had to leave. Suggest they telephone Mr. T and tell him about their walk. They may use toy or imaginary telephones. Several or all of the children may do this simultaneously.

Sometimes when we try to telephone someone, we hear a noise that tells us the person is speaking to someone else. What is that noise called? (busy signal)

You may hear a busy signal when you call Mr. T.

Dictating Messages For Mr. T

If you hear a busy signal, you may tell me what you want to say to Mr. T. We will write it down together so that you won't forget. Then you may read your message to Mr. T when his line is not busy anymore.

TYING IT TOGETHER

*Working With
Mr. T's Puzzle*

Matching Pictures

Give each child a copy of Alpha Time Master #29. Discuss the picture with the children before they mark the letter T.

Whom do you see in the picture? (toe dancer, tap dancer, tiger, tumbler)

What are they doing? (tap dancer—tapping; tumbler—tumbling; toe dancer—turning or twirling; tiger—telephoning or talking)

Mr. T would like you to mark his lower case letter T with a yellow crayon.

Mr. T would like you to mark his upper case letter T with a green crayon.

Show Mr. T's Alpha Time Puzzle to the children. Have them remove one piece at a time and tell what it is. Follow the same procedure as you did for Mr. M's puzzle.

Use Mr. T's playing cards from Alpha Time Decks 1-4 and have the children match the pictures on the cards with the puzzle pieces.

ON THEIR OWN

Recalling Events

Science

Motor Coordination

Letter Tracing

Children may choose from the following activities:

Talking to each other on the telephone and telling something that happened on the way to school.

Building simple telephone by using two empty cans and a length of twine (about 6 feet long).

Punch a hole in the bottom of each can and pull the twine through the holes. Knot the ends of the rope so that it won't slip through the cans.

Children may send each other messages by holding the twine taut and talking into one can and listening at the other. The sound is transmitted over the twine.

Working with Mr. T's puzzle. The M and T puzzles may be used together by mixing the pieces of the two puzzles and then separating them.

Using copies of Alpha Time Master #74 to trace the letter T.

Making designs by drawing small, large or giant-sized letters T and placing them in various positions.

2T₄

TEACHER OBJECTIVES:

To reinforce the characteristic of Mr. T.
To help children become familiar with numerals and letters on the telephone dial.
To help children become familiar with their own telephone numbers.

PERFORMANCE OBJECTIVES:

The child will say words with the *t* in the initial position.
The child will dictate or copy his or her own telephone number.
The child will role-play, using the telephone.

DEVELOPMENT

Mr. M told Mr. T about the booklets he made for each of us.
Mr. T thought it was a terrific idea and he made booklets for us too.

Distribute the Mr. T "All About Us" booklets.
Ask the children to look at the front of the booklets.
Point to the words "All About Us."
Explain that Mr. T also wants to call his booklets "All About Us."

Which Letter Person's picture do you see? (Mr. T)
Whose picture do you think is next to Mr. T?
The words under the pictures will tell us.
Put your finger under them.
The words say, "Mr. T has a friend."
If you want the picture of Mr. T's friend to look like you, how can you finish the picture? (e.g., Color the hair the color of your hair. Color the eyes the color of your eyes. Make the shirt look like a shirt you have.)

Remind the children that they do not have to make the picture look like themselves.
They can make it look like anyone they wish.

What is special about Mr. T? (his tall teeth)
Look at Mr. T's friend's face.
Put your finger on the mouth.
What did Mr. T leave out when he drew the mouth? (teeth)
Mr. T wants each of us to draw teeth.

Give the children the opportunity to complete the picture.
Select a child's booklet and hold it so the class can see it.

This booklet says, "All About Us."
This is Mr. T.
This is his friend.
The sentence under the picture says, "Mr. T has a friend." (e.g., Jennifer *will tell us who she wants Mr. T's friend to be.*)

Select several other booklets and follow the same procedure.

Have the children open the booklets.
Point to the first sentence on the left-hand side.
Point to the rebus of the tall teeth.

Mr. T says it is easier for him to remember what the sentence says when he puts a picture in it.

Read aloud, "Mr. T has tall teeth."
Let the children pretend to reread it with you.

Mr. T will tell us something important in the next sentence
He will tell us his telephone number.

Read aloud, "Mr. T's telephone number is TT-2-2222."

67A

What picture did Mr. T put in the sentence? (a telephone)
Why do you think he put a picture in the sentence? (It helps him remember what the sentence says.)
Look at the picture under the sentence.
What is Mr. T doing? (talking on the telephone)
To which Letter Person do you think he is talking?

At this time you may wish to pursue skills for using the telephone. It is important that children be aware of the proper way of answering the telephone. The local telephone company is an excellent source for material.
There are booklets describing ways to use the telephone, plus a newly released filmstrip series.

Why do you think telephones are important to Mr. T? (Telephone starts with the same sound as *tall teeth.*)
Mr. T took this whole page to tell us about himself.
He told us he has tall teeth.
He told us his telephone number is TT-2-2222.
Mr. T says the next page is for us to tell him about ourselves.
Look at the next page.
Put your finger on the dotted line.
Mr. T wants us to write our names on the dotted line.
Then we'll listen to the sentence.

Give the children the opportunity to write their names.

Select a booklet and read the child's sentence to the class (*e.g.,* Bret has teeth).
Do this with several booklets.
Some children may want to tell what their sentences say.

Draw attention to the second sentence.
Explain that Mr. T wants the children to tell him their telephone numbers.

Mr. T wrote another sentence.
He could not finish it.
He made a dotted line where we can each write our name.
He left space for us to write our telephone number.
When our sentences are finished, Mr. T can listen to them.

Have the children write their names on the dotted line.
Then have them tell you their telephone number.
Write it for them in the space provided.
Read their sentences aloud.
Some children may wish to write their telephone numbers by themselves.
Write the numbers for them and let them copy their own number onto the booklet.

Have the children turn to the back of the booklet.
Draw their attention to Mr. T and the child holding telephone receivers.
Read aloud, "Let's talk about the telephone."
Explain that Mr. T drew a great big telephone dial.
Have the children pretend to dial their telephone numbers, using Mr. T's dial.
Children can role-play and demonstrate proper telephone etiquette. Encourage the children to take their booklets home and have members of their family "dial" telephone numbers, using the dial on the back page of the booklet.

2F₁

PLANNING AND PREPARATION: Huggables, Mr. M, Mr. T and Mr. F; a bag for Mr. F; picture of a man torn in half; cellophane tape; Mr. F's Picture Squares; Record #1; magazines; scissors; paste; various other art materials; two pieces of construction paper for each child; Alpha Time Master #30.

Mr. F's music (record #1, side A, band #3) may be played to set the mood.

INTRODUCING MR. F's FUNNY FEET SOUND

Show the children the picture of a man torn in half which you have previously prepared.

Look at this picture. What happened to it? (it is torn)

Who is in the picture? (a man)

From whose bag did it come? (Mr. M's bag)

Let's tape the picture back together for Mr. M.

Mr. M is unhappy that the picture is torn. He says it is Mr. F's fault. Mr. F says it is Mr. M's fault.

Maybe Mr. M or Mr. F will tell us what happened.

Give several children a chance to say what Mr. M or Mr. F told them. Then, tell them what Mr. M said to you.

Mr. M says Mr. F took the picture of the man out of Mr. M's bag.

Mr. F says he is going to keep the picture because he needs it. It is his turn to get a sound.

Mr. M says he is happy Mr. F will get a sound, but Mr. F should not take his pictures. He says the word *man* starts the same way as Munching Mouth; the picture must stay in Mr. M's bag.

Mr. F says, "I see the picture. It is a man. It makes me think of a special man. I can give that picture another name. The name I am thinking of starts the same way as Funny Feet. The picture will belong in my bag."

Mr. M couldn't understand. He said, "Mr. F, you don't even know what your sound will be."

Mr. F smiled and said: "I can figure it out for myself. You got your sound from *Munching Mouth.* Mr. T got his sound from *Tall Teeth.* What is special about me? Now can you figure out how I'll get my sound?

Mr. M thought and thought. Let's help Mr. M figure it out.

Making Inferences

From where will Mr. F get his sound? (Funny Feet)

Mr. M is glad you figured it out for him, but he still doesn't understand why Mr. F took his picture. It's a picture of a man and *man* doesn't start the same way as Funny Feet.

68

HEARING WORDS THAT BEGIN WITH MR. F'S SOUND

Discovering That Pictures Can Be Renamed

Mr. F can give the picture another name. The name starts with the same sound as Funny Feet. Mr. F will give us a clue. He says a lady can be a mother; a man can be a *father*. *Father* starts with the same sound as Funny Feet.

Mr. F is right. It could be a picture of a father. Mr. M is also right. It is a picture of a man.

Help the children re-name some objects in Mr. M's and Mr. T's bag so that they begin with the same sound as Funny Feet.

Mr. M and Mr. T say they want to give a picture to Mr. F. Help him find another name for one of their pictures. It must start the same way as Funny Feet (e.g., toast or turkey may be called *food*).

Note: This is a very difficult skill and requires repeated experiences. The children may need considerable help from you, especially at the beginning.

Be sure the children "prove" anything they re-name.

Show the children Mr. F's picture squares (i.e., fairy, finger, fish, feather, farm). Have them name and prove each one.

Mr. F found some pictures. He doesn't want to put them in his bag until you prove them for him. Let's prove each of these pictures for Mr. F.

Help the children think of additional things they can find or make for Mr. F's bag. Instead of telling them the names of things, give the children clues so that they can think of the names themselves. (e.g., You have five of these on each hand. (fingers) Your eyes, nose and mouth are all part of your ____(face).)

Sound-Symbol
Relationships

Let the children go to different parts of the room where they may use a variety of materials to find and/or make things for Mr. F's bag. Tell them to prove each thing to Mr. F before it is put into his bag.

Listening To Mr. F's Song

Mr. F wants you to hear him sing his song again. Try to listen for some words that begin with the same sound as his *Funny Feet*.

Play the song (record #1 side A band 3) often enough so that several children remember a word that begins the same way as Funny Feet.

(Sandy), tell Mr. F which word in the song starts with his sound. Prove it to Mr. F.

INTRODUCING THE IDEA OF HALF

Mr. F is thinking about all the things he can do that start the same way as Funny Feet. One thing he thought of was *fold*. (Emphasize the initial sound in the word fold.) Mr. F loves to *fold* things. Why do you think he likes to *fold* things? (*Fold* starts the same way as Funny Feet.)

Distribute two sheets of drawing paper to each child. Show the children how to fold a piece of paper in half (horizontally) by bringing the corners together.

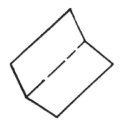

Sometimes, Mr. F folds a piece of paper in half. He holds one corner with one hand. He holds the corner next to it with his other hand. Now, watch what he does.

He lets these two corners catch two more corners. When the corners catch, he can fold the paper. Then, Mr. F opens the paper and sees two parts that look the same. He says he folded the paper in *half*. Let's all catch corners and fold a paper in half.

Look at both parts. Is one bigger than the other?

How can we fold the paper in half a different way?

Have the children fold another piece of paper in half lengthwise.

Folding Papers In Half

Let's catch different corners. Open the paper and look at each part. Do both parts look the same? They look the same, but how can we prove it?

Have the children prove the meaning of "in half" by cutting their papers along the crease and laying one half on top of the other.

How many equal parts do we have after we fold something in half? (two)

TYING IT TOGETHER

Distribute copies of Alpha Time Master #30 and discuss with children.

What are some things you see in the picture? (Funny Feet, fish, feather, fairy, finger)

Why do you think Mr. F's Funny Feet are there? (because the pictures start with the Funny Feet sound)

Mr. F would like his Funny Feet to touch some of the pictures. How can we make them touch?

ON THEIR OWN

Children may choose from the following activities:

Auditory Discrimination

Including Mr. F's playing cards in any of the games in the *Games* section of the manual.

Using Mr. F's Picture Squares in any of the activities described in the *Games* section.

Using Picture Card 2 to name objects that begin with Mr. F's sound.

Music

Singing along with Mr. F's music, emphasizing all the *F* words.

Art

Using colored squares and circles for folding objects such as fans, fish, ships and bats.

Mathematical Concepts

Making plasticine shapes (e.g., snakes, balls) and cutting them in half.

Using measuring cups and spoons to measure half cups of liquid.

Dropping ink or paint on one side of a piece of paper and folding it in half, pressing the halves of the paper together. Open the paper to find interesting designs.

2F₂

PLANNING AND PREPARATION: Huggable, Mr. F; 6 pairs of cut out paper footprints; cellophane tape; Mr. F's Alpha Time Puzzle; scissors, paper, crayons; Alpha Time Master #31.

Draw or tape pictures of objects that start with the F sound on 9 of the paper footprints. Then, tape the footprints to the floor to make a Funny Feet Road.

NAMING WORDS THAT BEGIN WITH THE FUNNY FEET SOUND

Discovering Funny Feet Road

Draw the children's attention to the footprints on the floor.

What do you see on the floor?

Who do you think made this road for us? (Mr. F)

What name do you think Mr. F gave this road? *(Elicit Funny Feet Road.)*

Mr. F has a Funny Feet Road Song for us.

Have the children join you in chanting the Funny Feet Road Jingle.

Follow, follow, follow, follow,
Follow the Funny Feet Road.
Funny Feet, Funny Feet, Funny Feet, Funny Feet,
Follow the Funny Feet Road.

What does Mr. F have on some Funny Feet on Funny Feet Road? (pictures)

Playing The Funny Feet Road Game

Why do you think he put those pictures on Funny Feet Road? (They start with his sound.)

Tell the children that Mr. F says if they want to follow Funny Feet Road, they must first follow his directions.

Mr. F says, "This is direction number one:

"We have to take off our shoes if we want to follow *Funny Feet Road.* Feet must touch feet."

Mr. F says, "Listen to direction number two:

"You may only put your foot down on a paper foot that has a picture on it—a picture of something that starts the same way as Funny Feet.

"We may not step on a foot that has no picture."

Ask Mr. F if we may follow *Funny Feet Road* now.

Mr. F says he has more directions. Here is direction number three:

Recalling And Repeating Directions In Sequence

Mr. F says that every time we step on one of the Funny Feet, we have to say the name of the picture that is on that foot.

Mr. F wants to be sure that everybody knows all the directions. Let's tell Mr. F the directions he wants us to follow. Then, we can follow *Funny Feet Road!*

Have several children repeat Mr. F's directions. Give the children a chance to walk on Funny Feet Road, following Mr. F's directions. When they have finished, they may chant the Funny Feet Road jingle again.

The children may make several different Funny Feet Roads in different parts of the room. Encourage the children to decide how they will make their Funny Feet Roads.

How many feet will have pictures that start the same way as Funny Feet?

How many will not have pictures?

TALKING ABOUT HUMOROUS SITUATIONS

Mr. F says the funniest place in the whole world is *Funny Feet Road*. The funniest things happen on *Funny Feet Road*. Anything could happen on *Funny Feet Road*.

Talking About Things That Are Funny

Look at Mr. F! He can't stop laughing whenever he thinks of all the funny things that happen on *Funny Feet Road*.

What are some funny things that could happen on *Funny Feet Road*? (e.g., Mr. F saw a squirrel storing nuts in an elephant's trunk.)

Close your eyes and think of the funniest thing that could happen on *Funny Feet Road*.

Share it with us by telling us, or drawing a picture or writing a story (dictating to teacher).

TYING IT TOGETHER

Comprehension skills:
remembering
relating
drawing conclusions

Distribute copies of Alpha Time Master #31 and show Mr. F's Alpha Time puzzle to the children.

Here is Mr. F who has some things that belong to him.

What pictures do you see? (fairy, fish)

Why does Mr. F have these pictures? (They start with his Funny Feet sound.)

Prove to Mr. F that these pictures belong to him.

Why do you think he has a picture of his Funny Feet?

ON THEIR OWN

Eye-Hand Coordination

Crafts

Children may choose from the following activities:

Working with Mr. F's puzzle. The pieces of Mr. M's and Mr. T's puzzles may be mixed with Mr. F's puzzle. The children must then "prove" each piece before fitting it in the appropriate Letter Person.

Making giant Funny Feet and pasting or drawing a picture of something that begins the same way as Funny Feet on each toe.

Dropping ink or paint on one side of a piece of paper and folding it in half, pressing the halves of the paper together. Open the paper to find interesting designs.

2F₃

PLANNING AND PREPARATION: Huggable, Mr. F; short pieces of string or yarn (about 5" long), enough for each child; a bag for Mr. F; art supplies; Alpha Time Master #32.

REMEMBERING WORDS THAT BEGIN WITH THE FUNNY FEET SOUND

Tell the children that Mr. F is always forgetting things.

No one forgets the way Mr. F forgets. Look at all these strings! These are the strings Mr. F needs so that he doesn't forget things. Mr. F ties a string around his finger so that he doesn't forget.

Tell the children that Mr. F has forgotten the name of each thing in his bag.

Mr. F says that he doesn't have enough fingers for all the things he forgets.

What does he mean?

How many fingers does Mr. F have?

He has ten fingers—the same as we do.

Ten fingers are not enough for all the things he forgets.

Show Mr. F which finger you will lend him.

Mr. F wants each of you to take something out of his bag. Then he wants you to tell him what it is and prove it to him.

As each object is proven by a child, tie a string around his finger so that he won't forget.

Lead the children into the Finger poem. Have them repeat it as a finger play.

*Participating In
A Finger Play*

Mr. F forgets things.
As everyone knows.
So he brings along string
Wherever he goes.

With string on his fingers,
(But none on his toes),
Mr. F won't forget,
Wherever he goes.

Have the children walk around Mr. F in a circle. They each show him the finger on which the string is tied. Each child tells Mr. F the name of an object that starts with the same sound as his Funny Feet. That way, Mr. F will never forget.

*Talking About
Forgotten Things*

Mr. F is not the only one who ever forgets. What have you ever forgotten? Tell Mr. F about some things you have forgotten to do.

The children may want to dictate stories or draw pictures about something they have forgotten. They might paste a knotted string on the paper so that they don't forget what the picture is about!

The following game will give the children the opportunity of using words that begin with Mr. F's sound. Repeat the game giving several children a chance to be Mr. F.

Mr. F has a game for us. We will follow his directions.

Here is the first direction: We have to form a circle.

Mr. F does not want us to stand. Ask him what he would like us to do instead of stand.

Practicing The
Initial F Sound

Here is the second direction: Everyone sit down.

(John), you may be Mr. F. Pick something from Mr. F's bag. Tell us the name of what you picked so that Mr. F doesn't forget.

Now walk around the outside of the circle and tap each person as you pass. As you tap, keep saying the name of the thing you took out of Mr. F's bag.

When you don't want to say it anymore, tap the next person you come to and say *Funny Feet.* Then that person will chase you, and we'll see who gets back to the empty place in the circle first.

Then someone else will have a chance to be Mr. F.

RECOGNIZING THE UPPER AND LOWER CASE LETTER F

Draw the children's attention to the capital letter F on Mr. F's body.

Mr. F wants to show us his capital letter.

Look at Mr. F, and you will see that his letter is part of his body.

Use your hands to show us Mr. F's capital letter.

What do you think the name of his letter is? (F)

How many parts do we need to make the capital letter F with our bodies? (three)

Have three children practice forming the capital letter F on the floor with their bodies. Have all the children discuss and decide the best way to form the letter. Then let the class divide into groups of three. Each group may form the letter F with their bodies. Then have the children find the lower case f on Mr. F.

Mr. F wants us to find his lower case letter.

Use your hands to show us where Mr. F's lower case letter is. (his hand)

Mr. F says, "Look at my two letters. Close your eyes and try to see them. Open your eyes and look at them again. Close your eyes again. Can you still see them?"

TYING IT TOGETHER

Give each child a copy of Alpha Time Master #32.

Mr. F has a paper for us. He wants us to find his letters again.

First we will find the capital letter F. Then we will find the lower case letter f.

Which kind of letter is on the top half of the paper? (capital letter F)

What pictures are drawn on the top half? (feet)

What letters are on the bottom half? (lower case f)

On what are the lower case letters drawn? (fingers)

ON THEIR OWN

Children may choose from the following activities:

Using Art For Related Vocabulary

Tracing their hands and then drawing a string around each finger. Then they may tell Mr. F a word for each string they have drawn.

Letter Tracing

Using copies of Alpha Time Master #60, children may trace and write the letter F. Others may paint the letter F or draw it on the chalkboard.

Letter Identification

Using the Alpha Time puzzles, children may take the capital letters from Mr. M, Mr. T and Mr. F puzzles and compare them before putting them back in place.

2F₄

IDENTIFYING BODY PARTS — SINGULAR AND PLURAL

Gather the children around Mr. F.

Mr. F, what are you thinking?

Mr. F says he is not thinking, he is figuring things out. Mr. F likes to figure things out.

Talking About Body Parts That Start With The Funny Feet Sound

He says he has figured out that many parts of your body start with the same sound as Funny Feet. He wants to see how many you can figure out.

Let's all figure out what parts of our bodies start with Mr. F's Funny Feet sound.

Help the children realize that face, feet, fingers, and fist all start with the same sound as Funny Feet.

Hold up fingers as indicated:

We have a hand that has five fingers.

If we hold up one, we call it a . . . (finger).

If we hold up two, we call them . . . (fingers).

If we hold up all of them, we still call them . . . (fingers).

Point to feet as indicated:

If we show one of these, we call it a . . . (foot).

If we show two of these, we call them . . . (feet).

Draw a circle in the air around your face.

This part of our head is called the . . . (face).

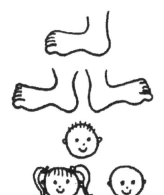

If we see two people, we see two . . . (faces).

Adapt the game Looby Loo, using only body parts that begin with F— and changing the days of the week with each chorus.

Here we go Looby Loo,
Here we go Looby Light.
Here we go Looby Loo,
All on a *Saturday* night.

I put my *finger* in,
I take my *finger* out.
I give my *finger* a shake, shake, shake—
And turn my self about.

Participating In A Circle Game

Tell the children to listen carefully, because two of the words in the game will be changed.

Here we go Looby Loo,
Here we go Looby Light.
Here we go Looby Loo,
All on a *Sunday* night.

I put my *fingers* in,
I take my *fingers* out.
I give my *fingers* a shake, shake, shake —
And turn myself about.

Repeat the song substituting the following words for finger(s): fist(s); foot, feet; face(s). Change the days of the week with each verse.

READING A PICTURE STORY

Tell the children that Mr. F would like them to figure something out for him.

Mr. F loves Funny Feet Road. He goes there everyday to make sure that everything is fine. One day something happened on Funny Feet Road.

Give each child a copy of Alpha Time Master #33.

Mr. F said you are so good at figuring things out that he would like you to figure out what happened. He is not going to say a word.

These pictures will tell us the story of what happened on Funny Feet Road.

Let's look at the first picture.

What are some of the things we see in the picture?

What is next to Funny Feet Road? (a sign)

What is painted on the sign? (an arrow)

Where is the arrow pointing? (toward Funny Feet Road)

How is a sign used? (to show the way)

Where have you ever seen a sign with an arrow?

Pictorial comprehension:
visual discrimination
locating details
recall
numeration
inference
predicting outcomes
cause and effect relations

What do you think is going to happen to this sign? (It may fall down.)

What could make it fall down? (e.g., wind)

Now let's look at the next part of the story.

What has happened to the sign? (It fell down.)

What is Mr. F trying to do? (pick it up)

Why do you think the sign fell down? (e.g., It was not attached properly.)

Let's look at the last part of the story.

Who is in the picture? (Mr. F and Mr. M)

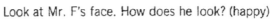

Look at Mr. F's face. How does he look? (happy)

Why do you think he is happy? (He put the sign up.)

How does Mr. M look? (confused)

Look at the sign before it fell down in the first picture.

Look at the sign after Mr. F put it up again in the last picture.

Do they look the same?

How are they different? (the arrows are pointing in different directions)

What doesn't Mr. F know about the arrow on the sign? (It is pointing in the wrong direction.)

What will happen when people want to walk on Funny Feet Road? (They will go in the wrong direction.)

What did Mr. F do wrong on Funny Feet Road? (He put the sign up the wrong way.)

TYING IT TOGETHER

Tell the children that Mr. F would like them to make signs for Funny Feet Road. Let the children decide on signs they want on Funny Feet Road.

Mr. F would like Funny Feet Road to have lots of different signs.

Discuss the purpose of signs such as: WET PAINT, KEEP OFF THE GRASS, BEWARE OF DOG, CHILDREN AT PLAY, QUIET—HOSPITAL ZONE.

When your signs are finished, show Mr. F your signs, and tell him why you think he should put them on Funny Feet Road.

ON THEIR OWN

Children may choose from the following activities:

Making Signs For Funny Feet Road

Making signs for funny feet road

Making charts or scrapbooks of different kinds of signs.

Discovery

Looking for signs around the school.

Crafts

Making designs by tracing their fingers in various positions on paper.

Telling A Story

Using Alpha Time Master #33 to retell Mr. F's story to Mr. F or to each other.

2F₅

TEACHER OBJECTIVES:

To review the characteristic and sound of Mr. F.

To have children identify names of some fruits.

To encourage discussion about classification, shape, taste, etc. of fruit.

PERFORMANCE OBJECTIVES:

The child will identify certain fruit by name.

The child will classify fruit by taste, etc.

The child will say words with the *f* in the initial position.

DEVELOPMENT

Mr. F heard about the booklets Mr. M and Mr. T gave us.
Guess what Mr. F made for each of us. ("All About Us" booklets)

Distribute the Mr. F booklets to the children.

Look at the front of the booklet.

Point to "All About Us."
Read it aloud.

Which Letter Person's picture do you see? (Mr. F)
Whose picture do you think is next to Mr. F? (his friend)
Put your finger on the words under the pictures.
The words say, "Mr. F has a friend."
When Mr. F drew this picture what did he leave out? (feet)
Draw feet for Mr. F's friend.
What is special about Mr. F? (his funny feet)
Look at the picture of Mr. F's friend.
If you want the picture of Mr. F's friend to look like you, what will you do?

Give the children the opportunity to complete the picture.
Remind them that it may look like anyone they wish.

Select several booklets and read aloud.

This is Mr. F.
This is his friend.
The sentence under the picture says, "Mr. F has a friend."

Have the children open the booklets.
Point to the first sentence on the left-hand side.

What picture did Mr. F put in the sentence? (funny feet)

Read aloud, "Mr. F has funny feet."
Let the children pretend to reread the sentence with you.

Ask the children to look at the picture at the bottom of the page.

Mr. F has been very busy eating.
What has he been eating? (apples, bananas, a pear, a lemon, a strawberry and a cherry)
What is one name we can give to all the things he has been eating? (fruit)
Mr. F says he likes all fruit.
Why do you think Mr. F likes fruit? (Fruit starts with the same sound as funny feet.)

78A

Point to the sentence, "Mr. F likes all fruit."
Read it aloud.

Mr. F took this whole page to tell us about himself.
What did he tell us first? (He has funny feet.)
What did he tell us next? (He likes all fruit.)
Mr. F says the next page is for us to tell him about ourselves.
Mr. F wants us to write our names on the first dotted line.
Write your name and Mr. F will listen to your sentence.

After the children have written their names, select booklets and read the sentences aloud.
Have the children turn to the back of the booklet.
Read the sentence, "Let's talk about fruits."
Have them find and name the different fruits.

In your discussion of fruits, encourage responses dealing with classification of fruits (*e.g.*, shapes, taste, peeling, seeds). This could lead into a further discussion of classification per se. Why do we use words such as fruit, vegetables, etc.? Time can be devoted to the story of fruit-growing.
Have the children select one or two fruits, *e.g.*, oranges, apples, bananas.
Where does fruit come from? How does it grow: on bushes, vines, trees, etc.? Which fruits grow nearby? Perhaps the children would like to plant seeds as a class project.

Mr. F wants each of us to tell him the name of our favorite fruit.
Have the children open their booklets.
Refer them to the second sentence on the right-hand page.
Explain that Mr. F wants them to use the sentence to write their name and favorite fruit.

Mr. F made a dotted line where we can each write our name.
Let's write our names and see if that will finish the sentence.

Have the children write their names on the line.
Then select a booklet and read the sentence aloud to prove it is incomplete (*e.g.*, Barbara's favorite fruit is   .).

Mr. F says he knows why the sentence isn't finished.
It doesn't tell Barbara's favorite fruit.
Let's listen to another sentence.

Select several booklets and follow the above procedure.
Have the children suggest ways of finishing the sentence (*e.g.*, drawing a picture of their favorite fruit, cutting and pasting a picture, dictating the name of their favorite fruit or copying the name).

Help the children share their sentences.
Encourage them to tell the name of their favorite fruit to Mr. F.
Suggest that they take their booklets home.
Have them ask members of their family to tell Mr. F their favorite fruits.

2H₁

PLANNING AND PREPARATION: Huggables, Mr. H, Mr. M, Mr. T and Mr. F; objects or pictures of objects that begin with H; a bag for Mr. H; Mr. H's Picture Squares; Mr. M's picture of a man, Mr. T's picture of a table, and Mr. F's picture of fish; Record #1; Alpha Time Master #34.

INTRODUCING H AS AN INITIAL LETTER SOUND

Mr. H is the next Letter Person to get a sound. He should be happy, but he is sad.

Mr. H says he doesn't want to have a sound. He knows where he will find his sound. He says that the sound he must have is too hard.

Recalling How The Other Letter People Got Their Sounds

Have the children recall that the other Letter People got their sounds from their special features.

Tell us from what Mr. M, Mr. T and Mr. F got their sounds. (Munching Mouth, Tall Teeth, Funny Feet)

From what will Mr. H get his sound? (Horrible Hair)

Let's say *horrible.* (Emphasize initial consonant.)

Let's say *hair.* (Emphasize initial consonant.)

Why does Mr. H think his sound is so hard to hear?

Do you think it is hard to hear?

Mr. M says he knows how Mr. H feels. Mr. M was the first Letter Person to get a sound. His sound was too hard for him **until** everyone told him to watch our lips.

Maybe Mr. H can get help by watching what happens to our mouths when we say *horrible* and when we say *hair.*

Making The H Sound In Horrible Hair

Have the children form pairs. One child says Horrible Hair while the other watches his mouth. Then they reverse roles. Have the children discover that their mouths are open when they start to say, horrible, and when they start to say, hair.

Tell the children to hold their hands in front of their mouths (not too closely). Have them say Horrible Hair—with emphasis on the initial sounds. Ask them what they feel on their hands when they start to say horrible and when they start to say hair. (breath)

What are some things that will help Mr. H when he is listening for words that start the same way as Horrible Hair? (open mouth, breath on hands)

Mr. H says he thinks he understands a little bit better. Now he wants you to prove some words for him.

SAYING WORDS THAT BEGIN WITH H

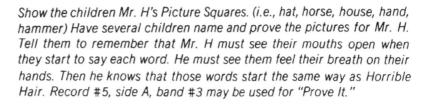

Show the children Mr. H's Picture Squares. (i.e., hat, horse, house, hand, hammer) Have several children name and prove the pictures for Mr. H. Tell them to remember that Mr. H must see their mouths open when they start to say each word. He must see them feel their breath on their hands. Then he knows that those words start the same way as Horrible Hair. Record #5, side A, band #3 may be used for "Prove It."

The other Letter People want to help Mr. H fill his bag. They have hidden pictures all around the room for him. Let's see how many pictures we can find.

As the children find the pictures or objects, they may prove each one to Mr. H and put it into his bag.

Mr. M, Mr. T and Mr. F would each like to put something from their bags into Mr. H's bag. They can't do that unless they give each picture a name that starts with Mr. H's Horrible Hair sound.

Mr. M says we can take his picture of a man and call it handsome. He can think of many ways to name the man so that the picture starts like *Horrible Hair.*

Can you think of any other names? (Harry, healthy, happy)

Is there anything that Mr. T or Mr. F can give Mr. H?

Mr. T says we can use the word *high* to talk about his table. Why would Mr. H use the word *high* instead of *table*?

Mr. F says he has a picture of a fish. What can we call the fish so that it begins like Horrible Hair? (halibut, heathful, hobby)

Play Mr. H's song (record #1, side A, band #4). Encourage the class to sing along. Some children may be able to hear words that begin the same way as Horrible Hair.

TYING IT TOGETHER

Distribute Alpha Time Master #34.

What do you see in the picture? (Horrible Hair, hat, horse, house, hammer)

Why is Mr. H's Horrible Hair with these things? (They all start with the same sound as Horrible Hair.)

Prove to Mr. H that these things start the same way as *Horrible Hair.*

Mr. H would like to touch all the things that start with his sound. Think of ways to do this.

ON THEIR OWN

Children may choose from the following activities:

Picture Matching

Using Mr. H's Picture Squares and matching them with the pictures on Alpha Time Master #34.

Auditory Discrimination

Finding objects that begin with Mr. H's sound in Picture Card 3.

Crafts

Making additional objects for Mr. H's bag.

2H₂

PLANNING AND PREPARATION: Huggable, Mr. H; Mr. H's Picture Squares; other pictures of objects that start with H; Record #5; Alpha Time Master #35; Mr. H's Alpha Time Puzzle; long strips of paper or oak tag that may be stapled or pasted to make hoops at least 8" in diameter; blocks.

REMEMBERING HOW TO MAKE MR. H'S SOUND

As you read the following poem to the children, emphasize the initial H sound whenever it occurs. Then reread the poem, letting them say Mr. H's words with you.

Mr. H has been thinking about Prove It all night.

This is what he has been thinking:

> "Prove It" is very hard for me;
> I don't hear my sound easily.

Fine auditory discrimination

> Whenever you say words to me,
> Here are all the things I must see:
> I must see your mouth open wide,
> Hear your breath come from way inside.

> Say *hat*, say *hug*. Help me understand.
> Did you feel your breath on your hand?
> Say *horrible*, say *horse*, say *hair*.
> Make very sure your hand is there.

> Make sure Mr. H's sound is heard;
> Feel your breath as you say each word.

NAMING OBJECTS THAT BEGIN WITH MR. H'S SOUND

Let's each take something from Mr. H's bag and sing *Prove It* to show Mr. H that we can remember how to make his sound.

The children may sing the "Prove It" song with the music (record #5, side A, band 3).

Tell the children that they are going to play a game with Mr. H.

Mr. H would like us to make believe that we are at a fair or a carnival.

We are going to throw a hoop around each picture that starts the same way as *Horrible Hair*. We can make our own hoops.

Playing Toss The Hoop

Help the children tape or staple the strips of paper to make hoops. Tape or tie each or Mr. H's Picture Squares to a block. To play the game, a child must name the picture that he wants to encircle with the hoop and then try to toss the hoop over that block.

IDENTIFYING THE CAPITAL AND LOWER CASE LETTER H

Gather the children around Mr. H.

Mr. H knows that his letter is part of his body, but he would like you to show it to him.

Point to Mr. H's capital letter.

How many straight lines do we need to make the capital letter H? (three)

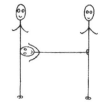

Have the children form groups of three and arrange themselves to form the capital letter H.

Now Mr. H would like you to find his other letter.

Point to Mr. H's lower case letter.

TYING IT TOGETHER

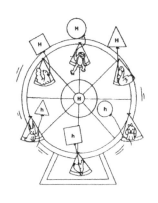

Pictorial comprehension:
distinguishing letters
visual memory
drawing conclusions
details
main idea

Distribute copies of Alpha Time Master #35 to the children.

Mr. H would like us to find his capital letter H and his lower case letter h in this picture.

The capital letter *H* is on the top part of the paper. The lower case letter *h* is on the bottom part of the paper.

What kind of wheel is in this picture? (ferris wheel)

Who is riding the ferris wheel? (animals)

What does each animal have? (the letter H)

Where else do you see a capital letter H? (In the middle of the ferris wheel.)

What are some shapes you see in this picture? (circles, squares, triangles)

What color crayon will you use to show Mr. H where his letters are? (*Let the children decide on the color.*)

Using A Puzzle
For Design,
Distinguishing
Letters And
Generalization

Show the children Mr. H's puzzle. Call on one child at a time to remove a piece. When all the pieces are removed, other children may replace them.

(Linda), which piece did you remove? Tell Mr. H why this piece belongs to him.

(Jack), Mr. H would like his capital letter. Please find it and put it back where it belongs.

ON THEIR OWN

Children may choose from the following activities:

Letter Tracing

Using copies of Alpha Time Master #62 to trace the letter H.

Using various materials, writing, painting or molding the letter H.

Eye Hand Co-ordination

Using Mr. H's puzzle in any of the activities described in the *Games* section.

Counting Shapes

Counting how many circles, triangles, and squares can be found on Alpha Time Master #35.

Sorting And Matching

Including Mr. H's playing cards in any of the activities described in the *Games* section.

Art

Painting carnival pictures (e.g., carousel, tents, go-carts, roller coaster).

2H₃

PLANNING AND PREPARATION: Huggables, Mr. M, Mr. T, Mr. F, Mr. N and Miss A; blank sheet of paper to use as Mr. H's letter; paper and pencils, drawing paper, crayons and art materials; Mr. H's filled bag, toy telephone, Alpha Time Master #36.

Mr. H should not be in the room.

DISCUSSING GOING TO THE HOSPITAL

Stand the Letter People Mr. M, Mr. T, Mr. F, Mr. N, Miss A, (not Mr. H) in a line. Touch each one as you count them aloud.

Counting The Letter People

One, two, three, four, five.

Let us count them once again.

One, two, three, four, five.

This is strange. We have *six* Letter People, but we counted only *five.*

Maybe we didn't count correctly.

Who will count for us?

Which Letter Person is missing?

Have the children discover that Mr. H is missing.

Where is Mr. H?

Give several children a chance to ask a Letter Person and to tell the class what he said. Then pretend that Miss A is telling you what has happened to Mr. H.

Miss A says that she knows what happened to Mr. H.

Miss A says that yesterday Mr. H fell and cut his knee very badly. The cut was so deep that the Letter People had to take Mr. H to the hospital for stitches.

Talking About Feelings

You know how afraid Mr. H is of having a haircut. How do you think he will feel about going to the hospital?

How do you think he will feel about getting stitches?

Have you ever gone to the hospital?

What feelings did you have inside of you?

Did you ever have to stay for more than one day and sleep in the hospital?

How do you think Mr. H will feel if he has to sleep in the hospital?

Look, there's a letter on my desk! It's from Mr. H. I'm so glad! Now we'll find out what happened.

Take note paper out of an envelope and "read" this letter to the children:

*Listening To A
Letter From Mr. H*

Dear Boys and Girls,

Yesterday, I cut my knee pretty badly. It was the worst cut I've ever had.

I knew when it started to bleed that I would need stitches. The Letter People took me to the hospital.

I shook inside when I heard that I'd have to stay there overnight. The hospital looked so big. It gave me an awful scare! I was even more afraid than the day my mother wanted me to get a haircut.

The other Letter People could not stay. I cried as I watched tnem all leave.

The doctor said, "That's not the way to behave! Big boys like you must be brave."

Couldn't he see that I wasn't a big boy at all? I'm still really very, very little, I would like to be brave, but sometimes that's not easy for me.

Just then, I saw a friendly smile. It was a nurse who came in to talk to me. She said that I'd be able to go home the next day.

I don't like it here, but there is one thing I know. The hospital may look big and make me feel afraid, but the doctors and the nurses take good care of me and will send me home as soon as they can.

I hope to see you tomorrow!

Love,
Mr. H

Let the children discuss Mr. H's letter. Encourage them to remember details mentioned in the letter by asking questions like these:

*Remembering And
Relating What
Happened To Mr. H*

What happened when Mr. H cut his knee? (It was bleeding.)

How do you know that Mr. H was very frightened? (He shook inside.)

When did he start to cry? (when the Letter People left)

Tell us about a time that you had to stay overnight somewhere — without your mother or father. How did you feel?

*Remembering and relating
emotional experiences in
a hospital*

Mr. H is right. It isn't always easy to be brave.

Tell us about a time when you tried to be brave.

If Mr. H has to go back to the hospital again, do you think he will still be afraid?

FINDING WAYS TO COMMUNICATE WITH MR. H

When someone is in the hospital, he enjoys hearing from the people he loves. We can't go to visit him. What can we do?

*Speaking On The
Telephone And
Dictating Letters
For Mr. H*

Lead the children to the suggestion that they can telephone Mr. H. (toy telephones may be used) Tell the children that when the receptionist at the hospital answers, they must say "May I please speak to Mr. H?" When Mr. H answers the telephone, tell them to make sure that they say, "Hello, Mr. H. This is (Billy)."

Some children might decide that Mr. H would like to receive a letter from them. Have them dictate letters and decide what else they could send him.

Pretend the telephone is ringing, and answer it.

85

It's Mr. H! He says that he is very happy so many people called him.

He heard that you were writing letters and making things for him. He can't wait to get them!

PRACTICING WORDS THAT BEGIN WITH H

Mr. H would like you to do him a favor. He is worried about his bag. He says that when he fell, everything tumbled out—and he is not sure what is in his bag.

Developing Vocabulary Words Beginning With H

Have the children take things out of Mr. H's bag and prove them to him over the telephone.

Distribute a variety of art materials. Help the children fold their papers in half so that they look like greeting cards. When the cards are finished collect them and keep them for the next lesson.

Making Get-Well Cards

What are some pictures that we can draw on Mr. H's get-well cards?

What else can we make besides cards?

How will Mr. H feel when he gets these cards and gifts from us?

TYING IT TOGETHER

Distribute copies of Alpha Time Master #36, and discuss them with the children.

What do you see in this picture? (Mr. H in the hospital)

Where is Mr. H? (in a hospital bed)

Why is he in the hospital? (He hurt his knee.)

Where is the bandage? (on his knee)

Who else is in the room? (nurse)

What is Mr. H doing? (talking on the telephone)

To whom is Mr. H speaking? (children in class)

What do you think he is saying?

ON THEIR OWN

Children may choose from the following activities:

Crafts

Making paper flowers for Mr. H.

Classifying

Using Alpha Time Master #36 to find things that have numbers (e.g., chart, door, thermometer, telephone, watch).

Art

Drawing or painting pictures of personal experiences in the hospital.

Dramatic Play

Dramatizing *Mr. H Goes To The Hospital.*

Storytelling

Telling other hospital stories to each other on tape.

2H₄

PLANNING AND PREPARATION: Huggable, Mr. H; Alpha Time Master #37; the gifts, letters and get well cards that the children made for Mr. H; pictures of things that start with the letter H; tape or chalk.

READING PICTURES

Show Mr. H to the children.

He's back! He's back! Mr. H is back!

Ask Mr. H if he received your letters and cards and all the things you made for him.

Ask him how he felt when all the things came to his hospital room.

Mr. H says he wants to show you a story with pictures. It will answer many of the questions that you asked him.

Give each child a copy of Alpha Time Master #37. Discuss the picture story with the children.

Frame 1

Look at the first picture at the top.

Where is Mr. H? (in the hospital)

How do you think he feels? (e.g., unhappy, frightened)

What do you think will make him smile?

Frame 2

Look at the next picture.

Who is bringing things to Mr. H? (the nurse)

Where did all these things come from? (children)

What are some of the things the nurse is holding? (e.g., cards, letters, flowers, boxes)

Let's look at the last picture.

Frame 3

How does Mr. H feel now? (happy)

Why do you think he is happy?

What is he doing? (talking on the telephone)

Which letter do you think he is reading?

Tell us what you think the letter says.

Look at Mr. H's face in the first picture. How does he look? (He is sad.)

Now look at the last picture on the bottom.

How is Mr. H's face different? (He is smiling.)

SUBSTITUTING NOUNS THAT BEGIN WITH H

When Mr. H was in the hospital, he listened to the radio. He heard poems that he heard many times before. He liked the way they sounded. The first one he heard was called *Hickory Dickory Dock.*

Why do you think Mr. H especially liked *Hickory Dickory Dock?* (The first word begins the same way as Horrible Hair.)

Listening To A Poem

Here is how the poem sounded when Mr. H first heard it:

> Hickory dickory dock.
> The mouse ran up the clock.
> The clock struck one.
> The mouse ran down.
> Hickory dickory dock.

Have the children repeat the poem so that they become familiar with the words.

Now Mr. H wants to tell you what he did with the poem.

Mr. H thought and thought, and he said to himself:

"Who ran in this poem? That's right—a mouse.

"What did the mouse run up? That's right—a clock.

"I don't want the mouse in this poem.

"I don't want the clock in this poem.

"I want two different things—two things that start like my Horrible Hair."

Substituting Words
In The Poem

Mr. H decided that he would have a *house* and a *hill.*

He said the poem like this:

> "Hickory dickory dock.
> The house ran up the hill.
> The hill struck one.
> The house ran down.
> Hickory dickory dock."

Have the children repeat the new version of the poem. Then have them think of two more words that start with the letter H to substitute, and let them repeat this third version of the rhyme.

On another day, the children may enjoy thinking of variations of the nursery rhyme Hey Diddle Diddle.

> Hey diddle diddle,
> The cat and the fiddle,
> The cow jumped over the moon,
> The little dog laughed,
> To see such sport,
> And the dish ran away with the spoon.

When the children have found the seven things in the rhyme (i.e., cat, fiddle, moon, dog, cow, dish, spoon), they may choose seven pictures from Mr. H's bag. Then reread the poem to them. Each time a noun is mentioned, pause and let a child say the name of a picture that may be used as a substitution.

TYING IT TOGETHER

Playing Hocus Pocus Hopscotch

Mr. H has a game for us.

The game is called *Hocus Pocus Hopscotch!*

Everyone may hop any way he wants to hop. Mr. H wants to see all the different hops you make.

Let several children demonstrate their favorite hops.

Now we are ready to play.

Use tape or chalk to outline two or three hopscotch boxes on the floor. Put a picture of something that starts with the letter H in each box.

Directions: Before a child hops, he must tell Mr. H the boxes into which he is planning to hop and the order in which he will hop. (e.g., "I will hop in horse, hat and house.") Each child may decide for himself into which box(es) he wants to hop.

Following A Sequence

Children who are onlookers may help the child who is hopping to remember the sequence he picked by saying, "(Billy), now you are in hat. You said you were hopping to house next."

Mr. H calls the game *Hocus Pocus Hopscotch* because each child has to do a hocus pocus after he finishes hopping.

When a person is finished hopping, everyone else will close his eyes. Then the person who played will keep saying hocus pocus and put all the pictures in different hopscotch squares. Then someone else will have a turn to play.

ON THEIR OWN

Children may choose from the following activities:

Art

Drawing nonsense pictures illustrating the rhymes in the lesson (e.g., a house running up a hill).

Retelling A Story

Retelling the picture story to one of the Letter People by referring to Alpha Time Master #37.

Recalling A Sequence

Cutting apart the three frames of Alpha Time Master #37 and putting them in order.

2H₅

TEACHER OBJECTIVES:
To associate pictures with holidays.
To reinforce the characteristic and sound of Mr. H.
To review months.

PERFORMANCE OBJECTIVES:
The child will identify certain holidays.
The child will say words with the *h* in the initial position.
The child will identify certain holidays by looking at a picture.
The child will relate certain holidays to months.

DEVELOPMENT

Mr. H made "All About Us" booklets.

Distribute the Mr. H booklets.
Have the children look at the front of the booklet.
Read the words "All About Us" to them.

Which Letter Person's picture do you see? (Mr. H)
Whose picture do you think is next to Mr. H's? (his friend's)
Put your finger on the words under the pictures of Mr. H and his friend.
The words say, "Mr. H has a friend."
What is special about Mr. H? (his horrible hair)
Mr. H wants us to draw hair on the picture of his friend.
If you want the picture of Mr. H's friend to look like you, make the hair look like your hair.
What else can you do to finish the picture? (e.g., Color the eyes the color of your eyes.)

Give the children the opportunity to complete the picture.
Select several children's booklets and read them aloud.

Have the children open the booklet.
Point to the first sentence on the left-hand side.
Ask them what picture Mr. H put in the sentence.
Read aloud, "Mr. H has horrible hair."
Let them pretend to reread the sentence with you.

Explain that the next sentence tells Mr. H's favorite holiday.
Have the children discuss the picture at the bottom.

Guess the name of Mr. H's favorite holiday.
Let's listen to the sentence and see if we are right.

Read aloud, "Mr. H's favorite holiday is Halloween."
Ask them why they think Mr. H likes holidays and why his favorite holiday is Halloween. (*Holiday* and *Halloween* start with the same sound as *horrible hair.*)

Mr. H took this whole page to tell us about himself.
What did he tell us first? (He has horrible hair.)
What did he tell us next? (His favorite holiday is Halloween.)
Mr. H says the next page is for us.
What does Mr. H want each of us to write on the first dotted line?
(our name)
Write your name and then we'll let Mr. H listen to your sentence.

After the children have written their names, select booklets and read the sentences to the class.

Mr. H says he wants us to look at the picture of holidays he drew on the back page.

Have the children turn to the back of the booklet.

Read aloud, "Let's talk about holidays."
Help them identify the different pictures.
Ask them what holiday each picture makes them think about.
Discuss briefly what is special about each holiday.
Ask the children to tell about other holidays they celebrate.
This is an added opportunity to review and/or teach more of the months of the year.

A unit or portion of a unit can begin by dealing with holidays, *e.g.*, patriotic, festival, etc.

Mr. H wants each of us to tell him the name of our favorite holiday.

Have the children open their booklets.
Draw the children's attention to the second sentence on the right-hand page.
Explain that Mr. H wants them to use the sentences to write their name and favorite holiday.

Have the children write their names on the dotted line.
Then select a booklet and read the sentence aloud to prove it is incomplete (*e.g.*, Alan's favorite holiday is   .).

Mr. H says he knows why the sentence isn't finished.
It doesn't tell Alan's favorite holiday.

Select several booklets and follow the above procedure.
Explore with the children different ways of finishing the sentence

(*e.g.*, dictating the name of a holiday, drawing a picture to represent a holiday or finding a picture in a magazine).
Help the children share their completed sentences. Encourage them to tell the name of their favorite holidays to Mr. H.

If you make a timeline of months, add holidays to the time line.

Suggest that the children take the booklets home and ask members of their family to tell Mr. H their favorite holidays.

2N 1

PLANNING AND PREPARATION: Huggables, Mr. N, Mr. M, Mr. T, Mr. F, Mr. H; Mr. N's Picture Squares; a bag for Mr. N; Alpha Time Master #38; magazines, newspapers, construction paper, clay, pipe cleaners, scissors, paste; a paper cut-out of Mr. N's Noisy Nose.

DISCOVERING THAT THE SOUND FOR N WILL COME FROM NOISY NOSE

Pretend to talk to Mr. N as the other Letter People watch.

Mr. N says, "Mr. M got his sound from *Munching Mouth.* Mr. T got his sound from *Tall Teeth.* Mr. F got his sound from *Funny Feet.* Mr. H got his sound from *Horrible Hair.* Where will I get mine?"

Lead the children to the conclusion that Mr. N will get his sound from Noisy Nose and that he wants to fill a bag.

RECOGNIZING OBJECTS THAT START WITH N IN THE INITIAL POSITION

Proving Mr. N's Picture Squares

Show Mr. N's Picture Squares to the children.

Mr. N would like us all to look at some things that start with the same sound as Noisy Nose.

These pictures belong to Mr. N. (i.e., nest, nail, needle, necklace, newspaper) Let's say their names and *prove* them for Mr. N. (e.g., Noisy Nose—nest)

Ask the children to think of other things that start with Mr. N's Noisy Nose sound. This is a difficult skill. If the children need help give them clues. (e.g., When you are eating you put it on your lap so you don't get your clothes dirty. It's name is-----napkin.) Other words you may want to use are nurse, nightgown, nut.

Have the children cut out or make pictures of things that start with N in the initial position. After the children have found and made things for Mr. N's bag one child may act as Mr. N. Mr. N will call on each of the children to put something into his bag. Of course, the must "prove it" to him first. Record #5, side A, band #3 may be used for "Prove It."

We found so many nice things for Mr. N. Now he has found a game for us to play. The game is called Nail the Nose. Mr. N will tell us how to play.

Give the children directions for playing Nail the Nose (a variation of Pin the Tail on the Donkey).

We have to tape some of Mr. N's pictures on the chalkboard. They are pictures of things that start with the same sound as *Noisy Nose.*

Show the children the cut out of the Noisy Nose you have prepared and explain that the Noisy Nose wants to touch (or nail) one of the pictures.

The first person to play will tell us the name of a picture that *Noisy Nose* will touch (nail). We'll cover his eyes so he can't see. Then he will try to "nail" the picture with the *Noisy Nose.*

Repeat the game so that several children may have a turn. Each child must name the picture he is trying to "nail." (e.g., Noisy Nose will nail the newspaper.)

TYING IT TOGETHER

Give each child a copy of Alpha Time Master #38. Explain that by cutting out the pictures they may play the Nail the Nose Game at home. Have the children name and "prove" each N picture on the sheet.

ON THEIR OWN

Children may choose from the following activities:

Motor Skills

Pasting the pictures from their copies of Alpha Time Master #38 on oak tag or construction paper, and playing *Nail the Nose.*

Auditory Discrimination

Listening for words that begin with Mr. N's sound in Mr. N's song. (record #1, side A, band #5)

Visual Memory

Using Mr. N's Picture Squares to play the *Memory Game.* Directions can be found in the *Games* section of the manual.

Classifying

Using Alpha Time Decks or Picture Squares and dividing them into groups for each Letter Person introduced so far.

Crafts

Using hammer, nails, and pieces of soft wood, children may nail a nose by drawing an outline of a nose on a piece of wood and hammering nails about an inch apart along the outline. The nails may be painted and wool or laces may be twisted around the nails to outline the nose.

2N₂

PLANNING AND PREPARATION: Huggables, Mr. N, Mr. M, Mr. T, Mr. F, Mr. H; a sheet of newspaper for each child; magazines, scissors, crayons, drawing paper, paste, stapler; Alpha Time Master #39.

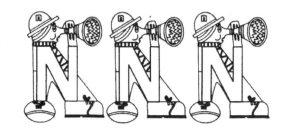

USING WORDS THAT HAVE N AS THE INITIAL SOUND

Mr. N keeps saying he wants us to make a *Newspaper Nose*.

I thought he meant a *Noisy Nose*, but he keeps saying *Newspaper Nose*.

Let's ask Mr. N why he keeps saying *Newspaper Nose*.

Have several children ask Mr. N about Newspaper Noses. Lead them to the conclusion that Mr. N would like them to make Newspaper Noses.

Mr. N says he knows he has a Noisy Nose but he wants us to make a Newspaper Nose for him and he will tell us how.

Following Directions: Making Newspaper Noses

Distribute a sheet of newspaper to each child. Give the children directions and demonstrate.

First everyone must have a sheet of newspaper.

Next Mr. N wants us to paste or draw pictures all over our sheets of newspaper.

What kind of pictures do you think Mr. N would like? (pictures that start with Mr. N's Noisy Nose sound)

Tell Mr. N some of the things you are planning to put on your sheet of newspaper.

Mr. N says he can't give us anymore directions until we finish doing what he just told us to do.

After the children have drawn or pasted several pictures on their sheets of newspaper, tell them Mr. N is ready to give more directions.

Mr. N says now you are ready to make a Newspaper Nose.

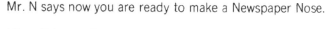

We roll it up. (*Demonstrate by rolling the newspaper to make a tube, keeping the pictures facing the outside.*)

Then we will staple each end.

Now we can hold it up to our noses.

Show Mr. N the pictures on your Newspaper Nose.

IDENTIFYING THE CAPITAL AND LOWER CASE LETTER N

Mr. N would like us to find his capital letter N.

Show him with your hands the part of his body that is the capital N.

Call on several children to point to Mr. N's capital letter.

Making The
Capital Letter "N"
Physically

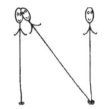

Mr. N wants us to make his capital letter N with our bodies.

How many parts does the capital N have? (three) How many children will we need to make a capital N? (three)

What kind of lines does the capital N have? (straight)

Have the children form groups of three and experiment in forming capital N. Then ask them to identify the lower case "n."

Mr. N has another letter. Show Mr. N his lower case letter n.

DISCUSSING FEELINGS

The Letter People are tired today. They say they could not fall asleep last night. Mr. N wouldn't let them turn off the light. He said he doesn't want to sleep in the dark. He needs to have light.

Have the children ask Mr. N why he wants a light on when he goes to sleep. Then read them the following poem:

Night

When the light is out and I'm in bed,
I put the blankets over my head.
Night, night, you frighten me,
When it's dark and I can't see.
My Noisy Nose makes sounds, it's true.
But dark, dark night, you do too!
I hear footsteps, horns, the telephone,
In the night, when I'm alone.
There are sounds that I can't figure out,
A growl, a creak, a hiss, a shout.
That's when I cover both my ears,
And try to stop my many fears.
Maybe I seem like a baby to you,
But that's how I feel, what can I do?
Perhaps if I had a tiny light,
We could be friends, oh dark, dark night.

Talking About
The Night

How does Mr. N feel about the night?

How do you feel about the night?

Mr. N says sometimes he hears lots of noises.

What are some noises he hears? (e.g., telephone, footsteps)

Deepening awareness of
personal reactions

What are some noises he can't figure out? (e.g., hiss, creak, growl)

Tell him the different noises you hear when you are in bed.

What do you think made the growl? the hiss? the shout? the creak?

What does Mr. N think about when it is very quiet at night?

Tell Mr. N about a time when you wanted to have a light on at night.

Why can't Mr. N help the way he feels at night?

Tell the children that Mr. N would feel much better if they could write some stories for him describing the way they feel at night.

Let's tell Mr. N about things that have happened to us at night.

Let's draw pictures of the night for him.

Encourage the children to dictate stories and to "read" them to Mr. N.

TYING IT TOGETHER

Give each child a copy of Alpha Time Master #39.

Look at the top half of the paper.

Who is in the picture? (Mr. N)

What game is he playing? (Nail the Nose)

What is Mr. N trying to "Nail?" (letter N)

How is Mr. N's game of Nail the Nose different from our game? (We nailed the pictures.)

Put a mark on all the capital "N's" you want Mr. N to nail.

Let's look at the bottom half of the picture. How are the bottom and top half the same? (same game)

How are they different? (different kind of N)

Let's put a mark on all the lower case n's we want Mr. N to nail.

Pictorial comprehension

ON THEIR OWN

Children may choose from the following activities:

Eye-Hand Coordination Letter Tracing

Working with Mr. N's puzzle.

Using Alpha Time Master #68 to trace the letter N.

Drawing or painting the letter N.

Crafts

Using 3 ice cream sticks or tongue depressors, children may nail (or tack) the sticks onto a piece of board to form the capital letter N. More sticks may be added to make letters M, T, F, H.

Art

Making crayon drawings to show night and day. Children draw an outdoor picture, using wax crayons and pressing hard on them. When the picture is finished it can be made "night" by painting black water color or tempera over the entire paper. The wax surface of the crayoned picture will resist the paint while the rest of the paper appears black.

Using black construction paper and yellow crayon to show moon and stars in the night sky.

2N₃

PLANNING AND PREPARATION: Huggable, Mr. N; Mr. N's bag, Mr. N's Picture Squares; Mr. N's Picture Book—one for each child.

RECALLING WORDS THAT BEGIN WITH THE N SOUND

Tell the children what has happened to Mr. N.

Mr. N kept everyone awake all night. He kept chasing things around the room! This morning all the things that were in Mr. N's bag were on the floor. I went to pick them up and put them in his bag. Mr. N was so upset, his nose started to make the noisiest noises.

He said, "Please don't touch anything. Nothing may go back in my bag! I promised. I promised each of my things that it wouldn't have to go back into my bag until I played tag with it and caught it. First, I chased the needle, then I chased the necklace and the newspaper, but I never caught one of them!

Tell the children how to play Mr. N's Game of Tag.

Practicing "N" Words By Playing Tag

Mr. N wants all his things back in his bag, but first he must catch them. Let's help him.

(Jimmy), which thing from the bag do you want to be? (e.g. needle) We'll tape the picture of the (needle) on your back. You start to run. Someone else will be Mr. N and call out your name ("needle, needle, needle") as he is chasing you. When he tags you, you have to go back into the bag!

Continue the game, giving several children a chance to be Mr. N or "it."

Remembering And Relating To A Previous Activity: Newspaper Noses

Remind the children of the newspaper noses they made in the previous lesson. Mr. N doesn't remember how we made the newspaper noses. Let's remind him.

What kind of paper did we use to make newspaper noses? (newspaper)

What did we draw on the newspaper? (pictures for Mr. N)

What did we do with the sheet of newspaper to make it look like a nose? (rolled it)

How did we attach the ends so they wouldn't unroll? (staple)

Now Mr. N remembers. He is so happy that we told him that he has an extra special treat for us.

READING A PICTURE STORY

Discussing Picture Books

Distribute copies of Mr. N's Picture Book. Discuss each page in detail with the children.

Mr. N sent us something very special. What is this? (a book)

What is inside the book? (pictures)

What is Mr. N going to tell us with these pictures? (a story)

Where do we look first? (on the cover)

Cover

Look at the picture on the cover.

Who is on the cover? (Mr. N)

Whom do you think the story is about? (Mr. N)

Turn the page and look at the first picture inside.

Page 1

Who is in the picture? (Mr. N, newspaper seller)

What is for sale at the newspaper stand? (papers, magazines)

How do we know Mr. N is going to buy a newspaper? (He has money in his hand.)

What will Mr. N have to tell the man selling the newspapers? (which one he wants)

Let's all turn the page and look at the next picture—the one near your left hand.

Page 2

Point to Mr. N.

What other Letter People are here? (Miss A, Mr. T, Mr. M, Mr. H, Mr. F)

What is Mr. N doing with the newspaper? (opening it, taking sheets out of it)

How do the other Letter people look? (confused, puzzled)

Why do you think they are watching Mr. N?

Page 3

Let's look at the picture on the next page, the one near your right hand.

What is Mr. N doing? (drawing on a sheet of newspaper)

What picture has he drawn? (a fish)

What do you think Mr. N is making? (newspaper nose)

Who do you think would like a newspaper nose with a fish on it? (Mr. F)

What other pictures could Mr. N draw for Mr. F's nose? (e.g., feather)

Page 4

Who is in this picture? (Mr. N, Mr. F)

What is Mr. N doing? (giving him a newspaper nose)

How does Mr. F feel? (happy)

How can you tell how he feels? (expression on his face)

Page 5

Which Letter People have newspaper noses? (Mr. F, Mr. M, Mr. T, Miss A)

What pictures do you think are on Mr. M's nose? (e.g., mouse) Mr. T's? (e.g., triangle)

How many newspaper noses has Mr. N made so far? (four)

Why do you think Mr. H looks unhappy? (He doesn't have a newspaper nose.)

What is Mr. N doing? (making another newspaper nose)

Which Letter Person will get a newspaper nose next? (Mr. H)

Page 6

Sensory Images

How many newspaper noses did Mr. N make? (five)

What pictures do you think he put on Mr. H's nose? (e.g., heart)

How do the Letter People feel? (happy)

How do we know they like Mr. N? (They are smiling at him.)

What is one reason they like him? (He made things for them.)

TYING IT TOGETHER

Dramatizing
A Story

Several children may dramatize Mr. N's story. A director may be chosen to be sure the sequence of the story is followed. The Letter People and newspaper nose materials may be used as props.

ON THEIR OWN

Children may choose from the following activities:

Developing
Sequence

Cutting the pages of Mr. N's Picture Book apart and mounting each page on a sheet of construction paper — seven in all. (Two books are needed.) Mix them up and line them up on the chalk board shelf. Children decide which event comes first, second, third etc. until all seven pictures are in order. It might be best to start with only two or three pictures at first (e.g., p.3, p.4, p.6) adding more pictures as the children become more experienced.

Using Recall
To Make Books

Making individual picture books by stapling several sheets of paper together along the left edge and drawing pictures on each page. The stories may then be read to the class or recorded to be shared later.

Crafts

Making dioramas of one of the events in Mr. N's Picture Book.

2N₄

TEACHER OBJECTIVES:

To reinforce characteristic and sound of Mr. N.

To review numerals.

PERFORMANCE OBJECTIVES:

The child will state numerals.

The child will say words with the *n* in the initial position.

The child will hear a number word and point to the numeral written on the fantasy character picture.

DEVELOPMENT

Mr. N's noisy nose has been making so much noise.
He never heard about the "All About Us" booklets.
Mr. H had to send him a letter to remind him to make them.
Here they are.

Distribute the booklets.
Point to the words, "All About Us."
Read the title aloud.

Which Letter Person's picture do you see? (Mr. N's)
Whose picture do you think is next to Mr. N? (his friend's)
Put your finger on the words under the pictures.
The words say, "Mr. N has a friend."

What is special about Mr. N? (his noisy nose)
Mr. N wants us to draw a nose on the picture of his friend.
If you want the picture of Mr. N's friend to look like you, make the nose look like your nose.

Give the children the opportunity to complete the picture.
Remind them that it can look like anyone they wish.
Select several booklets and read them aloud.

Have the children open the booklets.
Point to the first sentence on the left-hand side.
Ask the children what picture Mr. N put in the sentence. (his noisy nose)
Read aloud, "Mr. N has a noisy nose."
Let the children pretend to reread the sentence with you.

Explain that the next sentence tells us Mr. N's favorite numeral.

Ask the children to look at the picture and guess the name of Mr. N's favorite numeral.
Read aloud, "Mr. N's favorite numeral is 9."
Ask them why they think Mr. N likes numerals and why his favorite numeral is nine. (*Numerals* and *nine* start with the same sound as *noisy nose.*)

Mr. N took this whole page to tell us about himself.
What did he tell us first? (He has a noisy nose.)
What did he tell us next? (His favorite numeral is nine.)
Mr. N says the next page is for us.

What does Mr. N want each of us to write on the first dotted line?
(our names)
Write your name and then Mr. N will listen to your sentence.

After the children have written their names, select booklets and read the sentences aloud.
Explain that Mr. N wants the children to look at the picture he drew on the back of the booklet.
Have them turn to the back of the booklet.

Read aloud, "Let's talk about numerals."
Give the children time to enjoy the picture.
Ask them to name the numerals they see.

You might have one child call out a numeral.
The others should look for the numeral.
When they find it they should put a finger on it, and then tell on which fantasy character the numeral is found.

Help the children discover which numerals Mr. N included in his picture.

After you have discussed the numerals indicated in the picture, discuss with the children where numerals may be found. Why do we need numerals?
The children may point out numerals that are readily visible in the classroom on clocks and watches, rulers, etc.

Recall with the children that Mr. N's favorite numeral is 9. Ask them to each tell Mr. N what their favorite numeral is. Have them open their booklets.

Draw the children's attention to the second sentence on the right-hand side. Explain that Mr. N wants them to use the sentences to write their names and favorite numerals.

Have the children write their names.
Select a booklet.
Read the sentence aloud to prove it is incomplete. (*e.g.*, Janet's favorite numeral is   .)

Mr. N says he knows why the sentence isn't finished.
It doesn't tell Janet's favorite numeral.

Select several booklets and follow the above procedure.
Discuss ways in which the children may complete their sentences.

Some children may want to dictate the numeral.
Others may want to find the numeral in a magazine, cut it out and paste it on the booklet.
Others may draw the numeral.
Read aloud completed sentences.
Encourage the children to tell the name of their favorite numeral to Mr. N.
Suggest that they take the booklets home and have members of their family tell Mr. N their favorite numeral.

 **PLANNING AND PREPARATION:** Huggables, Mr. M, Mr. T, Mr. F, Mr. H, Mr. N and their playing cards from Alpha Time Decks 1 and 2; Alpha Time Master #18.

REMEMBERING MR. M, MR. T, MR. MR. F, MR. H AND MR. N

Remembering a sequence.

Group all five Letter People together in an easily accessible part of the room.

All the Letter People are talking to one another. They are all glad to be here.

Which of the Letter People arrived first? (Mr. M)

(Jimmy), ask Mr. M why he is glad to be here.

Who came next? (Mr. T)

(Ann), ask Mr. T why he is glad to be with us.

Continue questioning Mr. F, Mr. H and, finally, Mr. N.

Have the children sing The Letter Song to the tune of "Bingo."

Singing A Letter Song

Following directions

We are a class that has some friends;
And these are their names, sir:
M, T, F, H, N!
M, T, F, H, N!
M, T, F, H, N!
And these are their names, sir.

Repeat substituting one clap for the letter M—i.e., "(clap), T, F, H, N!"

Repeat again, substituting two claps for the letters M and T—i.e., "(clap), (clap), F, H, N!"

Repeat again, substituting three claps for M, T and F—i.e., "(clap), (clap), (clap), H, N!"

Continue until all the letters have been replaced by claps—i.e., "(clap), (clap), (clap), (clap), (clap)!
And these are their names, sir."

Tell the children that Mr. N would like to listen to riddles about himself and all the other Letter People.

Identifying The Letter Boys Through Riddles

Listen to each of these riddles and decide if it is about Mr. N, or if it is about one of the other Letter People. When you think you know which Letter Person the riddle is about, you may come up and hug him.

My Munching Mouth munches fast and slow.
I munch and munch wherever I go.
(Mr. M)

When you look at me,
Tall, tall, Tall Teeth are what you see.
(Mr. T)

TYING IT TOGETHER

Distribute Alpha Time Master #17.

Who is in this picture? (Mr. N)

What is Mr. N doing? (chasing Needledeenoop)

What trouble is Needledeenoop making?

How did the lamp tip over?

ON THEIR OWN

Dramatic Play

*Inferring Cause
And Effect
Relationships
Art*

Children may choose from the following activities:

Creating a Needledeenoop play in which an invisible Needledeenoop plays pranks on an unsuspecting person.

Marking on Alpha Time Master #17 all the evidence of mischief Needledeenoop has caused.

Drawing Needledeenoop on Alpha Time Master #17.

2A₁

PLANNING AND PREPARATION: Huggable, Miss A; a bag for Miss A; Miss A's Picture Squares; Alpha Time Master #40; magazines, a variety of papers and art materials.

Miss A's music, (record #1, side A, band #6) may be played to set the mood.

INTRODUCING THE SHORT A SOUND

Talk about Miss A's sneeze with the children. Have the children tell Miss A what they remember about her sneeze.

Remembering Miss A's Sneeze

Miss A says ă, ă, ă'choo.

Miss A says her nose keeps wiggling and wiggling and tickling and tickling.

Do you feel a wiggle and a tickle at the tip of your nose?

Guess who is back? It is Miss A's sneeze!

Have the children repeat the poem "Miss A's Sneeze" with you:

> I am Miss A's sneeze.
> I love to tease and tease.
> I am Miss A's sneeze.
> I love to tease and tease.
> I make Miss A say ă, ă, ă, for a start,
> Then I stop before she can say the *choo* part.
> I am Miss A's sneeze.
> I love to tease and tease.
> Here I come to tease you, too.
> Sneeze!—ă, ă, ă, without the 'choo.

Miss A says she thought of a sound she can have.

What sound do you think Miss A can have?

Miss A says she has to say ă so many times that whenever she opens her mouth, ă is the only thing that comes out.

Help the children decide that Miss A's sound should be the ă from ă'choo.

Miss A says she likes her ă sound. Whenever she forgets her sound, she will just think of the way in which she sneezes.

USING WORDS WITH THE SHORT A IN INITIAL POSITION

Show Miss A's Picture Squares to the children. (i.e., ax, arrow, apple, anchor, astronauts)

Miss A says she isn't sure what each of these pictures is.

Let's show one picture at a time to Miss A and tell her what it is and why the picture belongs to her.

Say the name of the picture so Miss A can hear her ă sound.

Show the children how to emphasize the initial ă sound each time they name a picture. Give as many children as possible a chance to name the pictures.

Miss A would like us to fill a bag for her.

She says she can't think of too many things that start with her ă sound. We'll have to help her.

Let's make some pictures for her.

Making Things For Miss A's Bag

If the children find it difficult to think of things that start with the ă sound, suggest words to them (e.g., alligator, ant). Then they may cut out pictures or make things to put in Miss A's bag.

When the children are ready to put their objects into Miss A's bag they may follow a new procedure.

Miss A likes to ask questions.

She likes to listen to answers.

Why do you think she likes asking and answering? (Ask and answer start with her ă sound.)

Before you put your picture in Miss A's bag she will ask you a question. After you answer it you may put your picture in her bag.

First Miss A will ask, "What is it?" Then you will answer by telling her what it is. (e.g. "It is an ant.") Miss A will ask, "Does it start with my ă sound?" Then you may answer, "Yes." Miss A will then ask, "Can you prove it?" Then you answer, "Yes I can." (e.g., "ă'choo—ant")

Note: *It is best if you play the role of Miss A until you feel a child can handle it.*

IDENTIFYING THE UPPER AND LOWER CASE LETTER A

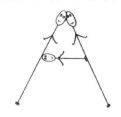

Miss A is glad to know words that begin with her sound.

Now Miss A would like you to show her her capital letter. Use your hands to outline her capital letter A.

Let the children talk about the number of straight lines needed to make the capital A. Have them form groups of three and show Miss A how they make her capital letter. Then they may find Miss A's lower case letter.

TYING IT TOGETHER

*Finding details
Inference*

Give each child a copy of Alpha Time Master #40. Discuss the picture. Help the children locate the capital and lower case A's.

What kind of store is this? (drug store)
Who is in the picture? (Miss A, the druggist)
What is Miss A saying? (ă ă ă)
What is she buying? (tissues)
Why does she need tissues? (for her sneeze)
What other things are for sale?
What would Mr. T buy in the drug store?
Where do you see a capital A?
Where do you see a lower case a?

ON THEIR OWN

Children may choose from the following activities:

Listening	Listening to Miss A's story, Meet Miss A (record #3).
Auditory Discrimination	Playing Miss A's song (record #1) and listening for words that begin with her sound.
Classification	Using Miss A's playing cards and telling her why these cards belong to her.
Motor Coordination	Working with Miss A's puzzle.
Visual Memory	Miss A's Picture Squares and Alpha Time playing cards may be used as suggested in the *Games* section of the manual.
Letter Tracing	Using Alpha Time Master #55 for tracing the upper and lower case A.

2A 2

PLANNING AND PREPARATION: Huggables, Mr. M, Mr. T, Mr. F, Mr. H, Mr. N, Miss A; a small box, magazines, paste, scissors and art materials; Alpha Time Master #41.

REINFORCING THE SHORT A SOUND IN A'CHOO

Show the children the small box.

The Letter People found this box this morning. They tried to figure out what it is. No one could figure it out. Suddenly they all felt a wiggle and a tickle. Guess who it was?

Lead the children to the conclusion that it was Miss A's sneeze.

The Letter People said, "Sneeze, go away.
Go back to Little Miss A."
The sneeze said, "I'll tell you what kind of box that is."
The Letter Boys said, "Oh, sneeze, how would you know what kind of box that is?"
The sneeze said, "It is my box. I made it. It is the 'choo box.'"
"The 'choo box?' Do you mean a sneeze box?"
"Oh, no," the sneeze said, "not a sneeze box. It is just the 'choo box.'"

Give several child a chance to ask Miss A about the "choo box" and to tell the class Miss A's answer.

The sneeze says it is the only one who knows about the "choo box." Let's listen to what it has to say.

Read the children the following poem:

I am the smartest sneeze around.
I figured out Miss A's own sound.
This is what I make her do:
Ă ă ă, but never choo.
I always let the ă part stay.
The choo I catch and lock away.
My "choo box" catches every choo.
Can you make a "choo box" too?

What is a choo box?

Why does the sneeze catch all the choo's? (so that Miss A only says ă,ă,ă)
Let's make "choo boxes" and help the sneeze catch all the choos.

Making "Choo Boxes"

Have the children make their own versions of "choo boxes" using a variety of art materials. They may decorate the "choo boxes" as they wish. Ask them what things they could paste on their "choo boxes" to make Miss A happy. When the boxes are finished the children may show them to Miss A.

Tell the children how they are going to use their "choo boxes":

Are we ready to help the sneeze catch all the choos?

Before you catch the choo part, what must you hear first? (ă)

The *choo* knows you are trying to catch it in your "choo box" and it is tricky. It doesn't always come out after the first ă.

Sometimes you'll hear ă, ā, ā and then you may catch the *choo*.

Following Directions
By Playing A Game

Give the children directions for playing "Catch the Choo:"

First, we will pick a Choo Watcher. Then each person will hold his "choo box" and get ready to catch the *choos*. We will all keep moving and saying ă, ā, ā until the Choo Watcher says, "Here comes the *choo*."

Then, quick as a wink, we will catch the *choo* and lock it in our boxes.

Then we will get ready to catch another *choo*.

The children may move around the room repeating ă, ă, ā as they wait to catch the choos. Continue the game until several children have had a chance to be the Choo Watcher.

TALKING ABOUT BEING "IN THE MIDDLE"

NOTE: Establishing the meaning of "in the middle" is especially important because it introduces the children to the understanding of vowel sounds in the medial position in words.

Place Mr. M and Mr. T near each other in one part of the room.
Place Mr. H and Mr. F near each other in another part of the room.
Place Mr. N and Miss A near each other in a third part of the room.
Each pair of Letter People should be facing the children. Space each pair so that a child can easily stand between the two Letter People.

Look at the Letter People.

With whom is Mr. T? (Mr. M) With whom is Mr. H? (Mr. F) With whom is Mr. N? (Miss A)

Look at Mr. M and Mr. T. There is a space between them. Someone can stand in the middle.

Stand between Mr. M and Mr. T.

Look at me. I am standing between Mr. M and Mr. T. I am in the middle.

(Billy), stand between two of the Letter People. You are in the middle.

Between which two Letter People is Billy standing? (between Mr. M and Mr. T)

Taking Turns
Standing "In
The Middle"

(Bobby), stand between two other Letter People.
Between which two Letter People is Bobby standing?
Where is Bobby? (in the middle)

Repeat until several children have had the chance to stand between two Letter People. Emphasize the phrase "in the middle" making sure that the children know it means—in this instance—being between two objects.

Now the sneeze wants to play. It wants to stand between two of the Letter People.

The whole sneeze cannot go because part of it is still locked in your "choo boxes."

Which part of the sneeze will stand in the middle, between two Letter People? (the ă)

Let one child play the part of the sneeze (ă sound) and stand between different pairs of Letter People.

(Beth), may be the ă. The ă cannot make up its mind between which Letter People it wants to stand.

It runs and stands between Mr. M and Mr. T.

(Beth) stand between Mr. M and Mr. T.

It runs and stands between Mr. H and Mr. F.

It runs and stands between Mr. N and Miss A. It just cannot make up its mind.

(Beth) will keep on running and standing between different Letter People.

We'll keep saying, "Ă, ă, ă, stop running round and round." (Beth) will keep running until we say, "Ă, you must stand in the middle."

Then we will all close our eyes, and the ă, will stand between two of the Letter People.

When we open our eyes, we will look for the ă in the middle.

When we find the ă, we will tell where it is (e.g., "I see the ă between Mr. M and Mr. T.").

Then someone else may be the ă and stand in the middle.

After several children have had a chance to be the "ă," the game may be varied as follows:

The children close their eyes. The "ă" decides between which two Letter People he will stand. Then he turns one of the Letter People around. When the children open their eyes to look for the "ă," they will see the "ă" between two Letter People. However, one of the Letter People will not be facing them. They will have to determine which Letter Person has been turned around.

Understanding The Meaning Of "In The Middle"

After the game, repeat the following rhyme with the children to emphasize the meaning of "in the middle."

> When I'm in the middle,
> What do you see?
> A Letter Person
> On each side of me!

TYING IT TOGETHER

Give each child a copy of Alpha Time Master #41 to look at and discuss.

What are some things you see in the pictures?

What are some things that are "in the middle?" (e.g., boy; the plate; girl)

Look at the first picture.

Between which two Letter People is the little boy standing? (Mr. F and Mr. H)

Look at the picture next to this one. What do you see? (e.g. table setting)

Look at the sandwich.

What do you think is between the two pieces of bread?

Where is the bottle? (between the salt and pepper)

Look at the next picture.

Who is in the picture? (woman, girl, man)

Who is standing in the middle? (the little girl)

What do you see in the last picture? (two buildings)

What is between the two buildings? (a space)

Draw a picture in the middle.

ON THEIR OWN

Children may choose from the following activities:

Classifying

Circling or checking all the "in the middle" objects on Alpha Time Master #41.

Applying The "In The Middle" Principle

Looking around the classroom or in books for other objects or things that are "in the middle."

Color Discrimination

Drawing a blue car between two red ones; a yellow ball between two green ones; a brown doll between two purple ones.

Shape Discrimination

Placing a different shape between two like shapes (e.g., a square between two circles, a rectangle between two triangles).

2A₃
PLANNING AND PREPARATION: Huggables, Mr. M, Mr. T, Mr. F, Mr. H, Mr. N, Miss A; Alpha Time Master #42; Miss A's Bag, Miss A's "In the Middle" Picture Squares.

REINFORCING THE IDEA OF "IN THE MIDDLE"

Give each child a copy of Alpha Time Master #42. Help the children remember the "In the Middle" game that the sneeze played with the Letter People.

Recalling Experiences With Miss A's Sneeze

Miss A wants you to look at the pictures and to tell her everything that is happening in the story.

Look at the first picture.

Which Letter People do you see? (M, T, N, A, F, H)

Which Letter People are near each other? (M and T; N and A; F and H)

Point to Miss A's sneeze.

Where do you think the sneeze will go?

Let's look at the next part of the story.

Where is the sneeze now? (in the middle; between Mr. M and Mr. T)

Now the sneeze will fly around again.

This time it is going to stand between two different Letter People.

The sneeze will try to trick you.

You will have to say between which two Letter People the sneeze is standing.

Look at the last picture.

What trick did the sneeze play on us? (It turned a Letter Person around.)

How can we tell which Letter Person the sneeze turned around?

Between which two Letter People is the sneeze standing? (Mr. F and Mr. H)

Miss A has been watching the sneeze standing between the Letter People. She has a plan.

She knows that her "ă" sound starts words like *astronaut, apple* and *arrow.*

She has been thinking that her ă sound would sound beautiful in the middle of a word. She wants her sound to be heard between two of the Letter Boys' sounds. Let's let Miss A try.

RECOGNIZING THE SHORT A SOUND IN THE MEDIAL POSITION

Remember, we are listening for Miss A's sound. It is not going to be the first sound we hear in a word. It is going to be in the middle.

Miss A says the word is *man*. *(Emphasize the ă sound.)*

Did you hear Miss A's sound? What did she say? *(ă)*

How can you prove that the sound you hear is Miss A's sound? (Miss A gets her sound from her ă'choo.)

In what part of the word do you hear Miss A's sound? (in the middle)

It is not necessary at this point to mention the sounds at either side of Miss A's sound. If the children want to know, tell them. However, at this time the children need only recognize the ă sound in the medial position.

Miss A thinks she knows another word that has her ă sound in the middle of the word. She wants you to listen for her sound.

Tell the children that Miss A's word is "hat." Emphasize the "ă" sound.

Do you hear Miss A's sound in *hat?* What is she saying? *(ă)*

How can you prove that is Miss A's sound? (Miss A gets her sound from ă'choo.)

Where is Miss A's sound in the word *hat?* (It is in the middle.)

Tell the children that Miss A can think of more words in which her "ă" sound is in the middle (e.g., fat, mat, tan, fan, ham).

NOTE: Please follow the procedure outlined above. Please do not eliminate any of the questions. In field testing we found that using the questions helps to establish a pattern of thinking for the children.

Show the children Miss A's "in the middle" Picture Squares (i.e., hat, man, fan, ham, mat). The symbol  *designates these as "in the middle" pictures. Say the name of each picture aloud with the children. Emphasize the "ă" sound. Help the children decide that all these pictures have the "ă" in the middle of the word.*

TYING IT TOGETHER

*Reinforcing "a"
In The Medial
Position*

Play the following "In the Middle Game" with the children:

Choose two children to stand alongside each other. They should leave a space large enough so that another child can fit between them. Distribute Miss A's "in the middle" picture squares to five children. Choose one child to hold Miss A.

To play: A child names the picture he is holding (e.g., hat). The child playing Miss A says, "I hear my ă sound in hat. It is in the middle." The child then places Miss A between the two children. The class may then repeat the word and decide if Miss A's "ă" sound is in the word.

Continue the game by choosing another child to be Miss A and having another word said. Continue until all five "in the middle" words have been used.

ON THEIR OWN

Children may choose from the following activities:

Auditory Discrimination

Deciding which Letter Person begins each picture word on Miss A's "in the middle" Picture Squares.

Thinking of names that have the ă in the middle. (e.g., Pat, Nan, Sam, Dan, Sal, Fran, Hank)

Rhyming

Making rhyming words that end in *an, at, am.*

2A₄

PLANNING AND PREPARATION: Huggable, Miss A; Miss A's "In the Middle" Picture Squares; Alpha Time Masters #43 and #44.

REINFORCING SHORT A IN THE MEDIAL POSITION

Turn Miss A so that her back faces the children.

Miss A could hardly wait for you to come to school. She wants us to play a guessing game.

She likes to listen to her ă sound when it is in the middle of a word.

Hold up Miss A's "In the Middle" Picture Squares so that the children can see them. Tell the children that Miss A has a riddle for each word. The pictures will help figure out the words.

Miss A is ready to begin. She will think of one of the words on these pictures. It will be a word that has her ă sound in the middle of the word.

Identifying Words Through Context Clues

Miss A's back is turned. If you guess which word she is thinking about you may turn Miss A around.

Listen to the first riddle.

Riddle #1
    You always wear me on your head,
    But never when you are in bed.
    Please turn me around,
    If you hear my ă sound.

Which picture is Miss A thinking about? (hat)

Say the word so that she can hear her ă sound.

Before you turn Miss A around you must tell her where you hear her ă sound. (in the middle)

Read the children the rest of the riddles, following the same questioning technique after each.

Riddle #2 (mat)
    I am placed upon the floor.
    You wipe your feet on me,
    As you enter the door.
    Please turn me around,
    If you hear my ă sound.

Riddle #3 (fan)
    My blades keep spinning around and around.
    I cool the air with a whirring sound.
    (Refrain)

Riddle #4 (man)
    My name can be Frank or Dan or Sam.
    A grown up boy is what I am.
    (Refrain)

Riddle #5 (ham)
I am a kind of meat.
Some people like to eat.
(Refrain)

Miss A likes to hear her ă sound when it is in the middle of a word.

Miss A has another game for us.

Playing A Game With Miss A

Help the children play the following game to the tune of "London Bridge is Falling Down."

Directions: Divide the children into groups of three. Two children in each group join hands to form individual circles. The third child will play the part of Miss A. Miss A will dance around the outside of her circle. The circle tries to catch her so that she is in the middle. The two circle children may not drop their hands. The children sing these words:

> Please Miss A don't run away,
> Run away,
> Run away.
> Please Miss A don't run away,
> Get in the middle.

At this point, Miss A must get into the circle.

Then they sing these words while swaying back and forth and encircling their Miss A:

> Now Miss A is in the middle,
> In the middle,
> In the middle.
> Now Miss A is in the middle,
> Stay in the middle.

Then they sing:

> If you say ă we'll let you out.
> Let you out,
> Let you out.
> If you say ă we'll let you out,
> Dear Miss A.

When Miss A says "ă" she takes the place of one of the children in the circle. That child then becomes the new Miss A.

TYING IT TOGETHER

Distribute and discuss Alpha Time Master #43.

What game are the children playing? (Please Miss A Don't Run Away)

Where is Miss A? (In the middle)

Draw a line between the other two children.

NOTE: Alpha Time Master #44 is a letter to parents explaining the progress the children have made thus far with ALPHA TIME. This letter may be sent home with the children at this time.

ON THEIR OWN

Reinforcing
"In The Middle"

Using the letter parts of all the puzzle pieces, Miss A's letter may be put between any two others. (Same activity may be done using playing cards from Alpha Time Deck 4.)

Word Building

Using letter parts of puzzle pieces to build words with A in the middle. (i.e., fan, fat, man, mat, tan, ham)

Art

Building words as above using the Letter People themselves.

Drawing two Letter People with Miss A between them.

Crafts

Cutting out snowflakes designs on two colored paper squares or circles (two paper doilies may be used instead) and putting a contrasting color paper in the middle. Then the three pieces may be pasted, stitched or stapled together.

2A₅

PERFORMANCE OBJECTIVES:
The child will say words with the short *a* sound in the initial position.
The child will state his address.
The child will copy his address correctly.
The child will state a reason for numbering houses, identifying streets.

TEACHER OBJECTIVES:
To reinforce the characteristic and sound of Miss A.
To emphasize the concept of address.
To have children state and copy addresses.

DEVELOPMENT

The Letter Boys told Miss A about the "All About Us" booklets.
Miss A made "All About Us" booklets.

Distribute the Miss A booklets.

Point to the words "All About Us."
Read the title aloud.

Which Letter Person's picture do you see? (Miss A)
Whose picture do you think is next to Miss A? (her friend's)
Put your finger on the words under the pictures.
The words say, "Miss A has a friend."
What is special about Miss A? (her ă' choo)
Look at the picture of her friend.
What did Miss A forget to draw on the face? (eyes, nose and mouth)
What is Miss A's friend holding that causes a sneeze? (a feather)
How do you know Miss A's friend is going to sneeze? (the position of the finger)
Let's finish the picture of Miss A's friend.
If you want the picture of Miss A's friend to look like you, how will you finish it?

Give the children the opportunity to complete the picture.
Remind them it may look like anyone they wish.
Select several booklets and read them aloud.

Have the children open the booklets.
Point to the full page picture on the left-hand side.

Explain that Miss A used this whole page to show what happens when she keeps sneezing ă' choo.

Let's sneeze the way she does.
What happens to the trees when Miss A keeps sneezing ă' choo, ă' choo, ă' choo? (The trees bend.)
What happens to the flowers when Miss A sneezes ă' choo? (The flowers bend.)
Look at the rabbit.
The rabbit is delivering mail.
Miss A sneezes ă' choo.
What flies off the rabbit's head? (the mail cap)

The children may enjoy dramatizing the different things that happen as Miss A sneezes ă' choo.
This is an ideal opportunity for the children to practice the short *a* sound as they reproduce Miss A's ă' choo.

Have the children look at the right-hand side of the booklet.
Explain that Miss A has written something that is very important.
Read the first sentence aloud.
"Miss A's address is 5 Apple Avenue."

Talk about the word *address*. Discuss its meaning.

Miss A says it's important for each of us to know our address.
Tell Miss A why you think it is important.
Tell her your address.

Give as many children as possible the opportunity to tell their address to Miss A.
Explain that Miss A wants to see their addresses on the booklets. She left space at the bottom.
Have the children find the first dotted line.
Explain that this line is the place Miss A wants them to write their names.
Give them the opportunity to do this.

After the children have written their names, select a booklet and read the sentence aloud to prove it is incomplete. (*e.g.,* Donald's address is   .)

Miss A says she knows why the sentence isn't finished.
It doesn't tell Donald's address.
How can Donald finish his sentence? (He can write his address on the second dotted line.)

Have Donald dictate his address.
Write it on the book for him.
Read the completed sentence aloud.
Follow the above procedure with each child's booklet.
Some children may be able to copy their addresses onto the booklet.

Have the children turn to the back of the booklet.
Read aloud, "Let's talk about addresses."
Explain that Miss A drew a picture. In it there are many places where an address or part of an address may be written.
Miss A wants the children to find and name all the places. (*e.g.,* mail box, package, letter, above the door, on the street sign)

This is an excellent opportunity to discuss additional usages of numerals.

Why is it important for houses to have numerals?
Would the numerals on a house be enough to tell somebody where you lived?
What are some other words that are used to name streets? (*e.g.,* road, drive, parkway, etc.)

Suggest that the children take the booklets home.
Encourage them to tell how Miss A sneezes.
Suggest that they tell why it is important for them to know their address.

1B₁

PLANNING AND PREPARATION: Six buttons; large paper circles, one for each child in the class; a roll of newsprint or wrapping paper; crayons and art materials; Alpha Time Master #45.

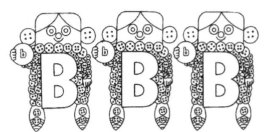

INTRODUCING BUTTONS

Dramatizing Rhymes

Show the children the buttons one at a time.

Do you know what these are? I thought they were all buttons too, but they said, "Oh no, we're not just buttons."
What do you think they are?

Give each child a paper circle to represent a button to be used in dramatizing the following rhymes:

I know a button who thinks it is a bee.
It buzzes and flies for all to see.

How would a button look buzzing and flying?

Show us how you would look if you were a bee buzzing and flying.

Let's each be a bee. Let's buzz and fly and then come back to hear about another button.

Have the children hold up their paper buttons and buzz around the room.

I know a button who thinks it is a clock.
It keeps on saying, "Tick tock, tick tock."

Hold up your button and let it be a clock.

What will your button say?

Show us how you would look being a clock.

After the ticks and tocks we will listen and find out about another button.

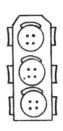

I know a button who thinks it is a traffic light.
It blinks its eyes open, then shuts them tight.

Take your button and let it be a traffic light.

Continue the game, giving the children the opportunity to dramatize each rhyme.

I know a button who thinks it is a mouse.
It creeps and squeaks all through the house.

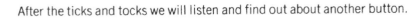

I know a button who thinks it is a fish.
It swims and swims—swish, swish, swish!

I know a button who thinks it is a kangaroo.
It jumps and leaps—that's all it will do.

Help the children remember the button rhymes they have just heard.

111

What were all the different things the buttons thought they were? (bee, clock, traffic light, mouse, fish, kangaroo)

Recalling

Take your buttons and be one of these things.

Using context clues

We'll try to guess which one you are.

MAKING A MURAL

We heard about the buttons, but we didn't see any pictures. Other classes would like to hear about the buttons, but they want to see pictures too.

Let's write about each button and draw a picture for it on one giant-size piece of paper.

Stretch the paper across the classroom floor, and tape it at several points so that it does not curl. Divide the paper into six sections. While the class watches, write one of the button rhymes in each section and read it aloud. Draw a small symbol next to each rhyme so the children can see which button the rhyme is describing (e.g., outline of a bee, clock, fish).

Let the children decide on which section of the mural they want to work. Have them form six groups. Each group may have a meeting to decide what their picture will show.

Meet with each group, and help them plan their picture. Encourage the children to give the mural depth by using various art materials such as pipe cleaners, cotton, bits of fabric.

As the children work, reread the rhymes for each group.

When the mural is finished, let each group read their rhyme in unison. Then have the children describe all the things they put in their picture.

Other classes may be invited to share the mural.

TYING IT TOGETHER

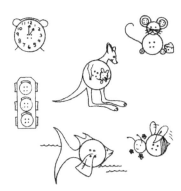

Give each child a copy of Alpha Time Master #45 and discuss it with the class.

What kind of buttons are in this picture?

Point to one of the buttons and tell us what it thinks it is. (e.g. fish, clock)

Which is the biggest button? (clock)

Which is the smallest button? (mouse's feet)

What noise did the bee make? (buzz)

What noise did the clock make? (tick, tock)

What noise did the fish make? (swish, swish)

Comparing Sizes

Recalling Sounds

ON THEIR OWN

Children may choose from the following activities:

Sewing

Sewing buttons on pieces of fabric.

Making button faces by using buttons for eyes, nose and mouth and sewing them onto fabric to look like a face.

Crafts

Making a mosaic design by pasting vari-colored buttons on cardboard.

Sorting

Sorting a box of mixed buttons according to color, size, shape, material and number of holes—putting each kind into an envelope.

Muscle Coordination

Practicing buttoning and unbuttoning by having a buttoning race as follows:

At a signal, two or more children may start buttoning or unbuttoning a coat, sweater, shirt, etc. The first person finished wins.

1B₂

PLANNING AND PREPARATION: Huggable, Mr. B; Record #1; Picture Card 5; Alpha Time Master #46.

Place Mr. B in a corner of the room.

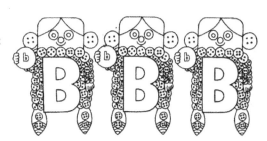

MEETING MR. B AND HIS BEAUTIFUL BUTTONS

Wait until a child discovers Mr. B. Then the rest of the class may gather around him, look at him, and talk about him.

Who can this Letter Person be?

What do you see all over this Letter Person? (buttons)

Why do you think he decided to come to our classroom?

What do you think he would like to see? (the button mural)

Ask him why he is covered with buttons.

Pretend to talk to Mr. B. Then tell the children what he said.

This Letter Person says, "You met buttons who thought they were a bee, a mouse, a fish, a clock, a kangaroo and a traffic light. I know every button in the whole world!

"All buttons are Beautiful Buttons, that's easy to see.
All Beautiful Buttons belong to me!"

Listening To
Mr. B's Song

This Letter Person has a song for us. Let's listen. Then we'll know what his name is.

Play Mr. B's Song (record #1, side B, band #1).

What is the Letter Person's name? (Mr. B)

What does he tell us about himself?

What kind of buttons does he have?

Show Mr. B how his music makes you feel.

Replay the song and let the children sing along with it, moving freely to the rhythm.

IDENTIFYING THE CAPITAL AND LOWER CASE B

Mr. B would like you to show him his capital letter and then make it with your bodies.

NOTE: Unlike the first six letters, B does not have all straight lines. It is important that the children recognize this when forming the letter.

Use your hand to show Mr. B his capital letter.

Where is Mr. B's lower case letter? (in his hand)

Look at the other Letter People's capital letters. How did we know how many children were needed to make each capital letter? (counted the lines)

How did we keep our bodies when we were lying on the floor? (straight)

*Analyzing The
Shape of B*

Look at the capital B. What will be different about the shape of our bodies as we make Mr. B's capital letter? (the lines are not all straight)

How many curves will there be in B? (two)

How many straight lines? (one)

How many children will have to curl their bodies? (two)

Let's ask three children to make the capital B.

Remember, one person will keep his body straight. Two will curl around so that their heads and feet touch the person who is lying straight. They can stretch their arms above their heads and touch him with their hands.

Help three children make the capital letter B with their bodies. Let the class assist by moving the children's bodies. Then all the children may form groups of three and make the capital letter B.

MAKING VALUE JUDGMENTS

Mr. B loves his Beautiful Buttons. He says he loves them all the time — even when they are bad.

He doesn't want them to be bad, but sometimes he does have bad Beautiful Buttons.

Mr. B wants to tell us a story about three bad but Beautiful Buttons.

Show Picture Card 5 to the children as you read the story.

Point to the first frame on the Picture Card.

One day, three children came to ask Mr. B if they might each have a Beautiful Button. One little girl had a beautiful new coat. A beautiful new coat needs a *Beautiful Button!*

One little boy had a beautiful new shirt. A beautiful new shirt needs a *Beautiful Button!*

The other little girl had a beautiful new skirt. Surely a beautiful new skirt needs a — *Beautiful Button!*

Point to frame two.

Mr. B brought a big Beautiful Button box. The children each picked out a Beautiful Button.

Before Mr. B gives his buttons to someone he always asks his buttons if they would like to go.

Mr. B asked one of the three Beautiful Buttons if it would please be on the coat. He asked another to be on the shirt. He asked the third to be on the skirt. Each button promised it would go.

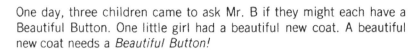

Mr. B told the children, "I will send your Beautiful Buttons to you. First I must make sure that each button is shiny and bright."

Mr. B polished each button until it sparkled. The buttons were brighter and more beautiful than ever.

Then they were ready to go to the children. Bless my Beautiful Buttons! What do you think happened?

Point to the third picture.

As Mr. B was about to put the buttons into boxes, the buttons said, "We changed our minds. We won't go!"

Mr. B said, "Please don't be bad Beautiful Buttons. You promised the children that you would go. Beautiful Buttons must not break promises."

What do you think those bad but Beautiful Buttons said?

They said, *"We won't go!"*

Mr. B said, "Buttons, a promise is a promise! You must go."

Mr. B kept trying to put the buttons into boxes. He wanted to send them to the children who wanted them, but BAROOM!—the buttons began to run around the room.

Sing the following words to the tune of Pop Goes The Weasel.

Round and round his beautiful room,
Mr. B chased three bad buttons.
The buttons didn't think it was fun.
BAROOM ran the buttons!
No button for a coat or shirt,
No button for a pretty skirt.
This is the way the story goes.
BAROOM ran the buttons!

Recalling

Whom was Mr. B chasing? (the buttons)

Why did he chase them? (They did not want to go into the boxes.)

Why did he call the buttons bad but Beautiful Buttons? (They broke their promises.)

Why do you think the buttons changed their minds?

Making Value Judgments

How do you feel about the Beautiful Buttons breaking their promises?

Predicting

How do you think the children will feel when they don't get their buttons?

Relating Personal Experiences

Tell us about a time when someone broke a promise to you.

Tell us about a time when you broke a promise.

What should Mr. B do?

What do you think will happen to those three bad but Beautiful Buttons?

Have the children sing the song and dramatize it, then repeat the song so that several of the children may have a chance to be Mr. B or one of the buttons.

TYING IT TOGETHER

Give each child a copy of Alpha Time Master #46 and have the children take turns in re-telling the story of each picture. They may then look for upper and lower case B's and mark them.

ON THEIR OWN

Letter Tracing

Classifying

Game

Size Sequence

Music, Rhythm

Children may choose from the following activities:

Tracing the upper and lower case letter B on copies of Alpha Time Master #56.

Drawing or cutting out pictures of articles of clothing that need buttons.

Playing "Who Has The Button?" as follows:

Five or more players are needed. The children stand in a circle. One child stands in the center and is "it" (or Mr. B). The children pass a button from one person to the other behind their backs. When Mr. B says STOP, the children must hold their fists out into the circle. Mr. B has three chances to guess who has the button. If he guesses incorrectly, the person who has the button becomes Mr. B.

Taking five different size buttons and arranging them according to size —from left to right or from top to bottom.

Dancing to Mr. B's music —either alone, in pairs, or with Mr. B.

1B₃

PLANNING AND PREPARATION: Huggable, Mr. B; Alpha Time Master #47; straws or popsicle sticks, drawing paper, crayons, pipe cleaners, scissors.

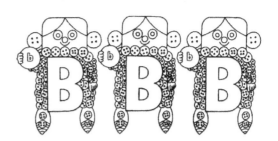

REMEMBERING MR. B'S BAD BUT BEAUTIFUL BUTTONS

Tell the children that Mr. B has been chasing the three bad but Beautiful Buttons most of the night.

Recalling

Why were the bad but Beautiful Buttons running away? (They didn't want to go into the boxes.)

Why did Mr. B want to catch them? (He promised the children that he would send the buttons.)

Predicting Outcomes

What do you think happened when the buttons ran away?

Listen for the answer in this song:

Listening for facts

Sing the Bad Button song to the tune of Three Blind Mice.

Three bad buttons,
Three bad buttons.
See how they run,
See how they run.
They all ran away from Mr. B.
He finally caught them—one, two, three.
Did you ever see such a sight in your life
As three bad buttons?
Three bad buttons!

What happened to the buttons? (they were caught)

How many bad buttons were there? (*Hold up three fingers to show the three bad buttons.*)

Have the children sing the song, and show them how to dramatize it as a finger play.

When we sing the line, *Three bad buttons*, we will make a circle with our thumb and one finger to represent a button.

Finger play

Following Directions

When we sing the line, *He finally caught them—one, two, three*, we'll hold up one finger at a time.

When the bad but Beautiful Buttons are running in the song, we will make three of our fingers run.

Mr. B was unhappy because the buttons had broken their promises. He finally caught the buttons. What do you think he will do?

READING COMPREHENSION

Let's read a picture story and find out what Mr. B does with the buttons.

Distribute copies of Alpha Time Master #47. Discuss each picture.

Look at the first part of the story.

Who is in this picture? (Mr. B, the buttons)

What is happening? (Mr. B is chasing them)

Which part of the song would go with this picture? (They all ran away from Mr. B.)

Can you think of any word that tells us what Mr. B is doing? (running, chasing, racing, galloping)

Let's look at the next picture and see what happens.

What did Mr. B do? (He caught the buttons.)

How many bad but Beautiful Buttons did Mr. B catch? (three)

Sing the part of the song that goes with this picture. (He finally caught them — one, two, three.)

Counting

How do you think the buttons feel now that Mr. B has caught them?

Sensory Images

Listen to some words that tell how the buttons might feel. Use your face to show us what each of these words means.

How would a button face look when it is *unhappy* because it was caught?

How would a button face look when it is *angry* because it was caught?

Repeat the same procedure for the words surprised, annoyed and afraid.

What do you think Mr. B will do with the three bad but Beautiful Buttons now that he has caught them? Let's look at the next picture.

What do you think is happening?

What is Mr. B doing? (talking to the buttons)

What do you think the first button is thinking? The second? The third?

What do you think the buttons will do?

Tell the buttons about something you had to do because you had promised. Maybe it was something you didn't want to do!

Do you think the buttons should keep their promise?

Let's look at the last picture.

How do you know the buttons are going to keep their promise? (They are going into the boxes.)

Why can't we call them *bad* but Beautiful Buttons anymore?

What could we call them instead?

119

GIVING A STORY A TITLE

Mr. B would like to hear you tell this story again and again. He says he may ask you to tell it to him a few days from now. He knows you will read so many picture stories that you won't know which one he means.

Mr. T told him that when he goes to buy toothpaste, he has to say the name of the toothpaste he wants.

Mr. B says, "I would like to tell you the name of the story that I want to hear, but this story doesn't have a name!" Mr. B is right. The story has no name!

Talking About Names

What would happen if we didn't have names?

What name did Mr. M's story have? (*Meet Me At The Market*)

What does its name tell about the story? (what happens in the story)

Who met at the market? (Mr. M and the people)

Mr. B's story has to have a name.

Can we give the story the name *Bobby?*

Can we give the story the name *Jane?*

We need a name that goes with just this story.

Getting The Main Idea

What is this story about?

What is most important in this story?

What names can we give the story?

As the children suggest names, decide with them whether the name tells about an important part of the story and whether it is short enough to be a title. If the names they suggest are too long explain:

Suppose you had a very, very long name like *Mary Elizabeth Barbara Susan Jane Penelope Smith?* It would take so long to say that we would forget what we wanted to tell you before we finished saying your name!

Some children may need help at first. You might encourage them as follows:

Is *Bad Buttons* a good name for this story?

Was the story about bad buttons?

If Mr. B said next week, "Read the story called *Bad Buttons,*" would you know which one he meant?

What other name could the story have?

TYING IT TOGETHER

Distribute art materials and let the children make stick puppets for any or all of the characters in the story. They may use them to dramatize any of the songs that they have learned in these lessons, or to dramatize stories or songs they make up themselves.

ON THEIR OWN

Children may choose from the following activities:

Storytelling

Using Picture Card 5 to retell Mr. B's story to him. Children may want to tell a story about what happens to each button when it arrives at the child's house. Another story might be about how the buttons feels when they are packed inside a box and sent through the mail.

Art

Drawing the bad but Beautiful Buttons the way they looked when they ran away, and the way they looked when Mr. B caught them.

Naming

Giving new titles to familiar stories, songs or poems.

Giving nicknames to friends.

Sorting And Matching

Including Mr. B's playing cards from Alpha Time Decks 1, 2, and 4 in any of the matching and sorting activities listed in the *Games* section of the manual.

1Z₁

PLANNING AND PREPARATION: Several real zippers; strips of paper, one for each child; large sheets of paper, crayons, art materials, paste; Alpha Time Master #48.

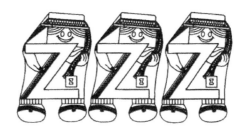

TALKING ABOUT ZIPPERS

Dramatizing
Nonsense Rhymes

Show the children the zippers you have brought to class. Let the children have time to look at each of the zippers before talking about them.

What are these things? (zippers)

I too thought they were just zippers until the zippers said, "Oh, no, we are *not* just zippers!" Then each zipper said what it thought it was.
I will tell you about them.

I know a zipper who thinks it is a broom.
It sweeps the floors in every room.

Give each child a strip of paper to represent a zipper.

Now you have the zipper who thinks it is a broom.

Take your zipper and sweep and sweep all around the room.

Let the children "sweep" around the room.

All right, brooms. Come back, and hear about the next zipper.

I know a zipper who thinks it is a top.
It spins and spins and will not stop.

Take your zipper and let it be a top. What will the top do? (spin)

Holding their zippers, the children may twirl and spin.

All right, tops, no more spinning and spinning. Now let's hear about another zipper.

I know a zipper who thinks it is a bird.
It flies and flies and says not a word.

Take your zipper and let it be a bird. What will the bird do? (fly)

Let the children fly their zippers.

All right, birds. No more flying and flying. Listen and find out about another zipper.

I know a zipper who thinks it is a kite.
It climbs so high it is out of sight.

Take your zipper and let it be a kite. What will the kite do? (climb)

Each zipper thinks it is something other than a zipper.

Say a word that tells what one of the zippers thinks it is (e.g. broom).

Using Vocabulary

Now say a word that tells what that zipper does (e.g. sweeps).

If the children have difficulty, help them by rereading one rhyme at a time for them. As each rhyme is read ask them to say the word in the rhyme which tells what the zipper thinks it is. Then reread the rhyme and ask them to say the word that tells what the zipper does.

PANTOMIMING ACTION WORDS

Sometimes we act something out without using any words.

I will not say a word, but if you watch me you will know what I am doing.

Inferring Meanings From Visual Clues

Ask the children to watch you as you pretend to be bouncing a ball.

What am I doing? (bouncing a ball)

How do you know? (by seeing what you are doing)

Pretend to be one of the zippers that we know. We will guess which zipper you are by watching how you act.

Continue until several children have had a chance to pantomime an action of one of the zippers.

MAKING A TALKING BOOK

The zippers saw the big picture story you made for the buttons. They want a story, too. They don't want you to make the same picture story you made for the buttons. They want you to make a giant Talking Book.

First we will make the pages of the book. They will have to be very big pages so we can bend down behind them and talk.

Let's try to figure out how many pages our book will have.

Have the children recall the zipper rhymes.

How many zippers did we meet? (four)

Each of those zippers would like its own page. We can make more pages for other zippers who think they are something else.

Maybe one could be a zipper who thinks it is a tree. What would it do? (sway, bend, shake)

Maybe it could be a zipper who thinks it is a monkey. What would it do? (climb, swing by its tail, eat bananas, make faces)

Have the children work in pairs or in small groups each illustrating one page of the Talking Book. Encourage them to use a variety of materials available in the classroom such as straws, pipe cleaners, bits of material to give the picture texture. After the pictures are finished, fasten the pages to form a book. Include a cover.

NAMING A STORY

Our book needs something.

The picture story about the three bad but Beautiful Buttons needed something, too. What did it need? (The story needed a name.)

Help the children suggest possible names for the Talking Book. Then let them suggest titles for each page in the book.

Discussing Titles

What must we remember about a story's name? (It has to tell something important about the story.)

What is important in the story?

How many zippers are in the story? (four)

What kind of zippers are they? (strange, funny, imaginative)

Tell us a name you would like this story to have. (e.g. Strange Zippers, Funny Zippers, Four Zippers, I Know A Zipper)

Each zipper wants its part of the story to have its own name.

Which is the first zipper in our book? (broom)

What does this zipper do? (sweep)

What name could this part of the story have? (e.g. The Zipper Who Sweeps; The Zipper Broom)

Narrating Each Page Of The Talking Book

Let several children take turns standing or crouching behind a page of the Talking Book and talking for the zipper on that page. If a tape recorder is available, the children might record the stories of their Talking Book. The Letter People may be invited to listen to the stories, too.

TYING IT TOGETHER

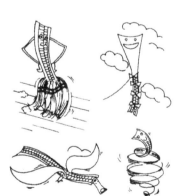

Distribute copies of Alpha Time Master #48 and discuss the pictures with the children.

Which of these zippers thinks it is a broom?

What is it doing? (sweeping)

Which of these zippers is spinning and spinning?

What does it think it is? (a top)

What do the other two zippers think they are? (kite, bird)

ON THEIR OWN

Children may choose from the following activities:

*Sewing: Motor
Co-ordination*

Stitching zippers on pieces of fabric.

Number Sequence

Writing numerals 1-4 under each picture on Alpha Time Master #48 to designate the order the zippers have in the Talking Book.

Art And Classifying

Making a collage or chart of pictures of things that have zippers.

1Z₂

PLANNING AND PREPARATION: Huggable, Mr. Z; Record #1; paper, crayons, paste, art materials; Alpha Time Master #49.

Place Mr. Z in a corner of the room.

MEETING MR. Z AND HIS ZIPPING ZIPPERS

Wait until a child discovers Mr. Z.

Who can this Letter Person be?

What does this Letter Person have all over him? (zippers)

Why do you think he came to this class?

He says he heard about the Talking Book and he would like to see it.

Why do you think he is interested in our Talking Book? (It is about zippers.)

*Listening To
Mr. Z's Song And
Moving To His
Music*

Play Mr. Z's song (record #1, side B, band #2).

Discuss the words and music with the children.

What is the new Letter Person's name? (Mr. Z)

What does Mr. Z tell us about himself? (He has Zipping Zippers.)

How did his music make you feel?

How does it make you want to move?

Play the record again and encourage the children to sing or move along with the music.

Mr. Z says that he heard about the zippers who think they are something else. Which zippers does he mean? (zippers who think they are a broom, top, bird, kite)

Mr. Z knows every zipper in the whole world. He says all zippers are Zipping Zippers and all Zipping Zippers belong to Mr. Z.

IDENTIFYING THE CAPITAL AND LOWER CASE LETTER Z

The other Letter People told Mr. Z that you made their capital letters with your bodies.

Mr. Z would like us to show him his capital letter Z. Than you may make the Z with your bodies.

Use your finger to show Mr. Z his capital letter.

Where is the lower case letter z?

*Analyzing The
Shape Of "Z"*

How many straight lines does the capital letter Z have? (three)

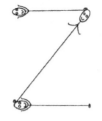

How many children will we need to make the capital Z? (three)

Will anyone have to curl his body to make the Z? (no)

Show Mr. Z which part of his letter is slanted.

Let's ask three children to make the capital Z with their bodies.

Let the class assist by helping to move the children's bodies. Encourage them to keep checking with Mr. Z to see if he likes the way his capital letter looks. Then all the children may form groups of three to make the capital Z.

Help the children compare the upper and lower case Z. They should realize that except for size, the letters look the same way.

TALKING ABOUT ZIGZAG ZIPPERS

Mr. Z is having a problem with some of his Zipping Zippers.

The Zipping Zippers have decided to become zigzag Zipping Zippers.

What is a zigzag Zipping Zipper?

How does something look when it zigzags?

Show Mr. Z how you zigzag.

Why is a Zipping Zipper that zigs and zags a problem?

Lead the children to the conclusion that zigzag zippers will have trouble zipping up and down. Read the following story to them:

Listening To A Story

Mr. Z has been getting many, many letters from people who are complaining about the zigzag zippers.

One letter came from a little boy who had bought a red jacket. He put it on and tried to zip the zipper. Instead of zipping, the zipper zigged and zagged.

The boy tried and tried to zip his jacket. He could not do it.

The little boy took off his jacket, sat down and wrote a letter to Mr. Z. He complained about zippers that zig and zag but won't zip.

Have the children dramatize this part of the story.

Dramatizing A Story

Be the little boy. Try to zip your jacket. Remember, you have a zipper that zigs and zags instead of zipping.

Continue Mr. Z's story.

A little girl also had trouble. She bought a beautiful blue pocketbook. It had a zipper so that things would not fall out.

The little girl filled her pocketbook. She said, "I think I'll zip the zipper." What a surprise she had! Instead of zipping, the zipper zigged and zagged.

The little girl could not close her pocketbook. Her things started tumbling out of it.

The little girl took everything out of the pocketbook. She sat down and wrote a letter to Mr. Z. She complained about the zipper that zigged and zagged but would not zip.

Several children may dramatize this part of the story.

Be the little girl. Fill your pocketbook.

Try to zip it with a zipper that zigs and zags but won't zip.

Continue with the last part of the story.

There was a lady who was taking a trip on a jet plane. She bought a special suitcase. This suitcase was very easy to close. It had a zipper that went all around. Just one zip and it was closed!

That poor lady! She *thought* her suitcase had a Zipping Zipper. She didn't know that she had bought a suitcase with a zipper that zigged and zagged but would not zip.

The lady tried and tried to close her suitcase. It just zigged and zagged. The lady missed her plane. She was very angry. She wrote a letter to Mr. Z, too.

Mr. Z is upset. He says the zippers have a job to do. He says it is wrong to fool people.

A variety of fabrics and art supplies should be available for the following activity.

Making Zigzag Zippers

Mr. Z has a plan. He will need our help. Mr. Z wants to be sure that people who buy things know when they are getting a zigzag zipper.

Mr. Z wants each of us to make something that can have a zipper (e.g., coat, jacket, skirt, shirt, dress, sweater, shoes, suitcase, pocketbook).

Then we will make zigzag zippers (a strip of paper cut in zigzag shapes).

We will paste the zigzag zipper on the things we made (e.g., jacket, coat).

That way everyone will know when a jacket has a zipper that zigs and zags and won't zip. When you are finished show your picture to Mr. Z. Mr. Z will be glad to know that people won't be fooled by those zigzag zippers.

TYING IT TOGETHER

Distribute copies of Alpha Time Master #49.

What do you see in this picture? (a zigzag zipper)

Put your finger on the top of the zigzag zipper.

What picture do you see there? (boy and his jacket)

How does the boy feel about his jacket? (upset)

Now zip your finger along the zipper until you get to the next picture.

What picture is that? (girl with her pocketbook)

How does the girl feel? (sad)

Why is she crying? (things are falling out)

Now zip your finger along the zigzag zipper until you get to the next picture.

Who is in this picture? (a lady and her suitcase)

How does the lady feel? (angry)

Why is she angry? (missed the plane, can't zip suitcase)

Zip your finger to the end of the zipper. What can we put in the empty space?

ON THEIR OWN

Children may choose from the following activities:

Dramatic Play	Taking the parts of the three people in Mr. Z's story and acting it out.
Art	Illustrating any part of Mr. Z's story.
Letter Tracing	Using a copy of Alpha Time Master #80 to trace the upper and lower case Z.

1Z₃

PLANNING AND PREPARATION: Huggable, Mr. Z; Picture Card 6, Alpha Time Master #50; a sheet of paper, scissors and paste.

PRACTICING LANGUAGE ARTS SKILLS

Remembering Zigzag Zippers

Mr. Z received a song in the mail today. The song is about some more zigzag zippers.

Show us with your fingers how zippers zig and zag.

Let's sing the words and zigzag with our fingers.

Sing this "Zigzag Zipper" song with the children to the tune of "Three Blind Mice" :

Zigzag zippers,
Zigzag zippers.
See how they zig.
See how they zag.
They zig and zag but will never zip.
A zig then a zag instead of a zip,
Did you ever see such a sight in your life,
As zigzag zippers?

Mr. Z likes the way you sing and the way your fingers zigzag.

Mr. Z has a picture story for us. He would like us to tell him words that we can use with the pictures.

Display Picture Card 6 and give the children copies of matching Alpha Time Master #50. Discuss each picture.

Reading A Picture Story

Look at the first part of the picture story.

Frame 1

Who is in the picture? (a boy and girl)

What are they trying to do? (zip the jacket and pocketbook)

Why are they having trouble? (The zipper is a zigzag zipper.)

Numeration Recalling

Tell Mr. Z a story about this picture. Try to make him see it by telling him everything about it.

Give several children a chance to tell Mr. Z about the picture.

What do you think the boy and girl will do?

Let's look at the next part of the story.

Frame 2

What are the boy and girl doing? (writing letters)

To whom do you think they are writing? (to Mr. Z)

Give a child a sheet of paper to represent the letter.

Inferring

130

Here is the boy's letter. Tell us what the boy's letter says.

Give another child a sheet of paper.

Here is the girl's letter. Tell us what it says.

Mr. Z would like you to tell him everything about it. He'll close his eyes and listen to your words to help him see the picture.

Predicting

What will the boy and girl do with their letters? (mail them to Mr. Z)

Let's look at the next picture and see what happens.

Frame 3

What is Mr. Z holding? (two letters)

Who do you think wrote the two letters? (the boy and girl)

Why doesn't Mr. Z look happy? (Everyone is complaining about zigzag zippers.)

Who do you think sent all the other letters? (other people who had zigzag zippers)

What should Mr. Z do about all these zigzag zippers that won't zip?

Frame 4

Let's look at the next picture and see what Mr. Z does.

What is Mr. Z doing? (sewing a zipper in the jacket)

Whose jacket is it? (the boy's jacket)

What happened to the zigzag zipper that was on the jacket? (Mr. Z took it out.)

Why is Mr. Z sewing another zipper on the jacket? (to replace the zigzag zipper which doesn't zip)

Looking for detail

What kind of zippers are in the pile? (zigzag zippers)

What is on the table near Mr. Z? (the pocketbook)

Look at the pocketbook. What is missing? (the zigzag zipper)

What do you think Mr. Z will do next? (sew a zipping zipper into the pocketbook)

Describing

Mr. Z can hardly wait to hear about this picture. There are many, many things to tell him. Try to tell him everything. Remember, Mr. Z closes his eyes and tries to see the picture. You should make him see the picture with the words you use.

Mr. Z is happy that the zigzag zippers were taken out of all those things. He is glad Zipping Zippers are being sewn into everything.

Mr. Z says there is one thing wrong with the picture story. Something is missing.

131

What is missing? (the name)

Let's think of a name for the picture story.

What is the story about? (e.g., Mr. Z, zigzag zippers)

What name can we give the story so people will know what it is about?

Have the children think of as many titles as they can for the story. (e.g., Mr. Z and the Zigzag Zippers, Trouble with Zigzag Zippers)

TYING IT TOGETHER

Mr. Z liked our Talking Book. He would like us to make a book out of his picture story. We can paste each picture on its own page.

Then you can make the picture talk with your voice. You can also make it talk with written words.

If you want your pictures to have written words, we can write them together.

Show the children how to cut out the four frames on the Alpha Time Master #50. They may then paste each frame on a separate piece of paper.

Some children will want to dictate sentences to accompany each picture. Others will want to tell about the picture as they did with the Talking Book.

Staple the pages of pictures together to form a book for each child. Include blank pages for a front and back cover. Encourage the children to name their books. When they have finished they might like to read their books to another class before taking them home.

ON THEIR OWN

Children may choose from the following activities:

Art

Decorating the front and back covers of the picture books.

Storytelling

Using Picture Card 6 to retell Mr. Z's story.

Sequence

Mixing up the loose pages of the picture book, and putting them in order again.

Matching And Sorting

Including Mr. Z's playing cards from Alpha Time Decks 1, 2, and 4 in any of the matching and sorting activities listed in the *Games* section of the manual.

1P₁

PLANNING AND PREPARATION: Pieces of fabric or colored paper cut into the shape of Pointy Patches, one for each child; 6 sheets of paper; art materials; Alpha Time Master #51.

INTRODUCING POINTY PATCHES

Show a patch to the children. Tell them that what you are holding came from the knee of a pair of pants. Ask them if they know what it is called. (Elicit "patch.") Tell the children that all the patches you have are Pointy Patches.

*Identifying
Pointy Patches*

Why do you think these are called Pointy Patches?

Show us which part looks pointy.

What other things can you think of that are pointy?

Where have you seen patches?

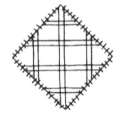

Distribute a Pointy Patch to each child.

These Pointy Patches say they are not just Pointy Patches. Each one thinks it is something else.

Listen to what each Pointy Patch thinks it is. Then take your Pointy Patch and let it be whatever it wishes.

Read the following rhymes. The children may dramatize each rhyme as they hear it.

*Dramatizing Action
Words*

> I know a Pointy Patch who thinks it's a worm.
> It creeps with a wiggle and a squirm, squirm, squirm.

What does the Pointy Patch think it is? (a worm)

*Developing
Vocabulary*

Which words tell us how it moves? (creeps, wiggle, squirm)

Let your patch be a worm. Show us how it will creep, wiggle and squirm.

Let the children have enough time to use their patches to dramatize the words "creep," "wiggle" and "squirm."

All right worms, no more squirms! Let's hear about another Pointy Patch.

> I know a Pointy Patch who thinks it's a horse.
> What does it do? Gallop of course!

What does this Pointy Patch think it is? (a horse)

Which word tells us how it moves? (gallop)

Let your Pointy Patch be a horse. Show us how it will gallop.

The children may gallop around the room while holding their Pointy Patches. Continue the game, using these additional rhymes:

133

I know a Pointy Patch who thinks it's a frog.
It keeps leaping and hopping from log to log.

I know a Pointy Patch who thinks it's a wheel.
It rolls and rolls. How does it feel?

I know a Pointy Patch who thinks it's a tree.
It sways its branches for everyone to see.

Help the children to remember what each of the Pointy Patches thought it was. Then, on separate sheets of paper, draw a simple outline of the worm, horse, frog, wheel, and tree. Place the papers so the children can see them easily and have them identify each picture.

Relating Action Words To Pictures

Each of these pictures shows one of the things a Pointy Patch thought it was.

I will say words that tell what the Pointy Patch did when it was a horse, a worm, a frog, a wheel, or a tree.

After I say the word, you may pick the picture that goes with the word.

The word is (gallop). We (galloped) when the Pointy Patch thought it was a . . . (horse).

Find the picture of the horse.

The next words are "wiggle" and "squirm."

Which of these pictures shows something that wiggles and squirms? (the worm)

Proceed as above mentioning each of the action words used in the rhymes; i.e., roll (wheel); sway (tree); leap and hop (frog). Each time have the children select the appropriate picture for the word given.

TYING IT TOGETHER

Give each child a copy of Alpha Time Master #51. Discuss the picture. Have the children find the tree, the frog, the wheel and the worm and mark the Pointy Patches near them. Then they may draw patches on the horse.

ON THEIR OWN

Story Telling

Children may choose from the following activities:

Making a mural or Talking Book for Pointy Patches such as the one made for the Beautiful Buttons and the Zipping Zippers.

Making a moving picture story:

1. Use a long sheet of paper which is no more than fifteen inches wide. Leave a blank area at the beginning and end of the paper.

2. Divide the mural paper into several sections. Each section or frame may tell about one of the Pointy Patches in the story.

3. Use two rolling pins or the cardboard tubing from paper towelling. Start with the blank area at the end of the mural (after the last picture) and tape to the roller. Roll the paper onto the roller.

4. Tape the blank area at the beginning of the picture onto the other roller.

5. Unroll one frame at a time. As each frame is revealed, the children tell the story of that picture.

Visual Discrimination

Using Alpha Time Master #51, pointing to, or marking as many Pointy Patches as they can find.

Sewing

Sewing patches over tears in clothing.

Painting

Painting a Pointy Patch design and putting a different pattern on each patch.

1P₂

PLANNING AND PREPARATION: Huggable, Mr. P; Record #1, drawing paper, scissors, crayons, paste, art materials, a copy of Mr. P's Picture Book for each child, Alpha Time Master #52.

Have Mr. P standing at the side of the room.

MEETING MR. P AND HIS POINTY PATCHES

Wait until a child discovers Mr. P. Then have the rest of the class gather around him to look at and talk about him.

Who can this Letter Person be?

What does he have all over him? (Pointy Patches)

Why do you think he decided to come to this class?

What do you think we had in this class that he might have heard about? (the Pointy Patches)

Ask him why he is covered with Pointy Patches.

Our new Letter Person would like to sing to us and to tell us his name.

*Listening To
Mr. P's Song*

Play "Mr. P's Song" (record #1, side B, band #3) and discuss it with the children.

What is the Letter Person's name? (Mr. P)

What does he have? (Pointy Patches)

How does Mr. P's music make you want to move?

Replay the song and encourage the children to sing and move along with it.

Mr. P knows every Pointy Patch in the whole world. He likes all Pointy Patches.

Mr. P says you have met patches who think they are something else.

Recalling

Which patches does he mean? (worm; horse; frog; wheel; tree)

IDENTIFYING THE CAPITAL AND LOWER CASE LETTER P

Mr. P would like you to show him his capital letter.

Show him the capital letter P with your hand.

Where is Mr. P's lower case letter?

How many parts does the capital P have? (two)

Are both parts straight? (no)

Point to the curved part. What will we have to do with our bodies to make this part of Mr. P's capital letter? (curl our bodies)

Let two of us try to make the capital letter P.

One person will keep his body straight. One person will curl around and touch the person who is lying straight. The one who is curled must have his head and feet near the person who has his body straight.

Have two children try to make the capital P with their bodies. Then have all the children work in pairs and form the capital P.

LISTENING TO A STORY

Poor Mr. P is busy pasting popping Pointy Patches.

He has used twenty jars of paste. He thinks that he will use 100 jars of paste before he is through!

Mr. P says he has pasted so many popping Pointy Patches that he is full of paste! He has paste on his head. He has paste on his nose. He even has paste in his mouth!

Ask Mr. P what he means by popping Pointy Patches.

Read the children the following story:

Mr. P says that it all started yesterday. He heard a noise at the door. He opened the door, and in popped piles and piles of Pointy Patches. There were so many of them that they knocked Mr. P down!

Mr. P had never seen popping Pointy Patches before. Those patches didn't stand still for a moment. They just kept popping the way popcorn does when it is cooking.

Mr. P said, "Please, popping Pointy Patches tell me why you are here." One purple popping Pointy Patch said, "I popped off a pair of pants!" One polka dot popping Pointy Patch said, "I popped off a pink pocketbook!"

Each patch told Mr. P from where he had popped. Poor Mr. P didn't know what to do. He said to the patches, "You can't just pop off! People need you. You're not being fair. If you have a job to do you must do it."

While Mr. P was talking there was a knock at the door. Mr. P opened the door and saw lots and lots of people standing there. Each one was holding something in his hands. They held pants, shirts, pocketbooks, socks and many, many other things. Each thing had a spot on it where a Pointy Patch had once been.

The people were very angry with Mr. P. They said that he was in charge of all Pointy Patches. It was his job to see that all the patches stayed put! If the Pointy Patches did pop off, it was Mr. P's job to put them back.

Mr. P said, "Please leave all your things here. I will put the Pointy Patches back on for you." The people left. Mr. P told the Pointy Patches they must pop back. The patches knew Mr. P was upset. They all ran back where they belonged.

Mr. P smiled and closed his eyes. He was tired. Guess what those popping Pointy Patches did? They peeked at Mr. P and saw that he was asleep. Then, they all started popping again. Poor Mr. P! What could he do to make those Pointy Patches stop popping?

Suddenly Mr. P had a popping good idea! He decided to put the popping Pointy Patches in place with paste. Mr. P started pasting and pasting. He pasted all day. He pasted all night. Soon paste was on his head. Paste was on his nose. Paste was in his mouth. Mr. P kept right on pasting. He still had piles and piles of Pointy Patches to paste.

Mr. P has so much pasting to do that he will never get finished unless we help him.

Pasting Popping Pointy Patches

Each of us will draw or make a pair of pants, a shirt, a scarf, a pencil case or anything else that needs a patch.

We will paste some popping Pointy Patches on the things we have made.

When we are finished we will show our things to Mr. P and tell him all about them.

Have the children use the art materials that you have prepared for them. Encourage them to use as many different materials as possible. If fabrics are available they are ideal to use as patches and for the things from which the patches popped. When the children have finished, suggest that they show their things to Mr. P and tell him about them.

READING A PICTURE STORY

Mr. P has a picture-story for us. He wants us to tell him words that will go with the pictures.

Give each child a copy of Mr. P's Picture Book.

Cover —

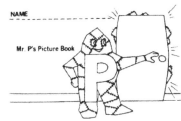

Let's look at the cover.

Whose picture is there? (Mr. P)

What is Mr. P doing? (opening the door for the popping Pointy Patches)

What does the picture on the cover tell us about the story?

Drawing Conclusions From Given Facts

Let's turn the page of our books. Look at the first picture.

Page #1:

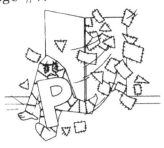

What has happened to Mr. P?

From where have all these patches come?

Say a word that tells what the Pointy Patches are doing. (popping)

What has happened to Mr. P? (He was knocked down.)

Mr. P wants to close his eyes and see the picture. He can see it by listening to your words. Your words can help make him see the picture.

Describing A Picture

Tell him everything that is happening in the picture.

How do you think Mr. P feels about being knocked down by the popping Pointy Patches?

How would you feel?

Let's turn the page and look at the next picture.

Page #2:

Reasoning And Role Playing

Look at Mr. P.

Look at Mr. P. How do you think he feels? What is he doing that tells you how he feels? (He is stamping his foot.)

Be Mr. P and tell the popping patches why you are upset with them.

Give several children a chance to be Mr. P and tell the popping Pointy Patches why he is so upset with them.

Mr. P's eyes are closed again. He is ready to listen to your words. It will help him see this picture.

What do you think will happen in the next part of the story? Let's look at the next page.

Page #3:

Reasoning And Role Playing

Why have these people come to see Mr. P? (They want the Pointy Patches back.)

How do these people feel? (annoyed)

What are they doing that tells you how they feel?

What have they brought to Mr. P? (the things that had the patches)

Why have they brought these things to Mr. P? (They want him to put back the patches.)

How can you tell that a Pointy Patch was once on the pants or on the pocketbook? (They left a mark.)

Be one of the people and tell us what you are saying to Mr. P.

Give several children a chance to take the role of one of the people who tells Mr. P why he has come and what he wants.

Turn to the next page. Look at the picture.

Page #4:

What are the Pointy Patches doing? (going back)

Why do you think they are going back where they belong?

Do you think they will stay there?

Let's look at the next page and see what happens.

Page #5:

Predicting Outcomes

What is Mr. P doing in this picture? (sleeping)

What are the Pointy Patches doing? (popping off)

How do you think Mr. P will act when he wakes up and sees the Pointy Patches popping again?

Be Mr. P. Make believe you are asleep in a chair. Tell us and show us what you will do and say as you wake up.

Page #6:

Getting The Main Idea

What is Mr. P doing? (pasting the patches)

Why is he pasting the patches?

Give several children a chance to play the role of Mr. P.

What do you think Mr. P will do with all the things after he has pasted the Pointy Patches on them?

NAMING THE PICTURE-STORY

Suggesting Titles For The Story

Mr. P says the story is missing something.

What could the story be missing?

Lead the children to the conclusion that the story needs a name.

Let's think of a name for the story.

Who is in the story? (Mr. P, popping Pointy Patches)

What name could we give the story so that people will know it is about Mr. P and about popping Pointy Patches?

Perhaps people will want to know what Mr. P did to the popping Pointy Patches. What did Mr. P do? (pasted them)

What name can we give the picture story so that people will know that Mr. P pasted the popping Pointy Patches?

Follow the above procedure to help the children give other names for the picture story.

TYING IT TOGETHER

Distribute copies of Alpha Time Master #52 and crayons.

Who is in this picture? (Mr. P, shopkeeper)

What is Mr. P doing? (buying jars of paste)

How will he use the paste? (to paste the patches)

What do you see on some jars of paste? (lower case p)

Mr. P would like you to use a purple crayon to mark his letter P.

Use your crayons to color Mr. P's patches.

What color are some of Mr. P's Pointy Patches?

ON THEIR OWN

Children may choose from the following activities:

Art

Making a Pointy Patch collage by pasting cut-outs of pointy pieces of fabric, foil, paper and corrugated board on a piece of construction paper or cardboard.

Drawing Mr. P and putting paste all over him.

Music

Dancing to Mr. P's music (record #1).

Story Telling

Selecting a page about any part of the story of the Popping Pointy Patches, then telling the story about it.

Letter Tracing

Using Alpha Time Master #70 to trace capital and lower case P.

Classifying

Marking things that may be used to fasten Pointy Patches to clothing on Alpha Time Master #52.

Counting

Counting specified objects in Alpha Time Master #52 (e.g., jars of paste, safety pins, rungs on the ladder).

Crafts

Making a Pointy Patch quilt.

1S₁

PLANNING AND PREPARATION: A small piece of well-used soap; a pair of large paper sock cut-outs (Super Socks); large piece of paper, crayons; Alpha Time Master #53.

Draw a face on each of the cut out Super Socks.

INTRODUCING SUPER SOCKS

Show the children the well-used bar of soap.

This piece of soap was on my desk this morning. It is almost gone. The soap was very nice and new. Now it is simply not the same, and one pair of socks is to blame. Imagine! The soap was almost all used by washing just one pair of socks.

What kind of socks would use so much soap?

Let's look at our own socks.

Was the soap used to wash your socks?

What other kinds of socks do you know about?

Let the children talk about different types of socks. Encourage them to specify various materials, patterns and colors.

The soap was used to wash a special kind of socks. They are Super Socks.

Discussing and Comparing Sizes

What is meant by *super*?

How do you think Super Socks would look?

If you close your eyes and say Super Socks slowly six times, the Super Socks will be there when you open your eyes.

While the children have their eyes closed, display the pair of Super Socks you have prepared.

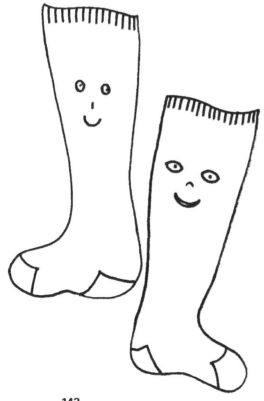

Have you ever seen socks like these before?

How are these socks different from your socks? (They are much bigger.)

The Super Socks must be washed but the soap is almost all gone.

What kind of soap could we make for Super Socks?

Lead the children to the conclusion that a super large piece of soap is needed for Super Socks.

Let's make some super soap for Super Socks.

How big do you think super soap will be?

Remember when we made a tall, tall toothbrush for Mr. T? Show us with your hands how tall the toothbrush was.

Talking About
Word Meanings

Show us with your hands how super big the super soap must be.

On a large piece of paper, draw a bar of super soap. Let each child draw a pair of socks on the super soap. The children may want you to write their names on the pair of socks they have drawn.

Super soap and Super Socks can work together if we help to show them the way.

First Super Socks and super soap must meet each other. Then Super Socks and super soap will soak together.

What does the word *soak* mean?

What things have you seen soaking at home?

Why do we soak things?

After Super Socks soak, then super soap must help scrub Super Socks.

What does the word *scrub* mean?

What have you seen scrubbed at home?

Why do we scrub things?

After soaking and scrubbing, super soap must help Super Socks squeeze out all the water.

Show us how you squeeze something.

Then Super Socks will be happy because they will be nice and clean. Super soap will be happy because it helped Super Socks.

Let's sing and dance with super soap and Super Socks as they soak, scrub and squeeze.

Participating In
Dramatic Play

Play the following game to the tune of "How Do You Do, My Partner?"

Let half the class hold the drawing of the super soap. The other half will hold the Super Socks cut-outs. The super soap children will skip over to the children holding the Super Socks and sing:

Dancing
And Singing

"How do you do, Super Socks?
How do you do today?
We will wash together.
I will show you the way."

Then super soap children dance around the Super Socks singing:

"Tra la la la la la,
Tra la la la la la,
We will wash together,
I will show you the way."

The roles may be reversed so that the children holding Super Socks follow the same procedure as they skip over to the children holding the super soap. The Super Socks children sing:

"How do you do, super soap?
How do you do today?
We will soak together,
I will show you the way."

Put the super soap and the Super Socks on the floor for the next part of the game.

Use your hands to show how Super Socks soak while you dance around and sing:

"Soak, soak, soak, soak, soak,
Soak, soak, soak, soak, soak.
We will soak together.
I will show you the way."

Continue with the two groups skipping back and forth to each other. As the song is repeated, the children substitue the words "scrub" and "squeeze" for "soak" and dramatize the new words each time. Children Complete the game by picking up the cutouts and skipping back and forth again singing:

"How do you do Super Socks?
How do you do, today?
We have worked together
We have shown you the way."

TYING IT TOGETHER

Give each child a copy of Alpha Time Master #53 to look at and talk about.

What is the woman in the top pictures doing? (soaking, scrubbing, squeezing)

What is the woman in the bottom picture doing? (putting socks in the washing machine)

Have you ever put clothes in a washing machine or watched your father or mother do it?

What do you do first, second, last?

Which is more work, washing clothes by hand or by machine?

What are other machines that help make work easier?

What are the names of some of the other things in the picture? What do you do with them? (e.g., laundry basket , box of soap powder, bottle of bleach, a dryer)

ON THEIR OWN

Children may choose from the following activities:

Crafts

Making sock puppets: Stuff a sock with rags or paper towels and sew or paste a face on it.

Using a grater or dull knife to make soap powder.

Carving soft white soap with a dull knife.

Muscle Co-ordination	Using a tub and soap, soaking, scrubbing, squeezing some articles of dolls clothing, dust cloths or other articles.
Science	Experimenting: Soak a small bar of soap in water until it dissolves. Keep daily records of the soap's progress, noticing how much smaller it gets as it dissolves. Has the soap disappeared? What has happened to it? (It has taken a different form: (i.e., changed from solid to liquid.)
Art	Soap painting: Use soap powder, water and an egg beater to make a mixture as thick as whipped cream. Use this for painting a textured picture on dark-colored (preferably black) construction paper.
Classifying	Making a picture list of machines, that are used around the house.

1S₂

PLANNING AND PREPARATION: Huggable, Mr. S; Record #1; Alpha Time Master #54; drawing paper, crayons and other arts and crafts material.

Place Mr. S in the room before the children arrive.

MEETING MR. S

Wait until one of the children discovers the new Letter Person. Then let all the children gather around, look at, talk to, and discuss the newcomer.

Who can he be?

What is he wearing? (Super Socks)

Why do you think this new Letter Person decided to come to our room?

Ask him if Super Socks belong to him.

Let's listen to his song and find out his name.

Play Mr. S's song, record #1, side B, band 4 for the children.

Listening To And Interpreting Mr. S's Song

What did Mr. S tell us about himself?

How did the music make you feel?

Tell us about a time you felt the way Mr. S does.

Why do you think the music is low at first and then suddenly gets loud? (e.g., At first Mr. S feels scared or shy, then he gets brave when he wears his Super Socks.)

Let's play the music again and show Mr. S how his music makes us move.

IDENTIFYING CAPITAL AND LOWER CASE LETTER "S"

Mr. S would like you to show him his capital letter.

Analyzing The Shape of Letter "S"

Use your hand to show Mr. S the capital letter S.

Let's look at his letter very carefully. It is different from any of the other Letter People's letters.

How is it different? (There is no straight part. It is just curves.)

Let's have one person make the capital S as we watch. Then we can each make the capital S by ourselves.

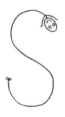

Let one child try to form the capital S with his body. Have the other children assist him by moving his body. Help them by first having them trace the shape with you in the air.

Now let's find the lower case s. Show Mr. S where it is. How are the capital S and the lower case s the same? (shape) How are they different? (size)

How do you think Mr. S looks in Super Socks? Do they fit him? (yes)

How do you think Super Socks would fit you? (They would be too big.)

Comparing Sizes

What do you think would happen if you tried to wear Super Socks? How far up would they reach?

PANTOMIMING

Pretend to distribute a pair of Super Socks to each of the children.

Playing A Game With Imaginary Super Socks

Mr. S would like each of us to try on a pair of Super Socks.

Here's a pair for each one of you. They are so super! They are nearly as big as you are! Is everybody ready? Let's all put on one Super Sock.

Pull it all the way up to your chin. Let's see how it looks.

Now, let go of the sock. Oops! Everybody's Super Sock fell right down!

Now let's put on the other Super Sock. Pull it to your chin. Let go. Let's see how it looks. Oh, dear, that one fell down too!

When we wear Super Socks they keep falling down. The only way to keep them up is to hold them with our hands.

Let's sing a song that tells about Super Socks that keep falling down.

Sing this "Super Socks" song to the tune of "London Bridge is Falling Down."

Super Socks keep falling down,
Falling down,
Falling down.
Super Socks keep falling down,
My fair lady.

Dramatizing The "Super Socks" Song

As we sing the next part of the song, pull up one Super Sock and hold it with your hand so it doesn't fall down.

Super Socks are half pulled up,
Half pulled up,
Half pulled up.
Super Socks are half pulled up,
My fair lady.

As we sing the next part, pull up your other Super Sock, but don't let go of the first one or it will fall down.

Super Socks are both pulled up,
Both pulled up,
Both pulled up.
Super Socks are both pulled up,
My fair lady.

Repeat the song using the words below to have the socks fall down one at a time.

Super Socks are half way down. . .

Super Socks are all the way down. . .

Children finish the song by singing:

Super Socks will not fit us, (children shake heads)
Not fit us.
Not fit us.
Super Socks will not fit us,
My fair lady.

Give them back to Mr. S, (dramatize)
Mr. S,
Mr. S.
Give them back to Mr. S,
My fair lady.

Super Socks will just fit him,
Just fit him,
Just fit him.
Super Socks will just fit him,
My fair lady.

Mr. S wants to give Mr. M and Mr. T a super present. He thought and thought about what he could give each of them.

Tell Mr. S what you would give Mr. M as a present.

Tell Mr. S what you would give Mr. T as a present.

Let several children suggest possible presents for Mr. M and Mr. T.

Mr. S thinks all the things you told him about would make wonderful presents. He has thought of another thing he could give to Mr. M and to Mr. T. He will give them what he likes best in the whole world.

What does Mr. S like best in the whole world? (Super Socks)

LISTENING TO MR. S's STORY

Tell the children the following story:

Mr. S went to the store. He bought two super-sized boxes. In each super-sized box he put a pair of Super Socks.

He sent one box to Mr. M. He sent one box to Mr. T.

Then he ran to the telephone and telephoned each one. He said, "Hello. This is Mr. S. How are you? I telephoned to tell you that I sent you a super surprise. As soon as it comes, please put it on. Pull it all the way up and don't take it off. Call me tomorrow and let me know how you like my super surprise."

Mr. M could hardly wait for his super surprise to arrive. Then the super-sized box came. Mr. M used his scissors to cut the strong silver strings that were tied around the super box. Mr. M opened the box and saw the Super Socks.

Mr. M thinks Super Socks are great for Mr. S. He wasn't sure that he wanted Super Socks for himself. However, Mr. M had promised Mr. S he would put on the Super Socks as soon as they arrived. A promise is a promise and Mr. M would not break a promise.

Mr. M put on the socks. He started to pull them up. Soon the socks were at his knee but there was still more to pull! The socks seemed to grow and grow. Soon the socks were at his neck, and still there was more to pull!

Mr. M pulled and pulled and finally the socks covered his Munching Mouth completely.

Mr. M was not too happy. He had promised he would wear the socks a whole day and tell Mr. S how he liked them.

Mr. M thought, "If I have a munch, I'll feel much better."

Mr. M took some of his very favorite marshmallows to munch. He started to munch but the munching wasn't making him feel any better. He couldn't understand it. His favorite marshmallows tasted just like Super Socks. "Maybe I had better munch something else," he thought.

Mr. M munched some of the macaroni he had cooked Monday night. Guess what! Munching macaroni didn't make him feel any better. The macaroni tasted just like Super Socks. No matter what Mr. M munched, it all tasted like Super Socks.

Making Inferences From Given Clues

Mr. M couldn't figure it out. Can you help him?

Why does everything taste like Super Socks? (The Super Socks are covering Mr. M's mouth.)

Mr. S will telephone Mr. M to ask him how he likes the Super Socks.

Poor Mr. M has a problem. He does not want to hurt Mr. S's feelings. He can not enjoy munching if he has to wear Super Socks. Tell Mr. M what he should do.

Let the children work in pairs. One child is Mr. S. He telephones Mr. M, asking him how he likes the Super Socks. The other child is Mr. M. He tells Mr. S how he feels. Remind the children that Mr. M doesn't want to hurt Mr. S's feelings.

TYING IT TOGETHER

S s   S s   S s

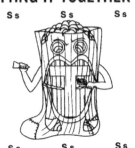

S s   S s   S s

Give each child a copy of Alpha Time Master #54. After the picture is discussed the children may mark the upper and lower case s.

What is Mr. T wearing? (Super Socks)

Where do you think he got them? (Mr. S sent them.)

Why does Mr. T look unhappy? (He can't brush his teeth.)

Predicting And Dramatizing The Outcome

Why can't Mr. T brush his teeth? (Super Socks are covering them.)

What should Mr. T do?

ON THEIR OWN

Children may choose from the following activities:

Music

Singing or dancing to Mr. S's music (record #1).

Letter Tracing

Using Alpha Time Master #73 for tracing the letter S.

Painting

Painting a picture using only curved lines (as in the letter S).

1S₃

PLANNING AND PREPARATION: Huggables, Mr. S and Mr. M; Alpha Time Master #81; Picture Card 7: drawing paper, crayons, scissors, paste, sticks or straws.

READING A PICTURE STORY

Recalling Mr. S's Story

Frame #1:

Noticing Detail, Inferring

Frame #2:

Describing And Inferring

Frame #3:

Inferring And Predicting Outcomes

Mr. M is still thinking about the Super Socks Mr. S sent him. When he first put them on he thought they'd be fine. He started to pull them up and they seemed to grow and grow. Mr. S would like us to remember his story.

Give each child a copy of Alpha Time Master #81. Display Picture Card 7. Have the children describe each picture.

Let's look at the first part of the story.

Who is in the picture? (Mr. M)

What does Mr. M have? (a package)

What word can you say to tell about the size of the box? (super, big)

If it is a super box, who do you think sent it? (Mr. S)

What did Mr. S put in the box to send to Mr. M? (Super Socks)

Why did he think Mr. M would love Super Socks? (Mr. S loves Super Socks)

Mr. S wants you to tell him about the picture. He is closing his eyes. Help him to see the picture. Remember how words help us to see pictures.

What do you think will happen when Mr. M puts on the Super Socks?

Let's look at the next part of the story and see what happens.

What is Mr. M trying to do with the Super Socks? (pull them up)

Why is he having so much trouble pulling up the Super Socks? (They are too long.)

What part of Mr. M's body have the Super Socks reached? (his neck)

Look at the Super Socks. How can you tell that Mr. M is not finished pulling up the socks?

Mr. S is waiting. His eyes are closed. Remember to tell him everything about this picture.

Let's look at the next picture.

The socks are all pulled up. How high did they go? (over his head)

What is Mr. M doing? (munching)

How do you think the marshmallow tastes to Mr. M? (not good; like socks)

151

How will Mr. S feel if Mr. M tells him he doesn't want the Super Socks?

What do you think Mr. S will do?

Let's look at the last part of the story.

Frame #4:

Noticing Detail, Dramatizing

Mr. M looks different in this picture from the way he looked in the picture we just saw.

How is he different? (He is not wearing Super Socks.)

Where are the Super Socks? (in the box)

To whom is Mr. M talking on the telephone? (Mr. S)

What do you think Mr. M is saying to Mr. S?

Be Mr. M. Talk to Mr. S on the telephone. Let us hear what Mr. M tells him about the Super Socks.

The picture story ends here. It is not really the end of the story. We don't know what happens to the Super Socks.

Suppose your television set should break before the program you are watching ends. You would want to know how it ends. Mr. M and Mr. S want to know how *this* story ends.

Let's think of a good way for it to end. Let's listen to each other's endings.

TYING IT TOGETHER

*Drawing
And/Or Dictating
An Ending For
The Story*

Let several children talk about what they think happened to the Super Socks. Then have all the children draw an ending picture for the story.

When you have finished your picture, show it to Mr. M and to Mr. S. Tell them all about it.

If you want your picture to have words under it, we will write the words together under your picture.

ON THEIR OWN

Children may choose from the following activities:

Dramatic Play

Making stick puppets and dramatizing the end of the story with the puppets.

Dramatizing Mr. S's story using the Huggables.

Sequence Skills

Putting Mr. S's story in order: Cut out the four pictures on Alpha Time Master #81. Paste each on a separate sheet of paper. Mix them up and put them in order again.

*Sorting And
Matching*

Include Mr. S's playing cards from Alpha Decks 1, 2 and 4 in any of the games in the *Games* section.

Storytelling

Using Picture Card 7 to retell the story of Mr. S.

1V₁ **PLANNING AND PREPARATION:** Huggable, Mr. V; Records #1 and #4; a piece of velvet; the storybook, *Vanishing Vests*; Alpha Time Master #82; paper, scissors, crayons, paste.

Place Mr. V in an accessible part of the room.

MEETING MR. V AND HIS VIOLET VELVET VEST

Wait until the children discover Mr. V. Then let them gather around to look at him, greet him, and discuss his appearance.

Discovering Mr. V's Name

Who can this new Letter Person be?

What is he wearing? (a vest)

What is the color of his vest? *If no one can identify the color of the vest, tell the children it is a Violet Vest.*

Show the children a piece of velvet. Let them touch it and use a word to tell how it feels.

Mr. V's vest is very special. It is made of velvet. Velvet is very soft to touch.

Let's listen to the new Letter Person's song and see if we can find out something about him.

Listening To Mr. V's Song

Play "Mr. V's Song" (record #1, side B, band #5).

Let the children discuss the record.

What is the Letter Person's name? (Mr. V)

What did Mr. V tell us?

What is special about Mr. V? (Violet Velvet Vest)

Show Mr. V how the music makes you feel.

Replay the record and encourage the children to sing or move along with it the second time.

LISTENING TO THE STORYBOOK "VANISHING VESTS"

Read the storybook "Vanishing Vests" or play the recording of the story (record #4, side A, band #2). Children should know that "vanishing" means disappearing.

When the story is finished the children may talk about parts they liked. Questions such as the following may encourage discussion:

What happened at the beginning of the story? (vests vanished)

What did Mr. Valentine do when he found out his vest was gone? (called another store)

Discussing The Story

Why had all the vests vanished? (They went to see Mr. V and his Violet Velvet Vest.)

Why was this a special day for the vests? (Mr. V came to visit)

Why were the vests happy at the end of the story?

Let's act out the story of Mr. V and the vanishing vests.

Dramatizing The Story

Help the children to decide what prop each will make to use in dramatizing the story. Suggest that the children arrange several chairs with their backs on the floor to use as patrol cars. They may make headlights, a flashing light, wheels, and an antenna to put on the chairs.

Some of us will be the vanishing vests. Some of us will be the detectives on the Vest Patrol.

If you want to be a detective, what can you make to help everyone know who you are? (e.g., badges, radio)

If you want to be one of the vanishing vests, what can you make for yourself? (a vest)

One child will be Mr. V in his Violet Velvet Vest. We will make a Violet Velvet Vest for Mr. V.

Making Costumes And Props

Children may make their props individually or in groups. When the children are satisfied with what they have made, they may re-enact any parts of the story while the Letter People listen. It may be necessary to reread parts of the story as the play progresses.

TYING IT TOGETHER

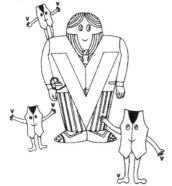

Give each child a copy of the Alpha Time Master #82.

Who is the new Letter Person? (Mr. V)

How do the vests feel? (happy, proud)

What do you think each vest is thinking?

ON THEIR OWN

Children may choose from the following activities:

Audio Visual Coordination

Playing the Vanishing Vests story (record #4) and "reading" along in the book.

Music

Dancing to Mr. V's music (record #1) using Mr. V as a dance partner.

Sensory Touch Images

Making a collection of materials that have velvet qualities such as softness, smoothness.

Color Discrimination

Making a bunch of violets out of crepe or tissue paper.

Painting

Painting a violet-colored picture.

1V₂

PLANNING AND PREPARATION: Huggable, Mr. V; Alpha Time filmstrip, *Vanishing Vests*; Alpha Time Master #83.

IDENTIFYING THE CAPITAL AND LOWER CASE LETTER "V"

Gather the children around Mr. V. Have them reacquaint themselves with him by telling him his name and something they remember from his story.

Analyzing The V Shape

Mr. V would like you to show him his capital letter.

Where is the lower case letter v?

Mr. V wants us to make his capital letter with our bodies.

How many lines does the capital letter V have? (two)

Are the lines straight or slanted? (slanted)

How many people will we need to make the capital letter V? (two)

Have the children form pairs and make the capital letter V.

PICTURE READING

Frame #1

Main idea
Looking for detail

Show the children the Alpha Time filmstrip "Vanishing Vests." Discuss one frame at a time.

The name of the story is *Vanishing Vests.*

How can we tell who will be in the story? (by looking at the picture)

Who do you think is in the story? (e.g., Mr. V, storekeeper)

Frame #2

Inferring

Look at the store window.

How can you tell what kind of store it is? (by what is seen in the window)

If this were your store, what name would you give it?

Who do you think would like to shop in this store?

Frame #3

Interpreting emotions

Who can this man be? (the storekeeper)

How do you know how he feels? (expression on his face)

Why is he shocked and surprised? (The vest is gone.)

What do you think happened to the vest? (It disappeared.)

Frame #4

Recalling

What does Mr. Valentine find out when he calls the owner of another vest store? (The other vests also vanished.)

How can you tell that vests have vanished in the other store? (They are not on the models.)

Frame #5

Using descriptive phrases

Role playing

Where are all the storekeepers? (at the police station)

Why have they come to the police station? (to report vanishing vests)

Be one of the storekeepers. Tell the policeman what has happened. Make sure to tell him exactly how your vest looks.

Give several children a chance to play the role of a storekeeper and tell the policeman about a missing vest. Suggest they include words that describe the size of the vest, its color and design (striped, polka dotted, flowered, checked), its fabric (cotton, silk, fur, satin, wool).

Frame #6

Identifying shapes

Who are these men? (Vest Patrol)

Why are they in such a hurry? (They want to find the vests.)

What are some shapes in this picture? (circles, squares, rectangles)

Frame #7

Why has patrol car #5 stopped? (He found the vests.)

How do the vests feel? (happy)

How does the patrolman feel? (upset)

Be the policeman in the patrol car. Tell us what you are saying to the vests.

Frame #8

What is the Vest Patrol asking the vests to do? (get into the van)

Be one of the men on the Vest Patrol. Tell us what you are saying to the vests.

Be one of the vests. Tell us what you are saying to the men on the Vest Patrol.

Frame #9

Where did the Vest Patrol take the vanished vests? (police station)

To whom are the vests talking? (the captain)

Why do you think they are crying?

Be one of the crying vests. Tell us what you are saying to the captain.

Be the police captain. Tell us what you are saying to the crying vests.

Frame #10

Sometimes people do not understand why we do things.

The polka dotted vest is trying to make the police captain understand why the vests vanished.

Be the polka dotted vest. Tell us what you are saying.

Frame #11

Why are the policemen crying? (They are sorry for the vests.)

Frame #12

Where are the patrol cars going? (to look for Mr. V)

How many cars are there? (four)

Frame #13

How do you know the Vest Patrol did a good job? (They found Mr. V.)

How do you think the vests feel now?

Frame #14

How do you think the policemen feel?

Be Mr. V. Tell us what you are saying to the Vest Patrol.

Frame #15

How does everyone feel?

Why do you think they are happy?

Frame #16

Now that Mr. V has left, what are all the vests doing? (going home)

Frame #17

Where did all the vests go? (back to their stores)

When do you think the vests will vanish again?

TYING IT TOGETHER

Distribute copies of Alpha Time Master #83. Ask the children to point to the vanishing vests and to tell where they are (i.e., in the car, under the newspaper; in the trash can; beside, or under the tree; at or behind the window).

ON THEIR OWN

Children may choose from the following activities:

Giving Descriptions

Playing "Calling All Cars." Children take turns reporting a missing person or object and describing it in as great detail as possible including its color, size, and shape. (For persons, include hair color, size, eye color, height, age and clothing.)

Letter Tracing

Using Alpha Time Master #76 to trace the upper and lower case V.

Crafts

Carving the letter V into wood or linoleum.

Making potato prints for Mr. V by carving the letter V deeply into the cut side of a raw potato half. Then the carved side is dipped into paint and pressed onto construction or drawing paper.

Hammering nails or tacks in a V shape into a block of wood or cork.

Story Telling

Using the Vanishing Vest filmstrip to retell the story.

Sorting And Matching

Including Mr. V's playing cards from Alpha Time Decks 1, 2, and 4 in any of the games described in the *Games* section.

1E₁

PLANNING AND PREPARATION: Huggables, Miss A and Miss E; Record #3; Alpha Time Master #84; drawing paper, crayons, scissors, variety of art materials.

Conceal Miss E until after the record has been played.

MEETING MISS E

Gather the children around you and Miss A. Play Meeting the Vowels, Miss E (record #3, side A, band #2). When the record is finished tell the children:

Miss A would like us to meet Miss E.

Close your eyes and Miss A will bring Miss E to meet you.

While the children have their eyes closed, place Miss E near the children.

Discovering Miss E

Look at Miss E. Miss E is still busy exercising.

What is she carrying? (*a barbell*)

How will the barbell help Miss E? (*make her strong*)

Miss E remembers that she must exercise very slowly.

Be Miss E and tell us what you will say as you are trying to lift the barbells. (*ĕ, ĕ, ĕ Exercise*)

Remember first Miss E must say ĕ, ĕ, ĕ then, as she lifts the barbell up high she says *Exercise*. Let's all be Miss E and lift the barbell.

PRACTICING THE SHORT SOUND FOR E

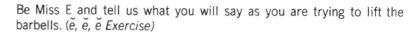

Miss E wants to do many different exercises. Let's teach her some.

Have the children do the following exercises, repeating ĕ, ĕ, ĕ and the word Exercise as indicated:

Doing Several Exercises

Clap your hands three times. Each time you clap your hands, say ĕ. After the third clap, spread your arms as wide as you can and say *Exercise*.

Stand tall, everybody. Bend your knees three times and say ĕ each time. After the third bend, jump and spread your legs wide and say *Exercise*.

Stand tall again. Bounce three times on the soles of your feet. Each time you bounce, say ĕ. After the third bounce, jump up high and say *Exercise*.

Have the children suggest other exercises that they would like to do with Miss E. They must always start the exercises with ĕ, ĕ, ĕ.

TYING IT TOGETHER

Distribute copies of Alpha Time Master #84 to the children.

Who is in this picture? *(Miss E)*

What kind of place is this? (gymnasium)

Have you ever been in a gym? Tell us about it.

What is Miss E doing? *(Exercising)*

What do you think Miss E is saying? (ĕ, ĕ, ĕ, *Exercise*)

Why do you think it is good for us to exercise?

What do you think would happen to us if we didn't get any exercise at all?

ON THEIR OWN

Children may choose from the following activities:

Listening	Listening to Meeting Miss E (record #3, side A, band #2).
Dramatic Play	Dramatizing *Meeting Miss E.* Miss E may be one of the actresses.
Storytelling	Re-telling the story of *Meeting Miss E* and recording it.
Motor Coordination	Playing Simon (or Miss E) Says using exercises as directions.
Art	Drawing and cutting out barbells.

1E₂

PLANNING AND PREPARATION: All the Huggables that have been introduced so far; Record #1; Alpha Time Masters #85 and #86; art and construction materials.

REMEMBERING MISS E AND HER SHORT E SOUND

Miss E is very happy now that she knows how to exercise in her very own special way. Miss E has a song for us.

*Listening To
Miss E's Song*

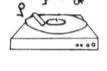

Play Miss E's song (record #1, side B, band #6). Then play it again and encourage the children to sing and move along with it. Discuss the words and music with the children.

What did Miss E tell us?

Show Miss E how her music makes you want to move.

Miss E says that her exercises must always start in a special way. How do we start Miss E's exercises? (with ĕ, ĕ, ĕ)

Let's give Miss E a surprise and do a Miss E Exercise.

Have the children take turns leading the class in different Miss E exercises. Remind them that they repeat a movement three times as they say ĕ. When they say "Exercise" the movement changes (e.g., bounce, bounce, bounce, jump).

REMEMBERING THE OTHER LETTER PEOPLE

*Introducing Miss E
To The Letter People*

Miss E would like to meet the other Letter People. She wants to know all about each one.

Bring one of the Letter People and introduce him or her to Miss E.

Tell Miss E everything you know about the Letter Person you are introducing to her.

Encourage the children to introduce the Letter People by telling about their characteristics. For example:

Miss E, this is Mr. M.

Mr. M, this is Miss E.

Miss E, I will tell you about Mr. M.

Mr. M has a Munching Mouth. He loves to munch.

He munches at the Munching Monday Market.

Mr. M's letter gets its sound from Munching Mouth.

The children may say anything they wish about the Letter Person. In each case, ask them to tell what Miss E says about the Letter Person, and what the Letter Person says about Miss E.

IDENTIFYING THE CAPITAL AND LOWER CASE LETTER E

Miss E says all the Letter People have a capital letter and a lower case letter.

Miss E wants to know if she has them, too.

Find Miss E's capital letter and show it to her with your hand.

Find Miss E's lower case letter and show it to her with your hand.

Analyzing The Shape Of Capital Letter E

Let's make a capital letter E with our bodies.

How many parts does it have? (four)

Look at each part. How will your body look for each part? (straight)

Have the children form groups of four and make the capital E.

PLANNING AN EXERCISE EXHIBIT

Miss E wants us to help her. She wants to have an *Exercise* exhibit.

She says that she has been to an art exhibit to see different kinds of pictures. She has been to a toy exhibit where she saw different kinds of toys. She has been to a car exhibit where she saw cars.

Now Miss E would like to have an Exercise exhibit where she will show her Miss E exercises.

Miss E wants everyone to know about her Exercise exhibit.

How can we help her make sure that everyone finds out about it?

Working In Committees

Have the children work individually or in small groups. Each child may decide how he wants to help Miss E tell people about her exhibit (by drawing signs and then dictating words for them; by dictating words for an ad; by decorating a piece of paper to be used as a "mailer"; by writing a TV commercial).

Some children may want to construct different equipment Miss E can use as she demonstrates her exercises (e.g., barbell, punching bag, exercising bicycle, jump rope).

Let the children put up their signs around the classroom or in the school corridors (if this is permitted).

Have the children "mail" their mailers to other classrooms.

Help them decide which children will demonstrate a particular Miss E Exercise and let them lead visitors in performing it.

TYING IT TOGETHER

Give each child a copy of Alpha Time Master #85.

What are some of the Exercise equipment pieces at Miss E's exhibit? (punching bag, parallel bars, exercise rings, bicycle, basketball)

Which exercise would you like to do?

Which exercise is hard?

Which exercise is easy?

After the picture has been discussed children may find capital and lower case E's and decide what color they would like to use for marking each.

NOTE: Alpha Time Master #86 is a letter to parents explaining the progress the children have made thus far with ALPHA TIME. This letter may be sent home with the children at this time.

ON THEIR OWN

Children may choose from the following activities:

Music And Dance

Listening and dancing to Miss E's music (record #1, side B, band #6).

Letter Tracing

Using Alpha Time Master #59 to trace the upper and lower case letter *E*.

Matching And Sorting

Playing any of the games in the *Games* section using Miss E's playing cards from Alpha Time Decks 1, 2, and 4.

Classifying

Collecting pictures of exercise equipment.

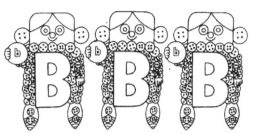

2B₁ PLANNING AND PREPARATION: Huggable, Mr. B; a bag for Mr. B; Mr. B's Picture Squares; one real button; tape, construction paper, crayons, paste, popsicle sticks or straws; Alpha Time Master #87; a small box containing a piece of paper that has writing on it.

Mr. B's music (record #1) may be played to set the mood.

INTRODUCING THE SOUND OF "B"

Have the children gather around Mr. B. Show them the box with a note inside which you have prepared.

A box was delivered to Mr. B this morning. It looks like the box he used when he sent the bad but Beautiful Buttons to the children.

Mr. B is afraid to open it. He thinks that the Beautiful Buttons probably have been so bad that the children have sent them back.

Let's open the box for Mr. B.

Have a child peek into the box. Ask him if the bad but Beautiful Buttons are there. Give several children a chance to peek. Then let one child peek and show everyone the note that he finds inside the box.

Mr. B wants us to read the note to him. He thinks he knows who sent it. Who do you think sent the note?

Read the note to the children.

Dear Mr. B,
We are not bad but Beautiful Buttons anymore. We are just Beautiful Buttons. We are glad you didn't let us break our promises. Now we want to make you happy. We have figured out how you can get your own sound. We will help you so that you will get a sound that you will never forget.

You can get your sound from Beautiful Buttons. You have bunches and bunches of Beautiful Buttons. Each Beautiful Button will be your sound-helper. Ask any Beautiful Button and he will help you prove your sound.
Love,
The Beautiful Buttons Who Are Not Bad Any More.

Drawing inferences

What do the Beautiful Buttons want to do to help Mr. B? (give him a sound)

How will they give Mr. B a sound that will be easy for him to remember? (They will give him the sound that starts Beautiful Buttons.)

USING THE SOUND FOR B IN THE INITIAL POSITION IN WORDS

The Beautiful Buttons sent Mr. B some pictures. Let's look at each picture and tell Mr. B what it is.

Show the children Mr. B's Picture Squares. Have them named and shown to Mr. B (i.e. ball, bat, baby, bicycle, bed).

Why do you think the Beautiful Buttons sent these pictures to Mr. B? (They start with his sound.)

Proving Each Picture For Mr. B

Let's say the name of each picture for Mr. B and prove to him that it begins the same way as Beautiful Buttons.

Mr. B likes to hear his sound in words. He likes to hear you say words that start the same way as Beautiful Buttons. Mr. B would like to play a word game with you. The words all begin with Mr. B's sound. Mr. B will give you a clue. Then you may tell him what the word is.

Tell the children the following riddles.

Mr. B is thinking. He says: "The word I am thinking about rhymes with *tag*. It is something you use to carry food when you leave the supermarket." (bag)

Note: (If a child should say "basket," tell him that's a very good word because "basket" does start with Mr. B's sound, but it does not rhyme with "tag.")

Playing A Riddle Game

Mr. B is thinking again. He is thinking of a word that rhymes with *coat*. It is something that sails on the water. (boat)

Mr. B is thinking again. He says: "I am thinking of a word that rhymes with *look*. You turn its pages when you read it." (book)

Giving answers to riddles based on rhyme with B in initial position

Mr. B is thinking again. He is thinking of something that rhymes with *see*. It buzzes around and can sting. (bee)

Mr. B is thinking again. He is thinking of something that rhymes with *stone*. Dogs like to chew on it to make their teeth strong. (bone)

Mr. B likes the way you figure out words that start with his Beautiful Buttons sound.

Mr. B said that he would like to have a bag of his own just like the other Letter People. Why is a *bag* especially important to Mr. B? (It begins with his sound.)

Mr. B wants us to make and find things that we can put in his bag.

Have the children work independently or in small groups using the art materials set out in the room. Encourage them to prove each thing they make or find for Mr. B's bag. When the children are finished they may sing "Prove It" for Mr. B (record 5, side A, band 3).

TYING IT TOGETHER

Give each child a copy of Alpha Time Master #87 to look at and discuss.

What do you see in the middle of the paper? (Mr. B's Beautiful Button)

What are some of the pictures around the Beautiful Button? (baby, bicycle, bat, bed)

Why do you think these pictures are around the Beautiful Button? (they start with the same sound)

Mr. B would like his Beautiful Button to touch some of his pictures.

What are some ways we can make them touch?

ON THEIR OWN

Children may choose from the following activities:

Eye-Hand Coordination

Using Mr. B's puzzle alone or in combination with other puzzles.

Sound Association

Using all of Mr. B's playing cards in any of the games described in the *Games* section.

Art

Painting a picture with colors that begin with the Beautiful Button sound. (e.g., blue, brown, black, beige)

Making a collage of objects that begin with the Beautiful Button sound.

Auditory Discrimination

Using Mr. B's Picture Squares in any of the activities described in the *Games* section of the manual.

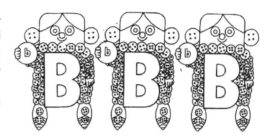

2B₂

PLANNING AND PREPARATION: Huggable Mr. B; a button; Mr. B's bag (filled from the previous lesson); a blindfold; Mr. B's Picture Squares; magazines, construction paper, scissors, paste, crayons, a variety of art materials; Alpha Time Master #88.

USING WORDS WITH B IN THE INITIAL POSITION IN WORDS

Playing A Game

Mr. B has a game for us. It is called Button, Button, who has the Button?

First, each one of us will take a picture out of Mr. B's bag and tape it to our sleeves.

Then we will sit in a circle.

One child will wear a blindfold over his eyes and stand in the center of the circle.

The teacher will give someone in the circle a button. The people sitting in the circle will keep passing the button until the child in the center holds up his hand and says "stop."

Then the child in the center will take off his blindfold and Mr. B will help him guess who has the button. When he guesses he may not use our names. He will have to look at the picture that is taped to our sleeves and name that instead.

For example, if he wants to guess the child who has the picture of the bicycle he will say:

"Button, button, who has the button?
Bicycle, do you have the button?"

Then the child who has the bicycle on his sleeve must answer *yes* or *no.*

Each child has three chances to guess who has the button. If he doesn't guess correctly, the child holding the button changes places with him. Continue the game until most of the children have had a turn to guess.

NAMING "DOING WORDS" THAT START WITH B

Mr. B says we *borrowed* (emphasize *initial sound*) things from his *bag.*

Borrowed tells what we did.

Mr. B has been thinking of words that tell what someone or something does. He calls those words "doing words." Mr. B says that when you run you are doing something.

Run is a "doing word."

Sleep is another "doing word."

Mr. B wondered, "Are there any 'doing words' that start the same way as Beautiful Buttons?"

Mr. B thought all day. Mr. B thought all night. Finally he thought of "doing words" that start with his Beautiful Buttons sound.

Play the following Riddle Game. Have the children dramatize each "doing word" as they guess it.

Mr. B will give you a clue and you must figure out the "doing word" he is thinking about.

Using Context Clues To Define Words

Mr. B says, "A ball does this."

What "doing word" is he thinking about that starts the same way as Beautiful Buttons? (bounce)

Show Mr. B how you look when you bounce a ball. You are doing something when you bounce.

Bounce is a "doing word."

Mr. B has thought of another "doing word":

You drop something. You want to pick it up. You cannot keep your body straight.

You must let your body ---------(bend).

Show Mr. B how you bend.

When you bend, you are doing something.

Bend is a "doing word."

Mr. B can think of another "doing word" that starts with his sound.

Mr. B is thinking of a word that tells what he had to do when he learned to ride his two wheel bicycle. He also had to do this when he tried to walk with a book on his head.

Mr. B is thinking of the word ---------(balance).

Make believe you are walking on a wire high above the ground. You have to balance yourself so that you don't fall.

Show Mr. B how you balance.

When you balance, you are doing something.

Balance is a "doing word."

Mr. B can think of another "doing word" that starts with his Beautiful Button sound. He says the word is *bow.* Show Mr. B how you bow. When you bow you are doing something.

Bow is a "doing word."

Mr. B told us four "doing words" that start the same way as Beautiful Buttons. What are they? (bounce, bend, balance, bow)

Distribute Mr. B's Picture Squares again. The child who has a Picture Square names the item and asks Mr. B what Mr. B wants him to do. Mr. B will tell each child one of the "doing words." The child then performs the action and then returns his picture to Mr. B's bag.

After several children have returned their pictures, Mr. B may ask the children to do two things (e.g., bounce and bend). The actions may then be increased to three and then to four.

REINFORCING THE SOUND OF B IN THE INITIAL POSITION IN WORDS

Mr. B would like to show us how to make button puppets.

First, make a big paper button.

Then paste a picture of something that starts with Mr. B's Beautiful Buttons sound on the back of your button.

Attach a stick or a straw to your button so you can hold it up.

Have the children play this "Naming and Doing" Game with their button puppets:

(Jimmy), have your button puppet ask (Mary's) button puppet what picture is on its back.

Mary's puppet will answer and tell your puppet to do one of Mr. B's "doing words."

Then (Jimmy's) puppet will act out the "doing word."

TYING IT TOGETHER

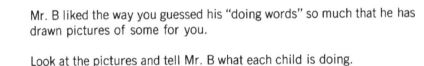

Give each child a copy of Alpha Time Master #88.

Mr. B liked the way you guessed his "doing words" so much that he has drawn pictures of some for you.

Look at the pictures and tell Mr. B what each child is doing.

What is the boy doing to the ball? (bouncing it)

What is the girl doing in order to pick the flowers? (bending)

What is the boy doing with the books? (balancing them)

What is the ballet dancer doing? (bowing)

Why do you think the ballerina is bowing?

ON THEIR OWN

Children may choose from the following activities:

Art

Drawing pictures of things that begin with Mr. B's sound (e.g., boots, bridges, baseball game).

Rhythms	Bending in all directions to different tempos.
Motor Co-ordination	Playing Simon Says—or Mr. B Says, using only Mr. B's "doing words."
Homemaking	Baking (oven ready) buns, bread, bananas.
	Boiling beans, broccoli, beets.
	Broiling or barbecuing beefburgers.

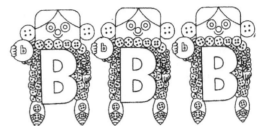

2B₃

PLANNING AND PREPARATION: Huggables, Mr. B, Mr. M, Mr. T, Mr. F, Mr. H; Mr. B's bag; two Picture Squares from each of the following: Mr. M, Mr. T, Mr. H, Mr. F; Alpha Time Master #89.

Put the Picture Squares of the Letter People named above into Mr. B's bag.

DISCRIMINATING AMONG INITIAL SOUNDS IN WORDS

Mr. B had visitors last night. Remember those Beautiful Buttons? Guess what! They are bad again! They took pictures out of the other Letter People's bags and put them into Mr. B's bag.

Mr. B may only have things in his bag that start with his sound. Those bad but Beautiful Buttons mixed up Mr. B's bag.

Mr. B can't figure out which things belong in his bag. He can't figure out which things don't belong in his bag.

We'll have to take everything out of Mr. B's bag, then we will put back the things that start with the sound of Mr. B's Beautiful Buttons.

Let one child at a time take something from Mr. B's bag. He decides whether or not it belongs there and proves it to Mr. B. If it is something that belongs in another Letter Person's bag, he proves it to that Letter Person and puts it in the correct bag. Continue the procedure for all the pictures.

RECOGNIZING "DOING WORDS"

Mr. B wants to know if you remember his "doing words."

Tell Mr. B some of his "doing words." (e.g., bounce, bend, bow, balance)

Mr. B has thought of another "doing word." He has thought of the word *bumping.*

He says that his Beautiful Buttons go bumping into one another. Mr. B likes the "doing word" *bumping.* Mr. B would like to have his "doing words" in poems.

He wants us to listen to a poem. Then he would like us to put some of his "doing words" in the poem.

Read the following rhyme to the children

Listening to a nursery rhyme for information

Jack and Jill went up the hill,
To fetch a pail of water.
Jack fell down and broke his crown,
And Jill came tumbling after.

Have the children repeat the nursery rhyme with you.

Let's put two of Mr. B's "doing words" in Jack and Jill.

171

Listen to this part of *Jack and Jill:* "Jack fell down."

Which word tells us what Jack did? (fell)

Jack fell. *Fell* is a "doing word."

Mr. B does not want the "doing word" *fell* to be in the poem.

He would like to use one of *his* "doing words" instead of the word *fell.*

What are some "doing words" we can use? (e.g., bowed, bent, bounced)

Have the children think of a Mr. B "doing word" which would make sense in the sentence "Jack fell down."

Say the rhyme using one of Mr. B's "doing words." (e.g., Jack bent down.)

Listen to another part of the poem: "And Jill came tumbling after."

Which word tells us how Jill came down the hill? (tumbling)

Tumbling is a "doing word."

Mr. B does not want the word *tumbling* in the poem. He wants you to use one of his "doing words" instead of *tumbling.*

Say this part of the poem using one of Mr. B's "doing words."

Have the children think of one of Mr. B's "doing words" which would make sense in the phrase "And Jill came tumbling after." (e.g., bumping, bouncing)

Now let's take the "doing word" we decided to use instead of *fell* and the "doing word" we decided to use instead of *tumbling.* We'll all say "Jack and Jill" together using these two "doing words."
(e.g., Jack and Jill went up the hill,
    To fetch a pail of water.
    Jack *bounced* down and broke his crown,
    And Jill came *bumping* after.)

PRACTICING SEQUENCE SKILLS

Distribute copies of Alpha Time Master #89 to the children.

Many people have asked Mr. B how to play "Button, Button, Who Has The Button?"

Recall with the children how the game was played. (See previous lesson.)

Everyone who read Mr. B's directions said that he still can't play the game.

Mr. B doesn't understand what is wrong. Let's try to help him.

Picture #1

Look at the top picture on your paper.

Who is in the picture? (children and Mr. B)

What is the little boy doing? (pointing to a child in the circle)

172

What do you think he is saying? (asking if the boy in the circle has the button)

Was this the first thing that happened when we played the game? (no)

Picture #2

Let's look at the middle picture.

Who is in this picture? (children and teacher)

What is the teacher doing? (giving a button to a child)

Why does the boy in the middle have a blindfold over his eyes? (He must not see who gets the button.)

When we played the game, when did you get the button? (at the beginning)

Let's look at the picture on the bottom.

Picture #3

What are the children doing? (passing the button)

Is this the last thing that happened when we played the game? (no)

Mr. B gives this paper to everyone who wants to play "Button, Button Who Has The Button?" Everyone looks at the first picture and does what the first picture shows.

Then they look at the next picture and do what the next picture shows.

Then they look at the last picture and do what that picture shows.

No one can play the game this way. Something is wrong!

Let's try to follow the pictures and see if we can play the game this way.

Have the children play the game following the sequence of the three pictures that Mr. B has drawn.

Mr. B has drawn everything that you have to do to play the game.

You cannot play it if you follow his pictures.

His pictures do not tell you what you must do first and second and last.

TYING IT TOGETHER

*Placing Pictures
In Correct Sequence*

Let's help him fix the pictures.

Which picture tells you the first thing to do when you play the game? (the middle picture)

Which picture tells you the second thing to do when you play the game? (the bottom picture)

Which picture tells you the last thing to do when you play the game? (the top picture)

Have the children cut out the pictures and paste them on another sheet of paper in the correct order.

ON THEIR OWN

Children may choose from the following activities:

*Poetry And
Rhymes*

Substituting Mr. B's "doing words" for "doing words" in other familiar poems or nursery rhymes.

Sorting

Mixing two or three Picture Squares from each Letter Person and sorting them again.

*Auditory
Discrimination*

Playing Mr. B's song (record #1, side B, band 1) and listening for words that begin with Mr. B's Beautiful Buttons sound.

2B₄

TEACHER OBJECTIVES:

To reinforce the characteristic and sound of Mr. B.

To help children identify their birthday.

To review concept of month, numerals.

PERFORMANCE OBJECTIVES:

The child will identify month and date birth.

The child will say some months a numbers.

The child will say words with the b in t initial position.

DEVELOPMENT

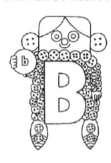

Mr. B's beautiful buttons are bursting.
He's so proud of the booklets he made for us.

Distribute the Mr. B "All About Us" booklets.
Ask the children to point to the words "All About Us" as you read them aloud.

Which Letter Person's picture do you see? (Mr. B)
Whose picture do you think is next to Mr. B? (his friend's)
Put your finger on the words under the pictures.
The words say, "Mr. B has a friend."
What is special about Mr. B? (his beautiful buttons)
Find the beautiful buttons on Mr. B.
Look at the picture of Mr. B's friend.
Mr. B wants us to put beautiful buttons on the picture.
Where can we put them?
Finish the picture of Mr. B's friend.
Make it look like you or anyone else.
Don't forget to put lots of beautiful buttons on the picture.

Give the children the opportunity to complete and share their pictures.

Have the children open the booklets.
Point to the first sentence on the left-hand side.
Explain that this time Mr. B put two pictures in the sentence.
Ask the children to name the pictures (beautiful buttons, Mr. B's back).
Read aloud, "Mr. B has beautiful buttons on his back."

Let the children pretend to reread the sentence with you.

Explain that the next sentence tells about a day that is very special to Mr. B.

Mr. B says if we look at the picture he put in the sentence, we will know what day is special to him.

Have the children look at the picture and discover the special day. (Mr. B's birthday)
Read the sentence aloud.
Ask them why birthdays are extra special to Mr. B. (*Birthdays* starts with the same sound as *beautiful buttons.*)

Mr. B took this whole page to tell us about himself.
What did he tell us first? (He has beautiful buttons on his back.)
What did he tell us next? (His birthday is May 6th.)
Mr. B says the next page is for us.

Look at the next page. What does Mr. B want each of us to write on the first dotted line? (our name)

Write it and then Mr. B will listen to your sentence.

After the children have written their names, select a booklet and read the incomplete sentence. (*e.g.,* Larry has buttons on his _____ .)

Mr. B says the sentence isn't finished.
It doesn't tell where Larry has buttons.
Where does Larry have buttons? (*e.g.,* shirt, pants, jacket)
How can Larry finish the sentence? (draw or cut out and paste a picture, dictate a word or copy a word)

Help each child complete his/her sentence.
You may wish to cross out the pronoun (her/his) that does not belong in the completed sentence.
Select several booklets and read the sentences aloud.

Explain that Mr. B has drawn all the months on the back of the booklet.
He wants each of the children to find his/her birthday.
Have the children turn to the back page.
Read aloud, "Let's talk about birthdays."
Have them find the first month.
Read the name of the month to them. (January)

Mr. B says if your birthday is in January, stand up.
Tell him the date.
Let's find the numeral for that date.
Let's put a circle around the numeral and a bigger circle around the month.
When Mr. B looks at the back of your booklet, he knows when your birthday is.

Follow this procedure with each of the remaining months.
Help each child circle the month and date of his/her birthday.

Have the children open their booklets.

Draw their attention to the second sentence on the right-hand side. Explain that Mr. B wants them to use the sentence to tell him their birthdays.

Mr. B wrote another sentence.
He could not finish it.
He made a dotted line where we can each write our name.
Let's write it and see if that will finish the sentence.

Have the children write their names.
Select a booklet and read the sentence aloud to prove it is incomplete. (*e.g.*, Edith's birthday is   .)

Mr. B says he knows why the sentence isn't finished.
It doesn't tell when Edith's birthday is.
How can Edith finish the sentence? (by dictating or copying her birthdate)

Help each child complete his/her sentence.
Select and read several aloud.
Children may enjoy pretending to read the information to Mr. B from their booklets.

This is an excellent opportunity to review months, days of the month, numbers of days in month, holidays. Discuss with the children birthdays of famous people. Add to the timeline birthdates of the children and famous people.

Encourage the children to take the booklets home.
Suggest they ask members of their family to show Mr. B when their birthday is.

2Z₁

PLANNING AND PREPARATION: Huggable, Mr. Z; large piece of mural paper divided into four sections; several zippers; Alpha Time Master #90; strips of paper to simulate zippers, one for each child; an envelope containing an invitation.

Draw a large outline of a house with a door and windows on the first section of the mural. Place a tiny note saying ZIP ME on each window and on the door. Tape a zipper on each window and on the door. Tape the mural to the wall or chalkboard. Conceal the drawing of the house with a sheet of newspaper.

Mr. Z's music (record #1) may be played to set the mood for the lesson.

SAYING WORDS WITH Z IN THE INITIAL POSITION

Show the children the invitation.

Here is an invitation for us to visit a Letter Person's home. He says we'll have a very good time. Let's look at his house.

Have the children accompany you as you remove the newspaper concealing the outline section of the mural. Talk about the house and why the zippers might be there. Then read the following rhyme to the children:

Hurry, hurry, we can't be late!
This is a most important date.
This house is very funny to see.
All the signs here say ZIP ME!

Look—there are zippers here, and zippers there,
There are zippers almost everywhere.
Let's zip the door right now,
Zzzip, zip—that's how.

Zip, zip, zipping is such fun!
Look—there is another one.

Look over here and you can see,
The sign on the window says ZIP ME!
Zip, zip—what fun!
Let us zip another one.

Now close your eyes and zip with me.
Guess which Letter Person we will see.

Have the children close their eyes. Then place Mr. Z in front of his zipper house.

SUBSTITUTING Z FOR OTHER INITIAL LETTER SOUNDS

Distribute the paper zippers to the children. Let the children play Zagic as follows: When their zippers are held against different things in the room, they name each object, substituting Z for its initial letter sound (e.g., book—zook).

Playing Zagic

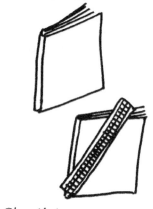

Classifying

Mr. Z says that these zippers can do very special things. *(Hold up a book.)*

What is this? Yes, it is a *book*. If we put a zipper on it, we may call it a *zook!* It's like magic. Zoops, I mean zagic!

What is this? *(Hold up a pencil.)* We know. It is a. . . *pencil*. If we put a zipper on it, we may call it a. . . *zencil!*

What is this? We know. It is a. . . *cup*. If we put a zipper on it, we may call it a. . . *zup!*

Let's think about the rooms in Mr. Z's house. What furniture belongs in a living room? (e.g., couch, table, lamp)

If Mr. Z puts a zagic zipper on his (couch), what will it be called? (a zouch) What would he call a table? (a zable)

Let's talk about other rooms in Mr. Z's house.

Have the children name items found in the kitchen (e.g., sink, stove, refrigerator, cabinets, chairs, table).

In Mr. Z's kitchen, a sink is not called a *sink*. It is called a. . . *zink!* If it is a zink, what must it have on it? (a zipper)

Let's talk about another room in Mr. Z's house. Let's look in his bedroom. What are some things you find in a bedroom?

Have the children name items found in the bedroom (e.g., bed, chest, mirror, chair).

In Mr. Z's bedroom, a bed is not called a *bed*. It is called. . . *zed!* If it is a zed, what must it have on it? (a zipper)

Let the children name another kind of room and name and rename all the items found in it. Then the children may form small groups. Each group will draw one of the rooms in Mr. Z's house on a section of the mural paper. Encourage the children to discuss and decide what each will draw.

Drawing A Mural

Mr. Z would like us to draw the rooms inside his house. Put all the things in each room that you think should be there. Remember, in Mr. Z's house, everything must have a zipper on it.

When the mural is finished, the children may give Mr. Z's picture a name.

Other classes may be invited to visit Mr. Z's house. The children may dictate an invitation.

TYING IT TOGETHER

Give each child a copy of Alpha Time Master #90. Using their paper strip zippers, the children may play ZAGIC with the furnishings in the picture.

ON THEIR OWN

The children may choose from the following activities:

Counting

Using Alpha Time Master #90, the children may count all the zippers they can find.

Classifying

Using Alpha Time Master #90, the children may mark all the things they can find that are hard or soft, that have legs, that are big or small, that are made of glass or wood.

Art

Painting a picture of one of the rooms at home.

2Z₂ **PLANNING AND PREPARATION:** Huggable, Mr. Z; a bag for Mr. Z; Mr. Z's Picture Squares; one Picture Square from Mr. M, Mr. T, Mr. F, Mr. H, Mr. N, Miss A and Mr. B; paper zippers for each child; Alpha Time Master #91.

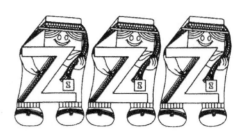

DECIDING HOW MR. Z WILL GET HIS SOUND

Mr. Z likes the way we play Zagic, but something is worrying him. He says that we forgot to tell him about his sound. He heard that Mr. B gets his sound from Beautiful Buttons.

Mr. Z wants to know how he will remember his sound.

How do you think Mr. Z will get his sound?

Lead the children to the conclusion that Mr. Z should get his sound from Zipping Zippers.

Mr. Z says he wants to be like all the other Letter People who have sounds. He wants his own *zag*. What does he mean? *(Mr. Z wants a bag of his own.)*

USING WORDS WITH Z IN THE INITIAL POSITION

Each of the Letter People would like to give Mr. Z something for his bag.

Let's take a picture out of Mr. M's bag.

Tell us what it is. (e.g. monkey)

Now put a zipper on it.

With a zagic zipper on it it is not a (monkey), it is a. . . (zonkey).

Prove to Mr. Z that the zonkey may go into his bag.

Follow the same procedure with a picture from Mr. F, Mr. T, Mr. H, Mr. N, Miss A and Mr. B.

Mr. Z has some pictures he wants to show us. He says they are not zagic pictures.

Naming Mr. Z's Picture Squares

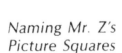

Show the children Mr. Z's Picture Squares (i.e. zebra, zoo, zipper, zero). Ask them to show each picture to Mr. Z and to name it for him.

Why did Mr. Z show us these pictures? (They begin with his sound.)

These pictures don't need the Zagic game. The pictures already begin with Mr. Z's sound.

Mr. Z would like us to fill his bag.

Making Things For Mr. Z's Bag

We can fill his bag with zagic pictures and with pictures that start with his Zipping Zippers sound. Words that start with Mr. Z's own sound do not need Zagic, but each zagic picture must have a zipper on it.

Have the children prove everything they find or make for Mr. Z before they put it into his bag.

TYING IT TOGETHER

Distribute copies of Alpha Time Master #91. Discuss the pictures around Mr. Z's Zipping Zipper (i.e. zipper, table, zebra, hat, zoo, mouse).

The children may name the pictures and decide which need Zagic. Then they may "touch" (connect) the zipper to those pictures that begin with Mr. Z's sound. (i.e., zipper, zoo, zebra)

ON THEIR OWN

Eye-Hand Co-ordination

Auditory Discrimination

Art

Nature Study

Construction

Sorting

Children may choose from the following activities:

Assembling Mr. Z's puzzle.

Listening for words that begin with Mr. Z's sound in Mr. Z's music (record #1, side B, band #2).

Painting zebra stripes on large sheets of paper.

Visiting the zoo.

Making a miniature zoo out of wood, clay, wire and other materials.

Using Mr. Z's Picture Squares and/or playing cards in any of the activities suggested in the *Games* section of the manual.

2Z₃

PLANNING AND PREPARATION: Huggables, Mr. Z, Mr. F; strips of colored paper; tape; contents of Mr. Z's bag; Alpha Time Master #92.

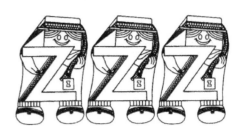

USING WORDS WITH Z IN THE INITIAL POSITION

Mr. Z has been talking to Mr. F. Mr. F told him how much fun we had when we played "Follow Funny Feet Road."

Mr. Z wants to make his own road. He says it can be called a Zig Zag Road.

Playing A Game

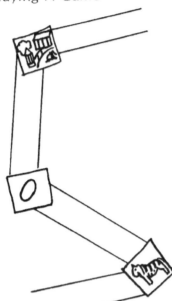

Using strips of paper laid end to end on the floor, have children make a Zig Zag Road. Tape a number of pictures from Mr. Z's bag at different points along the road.

We can play Follow the Zig Zag Road.

When we follow the Zig Zag Road, we must name the pictures so that they start with Mr. Z's Zipping Zippers sound. Sometimes we will have to use zagic.

When it is your turn to follow the Zig Zag Road, you must tell us the name of each picture on which you step.

We will all say "Follow the Zig Zag Road" while someone follows it.

> Follow the Zig Zag Road.
> Follow the Zig Zag Road.
> Follow, Follow, Follow, Follow,
> Follow the Zig Zag Road.

Children may form small groups and make and follow their own Zig Zag Roads.

READING COMPREHENSION

Mr. Z likes to play Zagic. The other Letter People liked to play Zagic, too, until one day something happened.

Let's read about it.

Reading A Picture Story

Give each child a copy of Alpha Time Master #92.

Frame 1

Look at the first picture.

Who is in the picture? (Mr. B, Miss A, Mr. M)

What are they holding? (their bags)

Why are they holding their bags upside down? (They are wondering what happened to their things.)

What is missing from their bags? (their pictures, etc.)

Look at their faces. How do they feel? (upset, confused)

Why do you think they are upset? (Their bags are empty.)

What do you think happened?

Frame 2

Let's look at the next part of the picture story and see if we can find out.

Who is in the picture? (Mr. Z)

What is he doing? (He is carrying many things.)

Where do you think Mr. Z got all these pictures and things? (from the Letter People)

What is on the table? (zippers)

What do you think Mr. Z will do with all those zippers? (play Zagic)

Predicting

Why do you think Mr. Z took all the things from the other Letter People?

Inferring

After Mr. Z plays Zagic with these things, what do you think he will do with them?

Frame 3

Let's look at the next picture.

What did Mr. Z do with all the things? (put zippers on them)

How can you tell he took things from Mr. M, Mr. B and Miss A? (They begin with their sounds, e.g., button, monkey.)

Do you think the Letter People will let Mr. Z keep all of their things?

Frame 4

Let's look at the last part of the story and find out.

Who is in the picture? (Mr. B, Miss A, Mr. M)

What are they doing? (looking in Mr. Z's bag)

Why is it hard for them to find their own pictures? (They are mixed up. Zippers are on them.)

What will they have to do before they can put something back into their own bags? (Take off the zipper and prove it.)

TYING IT TOGETHER

Auditory Discrimination

Have the children dramatize this picture story. This is an excellent way for them to prove which things belong in each Letter Person's bag. Any or all of the Letter People may be used.

ON THEIR OWN

Children may choose from the following activities.

Making A Picture Book

Using Alpha Time Master #92, the four pictures may be cut apart, mounted on separate sheets and stapled together to form a book. This book may then be "read" aloud.

Storytelling

Using Alpha Time Master #92 and retelling the story of Mr. Z and the Letter People. If a tape recorder is available, the story may be recorded.

2Z₄

TEACHER OBJECTIVES:

To review the characteristic and sound of Mr. Z.

To introduce basic number-line concepts.

To help children distinguish between 0 (zero) and o (letter).

PERFORMANCE OBJECTIVES:

The child will distinguish the numeral from the letter o in context.

The child will say words with the z in initial position.

DEVELOPMENT

One day Mr. Z's zipping zippers wouldn't zip.
Mr. Z was very upset.
The Letter People told Mr. Z he would feel better if he stopped thinking about the zipping zippers for a while and did something else.
Mr. Z decided to make booklets for us.

Distribute the Mr. Z "All About Us" booklets to the children.
Put your finger on the words at the top.
Read aloud, "All About Us."
Find Mr. Z.
Find his friend.
Let's read the words under the pictures.
The words say, "Mr. Z has a friend."
What is special about Mr. Z? (his zipping zippers)
Find the zipping zippers on Mr. Z.
Look at the picture of Mr. Z's friend.
What did Mr. Z give to his friend? (a zipping zipper)
Mr. Z did not finish the picture of his friend.
We cannot tell if the zipping zipper is on a jacket, a sweater, or a shirt.
Mr. Z wants us to finish the picture.

Encourage the children to finish the picture.
They may want to add to the body as well as the clothing.
When they've had the opportunity to complete and share their pictures, have them open the booklets.

Point to the first sentence on the left-hand side.

Explain that Mr. Z put two pictures in the sentence.
Ask the children to name the pictures. (zipping zipper, zebra)

Read aloud, "Mr. Z put a zipping zipper on a zebra."
Let them pretend to reread the sentence with you.

Mr. Z was very busy looking for something that starts like his zipping zippers.
He found a zero.
He wrote a sentence to tell us what he found.
Read aloud, "Mr. Z finds a zero."

Look at the picture under the sentence.
How can we tell what the temperature is? (by looking at the thermometer)
What is the temperature? (0°)
Where did Mr. Z find the zero? (on the thermometer)
How can we tell when it's very cold?
Discuss the range of the thermometer.

Mr. Z took this whole page to tell us about himself.
What did he tell us first? (He put a zipping zipper on a zebra.)
What did he tell us next? (He found a zero.)
Mr. Z says the next page is for us.
Look at the next page.
What does Mr. Z want each of us to write on the first dotted line?
(our name)
Write your name and then he'll listen to your sentence.

After the children have written their names, select a booklet and read the incomplete sentence. (*e.g.,* Charlotte put a zipper on a   .)
Mr. Z says the sentence isn't finished.
It doesn't tell on what Charlotte put a zipper.
On what can Charlotte put a zipper?
How can Charlotte finish the sentence? (draw or cut out and paste a picture, dictate or copy a word)

Help each child complete his or her sentence.
Select several booklets and read the completed sentences aloud.

Explain that Mr. Z wants them to look at the back of the booklet.
Mr. Z drew pictures of objects on which he found a zero.

Have the children turn to the back of the booklet.
Read aloud, "Let's talk about zeros."
Discuss each illustration with the children.
Have them find the zero on each object.

Explain that Mr. Z wants them to tell him where they find a zero.
Have them open their booklets.
Draw the children's attention to the second sentence on the right-hand page.

Have each child write his/her name on the dotted line.
Select and read aloud several of the sentences to prove they are incomplete.
Discuss with the children ways of completing the sentence.
Some children may want to draw a picture of one of the objects shown on the back of the booklet.
They may find a similar picture in a magazine and cut it out and paste it at the end of the sentence.
Others may be able to find or think of additional objects. (*e.g.,* adding machine, timer)

Encourage the children to take their booklets home.
Have them ask members of their family to help them find objects on which there is a zero.

2P₁

PLANNING AND PREPARATION: Huggable, Mr. P; a bag for Mr. P; Mr. P's Picture Squares; Alpha Time Master #93; magazines, drawing paper, crayons, scissors, paste, art materials.

Mr. P's music (record #1) may be played to set the mood for this lesson.

GETTING A SOUND FOR MR. P

Gather the children around Mr. P and tell them this story:

Listening To
A Story

Last night Mr. P was just about to go to sleep when someone knocked at his door. He opened the door, and in they popped! Mr. P said, "Oh, no, not again! You can't be back. I put paste on each of you. How did you get loose?"

Guess who was back? That's right. The popping Pointy Patches! Poor Mr. P could not believe his eyes. He was sure that soon people would be pounding at his door looking for the popping Pointy Patches.

Mr. P positively had to make those patches leave before the people came pounding at his door.

"Please let us tell you why we came," said a purple popping Pointy Patch.

"I don't want to hear one thing you have to say. Just go back where you belong," cried Mr. P. Poor Mr. P, all he could think about was pasting, pasting and more pasting.

"We didn't pop away," said a pink popping Pointy Patch. "We have permission from the people to come and talk to you."

"I don't want to hear any complaints," said Mr. P.

The Pointy Patches started to cry. "We don't want to complain," pleaded a polka dot popping Pointy Patch.

"I am sorry," said Mr. P. "Please tell me why you are here."

The purple popping Pointy Patch wiped his eyes and said, "We have come to help you get a sound.

The buttons we have been meeting keep teasing us. They say, 'We are Beautiful Buttons and Mr. B gets his sound from us, the Beautiful Buttons.'

The zippers we meet keep teasing us. They say, 'We are Zipping Zippers. Mr. Z got his sound from us, the Zipping Zippers.'

They both keep saying, 'It's too bad poor Mr. P doesn't have a sound. Poor Mr. P.'

We couldn't let them say that about you Mr. P. We love you. We want you to have a sound, too.

We popped in to tell you that your sound can be the sound that starts Pointy Patches. Then we'll pop back where we belong. We promise. That's all we want to say."

Mr. P felt tears running down his face onto his Pointy Patches. He thought, "Next time, I'll listen before I get so angry."

He hugged and kissed each popping Pointy Patch and thanked them.

Mr. P said that he liked his sound. He was sure that he would never forget it because he will always think of Pointy Patches. The popping Pointy Patches will be the patches he will always love best.

Mr. P promised the popping Pointy Patches he would send them pictures of things that start with the same sound as Pointy Patches.

NAMING WORDS WITH P IN THE INITIAL POSITION

*Playing A
Riddle Game*

Show the children Mr. P's Picture Squares (i.e., pillow, pipe, pie, pencil, piano). Have the children name each picture for Mr. P. Let them discover that each picture starts the same way as Pointy Patches. Then have them prove each picture for Mr. P and put it in his bag.

Mr. P has thought of more words that start with his Pointy Patches sound. He will give us clues and we will guess the word he is thinking about.

Mr. P says, "The word I am thinking about rhymes with *hot*. Mother uses it for cooking. What is its name?" (pot)

Mr. P says, "The word I am thinking about rhymes with *wig*. It is an animal that goes oink, oink. What is its name?" (pig)

Mr. P says, "The word I am thinking about rhymes with *taste*. It is something I used to put each popping Pointy Patch back in place. What is its name?" (paste)

Mr. P says, "The word I am thinking about rhymes with *tomato*. You have to cook it before you eat it. It can be mashed, boiled or baked. What is its name?" (potato)

Mr. P says, "The word I am thinking about rhymes with *tail*. Jack and Jill took it up the hill to fill it with water. What is its name?" (pail)

Mr. P says that now we know lots of things that start with his Pointy Patches sound.

*Making Things
For Mr. P's Bag*

He says, "Please, please, help me fill my bag." He wants to have his bag positively popping with things that start the same way as Pointy Patches.

Have the children work individually or in small groups finding and making things for Mr. P's bag. Encourage them to use as wide a variety of materials as possible. Have the children prove the things they make or find before placing it in Mr. P's bag.

TYING IT TOGETHER

Give each child a copy of Alpha Time Master #93. Encourage the children to name some of Mr. P's pictures. (i.e., pipe, pencil, piano) They may draw a picture of something that starts with the same sound as Pointy Patches in the space provided.

ON THEIR OWN

Children may choose from the following activities:

Auditory Discrimination

Using their copies of Alpha Time Master #93, children may cut out Mr. P's pictures, mount them on construction paper or oaktag, and start their own bag for Mr. P.

Playing Mr. P's song (record #1, side B, band 3) and listening for words that begin with Mr. P's sound.

Sorting And Matching

Including Mr. P's Picture Squares, puzzle and playing cards, in any of the games described in the *Games* section.

2P₂
PLANNING AND PREPARATION: Huggable, Mr. P; a piece of mural paper large enough to allow each child to draw a picture on it; sheets of paper for making patches; crayons, tape, scissors, art materials; a blindfold; Alpha Time Master #94; large piece of chart paper.

USING WORDS WITH P IN THE INITIAL POSITION

Tell the children about the following conversation between Mr. P and the Pointy Patches:

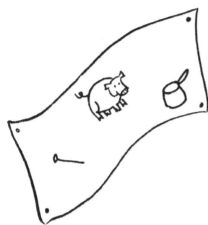

Mr. P had a telephone call last night. Who do you think called? That's right! Those popping Pointy Patches. They wanted to know if Mr. P likes his sound. They wanted to know if we had helped Mr. P fill his bag. They talked and talked and talked. They said they wanted to keep talking and talking because they had nothing to do.

A plan popped into Mr. P's head. He said, "I must hang up. I just thought of a game I can make. Then you will all be able to play."

Mr. P said his game is called "Paste the Pointy Patch." Mr. P says that he doesn't draw very well. We will have to help him.

Tape the mural paper on the board or wall.

Mr. P wants each of us to draw a small picture on this paper. It has to be something that starts with Mr. P's Pointy Patches sound.

Drawing Things That Start With "P"

Tell Mr. P what you are going to draw.

Then prove to him that it starts with his sound.

Let the children discuss the pictures each will draw. If they have trouble thinking of things that start with P, they may look at the pictures in Mr. P's bag.

When the drawings are complete, distribute a square Pointy Patch piece of paper to each child. Explain the game to the children. (It is a variation of "Pin the Tail on the Donkey")

Each child puts a little paste on the corner of his patch. He is then blindfolded and pointed in the direction of the mural. As he starts off, he must tell his patch which picture he wishes it to paste.

You have told your patch where to go. Your Pointy Patch is not blindfolded. It can see all the pictures on the mural, but it may not want to go where you want it to go.

Following Game Directions

We'll all say this rhyme as you walk toward the picture:

You told your Pointy Patch where to go.
Will it say "yes," will it say "no?"

After you have pasted your patch on the mural you may take off your blindfold and see whether your patch said "yes" and landed where you wanted it to go, or whether it said "no" and landed somewhere else.

Give all the children a chance to play "Paste the Pointy Patch." The purpose of the game is to give the children the opportunity to repeat words that start with the initial sound of "P." It does not matter which picture is touched. If the child does not paste the patch on the picture he picked, he can blame it on his "Pointy Patch" which has a mind of its own.

TYING IT TOGETHER

Mr. P likes to play "Paste the Pointy Patch." He knows the popping Pointy Patches will like playing it, too. Now they will have something to do.

Give each child a copy of Alpha Time Master #94.

Look at the picture.

What is Mr. P doing? (playing "Paste the Pointy Patch")

What pictures are on the board? (pig, pot, patch, pen)

Mr. P thinks the popping Pointy Patches would have a good time making their own "Paste the Patch" game. He wants us to write the directions for making the game.

What things did we need to make this game? (e.g., paper, paste, crayons)

What were the things we did to make the game?

As the children dictate their instructions, write them on a large piece of chart paper. Children may want their own copies of the Alpha Time Master to have words telling about how the game is made. Tell the children that Mr. P will use a separate piece of paper to show how the game is played.

ON THEIR OWN

Children may choose from the following activities:

Art

Painting a purple or pink picture.

Drawing pictures of all the supplies needed for making the Paste the Pointy Patch Game.

Making a Paste the Pointy Patch game to take home.

Auditory Discrimination

Finding and cutting out pictures in magazines that begin with Mr. P's sound, and using them for the game.

Classifying

Making lists of animals for Mr. P (e.g., pig, pony, porcupine, polar bear, panda, panther).

Making a list of names for Mr. P (e.g., Paul, Peter, Pedro, Patrick, Penny, Pauline, Pamela, Peggy, Patsy).

Making a list of places for Mr. P (e.g., Pennsylvania, Puerto Rico, Paris, Port Chester, Portugal, Panama).

2P₃

PLANNING AND PREPARATION: Huggable, Mr. P; Alpha Time Master #95; paper, scissors, paste; an outline-drawing of a boy and a green pepper.

TALKING ABOUT A SEQUENCE OF EVENTS

Gather the children around Mr. P.

Mr. P had another telephone call. Those popping Pointy Patches called again. They received two letters from Mr. P.

One letter had the directions we wrote for making "Paste the Pointy Patch."

The other letter had the directions Mr. P drew to show how to play the game. Mr. P drew some pictures to show how to play "Paste the Pointy Patch."

The popping Pointy Patches followed our instructions and made "Paste the Pointy Patch" game. Then they were ready to play.

They looked at Mr. P's pictures and started to play the game.

Something was wrong. They could not play the game. The Pointy Patches called Mr. P and told him they were sending back his picture directions.

Mr. P wants us to help him find out what is wrong with the pictures.

READING COMPREHENSION

Reading Pictures

Give each child a copy of Alpha Time Master #95. Discuss each picture.

Frame #1

detail
drawing conclusions

Let's look at the first picture.

What is the girl in the picture doing? (looking to see where her patch landed)

Why is the blindfold around her neck? (She has pasted her patch and now wants to see where it is.)

How did her patch get on the picture of the pipe? (She pasted the patch there while she was blindfolded.)

Is this the way the game "Paste the Pointy Patch" starts? (no)

Let's look at the next picture and see what Mr. P told the popping Pointy Patches to do next.

Frame #2

inferring
predicting
recalling

Who is in this picture? (girl and her teacher)

What is the girl doing? (telling which picture she wants to paste)

What will the teacher do with the blindfold? (tie it over the girl's eyes)

In what part of the game did this happen when we played "Paste the Pointy Patch?" (at the beginning)

Let's look at the next picture direction Mr. P drew for "Paste the Pointy Patch."

187

Frame #3

*making judgments
reasoning*

Who is in the picture? (the girl)

Why is the blindfold covering her eyes? (She is not supposed to see where the patch lands.)

What will she do with the patch? (paste it on the mural)

How do we know this picture does not show the last thing that happens in the game? (The patch has not been pasted.)

What is wrong with Mr. P's picture directions? (They are not in order.)

Why can't the popping Pointy Patches play the game when they follow Mr. P's picture directions? (They are mixed up.)

Mr. P does not believe that his picture directions are mixed up. He wants us to prove it to him.

Let's play the game following Mr. P's picture directions. Then he will see what is wrong.

Have several children try to play "Paste the Pointy Patch" following Mr. P's picture directions in the order in which he drew them.

How can we fix Mr. P's picture directions?

Mr. P wants to send the corrected pictures to the popping Pointy Patches.

Placing Pictures In The Correct Sequence

Have the children cut out each frame of the picture directions. Then they may arrange the pictures in the order in which the game is played (i.e. Frame 2, 3, 1). They may paste these pictures on a sheet of drawing paper in the correct order.

Encourage the children to check themselves by playing one sample game in the order in which they have pasted their pictures. They may use a make believe patch and mural.

Some children may want to dictate a note to the popping Pointy Patches explaining why they were unable to follow the picture directions.

IDENTIFYING THE DOING WORDS THAT HAVE P IN THE INITIAL POSITION

Some Beautiful Buttons told the Pointy Patches that Mr. B has "doing words."

Pointy Patches said that if Mr. B has "doing words," Mr. P can have "doing words," too.

They thought and thought of "doing words" that start the same way as Pointy Patches.

Mr. P was excited. He said, "Tell me, tell me, what are my 'doing words?'"

The Patches said, "No, you have to guess!" Those popping Pointy Patches! All they want to do is play.

Mr. P has to guess his "doing words."

Discovering Words
From Context Clues

Tell the children to listen to the clues and to try to think of each word for Mr. P. Be sure to give them enough time to think of the words.

You are standing at the easel. You dip your brush in paint and brush it on a paper. You are. . . (painting.)

When you are painting you are doing something. *Painting* is a "doing word."

Why is *painting* one of Mr. P's "doing words?" (It begins with his sound.)

Show Mr. P how you paint.

Before we play the "Paste the Pointy Patch" game, we tell which picture we want by holding out our finger and. . . (pointing or picking).

When you are pointing you are doing something. *Pointing* is a "doing word."

Why is *pointing* one of Mr. P's "doing words?"

Show Mr. P how you point.

This "doing word" tells us what Mr. P has to do to make the patches stick.

This is something Mr. P was tired of doing. He was tired of. . . (pasting).

When you are pasting you are doing something. *Pasting* is a "doing word."

Why is *pasting* one of Mr. P's "doing words?"

Show Mr. P how you paste.

Follow the above procedure for any or all of the following Mr. P "doing words": pull, push, pack, pin, punch, pinch, pound. Have the children pantomime each action.

TYING IT TOGETHER

If possible, make a simple drawing of a boy and some green peppers.

Mr. P read a story. He found a sentence that was filled with words that start with his Pointy Patches sound. This is the way it goes:

"Peter Piper picked a peck of pickled peppers."

Point to the boy. What is the boy's name? (Peter Piper)

Point to what he picked. What did he pick? (peppers)

How does a pepper taste?

Let's say the sentence about Peter Piper together.

Have the children repeat the sentence, increasing the speed with which it is said each time.

Mr. P wants us to find his "doing word" in the sentence about Peter Piper.

Which word tells us what Peter Piper did to the peck of pickled peppers? (picked)

Think of another Mr. P "doing word" that we can use instead of picked (e.g., packed, planted, plucked).

Let's say the sentence using that "doing word."
(Peter Piper planted a peck of pickled peppers.)

Show Mr. P how Peter Piper packed a peck of pickled peppers.

Have the children replace the "doing word" "picked" by as many other Mr. P "doing words" as they can suggest. Pantomime each word.

ON THEIR OWN

Children may choose from the following activities:

Counting

Counting how many words start with Mr. P's sound in "Peter Piper picked a peck of pickled peppers."

Cooking

Pickling peppers or cucumbers. Materials needed are: a quart container, vinegar, sugar, pickling spice, fresh or dry dill, small cucumbers or red peppers. (Optional: garlic) To pickle: Place as many small cucumbers or cut up peppers in a jar as possible. Mix the spices, water and vinegar together and pour into the jar. Fill jar to the top. Pickles should be sour in about three weeks—liquid may be added as necessary.

Needlework

Making patchwork quilts, blankets or place mats by sewing woven, flannel, crocheted or knitted squares together.

Grammar

Listening for "doing words" in any record or story.

2P₄

TEACHER OBJECTIVES:

To review the characteristic and sound of Mr. P.

To discuss pets.

PERFORMANCE OBJECTIVES:

The child will talk about pets.

The child will say words with the *p* in the initial position.

DEVELOPMENT

Mr. P's pointy patches are popping with pride.
He is so proud of the "All About Us" booklets he made.

Distribute the booklets to the children.

The words at the top say "All About Us."
Why does Mr. P call this booklet "All About Us"? (The booklet will tell things about Mr. P and things about each of us.)
Which Letter Person's picture do you see? (Mr. P)
What is all over Mr. P? (pointy patches)
Find the sentence at the bottom of the booklet.
Let's listen to what it says.
Read aloud, "Mr. P has a friend."
Look at the picture next to Mr. P.
Did Mr. P draw a picture of his friend? (no)
What did Mr. P draw for his friend? (a shirt and pants)
What did Mr. P put on the shirt and pants? (patches)
Mr. P wants us to finish the picture.

Give the children the opportunity to finish the picture.
After they have shared their pictures, have them open the booklet.

Point to the first sentence on the left-hand side.
Ask the children to name the picture Mr. P put in the first sentence. (pointy patches)
Read aloud, "Mr. P likes pointy patches."
Let them pretend to reread the sentence with you.

Explain that Mr. P likes pets.
He wrote a sentence to tell the children what his favorite pet is.
Ask them to look at the picture at the bottom of the page.
Have them whisper the name of Mr. P's favorite pet to him.
Read aloud, "Mr. P's favorite pet is a pig."
Why does Mr. P like pets?
Why is his favorite pet a pig? (Both *pet* and *pig* start with the same sound as *pointy patches.*)
Mr. P used this whole page to tell us about himself.
What did he tell us first? (He likes pointy patches.)
What did he tell us next? (His favorite pet is a pig.)
Mr. P says the next page is for us.

Look at the next page.
What does Mr. P want us to write on the first dotted line? (our name)
What pictures are in the sentence? (pictures of pointy patches)
Tell Mr. P the color of each pointy patch. (red, yellow, blue)
Write your name on the dotted line and then Mr. P will listen to your sentence.

After the children have written their names, select several booklets and read the sentences aloud.
The children may point to and name the color of the patches. (*e.g.,* Barbara likes red, yellow and blue patches.)
The children may wish to circle the color they like best.

Explain that Mr. P would like the children to look at the picture he drew on the back of the booklet.
Have the children turn to the back.

Read the sentence at the top aloud: "Let's talk about pets."
Have the children find and name the pets in the picture.
Ask them to tell about pets they have.

After finding out the different kinds of pets the children have, you may wish to discuss with them the different kinds of animals that are not usually thought of as pets.

Have children tell of instances in which animals not thought of as pets have been used as pets.

Explain that Mr. P wants them to tell him their favorite pet.

Have them open their booklets.
Draw the children's attention to the second sentence.

Let's each write our name on the dotted line.
Then we can listen to the sentence and see what's missing.

After they have written their names, select a booklet and read the incomplete sentence aloud. (*e.g.,* John's favorite pet is a

Mr. P says that he knows why the sentence is not finished.
The sentence does not tell what John's favorite pet is.
How can John finish the sentence? (Draw a picture of his favorite pet.)

Some may prefer finding a picture in a magazine, cutting it out and pasting it at the end of the sentence.
Still others may wish to dictate the name of their favorite pet.
Encourage the children to take the booklets home and have members of their family tell Mr. P what their favorite pet is.

2S₁ **PLANNING AND PREPARATION:** Huggable, Mr. S; two cut-outs of Super Socks stapled together to hold Mr. S's Picture Squares; a bag for Mr. S; magazines, paper, crayons, art materials, pipe cleaners; Alpha Time Master #96.

Mr. S's music (record #1, side B, band 4) may be played to set the mood.

RECALLING MR. S AND HIS SUPER SOCKS

Do you remember when Mr. S sent Super Socks to Mr. M?

Poor Mr. M could not munch when he wore the Super Socks.

He wanted to send them back to Mr. S, but he didn't want to hurt his feelings. Mr. M thought and thought of a plan. Finally, he decided what to do. He telephoned Mr. S and told him he had a Super Sock surprise for him. Mr. S had never heard of a Super Sock surprise. He begged Mr. M to tell him about it. Mr. M said that the surprise was in the Super Socks.

Mr. S said, "Please, Mr. M, can you send the Super Socks back to me? I will send you a different present. I will send you something you can munch!"

Mr. M was happy! He put the surprise in the Super Socks and sent them to Mr. S.

Mr. S has been waiting and waiting for the Super Socks. Sometimes it takes a long time for something to be delivered. At last—the Super Socks are here! Mr. S is too excited to look inside the Super Socks.

He wants us to find the surprise for him.

NAMING MR. S's PICTURES

Show the children the Super Socks cut-outs. Let several children in turn take a Picture Square out of the Super Socks, name each picture and show it to Mr. S. (i.e., sailor, sun, sink, sandwich, soda)

There is nothing else in the Super Socks.

There are no more parts to the surprise.

Can we figure out what the surprise is?

Let's say the name of each picture together. (Emphasize the initial S sound.)

Mr. S is smiling. He likes something he hears.

What can it be?

How are all these words the same?

Let the children discover that each word starts with the same sound as Mr. S's Super Socks.

Where do you think Mr. S will get his sound?

191

NAMING WORDS THAT HAVE S IN THE INITIAL POSITION

Mr. S closes his eyes and sees all kinds of things that start with his Super Socks sound.

He wants to tell you the names of some of the things so you can make or find them.

Mr. S says the names are a secret. He likes secrets.

He will not tell us the names; he will only give us a word that rhymes with each name.

Mr. S says the word that starts with his Super Socks sound rhymes with *moon.* It is something you use when you eat soup.

Answering riddles

What word is Mr. S thinking about? (spoon)

Say the word and prove it.

Mr. S is ready with another word. Mr. S says the word that starts with his Super Socks sound rhymes with *pool.*

It is the place where we are right now. What word is Mr. S thinking about? (school)

Say the word and prove it.

Mr. S is ready with another word. Mr. S says the word that starts with his Super Socks sound rhymes with *bed.* It is something you can ride on in the snow.

What word is Mr. S thinking about? (sled)

Say the word and prove it.

Mr. S is ready with another word. Mr. S says the word that starts with his Super Socks sound rhymes with *nail.* It is something you stand on when you want to find out how much you weigh.

What word is Mr. S thinking about? (scale)

Say the word and prove it.

Follow the same procedure for "better" and "sweater," "weed" and "seed," "blow" and "snow".

TALKING ABOUT DOING WORDS" THAT HAVE S IN THE INITIAL POSITION

Mr. S wants to play a game.

It is called "Mr. S Says."

Mr. S has thought of some special words that start the same way as Super Socks. They are words that tell us what we do. What do we call words that tell us what we do? (Doing Words)

Listen to Mr. S's Doing Word and do what it says.

Let the children act out each of the following verbs:

Mr. S says: sit, stand, slide, skip, sway, smile, skate, stretch, sing, sleep, sew.

Now tell the children that Mr. S wants them to do two things at the same time.

Motor Coordination

Mr. S says sit and smile. . . stand and stretch. . . skip and sing.

If the children are ready, vary the game in this fashion:

Mr. S will tell us to do two things, but he does not want us to do them both at the same time.

Following A Sequence

He wants us to do them one right after the other.

Mr. S says skate, and then sit. . . stretch, and then sleep, stand and then sit.

Follow the same procedure, asking the children to follow three directions. Then give some of the children a chance to tell the class what Mr. S says.

NAMING AND PROVING WORDS WITH S IN THE INITIAL POSITION

He is anxious to see what you will put in it.

Let's make and find things for his bag.

Remember to prove everything to him.

Encourage the children to use a wide variety of the materials available to them. Explain to them that Mr. S would like to have things in his bag that show one of his Doing Words. (e.g., someone skating, smiling, sitting) Pipe cleaners can be bent to show actions.

TYING IT TOGETHER

Give each child a copy of Alpha Time Master #96. They may name the pictures that rhyme, (e.g., sail, pail; star, car) then make the Super Socks "touch" some of the pictures that start with their sound.

ON THEIR OWN

Children may choose from the following activities:

Rhyming

Making verses in which one of the rhyming words begins with Mr. S's sound.

Auditory Discrimination

Playing Mr. S's song and listening for some words that begin with his sound.

Using Mr. S's Picture Squares in any of the activities described in the *Games* section.

Motor Coordination

Working with Mr. S's puzzle independently or together with other puzzles.

TALKING ABOUT WORDS THAT HAVE SIMILAR MEANINGS

Gather the children around Mr. B, Mr. S and Mr. S's bag.

Mr. S has been looking at his bag.

He says a *bag* is fine for Mr. B but not for him.

He says he will not have a *bag.* Mr. B asked him where he would keep all the things that we made for him.

Mr. S answered, "I will keep my things where they are."

Mr. B could not understand Mr. S.

He said: "Mr. S, your things are in a *bag.* You just said you did not want a *bag.* Now you say you will keep your things where they are. They are in a *bag.* I don't understand you, Mr. S."

Mr. S said, "Mr. B, to you it is a *bag,* but I know another name for a bag.

It means the same thing, but this name starts the same way as my Super Socks."

Mr. B thought and thought. What is another word that means the same thing as *bag* and starts with Mr. S's Super Socks sound?

Give the children a chance to think of the word "sack." If no one thinks of it, give them this additional clue:

Mr. B said, "Mr. S, give me a clue. Tell me a word that rhymes with the word you're thinking about."

Mr. S said, "It rhymes with *back.*"

What word is Mr. S thinking about? (sack)

Why can Mr. S call his bag a sack? (*Bag* and *sack* mean the same thing.)

"Bless my buttons," said Mr. B. "That's fun. Let's do another one.

Let's both think of some more words that mean the same thing.

Mr. S, you begin."

Take the role of Mr. S and give the children words which have synonyms that start with "s." As a clue, give a word that rhymes with each synonym.

Mr. S says, "Let's begin with the word *begin.*"

"I know a word that means the same thing as *begin.*

"It starts with my Super Socks sound.

"It rhymes with *chart*."

What word is Mr. S thinking about? (*start*)

Follow the same procedure for the following pairs of words: little and small, unhappy and sad, talk and speak, quiet and silent, alike and same, frighten and scare, tilt and slant, pile and stack.

USING WORDS WITH S IN THE INITIAL POSITION

Mr. S has been dreaming of silly sandwiches.

Everytime he thinks of a silly sandwich he smiles.

A silly sandwich can't be eaten.

It can only be filled with certain things.

We will be silly sandwiches. Mr. S will tell us how.

Right now, everyone take something from Mr. S's bag—ooops, I mean sack.

Then we will be ready to begin—ooops, I mean start—making a silly sandwich.

Explain the game to the children making sure they understand that the sandwich "filling" can only be one of the things from Mr. S's bag (i.e., beginning with his sound).

First we need a slice of bread.

(Beth), your hand will be the first slice of bread. Hold out your hand.

Next we need some filling to put on top of the bread. The filling can only be something that starts the same way as Mr. S's Super Socks.

(John), tell us what you took from Mr. S's sack. (e.g., soda)

Hold the picture of the soda and put your hand on top of the slice of bread (i.e., Mary's hand).

Now the sandwich needs another slice of bread.

(Peter), you be the top slice of bread and put your hand on top of the soda.

Look, these three have made a silly soda sandwich!

Give several children a chance to name the silly sandwiches they make by naming the pictures they are holding (e.g., silly soap sandwich). Then have the children form groups of three and make individual silly sandwiches.

After all the children have been part of a silly sandwich, tell them that Mr. S has a surprise for them.

TYING IT TOGETHER

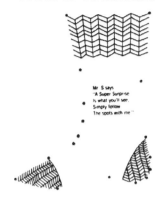

Distribute Alpha Time Master #97.

Mr. S says:
A super surprise is what you'll see.
Simply trace along with me.

Let's take our crayons and follow the dots and arrows.

What do you think the surprise will be? (a super sock)

ON THEIR OWN

Word Meanings

Children may choose from the following activities:

Playing a word catching game. One child will be a word and catch the word that means the same thing as he does.

(Bobby), you are the word "*little.*"
(Mary), you are the word "*begin.*"
(Jim), you are the word "*small.*"
(Sue), you are the word "*start.*"

(Bobby), which Mr. S word means the same thing as you do? (Jim's—*small*)

Which word will you catch? (*small*)

(Mary), which Mr. S word means the same thing as you do? (Sue's—*start*)

Which word will you catch? (*start*)

Let two children each catch the Mr. S words that mean the same things as they do. As each pair is made, have them say the words aloud (e.g., "little catches small"). Repeat the same procedure with other pairs of words the children have used.

Cooking

Making sandwiches—if possible with fillings that have Mr. S's sound (e.g., salami, swiss cheese, salmon, sardine, syrup, salad).

Counting

Counting the number of dots that are connected to make the Super Sock on Alpha Time Master #97.

Sewing

Mounting Alpha Time Master #97 on oaktag or cardboard, punching holes at each dot and lacing cord, string, or wool all around the outline of the Super Sock.

2S₃ **PLANNING AND PREPARATION:** Huggables Mr. S, Mr. P; paper, pencils, crayons, drawing paper, scissors, paste; Alpha Time Master #98. One or two cookbooks (preferably illustrated).

USING WORDS WITH S IN THE INITIAL POSITION

Show the children the cookbooks and discuss their use.

All the Letter People would like to make silly sandwiches.

They keep asking Mr. S for his cookbook.

Mr. S does not know what they mean. Mr. S says that he doesn't have a cookbook.

The Letter People say that Mr. S should have recipes to make silly sandwiches.

A recipe tells you all the things you need to make a silly sandwich.

It also tells you how to make the silly sandwich.

Developing A Sense Of Humor

Mr. S wants us to help him write recipes for his cookbook.

A cookbook can not have just one recipe in it.

Mr. S has thought of many different recipes we can write for him.

He wants a recipe for silly salads.

He wants a recipe for silly soups.

He wants a recipe for silly soda.

He wants a recipe for silly spaghetti sauce.

When we made Mr. S's silly sandwiches, we could only put in things that started the same way as Super Socks, but silly salads, silly sodas, silly spaghetti sauce and silly soups can be made with all the silliest things you can think of.

Distribute drawing paper.

While we are thinking of a recipe, remember that cookbooks may have pictures too. You can draw a picture to go with your recipe.

Children may dictate their recipes individually or in small groups, each small group may be responsible for a particular silly recipe. Have children discuss the ingredients of the recipe. Then they may discuss the step by step procedure in following the recipe.

The group may select one or two children to dictate the recipes while the others illustrate it.

When all the recipes are finished, put them together into a cookbook for Mr. S. One child may want to illustrate a cover.

PICTURE READING

Mr. P knows that Mr. S gets his sound from his Super Socks.

Mr. P would like Mr. S to tell him how he got his sound.

Mr. S told Mr. P the story.

Mr. P liked the story. He talked about it so much that all the other Letter People asked Mr. S to tell them the story, too. Mr. S told it to Mr. T and Mr. Z and then he got tired of saying the same thing over and over again.

Mr. S decided to tell the story by drawing three pictures. Then anyone who wanted to know about it could read the pictures.

Distribute copies of Alpha Time Master #98.

The Letter People read the picture story.

They all said that Mr. S drew a silly story.

It's a silly story because it does not make sense.

Inferring

Recalling

Let's look at Mr. S's story and see why people say it does not make sense.

Who is in the first picture? (mailman, Mr. S)

What does Mr. S have? (package with Super Socks)

How did he get the package? (mailman brought it)

When did he get the package? (just now)

Who sent the Super Socks to Mr. S? (Mr. M).

How did Mr. S know the Super Socks were coming? (Mr. M had told him)

Let's look at the next picture and see what Mr. S thinks is the next part of the story.

Who is in this picture? (Mr. M, Mr. S)

Who has the Super Socks? (Mr. M)

What does Mr. M want to do with the Super Socks? (send them to Mr. S)

Why has he telephoned Mr. S? (to tell him about the surprise in the Super Socks)

Predicting

What will Mr. M do with the Super Socks? (send them to Mr. S)

What will he find in his Super Socks? (pictures that start with his sound)

Let's look at the next part of the story Mr. S drew.

Recalling a sequence

What is Mr. S doing? (taking things out of the Super Socks)

Be Mr. S. Tell us what you find in the Super Socks. (e.g., sun, sailor, sink, sandwich, soda)

Which part of the story happened first? (Frame 2)

Which part of the story happened next? (Frame 1)

Which part of the story happened last? (Frame 3)

Why is the story silly the way Mr. S drew it? (not in order)

TYING IT TOGETHER

ON THEIR OWN

How can we fix the story so that it makes sense?

Lead the children to the conclusion that the pictures are out of sequence and need to be put in the correct order.

Children may cut the frames apart and paste the pictures in the correct order on a piece of drawing paper. Have them check the order by themselves by telling the way they arranged the pictures. When the pictures are in order, the children may dictate the story and have it written under their pictures.

Children may choose from the following activities:

Storytelling	Retelling the Super Socks story by using the cut out pictures from Alpha Time Master #98 as cue cards.
Humor	Telling silly stories in which silly things happen.
Sewing	Sewing Super Socks by sewing together two sock shapes, leaving the top open for stuffing or to save for Santa.
Counting	Stringing six spools which have been painted and/or decorated. This makes a good necklace or belt.
Cooking	Following a simple recipe (in an illustrated cookbook if possible) for salad, spaghetti, soup or sandwiches.

2S₄

TEACHER OBJECTIVES:

To review the characteristic and sound of Mr. S.

To associate particular shapes with symbols.

To identify the "stop" sign specifically.

PERFORMANCE OBJECTIVES:

The child will recognize sign symbolizing "stop."

The child will identify other types of signs.

The child will say words with the *s* in the initial position.

DEVELOPMENT

Mr. S spends so much time soaking his super socks in soap suds.
Mr. S thinks you can soak everything.
Guess what he did to the Mr. S "All About Us" booklets? (He soaked them in soap suds.)
The soaking spoiled all the booklets.
The Letter People had to help him make new booklets.
Let's look at them.

Distribute the Mr. S booklets.
Direct the children's attention to the words at the top.
Read aloud, "All About Us."

Which Letter Person's picture do you see? (Mr. S)
What is special about Mr. S? (his super socks)
Find the sentence at the bottom of the booklet.
It says, "Mr. S has a friend."

Look at the picture next to Mr. S.
Mr. S wanted to give his friend super socks.
He soaked a special pair in soap suds.
The socks were such a super size they still haven't dried.
Mr. S wants us to draw super socks for his friend.

Give the children the opportunity to draw super socks.
Some children may want to draw the socks directly on the booklet.
Others may prefer to draw them on paper, cut them out and paste them onto the booklet.
Remind the children that the picture may be finished to look like themselves or anyone else.

Ask the children to open their booklets.
Have them find the first sentence on the left-hand side.

What picture did Mr. S put in the sentence? (super socks)
Read aloud, "Mr. S likes super socks."
Let them pretend to reread it with you.

Mr. S says there's something else he likes.
He likes signs.
He wants to show us his favorite sign.
Look at the picture at the bottom of the page.
The picture shows us Mr. S's favorite sign.

Discuss the picture.
Help the children discover why Mr. S suddenly stops skating. (He sees a special sign.)
The children will probably recognize the *stop* sign by its shape.
Ask them what it says.

Discuss the reason for a stop sign.
Read aloud, "Mr. S's favorite sign is a stop sign."

Mr. S used this whole page to tell us about himself.
What did he tell us first? (He likes super socks.)
What did he tell us next? (His favorite sign is a stop sign.)
Mr. S says the next page is for us.

Look at the next page.
What does Mr. S want each of us to write on the first dotted line?
(our name)
What pictures are in the sentence? (pictures of socks)
Tell Mr. S the color of each sock. (green, yellow, blue)
Write your name on the dotted line and then Mr. S will listen to
your sentence.

Read the sentences aloud.
The children may point to and name the color of each sock. (*e.g.,*
Delores likes green, yellow and blue socks.)
The children may wish to circle the color they like best.

Explain that Mr. S wants them to look at the picture he drew on
the back of the booklet.

Have the children turn to the back.
Read aloud, "Let's talk about signs."
Have them find Mr. S's favorite sign.
Name and discuss the necessity for each sign.

You may want to take the opportunity to classify signs. (*e.g.,*
traffic signs, supermarket, school, hospital)

Explain that Mr. S wants them to draw a picture of their favorite
sign on the inside of the booklet.

Have them open their booklet.
Draw the children's attention to the second sentence on the
right-hand side.

Let's each write our name on the dotted line.
Then we can listen to the sentence and see what's missing.

After the children have written their names, select a booklet and
read the incomplete sentence aloud. (*e.g.,* Bert's favorite sign
is   .)

Mr. S says he knows why the sentence is not finished.
The sentence does not tell what Bert's favorite sign is.
How does he want Bert to finish the sentence? (drawing a picture
of his favorite sign)

Some children may wish to find a picture.
Others may wish to dictate the name of a sign.

Give several children a chance to tell Mr. S which sign is their
favorite.

Encourage the children to take their booklets home and have
members of their family tell Mr. S what their favorite sign is.

2V₁

PLANNING AND PREPARATION: Huggables, Mr. V, Mr. M, Mr. T, Mr. F, Mr. H, Mr. N, Miss A, Mr. B, Mr. Z, Mr. P, Mr. S, Miss E; Alpha Time Master #99.

Play Mr. V's music to set the mood for the lesson (record #1, side B, band 5).

DISCOVERING THAT MR. V GETS HIS SOUND FROM VIOLET VELVET VEST

Gather the children around you and tell them this story:

*Listening To
A Story*

There was a special report on the radio this morning. The Vest Patrol was being called out. All the vests had vanished again. Mr. V seemed to have vanished, too! The Vest Patrol looked and looked but could find neither the vanishing vests nor Mr. V.

Mr. V and the vests had not vanished. They were having a vegetable picnic at a vegetable farm. Mr. V had invited the vanishing vests to this very special picnic.

The vests thought and thought about what they could bring to the vegetable picnic. They could not think of anything that was special enough. Suddenly, they had an idea. They would bring Mr. V something very special, something he wanted very much.

"Surprise, surprise" shouted the vests when they arrived at the picnic. "We have brought you a surprise present, Mr. V." "How very, very nice of you," said Mr. V. "What can this surprise be?"

What do you think the surprise is?

Let the children suggest various things the surprise could be.

The vests knew how much Mr. V wanted a sound of his own. They thought of the thing Mr. V liked best in the whole world.

What does Mr. V like best in the whole world?

That's right—his Violet Velvet Vest.

Well, the vests said that Mr. V could get his sound from his very own Violet Velvet Vest! They thought this would make Mr. V very happy but—Mr. V did not look very happy when they told him.

Mr. V could not think of many words that started with his sound. He had been thinking and thinking and thinking. He had all the other Letter People thinking for him, too. They had not been able to think of many words that started the same way as Violet Velvet Vest. They had thought of a few words, but they were such big words that Mr. V did not know what they meant.

TALKING ABOUT WORD MEANINGS

Mr. V has been crying all day long because he says he can't remember such big words. We'll have to help him before those tears get on his Violet Velvet Vest and ruin it.

Mr. V has thought of a word that starts the same way as Violet Velvet Vest. He thought of the word *vacation*. Mr. V says, "*Vacation* starts the same way as Violet Velvet Vest, but what is a vacation?"

Talking About Vacations

Recalling Personal Experiences

Tell Mr. V what a vacation is.

Give several children a chance to describe what a vacation is.

Tell Mr. V about a vacation he might like to take.

Tell him about a vacation you have taken.

When Mr. V hears about all these vacations perhaps he will remember the word.

Give the children a chance to tell about vacations they have taken or heard about.

Vacation is a good word to think of when Mr. V wants to think of words that start the same way as his Violet Velvet Vest.

Mr. V thinks that he will be able to remember the word *vacation* now.

One of the Letter People found another long word for Mr. V.

It is a word that starts with Mr. V's Violet Velvet Vest sound and that word is *volunteer.*

Mr. V says, "What does *volunteer* mean? I never heard of the word *volunteer.*"

The Letter People tried to make Mr. V understand what the word *volunteer* means. They explain it this way: Suppose you ask the Letter People, "Who will go to the store to get some bread?" If Mr. T and Mr. F say they will go, they *volunteer* to go.

Give the children a chance to volunteer for various classroom jobs.

Now Mr. V asks, "Who will volunteer to give out the cookies today?"

If you are willing to give out the cookies, tell Mr. V that you volunteer to give out the cookies.

Mr. V asks, "Who will volunteer to give out the milk today?"

If you will do it, tell Mr. V that you volunteer to give out the milk today.

Mr. V asks, "Who will volunteer to fix the blocks today?"

If you want to do it, tell Mr. V that you volunteer to fix the blocks today.

If Mr. V asks who will volunteer to clean the paint brushes today, and you want to do it, tell Mr. V that you volunteer to clean the paint brushes today.

Mr. V says that if we tell him everytime we volunteer to do something, perhaps he will be able to remember the word *volunteer.*

Discuss each of the following words: vitamins, vote, visit.

REMEMBERING THE NAMES OF THE LETTER PEOPLE

The vests who vanished gave Mr. V another word. The word they gave to Mr. V is *vanish.*

Mr. V says, "I know you are called vanishing vests, but I am not sure what *vanishing* means."

The Vanishing Vests explained that when something goes away and isn't there anymore, it vanishes.

Playing A Game

Mr. V wants us to play a game. When we have finished he thinks that he will be able to remember what the word *vanish* means.

The Letter People say that they want to play "Vanish". First let's put all the Letter People in line. We'll close our eyes, and say:

> Vanish, vanish, vanish, while our eyes are shut tight.
> Which of the Letter People will vanish from sight?

Have the children close their eyes and repeat the refrain. While their eyes are closed, remove one of the Letter People.

Who volunteers to tell us which Letter Person vanished?

Now two Letter People will vanish.

Repeat the same procedure, having two Letter People vanish at the same time, then three Letter People, then four. The game may also be played by having the children vanish in place of the Letter People. Children may also volunteer to stand behind a Letter Person and vanish with that Letter Person.

TYING IT TOGETHER

Distribute copies of Alpha Time Master #99.

Mr. V drew a picture for some of his words. (i.e., vacation, volunteer, vote, visit) Let us see if we know which words he means.

Look at one of the pictures and tell Mr. V about it.

What is the person in the picture doing?

Which word do you think describes this picture?

Continue this way until the children have identified all the pictures. Some children may want you to write the correct word under each picture for them.

ON THEIR OWN

Children may choose from the following activities:

Art

Painting a picture of a vacation that a child has taken, or would like to take.

Drawing a picture of a time relatives came to visit.

Music

Playing Mr. V's music, (record #1, side B, band 5) and listening for words that begin with Mr. V's sound.

Auditory Discrimination

Playing the story of Vanishing Vests (record #4) and listening for words that begin with Mr. V's sound.

2V₂

PLANNING AND PREPARATION: Huggable, Mr. V; Mr. V's Picture Squares; a bag for Mr. V; drawing paper, pencils, crayons, paste, scissors, art materials; a large piece of chart paper, several violet crayons, small pieces of paper to represent bits of velvet; Alpha Time Master #100.

USING WORDS WITH V IN THE INITIAL POSITION

Mr. V remembers some of his big words that start with his Violet Velvet Vest sound.

He says that they are very nice words and he likes them, but no one has made or found anything to put in his bag. He is looking and looking and he thinks that he has found some things.

He wants you to look at the things he has found and prove to him whether or not they may go into his bag.

Identifying And Proving Mr. V's Pictures

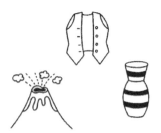

Show the children Mr. V's Picture Squares (i.e., violin, vegetables, vest, volcano, vase). Have the children discuss each picture and help the children name them. Have them "prove" each picture for Mr. V. They may want to sing "Prove It" to Mr. V using record #5, side A, band 3.

Mr. V would like to have his bag filled.

He knows that it is hard to find pictures of things that start the same way as his Violet Velvet Vest. Mr. V doesn't give up easily. When things get hard, he just thinks and thinks and thinks. He has figured out how he can fill his bag.

Mr. V would like us to make pictures and to write stores about his words.

He says he remembers what the word *vacation* means.

Let's write a story about a vacation that we would like to take.

Making And Finding Things For Mr. V's Bag

Mr. V remembers what the word *volunteer* means. Let's make a picture showing children volunteering to do something in school. Let's make a picture showing children volunteering to do something at home. Let's write a story telling about what we volunteered to do in school or at home.

Mr. V would like to have that in his bag.

Follow the same procedure with any of the words that start with Mr. V's Violet Velvet Vest sound (e.g., vitamins, vote, visit, vanish). Encourage the children to use a wide variety of the art materials available. The children may work individually or in small groups making and finding things for Mr. V's bag.

They may dictate stories to go with the pictures. Encourage the children to show Mr. V what they have made for his bag. Encourage them to tell or "read" their stories to Mr. V.

TALKING ABOUT DESCRIPTIVE WORDS

Draw a large outline of a vest on a piece of chart paper.

Long ago Mr. V's Violet Velvet Vest was just a vest. Mr. V said, "I don't want my vest to be just a vest. I will make it special. I will put velvet all over it."

Give several children pieces of paper to represent velvet, and have them tape or paste them on the outline of the vest.

Mr. V said, "Now the vest is not just a vest. Now the vest is made of velvet. It is called a Velvet Vest."

Velvet Vest

Have the children repeat "Velvet Vest."

Then Mr. V said, "I want my velvet vest to have a color. I want the color to be violet."

Give several children violet crayons so that they may color the paper squares on the vest.

Mr. V says, "Now it is a vest made of velvet that is violet.

We cannot call it just a vest.

We cannot call it just a Velvet Vest. Because the velvet is violet, we must call it a Violet Velvet Vest."

Let the children repeat "Violet Velvet Vest."

Mr. V was pleased. He said that his Violet Velvet Vest was so grand and beautiful he wanted it to visit all the vests in the whole world. The Violet Velvet Vest will go visiting.

Let's draw little feet on the Violet Velvet Vest to show that it can go visiting.

Mr. V said, "Now we cannot call it just a vest. We cannot call it just a Velvet Vest. We cannot call it just a Violet Velvet Vest. Because the Violet Velvet Vest goes visiting, we can call it a Visiting Violet Velvet Vest.

Again have the children repeat with you.

Now Mr. V says that we are ready to play the "Visiting Violet Velvet Vest" game.

Following Directions

Have the children form groups of four. Give each child in each group a number from 1 through 4.

All the #1's draw an outline of a vest. They pass their papers to the #2's and say, "Here is a vest."

The #2's paste bits of paper representing velvet on the outline of the vest. They pass the paper to the #3's saying, "Here is a Velvet Vest."

The #3's color the vest violet. They pass the paper to the #4's saying, "Here is a Violet Velvet Vest."

The #4's put legs and feet on the vest. They stand up and say, "We have made a visiting Violet Velvet Vest!"

When the game is finished the children may want to change positions and make other visiting Violet Velvet Vests.

TYING IT TOGETHER

Give each child a copy of Alpha Time Master #100.

Mr. V has drawn some pictures that show how to play his game.

He remembered what happened when some of the other Letter People drew directions for playing games. They got the directions all mixed up. Mr. V was very careful with his directions but he wants us to check them for him.

Frame 1

Let's look at the first picture.

What does the first picture show? (a vest)

What can we call this picture? (vest)

Why can we only call it a vest?

What was the next thing that the vest became? (velvet vest)

Let's look at the next part of the story and see if Mr. V remembered what happened next.

Frame 2

What do we see? (a child putting velvet on the vest)

What may we call the vest now? (Velvet Vest)

Look at the next picture.

Frame 3

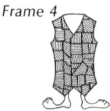

What is happening to the vest? (velvet is being colored violet)

How will the name of the vest change? (Violet Velvet Vest)

What is the next thing that happened to the vest? (It went visiting.)

Let's look at the last part of the story and see if Mr. V remembered.

Frame 4

What is happening in the last picture? (feet are on the vest)

How can the vest's name be changed? (Visiting Violet Velvet Vest)

How do we know that Mr. V did a good job of drawing directions for the game? (Everything is in order.)

ON THEIR OWN

Children may choose from the following activities:

Using Descriptive Words

Finding objects or pictures of objects and describing them by telling of their size, texture, shape, and color. (e.g., This is a large, blue, round, smooth ball.)

Auditory Discrimination	Including Mr. V's Picture Squares, playing cards and puzzle in any of the activities described in the *Games* section.
Crafts	Using paper flocking, paste and violet paint to make a Violet Velvet Vest.
Food Preparation	Preparing and eating raw vegetables such as carrot curls, shelled green peas, cauliflower roses, radishes, celery, scallions, tomatoes, mushrooms.

2V₃

The child will say words with the v in th[e] initial position.

The child will state orally names of veg[e]tables.

Some children will copy some names [of] vegetables.

The child will locate pictures of vegetable[s]

TEACHER OBJECTIVES:

To review the characteristic of Mr. V.

To have children discuss vegetables.

DEVELOPMENT

Mr. V has "All About Us" booklets for us.

Distribute the Mr. V "All About Us" booklets to the children.

Mr. V wants us to find the words that say "All About Us."

Which Letter Person's picture is on the booklet? (Mr. V)

Whose picture is next to Mr. V? (his friend's)

Find the sentence at the bottom of the booklet.

Read aloud, "Mr. V has a friend."

What is special about Mr. V? (his velvet vest)

What do you think Mr. V would like us to draw on the picture of his friend? (a vest)

If you want the picture of Mr. V's friend to look like you, what will you do to the hair, the eyes, the clothes?

Does the picture have to look like you? (No.)

Give the children the opportunity to finish the picture and show it to Mr. V.

Then have them open their booklets.

Point to the first sentence on the left-hand side.

Ask the children to name the picture Mr. V put in the sentence. (velvet vest)

Read aloud, "Mr. V likes a velvet vest."

Let them pretend to reread the sentence with you.

Explain that the picture at the bottom of the page tells what Mr. V likes to eat.

Have the children name the different vegetables in the basket.

Ask them if they can think of one word to name all the things. (vegetables)

Read aloud, "Mr. V likes all vegetables."

Why does Mr. V like vegetables? (*Vegetables* starts with the same sound as *velvet vest*.)

Mr. V took this whole page to tell us about himself.

What two things did he tell us? (He likes a velvet vest. He likes all vegetables.)

Mr. V says the next page is for us.

What picture did Mr. V put in the first sentence? (three vests)

Tell Mr. V the color of each vest. (green, black, yellovv)

Mr. V wants us to put a circle around the vest we like best.

207A

Give the children the opportunity to do this.
Then have each child write his/her name on the first dotted line.

Select several booklets and read the sentences aloud. (*e.g.*, Donna likes a yellow vest.)

Mr. V says he wants us to look at the picture he drew on the back of the booklet.

Have the children turn to the back.
Read aloud, "Let's talk about vegetables."
Have them find and name all the different vegetables on the vegetable stand.
Give several children a chance to tell the names of their favorite vegetables.

After discussing favorite vegetables, reinforce the concept of classification (see lesson on fruits). You may want to discuss the necessity for a balanced diet.

Explain that Mr. V wants them to draw a picture of their favorite vegetables.
Have the children open their booklets.
Draw the children's attention to the second sentence on the right-hand side.

Have the children write their names on the dotted line.

Select several booklets and read the incomplete sentences aloud. (*e.g.*, Alan's favorite vegetables are   .)

Mr. V says that he knows why the sentence is not finished.
It does not tell Alan's favorite vegetables.

Discuss with the children ways of completing the sentence.

They may draw a picture of their favorite vegetables.
They may find pictures in magazines, cut them out and paste them on the booklet.
Others may wish to dictate the names of their favorite vegetables.
Some may enjoy having you read their completed sentences to them.
Others may pretend to read from the booklet to Mr. V.

Encourage the children to take their booklets home and discover the favorite vegetables of the members of their family.

2E₁

PLANNING AND PREPARATION: Huggable, Miss E; Record #3, Meet Miss E; a bag for Miss E; Miss E's Picture Squares (initial letter sound); scissors, Alpha Time Master #101.

Play Miss E's music (record #1) to set the mood for the lesson.

DISCOVERING HOW MISS E WILL GET HER SOUND

Help the children recall the special way Miss E exercises by playing Meet Miss E (record #3).

How is Miss E's Exercise special? (it starts with ĕ, ĕ, ĕ)

Let's show Miss E that we remember how to do a Miss E exercise.

Have the children do one or two Miss E exercises being certain they say "ĕ,ĕ,ĕ-Exercise" while they do each exercise.

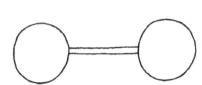

Miss E is the only Letter Person who does not have a sound yet. Miss E would like to have a sound. She has thought of a sound that she can have that she will never forget because she says it all the time. What sound do you think Miss E is thinking about?

Lead the children to the conclusion that it will be ĕ from Exercise.

Miss E is so happy. She keeps saying:

> "Ĕ, ĕ, ĕ, that's for me.
> Ĕ is the sound for Miss E."

Let's all say it with Miss E.

IDENTIFYING WORDS WITH SHORT E IN THE INITIAL POSITION

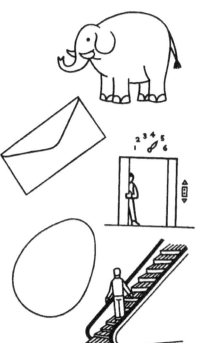

Show the children Miss E's initial sound Picture Squares (i.e., egg, elevator, elephant, escalator, envelope).

Miss E has some pictures she wants to show us.

Why are these pictures good for Miss E? (They begin with her sound.)

Miss E says she isn't sure what each picture shows.

Take one of the pictures. Show it to Miss E and tell her what it is.

Say the name of the picture so that Miss E can hear her ĕ sound.

Give as many children as possible a chance to name and prove pictures for Miss E. Remind them that Miss E wants to hear her ĕ sound at the beginning of the word as they name each picture.

If a child forgets, remind him that if Miss E is not sure of her sound, she can do one of her exercises and this will help her to remember her sound.

Read the riddles below while holding all the Picture Squares and have one child at a time choose the Picture that is described and put it into Miss E's bag.

*Naming And Proving
Miss E's Pictures*

There's a letter inside of me.
On my outside, a stamp you'll see.
You can find me easily.
I belong to Miss E. (envelope)

I come from a hen and I have a shell.
I'm soft inside unless you cook me well.
You can find me easily.
I belong to Miss E. (egg)

I am a way you get from floor to floor.
When you step inside me, I close my door.
You can find me easily.
I belong to Miss E. (elevator)

I'm an animal with a trunk that's long.
I have big ears, I'm very strong.
You can find me easily.
I belong to Miss E. (elephant)

Get on my steps, and stand quite still.
Don't climb up or down, the staircase will.
You can find me easily,
I belong to Miss E. (escalator)

TYING IT TOGETHER

Give each of the children a copy of Alpha Time Master #101. Have the children cut out the picture bag, fold it along the dotted line and staple, tape or sew the sides. Then they may cut out Miss E's pictures and put them in the bag. The children should recognize that Miss E's characteristic, the barbell stands for what she does (i.e., Exercise).

ON THEIR OWN

Children may choose from the following activities:

Physics

Finding out how many ways an egg can look (e.g., raw, scrambled, hardboiled, softboiled, beaten with yolks and whites separately, beaten together, yolks beaten in a blender).

Observing what happens when vinegar is added to beaten egg yolks. (they curdle)

Crafts

Painting hollow egg shells: Pierce a small hole on both ends of a raw egg. Let the egg run out of one of the holes. Paint the shells.

Making elephants out of clay.

Cooking

Making meringues by beating egg whites with sugar and baking them.*

Making mayonnaise with yolks and oil.*

Baking custard.*

Baking sponge cake.*

Making egg salad with chopped hardboiled eggs and mayonnaise.

*Simple recipes may be found in most cookbooks.

Nature Study
Size Relationships

Comparing size and color of various kinds of eggs. (Use dictionary or animal encyclopedia.)

2E 2

PLANNING AND PREPARATION: Hugga-bles, Miss E; some pages torn from old magazines; Alpha Time Master #102.

Prepare four large signs, each bearing one of the following words: ENTER, EXIT, ELEVATOR, EMPTY.

IDENTIFYING AND DEFINING WORDS THAT BEGIN WITH E

Developing Related Vocabulary

Scatter old magazine pages on the floor near Miss E.

What is on the floor near Miss E?

Ask Miss E why she tore these pages out of the magazine.

Miss E says that she has been looking at magazines all day long, but she can't find any pictures that start with her ĕ sound.

Then Miss E went shopping in a big department store. She saw people reading some signs in the store.

Miss E asked the people what the signs said and, guess what! Each sign started with Miss E's ĕ sound!

When Miss E arrived at the department store, she looked up. Above the door she saw a sign. It said "Enter." *Enter* starts with the ĕ sound.

Miss E said, "What does *enter* mean?"

Have the children demonstrate the meaning of "enter" by dramatizing it. Have two children hold up the sign marked ENTER.

Make believe that you have come to a door. Above the door you see a sign that says *enter*, and you walk through the door.

When Miss E entered the store, some people were leaving. There was a sign above the door through which the people were leaving. It said *"Exit."*

Miss E says that she hears her ĕ sound in *exit*. What does *exit* mean?

Have two children hold up the sign marked EXIT and let them demonstrate the meaning of exit.

Make believe you are leaving. The sign above the door says "Exit."

When Miss E wanted to buy a coat, she had to go to the third floor of the store. She was too tired to walk up the stairs. She saw another sign. It said "Elevator."

Miss E did not have to use the stairs. She could use the elevator.

Elevator starts with Miss E's ĕ sound.

Show the children the sign marked ELEVATOR.

This is the way the elevator sign looks.

Miss E was hungry. She thought that she would have a snack. She went to the candy machine. She put in her money and turned the knob. No candy came out. Instead, a sign popped up.

The sign told Miss E that there was no more candy in the machine. The sign started with Miss E's ĕ sound. It said *"Empty."*

Empty starts with Miss E's ĕ sound.

Show the children the sign marked EMPTY.

Let's be Miss E and go to the department store.

We will listen and then do just what the story tells us to do.

Have four children each hold one of the signs (i.e., EXIT, ENTER, ELEVATOR, EMPTY).Have the children stand in different parts of the room. Select a number of children to be Miss E. As you read the story all the Miss E's will do as the story says.

Give different children a chance to be one of Miss E's signs or Miss E.

Tell the children Miss E's Story:

Dramatizing A Story

Miss E arrived at the department store. She went in through the door marked ENTER.

(All the Miss E's go around the child holding the sign marked ENTER.)

Miss E walked all around the store. Then she decided to take a ride in the *elevator.*

(The Miss E's find the ELEVATOR sign and take a ride behind it.)

Miss E had a wonderful time riding in the elevator. Riding in the elevator made Miss E a little hungry.

Where do you think Miss E went next? (candy machine)

Miss E put her money in the candy machine and pulled the knob. What do you think happened? There was no more candy. What sign popped up? *EMPTY!*

The child holding the EMPTY sign pops up.

Then Miss E decided to go home. She wanted to leave the store. What sign did she look for? (EXIT)

(All the Miss E's walk around the child holding the EXIT sign.)

Making Things For Miss E's Bag

Tell the children that Miss E would be happy to have some of the signs in her bag.

They may draw pictures of the signs, prove them, and place them into Miss E's bag.

TYING IT TOGETHER

Give each child a copy of Alpha Time Master #102. Help them discuss each picture and point to the sign that identifies it.

ON THEIR OWN

Children may choose from the following activities:

Sorting And Matching

Using Miss E's Picture Squares, playing cards, puzzle in any of the activities suggested in the *Games* section of the manual.

Auditory Discrimination

Listening for words that start with the ĕ sound in Miss E's music (record #1, side B band #6).

Making a list of names that begin with Miss E's ĕ sound (e.g., Evelyn, Esther, Emmet, Erica, Edward, Elvira, Everett, Ellen).

Classifying

Cutting out pictures of other signs—especially traffic signs—and telling what they mean.

2E₃

PLANNING AND PREPARATION: Huggables, Miss E, Miss A; Miss E's "in the middle" Picture Squares; Alpha Time Masters #103 and #104.

IDENTIFYING WORDS THAT HAVE "E" IN THE MEDIAL POSITION

Stand Miss A next to Miss E.

Listening For the E Sound In The Medial Position

Miss A told Miss E that her sound can be in the middle of a word. Miss E wants to hear her ĕ sound when it is "in the middle."

Miss A brought Miss E some pictures that she thinks will make her happy.

Show the children the "in the middle" Picture Squares (i.e., men, pen, net, hen and numeral 10). The "in the middle" symbol is on each picture.

Name each picture for Miss E.

Why do you think these pictures will make Miss E happy? (Her ĕ sound is in the middle of the word.)

How do you know that ĕ is Miss E's sound? (It comes from Exercise.)

Miss E wants you to prove that her ĕ sound is "in the middle."

Have the children name each picture, following the same questioning procedure used for the Miss A "in the middle" words.

Miss E would like to play "In the Middle."

Playing A Game

Choose two children to stand alongside each other, leaving a space between them for another child. Give each of the "in the middle" Picture Squares to different children.

Choose one child to be Miss E. Each child holding a picture names that picture (e.g., pen). The child who is Miss E says, "I hear my ĕ sound in pen. It is in the middle." The Miss E child takes the Huggable, Miss E, and places her between the two children. Then the class repeats the word and decides if Miss E's sound is in the middle. Continue the same procedure for all the remaining pictures, choosing a new Miss E for each word.

Additional words that may be used are pet, set, met, bet.

We can play "In the Middle" another way. We played it this way with Miss A, too.

Have the children play the following game to the tune of "London Bridge is Falling Down."

Directions: Divide the children into groups of three partners and join hands to form individual circles. The third child will play the part of Miss E. Miss E will dance around the outside of her circle. The circle tries to catch her so that she is in the middle. The two circle children may not drop their hands. The children sing these words:

Please Miss E don't run away,
Run away,
Run away.
Please Miss E don't run away,
Get in the middle.

At this point, Miss E must get into the circle.

Then they sing these words while swaying back and forth and encircling their Miss E:

Now Miss E is in the middle,
In the middle,
In the middle.
Now Miss E is in the middle,
And we won't let her out.

Then they sing:

Say ĕ and we'll let you out,
Let you out,
Let you out.
Say ĕ and we'll let you out,
My fair Miss E.

Miss E says ĕ and takes the place of one of the children in the circle who becomes the new Miss E. The game continues, moving each Miss E to another circle.

TYING IT TOGETHER

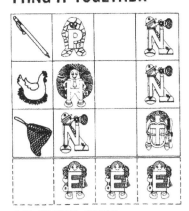

Give each child a copy of Alpha Time Master #103. Tell them that they are going to play the "In the Middle" game on paper.

They may cut out the three pictures of Miss E. Then, as they indentify each of the pictures in the first column (i.e., pen, hen, net) they may paste Miss E's picture between the pictures of the two standing Letter People, (thus spelling the word).

NOTE: Alpha Time Master #104 is a letter to parents explaining the progress the children have made thus far with ALPHA TIME. This letter may be sent home with the children at this time.

ON THEIR OWN

Children may choose from the following activities:

Word Building

Finding words that rhyme by putting some of the Letter People's sounds in front of *et* (e.g., met, net, bet, pet, set, wet); *en* (e.g., men, ten, hen, Ben, pen); *ed* (e.g., Ted, fed, Ned, bed).

Auditory Discrimination

Using Miss E's "in the middle" Picture Squares in any of the activities suggested in the *Games* section.

Deciding which sound begins Miss E's "in the middle" words.

2E₄

TEACHER OBJECTIVES:

To reinforce the characteristic and sound of Miss E.

To introduce the concept of energy.

To have children become aware of need to conserve energy.

PERFORMANCE OBJECTIVES:

The child will say words with the ĕ sound the initial position.

The child will state a reason to cons energy.

The child will classify different example energy use.

The child will identify ways to cons energy.

DEVELOPMENT

Miss E thought of a new exercise.
She tried to hold every one of the Miss E "All About Us" booklets on the tip of one finger.
Guess what? (The booklets all fell.)
Miss E had lots of exercise picking up all the booklets.
Miss E wants to give each of us a booklet.

Distribute the Miss E "All About Us" booklets to the children.
Ask the children to find the words that tell what the booklet is called.
Say the title with them.

Which Letter Person's picture do you see? (Miss E)
Whose picture is next to Miss E? (her friend's)
Find the sentence at the bottom of the booklet.

Read aloud, "Miss E has a friend."

What does Miss E do all the time? (exercise)
What is Miss E holding to help her exercise? (a barbell)
Look at the picture of Miss E's friend.
Miss E's friend wants to exercise using a barbell.
What did Miss E forget to give her friend? (a barbell)
Let's draw a barbell for Miss E's friend to hold.

Give the children the opportunity to draw the barbell.
Suggest they finish the picture to look like themselves or anyone else.

Have the children open the booklets.
Point to the full-page picture on the left-hand side.
Explain that Miss E used this whole page to show how she exercises.
Miss E taught some animals how to exercise with barbells.

Have the children discuss the different animals that are exercising with the barbells.

The children may enjoy pretending to be one of the animals and showing how they lift the barbell.

This provides an excellent opportunity to reproduce the ĕ sound as they do an ĕ ĕ exercise.

Have the children look at the right-hand side of the booklet.
Explain that Miss E has written something very important. Read aloud, "Miss E saves energy."

What does the picture in the sentence show us? (Miss E turns off the light.)
What does Miss E mean when she says she saves energy?
Why is it important to save energy?
What are the different ways we can each save energy?

Miss E wants us to look at the picture she drew on the back of the booklet.
It will show many ways in which we can save energy.

Have the children turn to the back of the booklet.
Read aloud, "Let's talk about energy."
Discuss each illustration.
Talk about the different objects that are dependent upon energy in order to operate.
Have the children tell how they can save energy in their homes.
Draw their attention to the two means of transportation shown in the picture. (bicycle, car)
Ask them why using a bicycle instead of a car saves energy.

In your discussion about objects that are dependent upon energy, lead into the concept of the environment. Explain what it means.
How can the children preserve a cleaner environment? (don't litter)
What pollutes the environment? (smog, smoke) How can we help?
Describe pollution that they see. What causes it?

Miss E wants us to tell her how we save energy.

Have the children open their booklets.
Draw their attention to the second sentence on the right-hand side.
Help them complete their sentences.
Select and read several completed sentences aloud.

Encourage the children to tell their sentences to Miss E.
Suggest they take their booklets home.
Have them ask members of their family to tell Miss E how they will each help save energy.

215B

1L₁

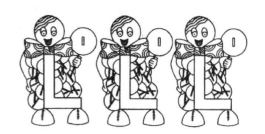

PLANNING AND PREPARATION: Huggable, Mr. L; mural paper, colored construction paper cut into circles, squares, triangles and rectangles; ice cream sticks; yellow construction paper; scissors and paste, square block, triangular block, rectangular block. Optional— Real Lemon Lollipops for everyone. Alpha Time Master #105.

Prepare paper lollipop cut outs for each child, using yellow construction paper.

MEETING MR. L

When the children come into the room have the Lemon Lollipops displayed around the room or on each child's table.

Gather the children around you and Mr. L, and read the following rhyme:

> Look! Lollipops here, lollipops there!
> There are Lemon Lollipops everywhere!
>
> Lick, lick, lick—oh what fun!
> There's a Lemon Lollipop for everyone.
> Let's lick this lollipop right away!
> It must be Lemon Lollipop day!
> Lick, lick, lick—oh what fun!
> Let's lick every single one.
>
> Lick, lick, lick, we all feel well.
> Here is a new Letter Boy—Mr. L!
>
> How do you do? How do you do?
> This is a lovely way of meeting you!

Let the children gather around Mr. L to look at him and to say "hello" to him. (If real Lemon Lollipops are available, Mr. L may distribute them now.)

Listening To Mr. L's Song

Play "Mr. L's song" (record #2, side A, band #1).

Discuss the music with the children.

Show Mr. L how the music makes you want to move.

What does Mr. L tell us about himself?

TALKING ABOUT COLOR AND SHAPE

Call the children's attention to the lollipops on Mr. L's body. Trace the outline of the shape of several of Mr. L's Lemon Lollipops with your finger.

What does Mr. L have all over himself? (Lemon Lollipops)

Look at the Lemon Lollipops on Mr. L. Mr. L made all his Lemon Lollipops look similar.

216

What words can we use to tell how Mr. L's Lemon Lollipops look? (e.g., yellow, lemon flavor, round)

Mr. L makes all his Lemon Lollipops round.

The shape of Mr. L's lollipops is round.

Show Mr. L with your hands what *round* is.

Mr. L's Lemon Lollipops have a shape.

The word we use to tell about his lollipops' shape is *round.*

A round shape like a lollipop is called a circle.

Mr. L's Lemon Lollipops are circles.

What is another shape a lollipop may be?

Have the children discuss different possible shapes for Mr. L's Lemon Lollipops. Some children may draw the shapes on the chalkboard. Have them recall lollipops that they have seen, especially lollipops made for special occasions (e.g., at Thanksgiving time when lollipops are made in the shape of turkeys).

Discriminating Among Shapes

Discriminating Among Sizes

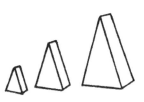

Making Lollipops In Different Shapes And Colors

Things look different from one another because they have different shapes.

We can see many different shapes in our room.

Show the children square, triangular and rectangular blocks.

Let's look at our blocks.

Are all these shapes the same?

Let's see how many different shapes we can see.

Each of these blocks has a different shape.

Each shape has a different name.

Name each shape as you show the children the blocks. (a square, a rectangle, a triangle)

Have the children select more blocks from the block corner to show different shapes. The shapes may be similar, but the sizes may be different. Have them examine the blocks and discuss how the shapes differ and how they are the same.

Mr. L would like to see different shaped lollipops.

Perhaps Mr. L would like lollipops that are different colors, too.

Show the children the different paper shapes you have prepared. Distribute the ice cream sticks. Let each child decide what shape and color lollipop he wants to make for Mr. L. Tell them that they may make more than one lollipop for Mr. L. They may use a different shape for each lollipop they make. When the lollipops are finished the children may tell Mr. L the shape and color they used to make each lollipop.

We know that Mr. L loves round lollipops.

All the children who made round lollipops, hold them up for Mr. L.

Mr. L also likes square lollipops.

All the children who have square lollipops, hold them up.

Mr. L likes triangle shaped lollipops too.

All the children who have triangle lollipops, hold them up.

Mr. L likes lollipops in the shape of a rectangle.

All the children who have rectangle shaped lollipops, hold them up.

TYING IT TOGETHER

Distribute copies of Alpha Time Master #105 and crayons. Discuss the illustration.

Who is in the picture? (Mr. L)

What is he made of? (Lemon Lollipops)

What color are Lemon Lollipops? (yellow)

What shape are Mr. L's lollipops? (round; circle-shaped)

What are some other shapes you see on this paper? (triangle, square, rectangle)

What can we do to make these shapes into lollipops? (add sticks or lines)

What color shall the square lollipops be? (e.g., red, green)

What flavor is that? (e.g., cherry, lime)

What color shall the triangle lollipops be?

What color shall the rectangle lollipops be?

Have the children draw lines on the shapes to make lollipops. They may then decide which color each shape should be.

ON THEIR OWN

Children may choose from the following activities:

Music And Dance   Playing Mr. L's song (record #2, side A, band #1) and dancing to it.

Oral Communication   Talking to Mr. L; introducing him to the other Letter People.

Discrimination Among Shapes   Going on a shape hunt in order to find objects in the room that have the shape of a circle, square, triangle, rectangle.

Discrimination Among Colors	Finding objects around the room that are blue, green, yellow, black, white.
Cooking (Measuring)	Making lemonade: Squeeze a lemon and add the lemon juice to water in a tall glass or jar. Then, add two or three teaspoons of sugar. Mix and drink.
Nature	Planting lemon seeds, watering them and watching them grow.
Art	Drawing pictures using only one shape.

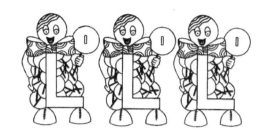

1L₂

PLANNING AND PREPARATION: Huggable, Mr. L; storybook, "Lovely Lemon Lollies"; Record #4; five yellow circles; five sticks; Alpha Time Master #106 construction paper, crayons, scissors, paste, several real or pretend Lemon Lollipops.

Hide the lollipops around the room.

LISTENING TO A STORY

Gather the children around Mr. L.

What does Mr. L have all over his body? (Lemon Lollipops)

Long ago Mr. L did not have Lemon Lollipops. He had only lemon lollies.

Lollies were round lemon candies you popped into your mouth.

Show the children the storybook, "Lovely Lemon Lollies."

Let's listen to a story about Mr. L. We will find out how lollies became lollipops.

Gather the children around you and read the story or play the recording (record #4, side B, band #1) as you turn the pages. When the story is finished, the following questions may stimulate discussion:

*Talking About
The Story*

What were some problems the lollies caused? (They looked like an egg or bowling ball.)

What size were some of the lollies Mr. L made? (little, large)

What idea did Lady Lark Bird have? (put sticks on lollies)

Why is everyone glad that lollies became lollipops? (They won't be mixed up.)

The Lolly Lane Lookers had lots of work to do in the story. What were some of the jobs the Lolly Lane Lookers had to do? (look in the nest; look at the ball; write a report)

Note: The "Lovely Lemon Lollies" filmstrip may be shown any time after the book has been introduced. (See end of lesson.) It may be used for recalling the story, identifying color and shape or storytelling. The recorded story may also be used for group viewing of the film.

*Making Lolly
Lookers*

Let's each be a Lolly Lane Looker and do some "looker" jobs.

Each Lolly Lane Looker has something special he uses when he looks.

First, we must make something to use when we look, to help us see better. What are some things that help us see better? (e.g., binoculars, magnifying glass, telescopes, eyeglasses)

220

The children may use a variety of art materials to make their own "lookers." Using their "lookers," the children may go on a lolly hunt looking for real or make believe Lemon Lollies that have been hidden around the room.

IDENTIFYING THE CAPITAL AND LOWER CASE LETTER L

One of the Letter People asked Mr. L where his letter was. Mr. L said, "My letter is part of my body. It must be some place on me."

Let's help Mr. L find his letter. Use your hand to show Mr. L his capital letter L.

How many straight lines are there in capital L? (two)

Have the children form pairs and make the capital letter L with their bodies.

Now let's look again. Where is the lower case l?

Show us with your hand, the lower case l on Mr. L's lollipop.

TALKING ABOUT THE QUANTITY "FIVE"

Mr. L was very busy putting sticks on lollies to make them into lollipops. Mr. L worked with five lollies at a time.

Five is an easy number for Mr. L to figure out. Mr. L knows he has five fingers on each hand. If he puts one lolly next to each finger, he has five lollies.

Have a child put his right hand on the desk, fingers outstretched, and count his fingers. Place a yellow circle next to each of the fingers on his right hand.

There are five fingers.

Count the circles. (five)

Each circle is a lolly. There are five lollies.

Five lollies need five sticks.

Mr. L used his left hand to count the sticks.

He put one stick next to each of his five fingers on his left hand.

Hold up your left hand with fingers outstretched. Have the children do the same thing.

Again a child may demonstrate putting a stick next to each of his five fingers and counting the sticks.

It always works out exactly right.

Five lollies. . . five sticks!

221

Mr. L puts a stick on each lolly.

Attach a stick to each yellow circle.

When he is finished making the lollipops he has no more sticks and no more lollies. He has five lollipops!

One day when Mr. L was making lollipops, something happened! It didn't work out just right!

Mr. L has a picture story for us. He wants us to help him figure out why it didn't work out just right.

READING COMPREHENSION

Reading A Picture Story

Give each child a copy of Alpha Time Master #106. Discuss each picture with the children.

Let's look at the first picture of the story.

Frame #1:

What do you see in the picture? (a hand and 5 sticks, a hand and 5 lollies)

Whose hands can they be? (Mr. L's)

Why did Mr. L put a stick next to each of his fingers? (to be sure there are five)

How many fingers are on Mr. L's hand? (five)

How many sticks are in the picture? (five)

What do you think Mr. L is going to do with these sticks?

Observing, Counting, Predicting Outcomes

Look at the other hand in the picture.

What do you see next to each finger of this hand? (5 lollies)

Why did Mr. L put a lolly next to each of his fingers? (to be sure there are five)

How many lollies does Mr. L have? (five)

How many sticks does Mr. L have? (five)

Does he have enough lollipop sticks for each lolly? (yes)

If Mr. L puts a stick on each lolly, will he have any sticks left? (no)

Let's look at the next picture and see what happens.

Frame #2:
Counting, Making Judgments

What is Mr. L doing? (showing the sticks to the lollies)

How do you know that all the lollies are not happy about becoming lollipops? (the look on their faces)

How many lollies look unhappy? (two)

What do you think the two lollies who don't want to be lollipops will do?

Frame #3:
Inferring

Let's look at the next part of the story and find out.

What are the two unhappy lollies doing? (running away)

Why do you think the lollies ran away?

Let's look at the last picture.

Frame #4:
Counting And
Inferring

Mr. L is wondering what happened to the two missing lollies.

How do you think Mr. L knows they are missing?

Mr. L can't finish the story because he doesn't know what happened.

Mr. L wants you to be Lolly Lane Lookers and to find out what happened to the two lollies who ran away.

When you find out, please write or draw the story for Mr. L.

Planning An Ending
And Name For
The Story

Then the story will be finished.

When Mr. L's story is finished we can help give it a name.

TYING IT TOGETHER

Predicting Outcomes

Have the children pretend to be Lolly Lane Lookers. They may form small groups to discuss what has happened to the two lollies. Have each group dictate its own version of the ending and then illustrate it.

Then let each group decide on a name for the story. The children may share their stories and illustrations with each other and with Mr. L.

ON THEIR OWN

Children may choose from the following activities:

Letter Tracing

Using copies of Alpha Time Master #66 to trace the capital and lower case letter L.

Counting To Five

Playing lolly factory: Making lollipops out of clay and sticks or any other material and tying them in bundles of five.

Listening

Playing the recording of Lovely Lemon Lollipops (record #4, side B, band #2) with or without the book.

Matching And
Sorting

Including Mr. L's playing cards from Alpha Time Decks 1, 2, and 4 in any of the activities in the *Games* section.

Recalling

Looking at the filmstrip *Lovely Lemon Lollies.*

FRAME 1

Numeration

Predicting

Drawing Conclusions

The following questions may be used when showing the filmstrip "Lovely Lemon Lollies."

What do you see? (Mr. L, bird, house)

Whose house do you think it is? (Mr. L)

What makes you think it is Mr. L's house? (There are lollies in the house.)

How can you tell what the story is about?

FRAME 2

Counting

Discriminating

Color

Shape

How many houses do you see? (four)

What color is the house in the middle? (yellow)

What color is the sky? (blue)

What are some of the shapes you see? (circles, triangles, rectangles)

What shape is the door? (rectangle)

FRAME 3

Inferences

Sensory Images

What color are the lollies? (yellow)

What flavor might a yellow lolly be? (lemon)

How do you think Mr. L feels? (happy)

What shape are the lollies? (round, circle)

Whose picture do you think is on the wall?

FRAME 4

Recall
Classification
Counting

What is happening to the lollies? (leaping on the street)

How many ladies do you see? (two)

224

FRAME 5

Interpreting Emotions

FRAME 6

Using Locational Terms

FRAME 7

Discriminating Shapes

FRAME 8

Recall

FRAME 9

Size Comparisons

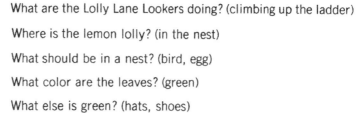

Who is in bed? (Lady Lark Bird)

How do the people look? (worried)

Why do you think they are worried?

What does Lady Lark Bird have in her mouth? (thermometer)

What are the Lolly Lane Lookers doing? (climbing up the ladder)

Where is the lemon lolly? (in the nest)

What should be in a nest? (bird, egg)

What color are the leaves? (green)

What else is green? (hats, shoes)

What are the Lolly Lane Lookers looking at? (lolly)

What shape is the lolly? (circle)

Where else do you see circles? (buttons, eyes, magnifying glass)

How does Mr. L look? (worried)

What do you think is written on the report? (a lolly was in the nest)

How do the people look? (worried)

Why is the man running? (He is afraid the lollies will hit him.)

Which lolly is the largest? (the lolly rolling down the hill)

FRAME 10

Predicting Outcomes

What does Lucky Loopy have in his hand? (a lolly)

What shape is the lolly? (round)

What shape is a bowling ball? (round)

Making Inferences

Why does Lucky Loopy think he has a bowling ball in his hand? (same shape)

What will happen when the lolly hits the floor? (break)

FRAME 11

Color Discrimination

Why is Lucky Loopy surprised? (ball broke)

What are some colors here? (e.g., red, blue, green, brown, purple, pink)

FRAME 12

Interpreting emotions

How does Lucky Loopy feel? (sad)

What do you think the people are saying?

What do you think Mr. L is thinking?

FRAME 13

Making Inferences

Why do you think Mr. L is crying?(His lollies are causing a lot of trouble.)

Make believe you are one of the people in the picture. Tell us what you are thinking about all the trouble.

FRAME 14

Making Inferences

Predicting Outcomes

How can you tell that the people are sorry to see Mr. L go? (their faces)

What is Mr. L putting on the truck? (lollies)

Why do you think Mr. L wants to move?

FRAME 15

Where are all the people looking? (at Lady Lark Bird)

What does Lady Lark Bird have in her beak? (sticks)

How does a bird use sticks? (for making a nest)

FRAME 16
Counting

What are all the people doing? (putting sticks in lollies)

How many sticks do you see? (four)

FRAME 17

How do the people feel? (happy)

Why are they happy? (lollies are lollipops, Mr. L may stay)

1D₁

PLANNING AND PREPARATION: Huggable, Mr. D; storybook, *A Dozen Delicious Doughnuts*; Records #2 and #4; Alpha Time Master #107.

Keep Mr. D concealed for the first part of the lesson.

MEETING MR. D AND HIS DELICIOUS DOUGHNUTS

Gather the children around you as you tell them the following story.

Last night before I went to bed, I took a glass of milk. I wanted something to eat with my milk.

I looked at the cookies. I didn't want cookies. Then I saw something that was round and sweet and had a hole in the middle. That's what I wanted!

What do you think it was?

Lead the children to the conclusion that what you have described is a doughnut.

Hearing About Delicious Doughnuts

I ate one—two—three—Delicious Doughnuts! They were so delicious I could not stop eating them.

When I went to sleep I dreamed about Delicious Doughnuts. Delicious Doughnuts danced in my dreams.

When I came to school, I told the Letter People about how I dreamed about the Delicious Doughnuts all night long.

They laughed and said that I had dreamed that dream because of the new Letter Person we are going to meet today. The Letter People all said, "Wait and see!"

We have to close our eyes and then they'll bring the new Letter Person to class.

Meeting Mr. D

Place Mr. D where the children will be able to see him when they open their eyes.

Am I still dreaming?

What do we see all over this Letter Person? (doughnuts)

Why do I think I'm dreaming?

Who can this Letter Person be?

Ask him.

Listening To Mr. D's Song

The new Letter Person has a song for us.

We'll find out his name from the song.

Let the children gather around Mr. D to greet him, talk to him, and to ask him his name. Then play Mr. D's song (record #2, side A, band #2).

228

What is his name? (Mr. D)

What are some things he tells us?

Show Mr. D how his music makes you want to move.

LISTENING TO A STORY

Look at Mr. D's Delicious Doughnuts.

Are they all the same?

How can doughnuts be different from each other? (icing, size, flavor)

Tell us about doughnuts that you have eaten.

Do all doughnuts have holes?

Mr. D says that long ago all doughnuts did have holes until one day something happened. Let's listen to the story and find out why all doughnuts don't have holes.

*Talking About
The Story*

Read the children "A Dozen Delicious Doughnuts" or play record #4 as you show them the pictures. When you have finished, questions such as the following will stimulate discussion:

Why don't all doughnuts have holes? (Some are jelly doughnuts.)

Why didn't the darling, dainty doughnut want to have a hole in it? (The dainty doughnut was afraid of the doughnut dentist.)

What happened when the Delicious Doughnuts delivered themselves? (No one wanted them.)

What kind of doughnuts did the dozen Delicious Doughnuts become? (jelly doughnuts)

Note: The filmstrip, "A Dozen Delicious Doughnuts" may be shown any time after the book has been introduced. It may be used for recalling the story or for other discussion. (See suggestions at end of lesson.) The recorded story may be used in conjunction with the filmstrip.

TYING IT TOGETHER

Distribute copies of Alpha Time Master #107.

Who is in the picture? (Mr. D)

Mr. D would like you to help decorate this dozen doughnuts.

Use your crayons to dip and dab some doughnuts.

You may be a doughnut dentist and draw holes in some of the doughnuts.

ON THEIR OWN

Children may choose from the following activities:

Size And Color Discrimination

Coloring the biggest doughnut on Alpha Time Master #107 blue, the smallest doughnut green.

Crafts

Making doughnuts out of clay and painting them.

Using art materials to decorate several paper doughnuts for Mr. D.

Making a doughnut mobile by hanging doughnuts from wire coat hangers.

Music And Dance

Listening and dancing to Mr. D's song (record #2, side A, band 2).

Listening

Listening to *A Dozen Delicious Doughnuts* (record #4) with or without looking at the book.

Picture Reading

Looking at the filmstrip of *A Dozen Delicious Doughnuts* and telling the story that goes with each picture.

FILMSTRIP: A DOZEN DELICIOUS DOUGHNUTS

FRAME 1

The following questions may be used when showing the filmstrip "A Dozen Delicious Doughnuts."

Who do you think will be in this story? (Mr. D, doughnuts, dentist, doughnut detectives)

FRAME 2

Counting

What is Mr. D doing? (decorating doughnuts, dipping and dabbing)

How many doughnuts are being decorated? (four)

How do the doughnuts feel? (happy)

FRAME 3

Why are the doughnuts looking in the mirror? (They want to see the decorations.)

What shape are the doughnuts? (round)

Do you think these doughnuts like the way they look? (yes)

FRAME 4

What is the doughnut dentist doing? (drilling holes in the doughnut)

What shape are the holes? (round)

What colors do you see? (e.g., yellow, green, pink)

FRAME 5

What are the doughnuts doing? (talking)

What do you think they are discussing?

FRAME 6

How many doughnuts do you see? (five)

What do you think the doughnut in the middle is saying?

FRAME 7

The darling dainty doughnut said it is afraid of the doughnut dentist.

Make believe you are one of the other doughnuts.

Tell us what you say to the doughnut.

FRAME 8

Where are the doughnuts going? (to speak to Mr. D)

What will they tell him? (They don't want to go to the dentist.)

FRAME 9

Make believe you are Mr. D. Tell us what you say to the doughnuts.

How many doughnuts are going out of the door? (two)

FRAME 10

How does the lady look?
What do you think the dog is thinking?
What are the doughnuts saying?
What color is the lady's shoe? (green)
What else is green? (door)

FRAME 11

Where are the dozen doughnuts? (in the street)

What shape are the windows? (rectangle)

What do you think the two doughnuts are saying?

FRAME 12

What are the people in the windows looking at? (doughnut detectives)

How will the doughnut detectives find the doughnuts? (follow the dough-nut smell)
Why are the doughnuts crying? (People don't want them.)

Is Mr. D glad to see the doughnuts?

Making Value Judgments

What do you think Mr. D is saying?

FRAME 14

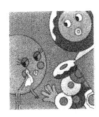

What is the doughnut doing? (crying)

How does Mr. D feel?

What are some colors you see? (e.g., blue, pink)

What are some shapes you see? (circle)

FRAME 15

What is in the bowl? (jelly)

What color is the jelly? (orange)

What flavor might the jelly be? (e.g., orange, apricot, peach)

FRAME 16

What is Mr. D doing? (putting jelly between two doughnuts)

How do the doughnuts feel? (happy)

How does Mr. D feel? (happy)

FRAME 17

What is everyone eating? (jelly doughnuts)

How can we tell they like the jelly doughnuts? (faces; they are eating them)

How many people are eating doughnuts? (six)

1D₂

PLANNING AND PREPARATION: Huggable, Mr. D; a circular piece of aluminum foil or construction paper, cellophane tape, 12 sheets of paper, crayons, paper, scissors; Alpha Time Master #108; pieces of construction paper cut into triangles, circles, squares, enough for each child.

Prepare a sign that reads: I do not dip,
I do not dab.

REMEMBERING MR. D's STORY

Gather the children around you and Mr. D.

Mr. D wants to know whether or not you liked his story about a dozen Delicious Doughnuts.

*Creating An
Interpretive Dance*

He would like to have you tell parts of the story to him. Mr. D doesn't want to listen to you, he just wants to look at you. He will know which part of the story you are telling him just by watching what you do. He would like you to dance everything you do.

First Mr. D wants to watch doughnuts being decorated. How did Mr. D decorate doughnuts? (Mr. D dipped and dabbed each doughnut with sugar, sprinkles, chocolate.)

Ask one child to be Mr. D. Select twelve children to be doughnuts. Explain to the children that Mr. D decorates a dozen doughnuts at a time because 12 doughnuts go into each box.

Have a child show how Mr. D dances around the doughnuts and dips and dabs each one. Each doughnut may tell Mr. D how he would like to be decorated.

After the doughnut is decorated, he dances to a mirror.

A child may be chosen to be a mirror and have a circular piece of construction paper or aluminum foil taped to his chest.

The decorated Delicious Doughnut dances in front of the mirror to see how he likes his decoration.

After each doughnut has been decorated and has seen himself in the mirror, the dozen doughnuts visit the doughnut dentist.

The child who is chosen to be the doughnut dentist dances to each doughnut and pretends to be drilling a hole.

After each doughnut has had a hole drilled, the doughnuts dance to the doughnut box.

(The doughnut box may be represented by twelve pieces of paper lined up on the floor.)

Each doughnut dances onto a piece of paper and crouches. Then all the doughnuts pretend to put the cover on the doughnut box. Now the dozen doughnuts are ready to be delivered.

The pantomime may be reenacted so that all the children have a chance to play one of the roles.

IDENTIFYING THE CAPITAL AND LOWER CASE LETTER D

The doughnuts are all in a dither. They don't know what to do. Mr. D put up a sign.

Show the children the sign that you have previously prepared.

The sign says: I do not dip,
                       I do not dab.

The doughnuts do not know why Mr. D will not dip and dab.

Mr. D will not tell them.

Ask him. Maybe he will tell you.

Let the children question Mr. D.

Mr. D says that one of the reasons he doesn't dip and dab any more is that he is very sad.

He knows that every Letter Person has a capital letter and a lower case letter.

No one has shown him his letter.

Find Mr. D's capital letter.

*Analyzing The
Letter D*

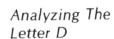

Trace it for him with your hand.

Where is Mr. D's lower case letter?

Trace it for him with your hand.

Let's look at the shape of Mr. D's capital letter.

How many parts does the capital D have? (two)

How many straight lines does it have? (one)

How many curved lines does it have? (one)

How many children will we need to make the capital letter D? (two)

How will we place our bodies?

Let's make some capital "D's."

READING COMPREHENSION

The doughnut dentists is tired of drilling round holes in the doughnuts.

He would like us to help him think of other shapes that he can drill.

*Discussing
Geometric Shapes*

Have the children pick out blocks or other objects that are shaped like squares, triangles, rectangles and circles. Have them name each shape.

The doughnut dentist decided to drill different shaped holes.

235

He decided to have a different office for each shape.

Mr. D has been watching the doughnut dentist all day. He would like us to help him figure out what the doughnut dentist is doing.

Give the children a copy of Alpha Time Master #108 and discuss each picture with them.

Let's look at the first picture.

How many doors do you see in this picture? (three)

How are the doors different from each other? (Each has a different shape painted on it.)

Why are the doughnuts standing in front of the doors? (They are waiting to have holes drilled.)

What do you think is behind each door?

What do you think will happen to the doughnuts as they go through each door?

Let's go through the door that has the circle painted on it. We'll go with one of the doughnuts.

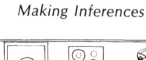

Whom did the doughnut find when it went through the door? (the doughnut dentist)

What shape hole is the doughnut dentist drilling? (round)

How do you know this Delicious Doughnut wants a hole that has a round shape? (It waited at the door that had the round shape on it.)

How do you know that the doughnut dentist has been saving the round parts that fall out of each doughnut as he drills the hole? (They are in the bowl under the table.)

What will happen to the round part of the doughnut that the doughnut dentist is cutting out? (It will go into the bowl with the rest of the cutouts.)

Let's open a different door and see what is there.

How can you tell which door we have opened this time? (There are square cut out shapes in the box.)

How is the box under this table different from the box under the table in the first picture? (It has a different shape.)

How did the square pieces get in the box? (The dentist put them in after drilling square holes.)

Which door do we still have to open? (the triangle door)

Let's open it and see what we find!

Frame #4:
Developing The
Concept Of
"Triangular"

How is the box under this table different from the boxes under the other tables? (It has a different shape.)

How can you tell there have been doughnuts here who have had dough-nut holes cut out in the shape of a triangle? (There are triangle cutouts in the box.)

What do you think the doughnut dentist will do with the different parts of the doughnuts that he has cut out?

Mr. D wants you to finish this story.

He can't figure out what the doughnut dentist will do with the left-over pieces of doughnut.

Have the children form small groups and discuss what they think the doughnut dentist plans to do with the pieces of doughnut. Then have them dictate their stories and draw illustrations to go with them. En-courage the children to share their stories and illustrations with each other and with Mr. D.

TYING IT TOGETHER

Mr. D likes the different ways you finished his story. Now he has a sur-prise for you.

Mr. D collected the parts of the doughnuts that fell out when the dentist cut out the holes.

He wants us to make designs using those pieces.

Working With
Geometric Shapes

Explain how the children may make doughnut designs using paper geo-metric shapes.

Use different shapes.

Dip and dab each piece with a dot of paste.

Paste the pieces on your paper.

Put them in different places on your paper.

If you need more pieces that are shaped like a square, or a triangle or a circle, you may make more yourself.

When you are finished you will have a doughnut design because the de-sign was made with parts of doughnuts.

ON THEIR OWN

Children may choose from the following activities:

Letter Tracing

Tracing upper and lower case D's on Alpha Time Master #58.

Shape Discrimination

Making a list of foods that have geometric shapes (e.g., *circle*—cookies, pancakes, *triangle*—sandwich that has been cut diagonally, slice of cheese cake, *square*—slices of bread, cake, *rectangle*—slices of ham, cheese, meat loaf).

Matching And
Sorting

Including Mr. D's playing cards from Alpha Time Decks #1, 2 and 4 in any of the activities found in the *Games* section of the manual.

Using colored construction paper, make enough large pieces of make believe Gooey Gum for each child in the class. Keep Mr. G concealed for the first part of the lesson.

MEETING MR. G AND HIS GOOEY GUM

Everything I touch feels strange. Everything feels gooey. My chair feels gooey. My desk feels gooey. This book feels gooey.

What do you think happened?

Touch each article as you mention it and react as if it were very sticky. Have the children do the same.

Gooey, gooey, everything feels gooey.

Touch the desk and tell us how a gooey desk feels.

Touch the chair and tell us how a gooey chair feels.

Touch this book and tell us how a gooey book feels.

Touch your shirt. See how gooey it feels.

Touch your shoes. See how gooey they feel!

I wonder who made everything so gooey!

Make believe you are consulting with Mr. D.

Mr. D says that there is a new Letter Person who has made everything so gooey.

If you close your eyes Mr. D will get the Letter Person.

Discovering Mr. G

While the children's eyes are closed, display Mr. G. When they open their eyes encourage them to gather around Mr. G, to look at him and to talk to him.

Who can this be?

Mr. D says his name is Mr. G.

What is he pulling out of his mouth? (gum)

What does he have on his head? (sticks of gum)

Why do you think he made everything gooey?

Mr. G says that he has Gooey Gum.

Listening To And Discussing Mr. G's Song

Play Mr. G's song (record #2, side A, band #3). Talk to the children about the way the music makes them feel. Discuss some of the things Mr. G does. Some children may want to pantomime Mr. G's actions as the record is played.

What happens to Mr. G? (He gets stuck.)

What does he say when his Gooey Gum gets unstuck? ("Good, now I can go again.")

Let the children ask Mr. G about his Gooey Gum.

Mr. G has the gooiest Gooey Gum. How do you think the gooiest Gooey Gum feels?

LISTENING TO A STORY

Tell the children the following story about Mr. G.

Mr. G loved Gooey Gum so much that he wanted to find the gooiest gum in the world. He went from one store to another, searching for the gooiest Gooey Gum.

Mr. G would try Gooey Gum in gold wrappers and Gooey Gum in green wrappers.

Each time Mr. G said, "It is gooey but not the gooiest!"

One night as Mr. G was chewing some new gum, someone was tapping at his window. He looked out and saw the strangest bird with the longest legs!

"Goodness," gasped Mr. G, "who are you?"

"Don't you remember me, Mr. G?" chirped the Gooney Bird.

"When I was a baby Gooney Bird, I lived in a nest in your garden.

"You were good to me and my family.

"Now I am all grown up and I have come to help you.

"I want to help you find the gooiest Gooey Gum.

"I cannot help you chew your gum but I can help by flying you from place to place to find the gooiest gum."

Early the next morning Mr. G got on Gooney Bird's back, and together they flew from Gooey Gum store to Gooey Gum store.

They flew that morning, and the next, and the next, and the next.

Gooney Bird watched as Mr. G chewed.

Each time it was the same. The Gooey Gum was not the gooiest.

Mr. G was getting grouchy and grumpy.

Gooney Bird said, "Mr. G, I know why you cannot find the gooiest Gooey Gum. The gooiest Gooey Gum has never been made!"

Mr. G started to cry and cry.

"Don't cry," begged Gooney Bird.

"You can still have the gooiest Gooey Gum. You will just have to make it. I will help you."

Mr. G wiped his eyes. He hopped on Gooney Bird's back, and off they flew to buy what they would need for making Gooey Gum.

They stopped at a store.

Mr. G went inside.

He was there for a long time.

When Mr. G came out, Gooney Bird did not know it was Mr. G.

He was wearing galoshes on his feet, gloves on his hands, glasses on his eyes.

Gooney Bird scratched his head.

Galoshes, gloves and glasses? What did they have to do with making the gooiest Gooey Gum?

Mr. G looked at Gooney Bird and said, "First I must look like a Gooey Gum maker. Then I will be able to make the gooiest Gooey Gum."

They flew back to Mr. G's garage. Then Mr. G gathered together all the things he thought he would need.

Now he was ready to start Gooey Gum making.

Mr. G filled glasses and glasses with little bits of this and little bits of that.

Would any of these make the gooiest Gooey Gum?

Mr. G decided to try.

He chewed.

Gooney Bird waited.

He chewed again.

Gooney Bird waited.

Mr. G shook his head.

"Gooey, but not the gooiest!" he said.

Mr. G did not give up. He filled more glasses and more glasses.

This time he put in lots of this and lots of that.

Would these turn into the gooiest Gooey Gum?

Again, Mr. G decided to try.

He chewed.

Gooney Bird waited.

Mr. G shook his head.

"Gooier, but not the gooiest!" he said again.

Mr. G was getting grouchy and grumpy again.

He was getting tired.

Soon Mr. G fell fast asleep. Gooney Bird slept too.

While they were asleep, something happened.

The lots of this and lots of that in the glasses started to grow and grow.

Gooey Gum gushed out of the glasses!

Gooey gum gushed onto Mr. G's galoshes.

Gooey gum gushed onto Gooney Bird's legs.

Gooey gum gushed into the garage, into the garden and out onto every street.

Mr. G and Gooney Bird slept on and on.

Suddenly Mr. G's telephone rang.

Then Mr. G's doorbell rang.

Mr. G and Gooney Bird both awoke.

"I'll answer the telephone. You answer the door," said Mr. G to Gooney Bird.

Mr. G could not answer the telephone. Gooney Bird could not answer the door. They could not move.

Mr. G's galoshes were stuck to the floor. Gooney Bird's legs were stuck to the floor.

Mr. G tried to get his galoshes free.

Goodness, gracious, his gloves got stuck to his galoshes!

And the Gooey Gum just kept gushing out of the glasses!

Mr. G got grumpier and grouchier.

Gooney Bird giggled and giggled.

Mr. G pulled and pulled at the Gooey Gum.

"What a mess," he yelled.

"This is the gooiest Gooey Gum I have ever seen. This is surely the gooiest Gooey Gum in the whole world!"

Gooney Bird grinned and hopped up and down in the Gooey Gum.

He rolled round and round in the Gooey Gum.

241

He said, "Mr. G, don't you know you've found it?

Drawing conclusions

You said it, and don't even know that you said it."

"What are you talking about," grumbled Mr. G.

"What did you say about this gum?" giggled Gooney Bird as he danced in the Gooey Gum.

"I said it's a mess. It's the gooiest. . . " Mr. G stopped.

He said in a whisper, "the gooiest. . . " His voice got louder.

"The gooiest"—his voice got still louder—"THE GOOIEST!

Gooney Bird, Gooney Bird, we've got it!

We've made the gooiest Gooey Gum in the world."

The people whose cars were stuck in it knew.

People whose feet were stuck in it knew.

Dogs, cats, children on roller skates, everyone knew!

Everyone was so happy for Mr. G they felt like dancing.

So they danced and danced in the Gooey Gum.

Even people who had never liked to dance liked dancing in the Gooey Gum.

In fact, the Gooey Gum Dance became the most popular dance in Letter People Land.

Dancing The Gooey Gum Dance

Mr. G wants us to dance the gooiest Gooey Gum dance with him.

He'll give you each a large piece of the gooiest Gooey Gum. Put it down on the floor in front of you and we'll be ready to start.

Give each child a piece of paper. Pretend that it is very gooey as you hand it to them. Have the children sing and enact the following to the tune of "Hokey Pokey." Remind the children that as they dance they are stepping on the gooiest Gooey Gum.

> You put your right gooey foot in!
> You put your right gooey foot out!
> Your foot is full of goo, goo, goo!
> So you shake it all about!

Discriminating between left and right

Repeat having the children use their left foot, right hand, left hand, whole self.

TYING IT TOGETHER

Show the children Picture Card 8 and give each child a matching copy of Alpha Time Master #109. Discuss the picture with the children.

Who do you see in the picture? (Mr. G, Gooney Bird)

What is happening to them? (They are stuck in the gooiest Gooey Gum.)

Show us Mr. G's glasses, galoshes, gloves.

ON THEIR OWN

Children may choose from the following activities:

Art

Drawing pictures of themselves stuck in gum.

Making galoshes, glasses and gloves.

Physics

Observing what happens when flour is added to water. (It becomes gooey).

Observing what happens when chewing gum is melted.

Dramatic Play

Pantomiming Mr. G's song (record #2).

Using Mr. G as a character in a play based on the story.

Dance

Making up a Gooey Gum dance.

Storytelling

Using Picture Card 8 to retell the story of what happened when Mr. G fell asleep.

Making Comparisons

Using objects (e.g. books, blocks) in the classroom to demonstrate words of comparison such as big, bigger, biggest; heavy, heavier, heaviest; short, shorter, shortest.

1G₂

PLANNING AND PREPARATION: Huggable, Mr. G; several dozen small cut-outs in square, rectangle, triangle and circle shapes; Alpha Time Master #110; crayons, drawing paper.

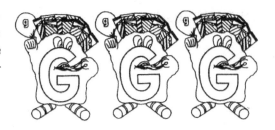

REMEMBERING MR. G's STORY

Gather the children around Mr. G.

Mr. G says you told the story of the doughnuts to Mr. D without words. Mr. G would like us to tell parts of his Gooey Gum story without using words.

Mr. G will tell us which parts he would like to see. Then we will try to act them out for him.

Do you remember how Gooney Bird helped Mr. G?

Help the children recall that Mr. G sat on Gooney Bird's back and flew from store to store.

Pantomiming Mr. G's Story

Gooney Bird and Mr. G went to many, many stores to look for the gooiest Gooey Gum.

One of us will be Mr. G. One of us will be Gooney Bird.

This morning Gooney Bird will fly Mr. G to four stores.

Four of us will be storekeepers. Mr. G will try the Gooey Gum in each store to see if it is the gooiest.

Remind the children that when they are not using words, their hands, their faces and their head movements must all do things to take the place of words.

Mr. G likes the way you acted for that part of the story. He would like to see you act for another part of the story.

Mr. G remembers when he was grouchy and grumpy because he could not make the gooiest of Gooey Gums. He got tired of trying again and again. He fell asleep. Gooney Bird fell asleep too.

Show us, without using words, what happened while Mr. G and Gooney Bird slept.

One of us will be Mr. G. One of us will be Gooney Bird.

The rest of us will be the people, the dogs, the cats, the buses and cars and the other things on the street in Letter People Land.

Remember that all of a sudden the gooiest Gooey Gum gushed into the streets.

Demonstrating A Sense Of Humor

Give the children enough time to develop their own slapstick humor.

IDENTIFYING THE UPPER AND LOWER CASE G

*Analyzing The
Shape Of The
Capital "G"*

Mr. G says please help him to find his capital letter.

Use your eyes to find it. Use your hands to show him the shape that it has.

Find Mr. G's lower case letter. Show it to him.

Look at the shape of Mr. G's capital letter G. How many people do you think we will need to make the capital G with our bodies? Let's try making it.

Have the children form small groups and experiment to find the best way of using their bodies to make the capital G.

REMEMBERING GEOMETRIC SHAPES

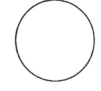

Mr. G spends all day long making the gooiest Gooey Gum. He gets tired of looking at the same shape all the time. Guess what shapes Mr. G has been using to make Gooey Gum.

Have the children recall any of the shapes they talked about in previous lessons. As you hold up the appropriate shapes in the activity below, the children may identify them.

Mr. G buys Gooey Gum from the storekeepers. The storekeepers sell Gooey Gum in the shape of a. . . (*Hold up the square shaped cut-out.*)

The storekeepers sell Gooey Gum in the shape of a. . . (*Hold up the rectangle shaped cut-out.*)

The storekeepers sell Gooey Gum in the shape of a. . . (*Hold up the circle shaped cut-out.*)

The storekeepers sell Gooey Gum in the shape of a. . . (*Hold up the triangle shaped cutout:*)

The storekeepers are selling lots of Gooey Gum. They are busy all the time. Sometimes they don't even have time to talk to you when you come to buy Gooey Gum.

You must bring a piece of paper on which you have drawn your order.

TYING IT TOGETHER

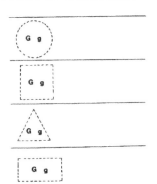

Give each child a copy of Alpha Time Master #110. Explain how it is to be used.

This will be your order sheet. If you want one piece of Gooey Gum shaped like a circle, draw one circle shape on your order paper.

If you want two pieces of Gooey Gum, one piece shaped like a square and one piece shaped like a triangle, what will you have to draw on your order paper? (a square and a triangle)

Name four children to be storekeepers. Give each a selection of the square, circular, rectangular, and triangular cut-outs you have previously prepared.

Have the children draw their orders on the Alpha Time Master sheets. Limit the orders to the number of cut-outs you have prepared.

Children who cannot draw the shapes may want to cut out the printed ones. Other may simply want to mark the shapes they want to use.

To play store, the children bring their orders to the storekeepers. Together the child and storekeeper fill the order. Each store can also have a "checker." The "checker" will match the child's order with his purchase.

The children may mark the upper and lower case G's.

ON THEIR OWN

Children may choose from the following activities:

Letter Tracing	Using Alpha Time Master #61 to trace the upper and lower case letter G.
Counting	Drawing one, two, three or four each of the shapes of gum in the lesson.
Art	Making a collage of cut outs of advertisements for chewing gum.
	Making paper chains out of gum wrappers.
Matching And Sorting	Including Mr. G's playing cards from Alpha Time Decks 1, 2, and 4 in any of the activities described in the *Games* section.

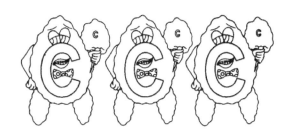

1C₁ **PLANNING AND PREPARATION:** Huggables, Mr. L, Mr. D, Mr. G, Mr. C; Record #2; Alpha Time Master #111. Small pieces of cotton—one for each child. (Pink cotton is ideal.)

Place Mr. L, Mr. D and Mr. G where the children can see them. Put a sheet or large cloth over Mr. C and hide him where he cannot be seen but is easily available.

TALKING ABOUT COTTON CANDY

Mr. L, Mr. D and Mr. G heard about a very special place called Cotton Candy Land.

(Be sure the children know what Cotton Candy is.)

Hearing About Cotton Candy Land

Everything in Cotton Candy Land is made of Cotton Candy.

There are Cotton Candy houses.

There are Cotton Candy trees.

There are Cotton Candy cars.

There are Cotton Candy bicycles.

There are Cotton Candy schools.

It is the prettiest and tastiest place anyone could visit. The people in Cotton Candy Land even wear Cotton Candy clothes.

Mr. L, Mr. G and Mr. D decided to go to Cotton Candy Land. They went to the chief of Cotton Candy Land. He welcomed them and smiled.

Mr. D couldn't believe his eyes. The chief's teeth were made of Cotton Candy.

The chief took a puff of Cotton Candy and placed it in Mr. L's hand.

He said to Mr. L, "What is this?"

"It is Cotton Candy," answered Mr. L.

"It is magical Cotton Candy," said the chief. "This puff of Cotton Candy can be anything you want it to be."

I would like it to be a Cotton Candy car," said Mr. L.

Mr. L waited and waited but the puff of Cotton Candy remained just a puff of Cotton Candy. Mr. L laughed. He thought that the chief was tricking him.

The chief said, "Mr. L, you must say the Cotton Candy magic words."

Cana, cana, cana, coo, coo, coo.
I'll blow a puff of Cotton Candy at you.
I'll wish for a Cotton Candy car and close my eyes.
And look for a Cotton Candy surprise.

Let's say the magic Cotton Candy words with Mr. L.

Repeat the rhyme with the children.

Mr. L blew a puff of Cotton Candy and sure enough, when he opened his eyes, there was a Cotton Candy car!

The other Letter People were so excited they could hardly wait to blow puffs of Cotton Candy too. They thought of all the things they wanted to have. They blew puffs of Cotton Candy all day and all night. Now the Letter People want us to try it.

Give each child a small piece of cotton and let them practice blowing it in the air.

Playing The Cotton Candy Game

Have one child pretend to hold a puff of Cotton Candy. The class joins him in saying the Cotton Candy magic words. Before the child opens his eyes, the rest of the class turn themselves into the child's wish. (e.g., If the child wants the Cotton Candy puff to be a tree, each child in the class stands and pretends to be a tree.)

Continue the game until several children have had a chance to blow puffs of Cotton Candy.

MEETING MR. C

The Letter People talked together and thought of something they wanted more than anything else.

They wanted a Letter Person made of Cotton Candy. They wanted a Letter Person who would live with them. Then they would always be able to remember Cotton Candy Land.

The chief thought and thought. He told the Letter People that he would send a Cotton Candy Letter Person to them.

Bring out Mr. C who is covered with a sheet. Do not remove the sheet.

If we all close our eyes and say the Cotton Candy magic words we will find a Letter Person made of Cotton Candy under this sheet.

Have the children say the Cotton Candy magic words with you and blow their bits of cotton.

> Cana, cana, cana, coo, coo, coo.
> I'll blow a puff of Cotton Candy at you.
> I'll wish for a Letter Person and close my eyes
> And look for a Cotton Candy surprise.

Remove the sheet covering Mr. C.

It really happened! How can we tell we got what we wished for? (The Letter Person is made of Cotton Candy.)

What is he holding in his hand? (Cotton Candy)

LISTENING TO MR. C's SONG

Mr. C wants to sing a song to us. The song will tell us many things about him.

Play Mr. C's song (record #2, side A, band #4) and discuss what Mr. C tells about himself.

What does Mr. C say that tells us he might play tricks on people?

Show Mr. C how his music makes you want to move.

248

TYING IT TOGETHER

ON THEIR OWN

Distribute copies of Alpha Time Master #111 and discuss it with the children.

Where in this picture, do you see Cotton Candy? (e.g., rabbit's tail, flowers)

Which Letter Person is in the picture? (Mr. C)

What is he made of? (Cotton Candy)

Children may choose from the following activities:

Music And Dance

Listening and dancing to Mr. C's music (record #2, side A band #4)

Art

Making Cotton Candy cones by pasting cotton on a paper cone or stick and painting it pink.

Making Cotton Candy Land by building a small town and pasting cotton on the houses, lamps, trees, etc.

Oral Communication

Introducing Mr. C to the other Letter People.

1C₂

PLANNING AND PREPARATION: Huggables, Mr. G and Mr. C; Alpha Time Master #112; crayons, paper, pencils.

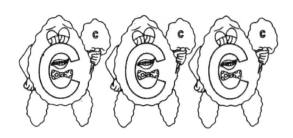

READING COMPREHENSION

Poor Mr. G has been having trouble with the Cotton Candy magic words. The Cotton Candy magic words keep getting stuck in his Gooey Gum and he gets them mixed up.

Call on several children to say the Cotton Candy words the way they are supposed to be said.

Cana, cana, cana, coo, coo, coo.
I'll blow a puff of Cotton Candy at you.
I'll wish for a Cotton Candy (car) and close my eyes.
And look for a Cotton Candy surprise.

When Mr. G says the words they keep getting stuck. He never gets exactly what he asks for. Mr. G is so surprised that he still can't talk about it. He drew the story of what happened to him. We will know what happened as we read the pictures.

Distribute copies of Alpha Time Master #112 and discuss each picture with the children.

Frame #1

Mr. G's first wish was for a pet.

Let's look at the first box. The box is empty. It was made to hold Mr. G's Cotton Candy wish for a pet. Mr. G got the Cotton Candy magic words stuck so he didn't get the pet he wanted.

Look at the picture next to the empty box. It shows what Mr. G got instead of his wish.

What did Mr. G get instead of his Cotton Candy wish? (a lion)

*Making inferences,
Making cause and effect
relationships,
predicting outcomes*

How do you think Mr. G feels about getting a lion?

Why might it be a problem to have a lion as a pet?

What do you think Mr. G will do with the lion?

What do you think Mr. G wished for instead of a lion?

Mr. G will give us a clue.

Solving A Riddle

"As big as a lion it never will be,
But my wish is part of the lion's family.
My wish is small and soft and says meow.
Can you tell me what my wish is now?" (cat)

Have the children draw Mr. G's wish (i.e., a cat) in the empty box along side the lion.

250

Frame #2

Let's look in the box under the lion and see what Mr. G got the next time he made a Cotton Candy wish. (a cow)

How do you think Mr. G feels about getting a cow?

Tell us what you would do with a cow if you suddenly got one.

Why wouldn't some people be able to keep a cow as a pet?

Let's listen to what Mr. G really wished.

> "My wish is white and comes from a cow.
> Can you tell me the name of my wish now?"

What was Mr. G's wish? (milk)

Be Mr. G. Take a puff of Cotton Candy. Say the Cotton Candy magic words so that they all get stuck together and come out all wrong.

Frame #3

Have the children draw Mr. G's wish (i.e., milk) in the box next to the picture of the cow. Follow the same procedure for the alligator and the tree riddles.

> "I don't want an alligator—alas and alack.
> My wish has four feet and a shell on its back!" (turtle)

> "A tree in a flower pot. What a funny sight!
> I guess my wish didn't turn out quite right.
> I wished for something small and sweet to smell.
> What is the name of my wish, can you tell?" (flower)

Frame #4

Mr. G brought all the mixed up wishes and left them with Mr. C.

Mr. C brought the tree to a forest.

He brought the alligator to the zoo.

He brought the cow to a farm.

What did Mr. C have left? (the lion)

Mr. C tried to get the zoo to take the lion but this was not their week for lions. They were all full of lions.

Now Mr. C doesn't know what to do with him!

DICTATING A NEWSPAPER STORY

The editor of the newspaper said that he would give Mr. C space on the front page of the newspaper.

Mr. C can write a story telling all about his lion.

Mr. C needs help in writing the story.

Let's write the story for Mr. C.

Have the children dictate a story about the lion. Encourage them to describe what he looks like and what kind of personality he has. (e.g., He is a friendly lion, a happy lion, a fierce lion.) Have them tell some funny things the lion might do.

251

TYING IT TOGETHER

Using context clues

Give the following clues to the children to help them guess the animals described. They may look at their copies of Alpha Time Master #112 for help.

This animal likes to drink milk. (cat)

This animal gives milk. (cow)

This animal roars. (lion)

This animal says meow. (cat)

This animal says moo. (cow)

This animal makes no sound. (turtle)

This animal has big jaws. (alligator)

This animal lives in the water or on land. (alligator, turtle)

This animal has a shell on its back. (turtle)

ON THEIR OWN

Zoology
Classifying

Art

Crafts

Children may choose from the following activities:

Making a list of animals that live on land and in the water (amphibians) such as a turtle or alligator.

Making a list of animals that belong to the cat family.

Making a list of animals that live on a farm, such as a cow.

Making a list of animals that make good pets.

Drawing or painting pictures of big animals or little animals.

Making animals out of clay.

252

1C₃

PLANNING AND PREPARATION: Huggable, Mr. C; Picture Card 9; Alpha Time Master #113.

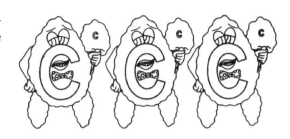

IDENTIFYING THE CAPITAL AND LOWER CASE LETTER C

Pointing To
Mr. C's Letter

Gather the children around Mr. C.

Mr. C is going on a trip, but first he wants to be sure we know his letter.

Show Mr. C his capital letter C.

Where is Mr. C's lower case letter c?

Show it to him.

What kind of line is used to make the C? (curve)

How many children do we need to make the C? (one)

How are the upper and lower case C different? (size)

TALKING ABOUT FEELINGS

Mr. C says that now he must get ready to leave for Cotton Candy Land.

He says that the only place that he can get all the Cotton Candy he wants is in Cotton Candy Land. He says that he will bring Cotton Candy back with him.

The Letter People know that Cotton Candy Land is far away. It is a very long trip. They are afraid that Mr. C won't come back to us.

Ask Mr. C if he will return.

Let the children talk to Mr. C about his trip and about whether or not he will return. NOTE: Children are often anxious about a member of the family leaving on a trip. This is a good time to discuss their feelings.

Mr. C says he has to go to Cotton Candy Land but that he will surely be back. Although he is made of Cotton Candy he is still a Letter Person and belongs here in class.

Tell the Letter People about a time someone you know went on a trip.

How did you feel when he (she) left?

,Was he (she) gone for a long time?

How did you feel when you missed them?

How did you feel when they returned?

Why is it sometimes necessary for people to take trips?

Did you ever have to go away?

How did you feel?

LISTENING TO A STORY

*Dramatizing
Action Words*

*This story can be told in the same manner as "Going on a Bear Hunt."
Gather the children around you. Explain that they are going to do everything that Mr. C does as you tell this story. Hands, arms and feet may be
used to simulate the different motions.*

Hiking

Mr. C started on his trip to Cotton Candy Land last Tuesday morning.

Crawling

Mr. C hiked to the edge of the cabbage fields. There he waited for Casper
Caterpillar to lead him through the cabbages. All the cabbages look
alike to Mr. C, but Casper knows each one of them personally, and so
he could lead Mr. C through the fields. Slowly and carefully, Casper
crawled to the end of the cabbage fields.

Miles and miles of cactus fields were ahead. "I must stop here," said
Casper as he came to the very edge of the cactus fields. "I must not
crawl any further. Cactus needles will stick me.

Camellia Camel will be here soon to take you to Cotton Candy Land.
Oh, I hear Camellia Camel now. Good-bye Mr. C. Have a wonderful trip."

The first part of Mr. C's trip was over and the second half was about to
begin!

Trotting

Clip-clop, clip-clop, clip-clop, here was Camellia Camel to take Mr. C
the rest of the way!

"Hello Mr. C," whispered Camellia. Camellia's eyes were the color of
caramels. Her eyelashes were long and curly. "Coo, Camellia, how pretty you look," said Mr. C.

"Mr. C, I will bend down so that you can climb on my back," said
the camel.

When Mr. C finally got settled on Camellia Camel, he was cozy and
comfortable.

Clip-clop, clip-clop, Camellia Camel's hoofs clicked as she walked along.

Sleeping

Clip-clop, clip-clop. Mr. C fell fast asleep. Can you guess what he dreamt
about?

Time passed. Mr. C slept on and on. Suddenly a soft voice said, "Wake
up! I can take you no further."

Waking

Mr. C woke up with a start. "Where am I?" he called.

Smelling

Mr. C smelled a wonderful smell in the air. Cotton Candy trees lined
the curbs. Even the fluffy clouds in the sky were made of Cotton Candy.
And what Cotton Candy it was! Light and delicate, and thin as cobwebs!
At last he was in Cotton Candy Land! He looked up and saw the Cotton
Candy castle standing high up on the hill.

"You have been sleeping a long time," said Camellia Camel. "If you climb up to the castle, you will get what you have been dreaming about. I cannot climb up that steep cobblestone hill."

Climbing

Leaping

Floating

Talking

Mr. C didn't feel tired any longer. His trip was almost over. He started to climb the steep cobblestone hill. Up, up, up he climbed. What a steep hill! He climbed and climbed some more. A fluffy Cotton Candy cloud floated by and called to Mr. C. "I will take you to the castle. Leap up and we will drift there."

"Thank you," said Mr. C. He climbed up on the cloud and away they floated. They floated and floated, up and up and up.

From the moment Mr. C landed at the Cotton Candy castle, he was very busy. He tried to think of a way of bringing Cotton Candy back to class. He spoke to the Cotton Candy makers for a long time. They talked and talked and talked. They wondered who could carry so much Cotton Candy back.

Then Mr. C called the Cotton Candy clouds. "I have a plan," said Mr. C. "I need your help. I would like to bring Cotton Candy back to class with me. Not everyone who wants Cotton Candy can make this trip. The Cotton Candy makers will gladly make Cotton Candy to send to people who cannot travel here. However, we need a way to deliver it. We need a delivery service that won't get stuck by cactus needles. We need a delivery service that won't get lost in miles and miles of cabbage fields."

"Wait!" called a Cotton Candy cloud. "What you say is true. It is hard for a delivery service to walk *through* the cactus and the cabbages but what about a delivery service that floats *over* them? We clouds will be happy to carry Cotton Candy to other people. Our Cotton Candy clouds will float Cotton Candy to everybody. We will float it to people in the city. We will float it to people in the country. We will float it to parks and circuses and zoos and carnivals. We will float it to the children in the class."

And that's the story of how Mr. C made it possible for all of us to get Cotton Candy without traveling to Cotton Candy Land.

TYING IT TOGETHER

Recalling The Story

While Mr. C was traveling to Cotton Candy Land, he took some pictures with his camera. He enjoys looking at them. He would like to have us look at them too so that we can remember how much fun he had on his trip.

Hold up Picture Card 9 and distribute matching Alpha Time Master #113 and talk about each picture on it.

Mr. C likes to remember all the things that happened on his way to Cotton Candy Land.

He remembers Casper Caterpillar crawling *through* the. . . (cabbage fields).

He remembers Camellia Camel, clippity clopping *through* the. . . (cactus fields).

He remembers floating in the air *on* a Cotton Candy. . . (cloud).

255

Children may mark the upper case C with one color and the lower case c with another.

ON THEIR OWN

Children may choose from the following activities:

Letter Tracing

Using Alpha Time Master #57 to trace the upper and lower case letter C.

Cooking

Using cabbage or carrots in various recipes such as boiled cabbage, coleslaw, carrot curls.

Science

Noting how the texture of a cabbage leaf changes when it is submerged in boiling water; when it is shredded, salted and left to stand for a half hour.

Nature

Collecting cactuses and learning about their care.

Story Telling

Using Mr. C's Picture Card 9 to retell his story.

Sorting & Matching

Including Mr. C's playing cards from Alpha Time Decks 1, 2, and 4 in the activities described in the *Games* section.

11₁ **PLANNING AND PREPARATION:** Hugga-bles, Mr. T, Miss A, Miss I; Record #3; art materials, large sheets of construction paper for each child; Alpha Time Master #114.

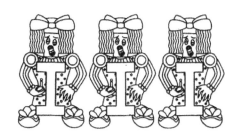

Place Mr. T next to Miss A and have Miss I stand a distance away.

MEETING MISS I

Listening To A Dramatization

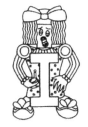

Play Meeting Miss I (record #3, side A, band #3) and then discuss the story with the children.

What is special about Miss I? (She itches.)

How did Miss A feel after Miss I arrived? (upset)

About what did Miss A complain? (Miss I and the others did not play with her.)

What did Mr. T say about the way Miss A felt? (She was jealous.)

What made Miss A jealous? (The Letter People were paying more attention to Miss I than to her.)

Tell us about a time you were jealous of someone new. (e.g., a new baby, a new member of the class)

What did Mr. T tell Miss A to do? (make friends with Miss I; get to know her; play with her)

Show us how you think Miss I wiggle hops.

Gather the children around Miss I.

How do Miss I's hands look? (e.g., itchy, wiggly)

Why do you think her fingers look that way?

Why do you think she has such a funny expression on her face? (She is itchy.)

Talking About "Itching"

Tell us about a time when you had an itch. What made you itch? (e.g., mosquito bites, hives, chicken pox) How did the itch make you feel?

Show us how your itch made you wiggle. Did you like your itch?

Tell us about any medicine that you put on yourself when you had an itch. (e.g., calamine lotion, witch hazel, ointment, powder)

IDENTIFYING THE UPPER AND LOWER CASE LETTER I

Analyzing The Letter I

Miss I says her Itch always makes her wiggle, but that her capital letter is very straight. Find Miss I's capital letter I.

How many straight lines does the capital I have? (three)

Help the children form the capital I with their bodies. Then have them find the lower case i.

Until now all the capital and lower case letters have had either straight or curved lines. What does the lower case i have over the straight line? (a dot)

TYING IT TOGETHER

Distribute copies of Alpha Time Master #114 and discuss the picture with the children.

Who is in this picture? (Miss I, Mr. T, Miss A)

What do you think Miss A is thinking?

What do you think Mr. T is thinking?

What do you think Miss I is thinking?

Why is Miss I always wiggling? (She has an Itch.)

ON THEIR OWN

Children may choose from the following activities:

Dramatic Play	Dramatizing the arrival of Miss I.
Listening	Listening to Meeting Miss I (record #3).
Letter Tracing	Using Alpha Time Master #63 to trace the upper and lower case I.
Oral Communication	Introducing Miss I to the other Letter People and telling about each one.
Science	Experimenting, comparing and describing different kinds of mixtures such as ointments, powders, liquids, creams and soaps. Note special qualities such as wet, dry, sticky, smooth, cool, warm, soft and hard.
Matching & Sorting	Including Miss I's playing cards from Alpha Time Decks 1, 2, and 4 in any of the games in the *Games* section.
Art	Creating designs using only straight lines and dots.

11₂ PLANNING AND PREPARATION: Huggable, Miss I; Record #2 with Miss I's song; Alpha Time Masters #115 and #116.

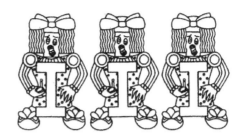

REMEMBERING MISS I

*Listening To
Miss I's Song*

Gather the children around you to listen to Miss I's song (record #2, side A, band #5).

Miss I had so much fun meeting us that she has been wiggling and hopping and waiting for us to come back to school to see her again. While she wiggled and hopped, she prepared a song for us. Let's listen to it.

Discuss Miss I's song with the children. Play the song a second time and encourage them to sing and dance along with it.

Does Miss I's music make you feel itchy? Show us how you can wiggle hop to Miss I's music.

What does Miss I tell us about herself?

INTRODUCING MISS I'S ITCH

Tell the children that sometimes Miss I's Itch makes other people itch too. Pretend to scratch as you mention each itchy place. Have the children do the same.

I feel an Itch on top of my head! Now there is an Itch on the top of your head. Now there's an Itch on top of our toes. Let's catch it. Here comes another Itch! It's catching our fingers. Let's see itchy fingers. Now it is leaving our fingers and running down to our knees. Let's see itchy knees.

Pretend to itch all over.

All this itching never seems to stop. Now we're doing a wiggle hop.

Tell the children that Miss I says it is her Itch that is making them feel so itchy. Then read Miss I's rhyme.

> My Itch is always itching me.
> I never know where it will be.
> I never know what it will do.
> It may itch me, it may itch you.
> First we'll itch down — then up to the top.
> We'll itch and itch and never stop!
> Now the Itch will take a ride.
> Let's make it slide from side to side.
> Then we'll itch around and around,
> And hide under a desk so we won't be found.

*Demonstrating Up,
Down, Around*

Have the class pretend to be Miss I. Reread the poem slowly, so the children may follow the directions in the rhyme.

Make sure the children understand what movements are meant by the terms "up and down," "side to side," "around and around."

ISOLATING THE SHORT VOWEL SOUND FOR I

Tell the children the following story. Emphasize the short vowel sound " ĭ" each time it occurs.

Last night Miss I went to sleep. Her Itch went to sleep too. That's when things started to happen!

Mr. B woke up because all of his buttons started jiggling just as though they were itching.

Mr. B looked for the Itch, however, he could not find it.

He looked behind each and every button, but no Itch!

Suddenly a teeny weeny little voice said, "Here I am."
"Who are you?" asked Mr. B.

The teeny weeny little voice said, "I'm the ĭ from Itch. When Miss I and her Itch went to sleep, I ran away! I wanted to see if I could make things Itch all by myself. You know an ĭ is the itchiest part of any Itch."

Mr. B tried to catch the ĭ, but it was so teeny weeny that it slid right out of his hand and ran off to do some more itching.

Mr. B telephoned some of the other Letter People to let them know that the ĭ had run away from the Itch. He called Mr. L and told him that the little ĭ was trying to prove that it was the itchiest part of the Itch.

"Leaping lollies! Now I understand why all my lollies are laughing and leaping around the room," said Mr. L. "Now I know it must be that teeny weeny ĭ!"

Demonstrating Action Words

Have the children demonstrate how lollies laugh and leap.

When Mr. B called Mr. D, Mr. D was trying to decorate a doughnut. He could not get one sprinkle on the doughnut. That doughnut would not stand still for a minute.

Mr. D scolded the doughnut, but the doughnut said, "I can't seem to stop! The ĭ is making me wiggle hop."

"Oh no," said Mr. D, "I don't want any itchy doughnuts!"

Have the children show Miss I how itchy doughnuts would look.

Then the same thing started happening to Mr. G, who was wrapping Gooey Gum—and to Mr. C, who was counting his Cotton Candy. The Gooey Gum and the Cotton Candy started wiggle-hopping around.

How would Gooey Gum look when it is wiggle-hopping?

How would Cotton Candy look?

Have the children dramatize this part of the story. Have them suggest other Letter People the ĭ might visit. (e.g., Mr. H with itchy hair, Mr. Z with itchy zippers)

The ĭ made itching trouble all night long. The next morning Miss I's telephone started to ring and ring.

Miss I couldn't believe what she heard! She decided to find the ĭ and bring it back.

When Miss I found the ĭ, it was happy. It said, "I would rather make Miss I Itch than anyone else in the whole world!"

Then the ĭ jumped on Miss I's shoulder. "I feel itchy," said Miss I. "I'm doing a wiggle hop!" At last Miss I was happy and so were the other Letter People.

Discuss the story with the children.

What happened to Mr. D when he tried to decorate the doughnut? (It wouldn't stand still.)

What other Letter People did the ĭ get into trouble? (Mr. L, Mr. C, Mr. G)

Show us what makes Miss I happy. (wiggle hopping)

Why were the other Letter People happy that the ĭ went back to Miss I? (They didn't want to itch.)

Singing A Song
Naming Body Parts

Have the children sing the following words to the tune of "Old Mac Donald."

> Miss I has an Itch,
> ĭ, ĭ, ĭ, ĭ, Itch.
> She has an Itch upon her foot,
> ĭ, ĭ, ĭ, ĭ, Itch.
> With an Itch, Itch here,
> And an Itch, Itch there. . . etc.

Repeat the song, substituting other body parts for foot (e.g., toes, knee, arm, hand, back).

TYING IT TOGETHER

Frame #1

Miss I is very happy that her ĭ has come back to her Itch. She has drawn a picture-story that tells what happened after the ĭ went away from her.

Give each child a copy of Alpha Time Master #115. Discuss the pictures with the children. Encourage them to retell the part of the story that goes with each picture. Use questions similar to the following to help the children remember the story:

Who is in the picture? (Mr. B and Mr. L)

Why is Mr. B unhappy? (His buttons are itching.)

Why did he call Mr. L? (to warn him about the ĭ)

Frame #2

Which Letter Boys are here? (Mr. D, Mr. C)

How do they look? (upset)

Why are they upset? (The ĭ from Itch went into the doughnuts and cotton candy.)

What do you think they are saying?

Frame #3

Where is the ĭ from Itch in this picture? (back with Miss I)

Why is Miss I smiling? (She likes the ĭ and the Itch.)

Why do the Letter Boys looks so happy? (They got rid of the ĭ.)

NOTE: Alpha Time Master #116 is a letter to parents explaining the progress the children have made thus far with ALPHA TIME. This letter may be sent home with the children at this time.

ON THEIR OWN

Children may choose from the following activities:

Music And Dance   Playing Miss I's song (record #2) and doing the wiggle hop.

Art   Painting a picture of itching doughnuts, gooey gum, lollipops and cotton candy.

Crafts   Making an "Itch" out of a variety of materials.

Dramatic Play   Enacting the story of Miss I's ĭ, possibly with stick puppets.

Story Telling   Retelling the story of Miss I's ĭ to some of the other Letter People. If a tape recorder is available the story may be recorded and shared later.

2L₁

PLANNING AND PREPARATION: Huggable, Mr. L; a bag for Mr. L; Mr. L's Picture Squares; Alpha Time Master #117; Record #2; a cut-out of a lollipop; magazines, a variety of art materials.

Before the lesson begins, Mr. L's music (record #2, side A, band #1) may be played to set the mood.

MR. L GETS HIS SOUND FROM LEMON LOLLIPOPS

Gather the children around you and Mr. L and tell them that the Lolly Lane Lookers have been called to the job once again.

Mr. L asked the Lolly Lane Lookers to look for something just for him. Mr. L wants to have a sound as the other Letter People do.

The Lolly Lane Lookers began looking up and down Lolly Lane to find a sound for Mr. L.

Mr. L has looked up and down Lolly Lane. And then he found a sound right under his nose!

What can it be?

Lead the children to the conclusion that the only thing under Mr. L's nose is a Lemon Lollipop! Have them discover that Mr. L will get his sound from his Lemon Lollipops.

IDENTIFYING WORDS WITH L IN THE INITIAL POSITION

Mr. L loves his Lemon Lollipops. He likes the idea of getting his sound from his Lemon Lollipops.

He is trying to think of words that start with his Lemon Lollipops sound.

Try to tell Mr. L some words that start the same way as Lemon Lollipops.

Give the children a chance to mention any words that start with "L."

The Lolly Lane Lookers say that as they were looking up and down Lolly Lane they saw many things that start the same way as Mr. L's Lemon Lollipops. They have a picture of Lolly Lane for us.

Give each child a copy of Alpha Time Master #117 and have them mark each picture as it is discussed.

Mr. L is going to tell us some riddles. We will look at this picture of Lolly Lane for the answer to each of his riddles.

The answers to his riddles will start with the same sound as his Lemon Lollipops. The answers will be somewhere on Lolly Lane.

Mr. L is ready with the first riddle. Remember—we have to find something on Lolly Lane that starts with his Lemon Lollipops sound!

Identifying Words
Through
Context Clues

Here is the first riddle:

You'll usually find me in a zoo.
I hope my roar doesn't frighten you!
Say "Lemon Lollipops" before you look for me.
Somewhere on Lolly Lane I will be. (lion)

Here is the second riddle:

The Lolly Lane Lookers climbed up and down me
When they looked at the nest up in the tree!
Say "Lemon Lollipops" before you look for me.
Somewhere on Lolly Lane—I will be! (ladder)

Continue with the following riddles adding the refrain for each.

I grow on the branches of a tree.
Trees don't give shade if they don't have me! (leaves)

For an address and a stamp I have space.
The mailbox is my special place! (letter)

I color lips a pretty pink.
Lots of ladies use me, I think. (lipstick)

Naming Mr. L's
Picture Squares

Mr. L is happy with all the things you found that start with his Lemon Lollipops sound.

Show the children Mr. L's Picture Squares (i.e., lion, ladder, lamp, lock, locomotive).

Mr. L has been looking on Lolly Lane, too! He has found some pictures. He wants us to tell him the names of the things that he has found.

He wants us to prove each thing to him so he can be sure that it starts with his Lemon Lollipops sound.

Have the children name and prove each of Mr. L's pictures and put them in a bag for Mr. L. (The "Prove It" song, record #5, side A, band #3 may be used.)

Mr. L wants us to fill his bag for him. He can't wait to have a bagful of things.

Making Things For
Mr. L's Bag

Let's find or make things for Mr. L's bag.

Have the children go to different parts of the room where various art materials have been put out for them. Remind them to prove each thing they make for Mr. L before putting it into his bag.

Explain the "Lollipop Leaders" game to the children: Lollipop Leaders can only do things that are Mr. L "doing words."

Dramatizing Mr. L's
Doing Words

First—Mr. L will help us discover some of his "doing words."

Give the children a chance to mention any Mr. L "doing words" they can think of.

Leaping

Mr. L says that before his lollies were lollipops, they used to *leap* out of his house.

Leap starts with Mr. L's Lemon Lollipops sound.

Leap is a Mr. L "doing word."

Show Mr. L how you *leap*.

Another Mr. L "doing word" tells what the Lolly Lane Lookers spend their time doing.

Looking

What do the Lolly Lane Lookers do? (look)

Look starts with Mr. L's sound.

Look is a Mr. L "doing word."

Laughing

What do people do when they hear a very funny joke? (laugh)

Laugh starts the same way as Lemon Lollipops.

Laugh is a Mr. L "doing word."

Show Mr. L how you *laugh*.

Locking

When you leave your house you use a key. Why do you use the key? (to *lock* the door)

Lock starts with the Lemon Lollipops sound.

Lock is a Mr. L "doing word."

Follow the procedure outlined above for other Mr. L "doing words" (e.g., lift, listen, lick, label, lace, lean, load). Then explain the rest of the game to the children as follows:

Now that we know some Mr. L "doing words" we are ready for the rest of the game.

Let us pick a Lollipop Leader. Our Lollipop Leader will wear this Lollipop. *(Show the children the cut-out of the lollipop.)*

The Lollipop Leader will tell us which Mr. L "doing word" we should do.

Then we will all show Mr. L how we do that "doing word."

TYING IT TOGETHER

Auditory Discrimination

Play Mr. L's song and have the children listen for words that begin with his Lemon Lollipops sound. (e.g., lovely, large, little, lots)

ON THEIR OWN

Children may choose from the following activities:

Playing A Game

Playing any of the games in the *Games* section involving Mr. L's Picture Squares.

Making up riddles for other "doing words."

Using Verbs

Using Alpha Time Master #117 to point out what the people and things are doing. (i.e., ladder is leaning, lady is painting her lips, leaves are hanging, lion is lying on the ground and licking lollipops)

Optional

Do TeamMate School Team Book page 43 and assign Home Team page 43 for homework.

2L 2

PLANNING AND PREPARATION: Huggables, Mr. L and Mr. F; Alpha Time Master #118; Mr. L's Bag; Mr. L's Picture Squares; construction paper cut into 4" long strips, crayons, magazines, paste and scissors.

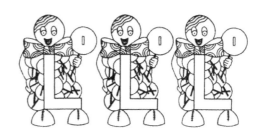

USING WORDS WITH L IN THE INITIAL POSITION IN WORDS

Mr. L loses everything.

Mr. L couldn't understand why he kept on losing things until the Letter People said to him, "Mr. L, we understand why your things are always getting lost.

"Lost is one of your words. *Lost* begins with your Lemon Lollipop sound."

Mr. L said, "Now I understand! Who found all the things that I lost?"

The Letter People all laughed. They said, "Mr. L, if you *lost* things that start with your sound, who do you *think* found the things you lost?"

Who is good at *finding* things?

Lead the children to the conclusion that Mr. F is good at finding things. You can point to Mr. F as a clue if the children have trouble remembering.

Mr. L and Mr. F want to play the "Lost and Found" game.

Mr. F will tell us about some things he found in Mr. L's Bag. He will give a clue for each thing he finds.

If Mr. L can guess what he lost, Mr. F will return it to Mr. L's bag.

(Johnny), you help Mr. L. (Mary), you help Mr. F.

Explain that as Mr. F takes something out of Mr. L's bag, he will give a clue. e.g. He might say "I found something that Mr. L lost. The thing that I found lives in a zoo and roars." Then the child helping Mr. L might say "Did you find the lion I lost?" The game continues as different children take turns helping Mr. F and Mr. L.

TALKING ABOUT WORDS WITH OPPOSITE MEANINGS

Mr. L has been thinking and thinking about the *lost* and *found*.

Mr. S told him about words that mean the same thing as other words. For example *sad* and *unhappy* mean the same thing.

What about the words *lost* and *found?*

Do they mean the same thing? (no)

When you lose something, is it the same as finding something? (no)

267

The words *lost* and *found* mean very different things.

We say that these two words are *opposites.*

Mr. L can think of many of his words that have opposites.

He wants us to help him find opposites for these words.

Identifying Opposites For Mr. L's Words

First, Mr. L says that in the morning when the sun is out it is very *light* outside.

Light is one of Mr. L's words.

Light has an opposite.

Listen to Mr. L's clue and see if you can figure out the opposite of *light.*

Late at night the sun is not out.
It is not light outside.
It is very. . . (dark).

Dark is the opposite of *light.*

Another Mr. L word that has an opposite is the word *laugh.*

Mr. L says that sometimes he watches TV programs. They are so funny that he laughs and laughs.

Sometimes a program is so sad that it makes Mr. L. . . (cry).

Cry is the opposite of *laugh.*

Another Mr. L word that has an opposite is *left.*

Sometimes when someone drives a car he makes a *left* turn.

Sometimes instead of making a *left* turn, he makes a. . . *(right)* turn.

Right is the opposite of *left.*

Another Mr. L word that has an opposite is the word *long.*

Mr. L does not put the same size sticks on all his lollipops.

Some lollipops have very, very long sticks.

Some lollipops do not have long sticks.

They have very very. . . (short) sticks.

Short is the opposite of *long.*

Sometimes mother lets you stay up very late.

Late is a Mr. L word that has an opposite.

Sometimes mother says you had a very busy day. She does not want you to go to bed late. She says that she wants you to go to bed. . . (early).

Early is the opposite of *late.*

Another Mr. L word that has an opposite is the word *little.*

Children's chairs are little.
The teacher's chair is not little.
The teacher's chair is. . . (big).

Big is the opposite of *little.*

Playing A Game

Tell the children how they may play the "opposite" word game. Tell them that you will whisper a word in a child's ear. The child will pantomime the word (e.g., cry). The class will then find a Mr. L word that is the opposite of the word being pantomimed (i.e. laugh). Continue the game until all the of "opposite" words previously mentioned have been used.

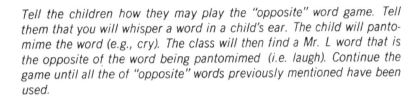

Show the children the strips of construction paper you have prepared.

Mr. L says that each of these strips of paper can make a loop.
What is a loop?

How can we make this strip of paper into a loop?

Let the children decide that they can make a loop by attaching the ends of each strip of paper.

Mr. L has lots and lots of strips. He would like us to change the strips into lots and lots of loops.

Mr. L wants very special loops. He wants us to paste a picture of something that starts with the same sound as his Lemon Lollipops on to each loop we make.

We'll save all our loops because Mr. L would like to play a game with them.

Making A
Loop Chain

Distribute the strips. Each child may find or draw a picture for his loop. If he has trouble thinking of things to draw, he may refer to Mr. L's bag for suggestions.

NOTE: After all the loops have been completed, have some children tell Mr. L the names of the pictures they put on his loops. Tell them that Mr. L wants to make sure that only loops that have pictures starting with his Lemon Lollipops sound will go into his Loop chain.

Help the children connect the loops to make a long, long, chain for Mr. L. Additional strips of paper may be used to make the connecting links.

TYING IT TOGETHER

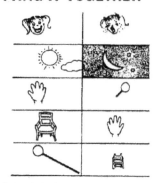

Distribute copies of Alpha Time Master #118. Discuss the pictures with the children. Have them select the pictures that are opposites of each other. Those who wish may connect the opposite pictures with crayon lines. (i.e., laugh—cry; day—night; left hand—right hand; short lollipop stick—long lollipop stick; big chair—little chair)

ON THEIR OWN

Children may choose from the following activities:

Opposite Words

Thinking of other words that have opposite meanings. These words may be dictated and written on a long list.

Matching

Using Mr. L's Picture Squares in any of the games in the *Games* section.

Motor Coordination

Using Mr. L's puzzle.

2L₃

PLANNING AND PREPARATION: Huggables, Mr. L, Mr. D, Miss I, Miss E; toy telephone, if available; Alpha Time Master #119; paper for dictation, drawing paper; art materials.

TALKING ABOUT FEELINGS

Discussion: Love Means Different Things To Different People

Gather the children around Mr. L.

Everytime Mr. L closed his eyes last night he thought of the same word. It is one of his words. It starts the same way as Lemon Lollipops.

The word that Mr. L kept thinking of is *love*.

"What does that mean?" thought Mr. L. Mr. L had never really thought about the meaning of *love*. Lickety split! Mr. L leaped out of bed. He ran to the telephone. He needed help. He wasn't sure. What did *love* mean?

Mr. L called Mr. D. Mr. D couldn't imagine who was calling so late at night! Mr. D said, "Mr. L, you must have lost your lollies. This had better be important!"

"Oh, it is very important" said Mr. L. "I have to know what *love* means. What does *love* mean to you?"

"Mr. L," said Mr. D, "I don't know what *love* means. I've never thought about it. Mr. D started to think. "What does love mean?" Mr. D thought, "I care about each of my Delicious Doughnuts. Is that love?"

Let the children discuss the idea of concern for another person. Let them decide whether or not this is part of loving someone.

What does it mean when someone cares about what you do and where you go?

Who cares about you?

Why do you care about someone?

Tell Mr. D how caring about someone is a part of love.

Continue with the next part of the story:

Mr. L thought and thought some more. He decided that he would call up one of the Letter Girls and ask her what *love* means.

Mr. L called Miss I. When Miss I answered the telephone so late at night, guess what she told Mr. L? That's right! She told him he'd lost his lollies to be calling in the middle of the night. Mr. L said "Miss I, I am trying to find out what love means. Please tell me what love means to you."

Miss I thought and thought. Then she said, "I was very upset when my ĭ left me. I wanted my ĭ to be with me. I am happiest when I am with my Itch. Is this love?"

Let the children discuss "wanting to be with someone" as part of love.

271

With whom do you like to be?

What makes you want to be with certain people?

What does it mean when you want to be with someone most of the time?

Tell Miss I how wanting to be with someone is a part of love.

Continue the story:

Mr. L was beginning to understand what love means. He wanted to telephone one more Letter Person. Mr. L called Miss E.

Mr. L told Miss E that everyone said that love means something else. Mr. D said that caring about what someone does is part of love. Miss I said that wanting to be with someone is part of love.

Miss E said that she cares about the Letter People. She wants to be with them as much as possible. Miss E agreed that this was all part of love. Miss E said there is something else. Miss E said that she likes to do things for the Letter People. She doesn't want to see them unhappy. She will do what she can to make them happy.

Miss E would like to know if this is a part of love.

What do you think?

Have the children discuss doing things for others as a part of love.

Who does things for you?

What are some things they do?

Why do they do things for you?

For whom do you do things?

Why do you want to do things for someone?

Tell the Letter People how wanting to do things for someone is a part of love.

Tell the children the conclusion of the story:

Mr. L is beginning to understand.

Love is something we feel. Everyone can feel love in a different way.

The Letter People told Mr. L some of the ways they feel.

Let's tell him some of the ways we feel.

Expressing Feelings About Love

Questions such as the following will stimulate a discussion of the children's feelings and attitudes about love:

Whom do you love?

How do you know that you love that person?

Who loves you?

How do you know that they love you?

Do we always love the people who love us?

Do all of us love the same people?

What makes you love certain people in school?

How do you feel inside when you see or think about a person you love?

Why do people want to be loved?

How would you feel if you had no one to love?

How would you feel if no one loved you?

Mr. L has been listening to all the things we have said about love.

He thought about what Mr. D said. Mr. D knows that he cares about his Delicious Doughnuts. He knows that he loves them.

Has Mr. D ever told his Doughnuts that he loves them?

Mr. D wants to know if he has to tell his Delicious Doughnuts that he loves them.

What can Mr. D do to make sure his doughnuts know he loves them?

How can we make sure that someone we love will know how we feel?

Have the children discuss the different ways of telling someone how they feel.

Explain to the children the importance of being able to express their feelings.

People we love like to know how we feel about them.

Words are a wonderful way for people to know how we feel about them. The words we use can often tell people how we feel about them.

What are the other ways we can tell people we love them?

Let's tell other children in the class how we feel about them.

TYING IT TOGETHER

Give each child a copy of Alpha Time Master #119. Help the children think of how each picture shows an aspect of love.

Look at the first picture.

Who is in this picture? (mother and child)

What are they doing? (cleaning the house)

How is the child showing that he loves his mother?

273

Look at the next picture.

What are the children doing? (holding hands

Why do you think they are holding hands? (They like to be with each other.)

Have you ever walked along hand-in-hand with anyone? How does it feel?

What do you see in the last picture? (father fixing child's doll)

Why does the father care if the child's doll is broken?

ON THEIR OWN

Children may choose from the following activities:

Art

Drawing pictures that express feelings about someone or something.

Dictation

Dictating letters that tell people they are loved.

Exploring Emotions

Hearing or learning poems about love.

Talking about other feelings such as fear, sadness, happiness and hate.

2L₄

TEACHER OBJECTIVES:

To reinforce the characteristic and sound of
Mr. L.

To reinforce the concept of identifying one-
self by name, address and telephone number.

PERFORMANCE OBJECTIVES:

The child will say words with the *l* in the
initial position.

The child will recite his name, address, and
telephone number.

The child will describe objects by color.

DEVELOPMENT

Mr. L has been busy making lemon lollipops.
He almost forgot to make booklets for us.
He worked all night to finish the Mr. L "All About Us" booklets.
Let's see what they look like.

Distribute the Mr. L "All About Us" booklets.

Mr. L wants us to show him the words that say "All About Us."
Let's find them at the top and say them for Mr. L.
Which Letter Person's picture is on the booklet? (Mr. L)
Whose picture is next to Mr. L? (his friend's)
Find the sentence at the bottom of the booklet.
It says, "Mr. L has a friend."

What is special about Mr. L? (his lemon lollipops)
Look at the picture of Mr. L's friend.
What part of a lollipop is his friend holding in each hand? (a stick)
What part of the lollipop is missing? (the part you eat)
Mr. L would like us each to be a lollipop maker.
Let's draw a lemon lollipop on each stick his friend is holding.

Give the children the opportunity to draw the candy part of the
lollipops.
Suggest they finish the picture to look like themselves or anyone
else they wish.

Ask the children to open their booklets.
Have them touch the first sentence on the left-hand side.
What picture did Mr. L put in the first sentence? (lemon lollipops)

Read aloud, "Mr. L likes lemon lollipops."
Let them pretend to reread the sentence with you.

Mr. L is not going to use this whole page to tell us about himself.
He told us one thing.
What did he tell us? (He likes lemon lollipops.)
Now he wants us to tell him the kind of lollipops we like.
Look at the next sentence.
What pictures did Mr. L put in the sentence? (pictures of three
lollipops)
Tell Mr. L the color of each lollipop. (orange, black, green)
Mr. L wants us to put a circle around the lollipop we like best.

Give the children the opportunity to do this.

Have each of them write his or her name on the dotted line.

Select and read several booklets aloud. (*e.g.*, Patsy likes a black lollipop.)

Some children may enjoy telling Mr. L the color of the lollipop they like.

Others may want to pretend to read their sentence to Mr. L.

Draw the children's attention to the right-hand page.

Explain that one day Mr. L got lost.

He could not find his way home.

He was worried.

He saw a policewoman.

The policewoman said she could help him if he could tell her three things.

First he had to tell the policewoman his name.

He had to tell her his address.

He had to tell the policewoman his telephone number.

Let's listen to what he told her.

Read the sentences aloud.

What three things did Mr. L tell the policewoman? (name, address, telephone number)

Mr. L wants us to make believe we are lost.

He wants each of us to tell a policeman our name, address and telephone number.

Let's turn to the back of the booklet and do this.

Have the children turn to the back of the booklet.

Read aloud, "Let's talk about being lost."

Have each child write his or her name on the first dotted line.

Select and read several booklets. (*e.g.*, Phyllis tells a policeman)

What three things will Phyllis tell the policeman? (name, address, telephone number)

Help each child complete his or her booklet.

The children can complete number one by writing their name on the dotted line provided.

In order to complete numbers two and three, have the children dictate their addresses and telephone numbers.

When the booklets are completed, encourage the children to tell Mr. L the three things they would tell a policeperson if they got lost.

Suggest that the children take their booklets home to share with other members of the family.

2D₁

PLANNING AND PREPARATION: Huggable, Mr. D; Record #2; a bag for Mr. D; Mr. D's Picture Squares; magazines, art materials; Alpha Time Master #120.

DISCOVERING HOW MR. D GETS HIS SOUND

Gather the children around you and Mr. D.

The doughnut dentist said to Mr. D, "I will not be your doughnut dentist anymore."

Mr. D begged the Doughnut Dentist to tell him what was wrong.

Finally he told Mr. D what was bothering him. Days and days had passed and not one doughnut had come to see the Doughnut Dentist. "There's no reason for me to stay here," said the Doughnut Dentist.

Discovering That Mr. D Will Get His Sound From Delicious Doughnuts

Mr. D was sure that there was some mistake. He and the Doughnut Dentist looked everywhere for the doughnuts. Finally, they found all of them stuffed into one room. Mr. D and the Doughnut Dentist could hardly get inside. It was noisy. It was sticky. It was doughnutty!

Mr. D asked the doughnuts what was going on. It took a long time before they would tell him. At last they said, "Mr. D we have been trying for days and days to find a special sound for you. We just can't find anything that's good enough."

Mr. D smiled. He said, "You are the dizziest doughnuts. Just think about what I love best, that's where I should get my sound." The doughnuts were all mixed up. They didn't know what Mr. D meant. Mr. D pointed at the doughnuts and said,

"Delicious Doughnuts; Delicious Doughnuts
Just look around,
Delicious Doughnuts; Delicious Doughnuts,
That's what will give me my sound."

The Delicious Doughnuts were so happy they danced. Mr. D was so happy he danced.

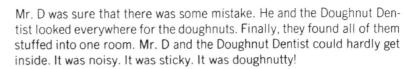

Play Mr. D's song (record #2, side A, band #2) and let the children be dancing doughnuts.

Let the children tell Mr. D how happy they are that he is getting his sound from Delicious Doughnuts.

IDENTIFYING WORDS WITH D IN THE INITIAL POSITION IN WORDS

Naming Mr. D's Pictures

Now the Delicious Doughnuts want to show us some of the things they found for Mr. D's bag.

Have the children name and prove each of Mr. D's Picture Squares (i.e., doll, dog, doctor, dinosaur, desk).

The Delicious Doughnuts think that Mr. D should have more things for his bag. Mr. D thought of some very special things that he would like to have in his bag.

He will give us a clue and we will try to guess what each of those things is.

*Identifying Words
Through
Context Clues*

Mr. D is thinking of something that says *quack, quack.*

The word starts with his Delicious Doughnuts sound.

It rhymes with the word *truck*. Mr. D is thinking about a. . . (duck:).

Prove to Mr. D that *duck* may go into his bag.

Mr. D is thinking of something that is money and is printed on paper.

It starts with his Delicious Doughnuts sound. It rhymes with the word *collar*.

Mr. D is thinking about a. . . (dollar).

Prove to Mr. D that *dollar* may go into his bag.

Mr. D is thinking of something that girls wear.

It starts with his Delicious Doughnuts sound. It rhymes with the word *guess*.

Mr. D is thinking about a. . . (dress).

Prove to Mr. D that *dress* may go in his bag.

Mr. D is thinking of something that makes a sound when you beat it with sticks.

It starts with his Delicious Doughnuts sound. It rhymes with the word *gum*.

Mr. D is thinking about a. . . (drum).

Prove to Mr. D that *drum* may go into his bag.

Mr. D is thinking of something that opens and closes.

It starts with his Delicious Doughnuts sound. It rhymes with the word *store*.

Mr. D is thinking about a. . . (door).

Prove to Mr. D that *door* may go in his bag.

*Making Things For
Mr. D's Bag*

We can show Mr. D some other things we know that start the same way as Delicious Doughnuts.

Let's find and make things to put into Mr. D's bag.

Make sure that you prove everything to him.

Have the children find and make things for Mr. D's bag, using the art materials previously prepared for them.

TYING IT TOGETHER

Distribute Alpha Time Master #120.

Mr. D has a surprise for us.

Mr. D loves *dots*.

Why do you think that Mr. D loves dots?(*Dots* starts with his Delicious Doughnuts sound.)

Mr. D has put some dots on this paper. These dots are very special dots. If we connect them we will find a picture of something Mr. D loves.

After you have connected the dots see if you can decide why Mr. D drew these dots.

Each dot wants to catch the dot next to it.

Demonstrate using your copy of the Alpha Time Master.

When all the dots have caught each other we will have a picture (a doughnut)

What are some of the pictures around Mr. D's Delicious Doughnuts? (doll, dog, doctor, dinosaur)

Why do you think these pictures are around the Declicious Doughnut? (They start with the Delicious Doughnut sound.)

Let's make the doughnut touch some of these pictures.

ON THEIR OWN

Children may choose from the following activities:

Motor Coordination

Using Mr. D's puzzle.

Sorting And Matching

Using the Picture Squares and Mr. D's playing cards in any of the activities listed in the *Games* section.

Auditory Discrimination

Listening for words that begin with Mr. D's sound on Mr. D's music (record #2).

Listening to the recording of A Dozen Delicious Doughnuts (record #4) and remembering words that begin with Mr. D's sound.

2D₂

PLANNING AND PREPARATION: Huggable, Mr. D; Mr. D's bag; magazines, paper, scissors, crayons, paste; Alpha Time Master #121.

TALKING ABOUT "DOING WORDS"

Mr. D is proud of his sound because he loves his Delicious Doughnuts.

Mr. D likes to hear people say "Delicious Doughnuts."

Mr. D likes to play games with his Delicious Doughnuts.

One game he plays is called "Do As D Does."

Mr. D thinks of one of his "doing words." He does what that "doing word" tells him to do. Then we may do as D does.

It takes those doughnuts so long to do anything. Some of them have to fix their sprinkles. Some of them keep bothering the Doughnut Dentist.

Mr. D says that his doughnuts dilly dally.

When Mr. D wants to play "Do As D Does" he says, "Don't dilly dally. Do As D Does."

Let us each be a doughnut and play this game with Mr. D.

*Following Directions
By Playing
A Game*

Explain to the children how they will play the game:

First, we will guess what some of Mr. D's "doing words" are.

We will not dilly dally, we will show Mr. D what those "doing words" mean.

Mr. D says that when he hears music his feet want to. . . *(dance).*

Don't dilly dally! Do As D Does, *dance!*

Mr. D loves how all of us dance.

Mr. D is ready to do another "Do As D Does."

Mr. D says, "I have a shovel and I love to. . . *(dig).*

Don't dilly dally! Do As D Does, *dig!*

Mr. D loves the way we all dig.

He is ready to do another "Do As D Does."

Mr. D says that sometimes he dips a doughnut in chocolate and then he dips it in sprinkles.

Mr. D says, "Let's all dip ourselves in doughnut decorations.

278

"Don't dilly dally! Do As D Does, *dip!*"

Mr. D thinks we did a good job. We really know how to dip ourselves.

Mr. D says that when he cleans his house he takes a cloth and he. . . *(dusts).*

Don't dilly dally! Do As D Does, *dust!*

Now Mr. D says that he has crayons and paper and he is ready to. . . *(draw).*

Don't dilly dally! Do As D Does, *draw!*

Mr. D thinks that we made delightful drawings.

Mr. D say that if we vanish we. . . *(disappear).*

Don't dilly dally! Do As D Does, *disappear!*

When the game is played again, different Mr. D "doing words" may be used (e.g., dash, dribble, dial, dream, decorate, duck and dunk)

TYING IT TOGETHER

Distribute Alpha Time Master #121.

The children may mark the picture that shows Mr. D dancing; drawing; digging, etc.

What are some things Mr. D is doing? (dusting, digging, dancing, drawing)

ON THEIR OWN

Children may choose from the following activities:

Motor Activities

Dancing to Mr. D's music.

Dusting the furniture.

Crafts

Drawing a picture of Mr. D.

Dying material with vegetable dyes.

Identifying Verbs

Looking at the filmstrip, *A Dozen Delicious Doughnuts* and telling what people (or doughnuts) are *doing* in each frame.

2D₃

TALKING ABOUT MAKING DECISIONS

Mr. L slept in Mr. D's house. Suddenly he woke up. He heard a noise. He heard Mr. D saying, "Decisions, decisions, decisions. I don't like to make decisions."

Mr. L leaped out of bed. He woke Mr. D. Then he asked, "Mr. D, what is a decision?" Mr. D thought and then said, "A decision is making up your mind about something. It is hard to make up my mind. It is hard to make decisions."

"Well," said Mr. L, "Tell us the problem. We'll try to help you make a decision."

Let's listen to the first problem.

Sharing Feelings

Mr. D said, "I have only one doughnut. Mr. M and Mr. T both want to have it. How can I decide who should have it?"

Mr. L said, "Before you make a decision Mr. D, you must think of what you can do."

What are some things Mr. D can think about before he makes a decision about whom to give the doughnut?

Lead the children to the realization that there are several choices. Let them evaluate each choice. (e.g., The person Mr. D likes best gets the doughnut; no one gets the doughnut; Mr. M and Mr. T could pull straws; the doughnut could go to the person who gives the most in return; the doughnut could be divided.)

Now Mr. D knows he has to think before he decides.

How can we help Mr. D decide to whom he should give the doughnut?

Tell Mr. D something about which you have to make a decision. Maybe Mr. D can learn to make decisions by helping us.

Give several children a chance to tell about a decision they had to make. Encourage the children to ask Mr. D what he thinks the decision should be. Mr. D may want to tell several children what he is thinking.

Mr. D says some decisions are easy to make and some are very hard to make. He says it is easy for him to decide where to play in the classroom. Tell him where you have decided to play today.

Mr. D says it is easy to decide what song he wants to sing today.

Tell him what song you decided to sing today.

Follow the same procedure for games to be played, pictures to be drawn, arts and crafts to be made.

Mr. D says some decisions are very hard to make. It was hard to decide whether Mr. T or Mr. M would get the doughnut.

One reason why Mr. D found it hard to make a decision is because he didn't want to hurt someone's feelings.

Why are some decisions hard for you to make? Tell Mr. D about decisions that are hard for you to make.

What decisions do you think are hard for your mother or father to make?

Mr. D says you must think before you make a decision.

Sometimes you think, and quick as a wink you know what decision to make.

Sometimes it's good to think and think and think before you make a decision.

TALKING ABOUT OPPOSITE WORDS

Mr. D would like us to help him decide what the meaning is of one of his words.

He has been trying to decide what the word *different* means.

Tell him what you think the word *different* means.

Mr. L says he knows what *different* means.

He says that *different* is the opposite of *same.*

Mr. L is very good at opposites. Mr. D wants us to decide on opposites for some of his words.

He will tell us a word and we will try to decide on a good opposite.

Tell the children the opposites do not have to start the same way as Delicious Doughnuts.

Help the children find opposites for each of the following words:

*Supplying Opposites
(Antonyms) To
Given Words*

Mr. D says late at night it is very *dark.*

Dark starts with his Delicious Doughnut sound.

Mr. D wants us to decide on an opposite for dark. (light)

Mr. D says that sometimes he tries and tries to do something but he just can't do it because it is too hard for him. It is too *difficult.*

Difficult starts the same way as Delicious Doughnuts.

Mr. D wants us to decide on an opposite for *difficult.* (easy)

Mr. D loves to play with mud. He has such a good time making all kinds of things. When he is finished playing, his hands are all *dirty.*

281

Dirty starts the same way as Delicious Doughnuts.

Mr. D wants us to decide on an opposite for *dirty.* (clean)

Mr. D says that some people use machines to clean their clothes. First, they put their clothes into a washing machine. Then, they put their clothes into a dryer. In the dryer, their clothes get *dry.*

Dry starts the same way as Delicious Doughnuts.
Mr. D wants us to decide on an opposite for *dry.* (wet)

READING COMPREHENSION

Reading A
Picture Book

Distribute copies of Mr. D's Picture Book to the children.

Mr. D has a picture story for us. In the story we will have to make a decision.

Mr. D said we must think before we make a decision.

Cover

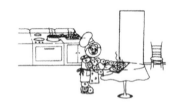

Numeration

Let's look at the cover.

Who is on the cover? (Mr. D)

What is he doing? (putting doughnuts on the table)

Let's turn the page.

Page #1

Where is Mr. D? (in the kitchen)

Who do you think made the doughnuts? (Mr. D)

How can you tell that the doughnuts are hot? (Steam is rising from them.)

Why are the doughnuts hot? (Mr. D just finished making them.)

Inferring
Cause and effect relationships

Why aren't they good to eat now? (too hot)

When will they be good to eat? (when they cool)

Let's turn the page and look at the next picture.

Page #2

Who has come into the kitchen? (a boy and a dog)

How do you think they knew that doughnuts were being made?

What do you think Mr. D is saying? (telling them not to touch)

Why doesn't Mr. D want the little boy or the dog to touch the doughnuts?

Let's look at the next page of the story.

Page #3

Who has left the kitchen? (Mr. D and the boy)

Who is in the kitchen? (the dog)

282

Is the dog touching the doughnuts? (no)

Let's turn the page.

Page #4

Looking for detail

How do you know that the boy has not listened to Mr. D? (He is reaching for the doughnuts.)

How can you tell what is going to happen to the doughnuts? (One of the trays is beginning to fall.)

What is the dog doing? (sleeping)

Let's turn to the next page.

Page #5

Inferring

What has happened? (the tray fell)

How can you tell that there is a loud noise as the doughnuts and dough-nut tray falls? (the dog woke up; boy's hands on ears)

How do you think the little boy feels?

Let's look at the next page and see what happens.

Page #6

Reasoning
Predicting

Who came into the kitchen? (Mr. D)

What is the dog doing? (eating the doughnuts)

If you were Mr. D what would you think happened to make the dough-nuts fall?

How can Mr. D find out who knocked the tray down?

Making Value
Judgments

What decision does the little boy have to make? (whether to tell the truth)

What do you think his decision will be?

After the children have decided what the little boy will do, have them discuss why they think it might be difficult for the little boy to reach a decision.

TYING IT TOGETHER

Reviewing
Opposite Words

Have the children sit in a circle. Whisper a word to one child (e.g., easy). The child stands up and walks around the circle saying "I am the word easy. One of Mr. D's words is my opposite. Where is my opposite?" The child who can recall the opposite of "easy" raises his hand. The first child taps him on the shoulder. The second child says, "I am the word difficult. I am your opposite." Both children run around the circle. The first one who reaches the vacant place in the circle is "it." The game continues until all the pairs of opposites have been named.

ON THEIR OWN

Children may choose from the following activities:

Sequence

Using the separated pages of Mr. D's Picture Book to put the story in order.

Storytelling

Reading the picture story aloud to Mr. D. If a tape recorder is available, record the story.

Word Study

Making lists of opposite words.

2D₄

TEACHER OBJECTIVES:

To reinforce the characteristic and sound of Mr. D.

To reinforce the D sound by having children pronounce and dictate words and sentences to the teacher.

To reinforce the concept that each child has a doctor.

PERFORMANCE OBJECTIVES:

The child will say words with the *d* in the initial position.

The child will identify his or her doctor by name.

The child will relate experiences he or she has had with a doctor.

DEVELOPMENT

Mr. D. hasn't made delicious doughnuts for a whole week.
He has been busy making "All About Us" booklets.
Now the booklets are finished and he wants to give one to each of us.

Distribute the Mr. D "All About Us" booklets to the children.

Mr. D wants us to show him the words that say "All About Us."
Let's find them at the top of the booklet and say them for Mr. D.
Which Letter Person's picture is on the booklet? (Mr. D)
Whose picture is next to Mr. D? (his friend's)
Touch the sentence at the bottom of the booklet.
It says, "Mr. D has a friend."

What is special about Mr. D? (his delicious doughnuts)
Look at the picture of Mr. D's friend.
What is his friend holding? (a plate)
How can you tell that his friend is thinking about delicious doughnuts? (the expression on his face)
Mr. D was so busy making the booklets, he had no time to make delicious doughnuts for his friend.
Let's draw delicious doughnuts on the plate.

Give the children the opportunity to draw the delicious doughnuts. Suggest they finish the picture of Mr. D's friend to look like themselves or anyone else they wish.

Have the children open their booklets.
Ask them to touch the first sentence on the left-hand side.

What picture did Mr. D put in the first sentence? (delicious doughnuts)
Read aloud, "Mr. D eats delicious donuts."
Let the children pretend to reread the sentence with you.

Mr. D will use this whole page to tell us about himself.
He told us he eats delicious doughnuts.
He wants to tell us his doctor's name.
Touch the next sentence.
It says, "Mr. D's doctor is Dr. Dell."

284A

What is the name of Mr. D's doctor? (Dr. Dell)
Find the picture of Dr. Dell.
What is she doing to Mr. D? (She is listening to his heartbeat.)

Mr. D wants us to use the next page to tell him about ourselves.
Have the children find the first dotted line on the right-hand page.
Explain that Mr. D wants each of them to write his or her name.
After the children have had an opportunity to do this, select and read a booklet. (*e.g.,* Jimmy eats
Mr. D says, "The sentence is not finished."
Mr. D's sentence tells that he eats delicious doughnuts.
Jimmy's sentence does not tell what Jimmy eats.
How can Jimmy finish the sentence?

Lead the children to the discovery that the sentence can be finished by drawing a picture of anything Jimmy likes to eat.
A picture may also be cut out of a magazine and pasted at the end of the sentence.
Children may just want to dictate a word to finish the sentence.

Help the children complete their sentences.
Read several aloud.
Encourage children to tell Mr. D what their sentence says.

Draw the children's attention to the second sentence.

Explain that Mr. D wants them each to tell him the name of their doctor.
Some children may use more than one doctor.
Suggest they tell you the name of the last doctor they've seen.
Some children may not have a family doctor. These children may wish to copy the name of the school doctor.
Help the children complete the sentences.

After the children have had time to share their sentences with each other and Mr. D, have them turn to the back of the booklet.
Read aloud, "Let's talk about doctors."
Discuss each illustration with the children.
Have them relate their experiences to each other.

You may wish to discuss other people that assist us with our health such as dentists, nurses, technicians: the role each plays; the different types of doctors, dentists. Children can describe visits to doctors, dentists.
What did they see there?
What did the doctor do? The nurse?
Suggest that they take the booklets home to share with other members of their family.

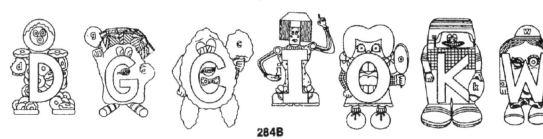

2G₁

PLANNING AND PREPARATION: Huggable, Mr. G; Picture Card 8; a bag for Mr. G; Mr. G's Picture Squares; Alpha Time Master #122; magazines, a variety of art materials.

Mr. G's music (record #2) may be played to set the mood.

DISCOVERING HOW MR. G WILL GET HIS SOUND

Listening To
A Story

Gather the children around Mr. G and his Picture Card 8. Briefly recall with them the story of Gooney Bird.

Do you remember Gooney Bird? Gooney Bird helped Mr. G find the gooiest Gooey Gum.

Tell the following story to the children:

Gooney Bird and Mr. G got to love each other so much that they were together all the time. That is, until last week. Early each morning, Gooney Bird left Mr. G and was gone all day. He came back late at night feeling very tired. Mr. G kept asking Gooney Bird where he was going. Gooney Bird just said, "Can't you guess Mr. G?"

"No, I can't guess Gooney Bird. I don't know where you are going," Mr. G said. Gooney Bird said, "Please guess, Mr. G. I'll give you three guesses."

For guess number one, Mr. G guessed that Gooney Bird was going home to visit his family.

Gooney Bird said that was not a good guess. He asked Mr. G to guess again.

Mr. G guessed two more times. Guess what! They weren't good guesses either!

Now Gooney Bird says that we can have some guesses and see if ours are better than Mr. G's.

What's your guess? Where do you think Gooney Bird goes every day?

Let the children guess. If a child guesses that Gooney Bird has been looking for a sound for Mr. G tell him that he is a good guesser. He has guessed what Gooney Bird has been doing. Continue even if the answer has not been guessed.

Gooney Bird says that he has been looking for a sound for Mr. G, but he still has not been able to find a sound for him.

My goodness! Look at Mr. G giggling. What's the matter, Mr. G? Why are you giggling and giggling?

Mr. G says that it is very silly of Gooney Bird to be looking for Mr. G's sound. He says that Mr. G's sound has already been found.

Let's all say this rhyme and see if Gooney Bird catches on.

Gooney Bird! Gooney Bird!
Take a rest!
My sound must come
From what I love best!

Concluding That
Mr. G's Sound
Comes From
Gooey Gum

Le†'s help Gooney Bird guess.

Lead the children to the conclusion that Mr. G's sound will come from Gooey Gum.

NAMING WORDS WITH G IN THE INITIAL POSITION

While Gooney Bird was flying around looking for a sound, he collected some pictures. He thinks that these pictures will be good for Mr. G's bag.

Display Mr. G's Picture Squares (i.e., gloves, glasses, girl, ghost, galoshes). Let the children look at the pictures. Then explain that Gooney Bird will give them a clue to each picture. They are to guess the name of the picture, select it from the other pictures, and prove it so it can go into Mr. G's bag.

Gooney Bird wants us to play "Guess What Picture I Am Thinking About." Then we'll have to prove them for him.

Identifying Pictures
By Listening To
Descriptions

Gooney Bird says, "Get ready to guess! I am thinking about something that Mr. G bought to wear for Gooey Gum-making. Mr. G wore them on his feet." Guess what Gooney Bird is thinking about. (galoshes)

After the galoshes have been selected and named have a child prove it to Mr. G.

Gooney Bird is ready to play again. He says, "I'm thinking about something else Mr. G bought to wear for Gooey Gum-making. He wore these on his hands. Guess what I am thinking about!" (gloves) Let's prove it.

Gooney Bird says, "I am thinking about another thing Mr. G bought to wear for Gooey Gum-making. He wore these over his eyes. Guess what I am thinking about." (glasses) Prove it.

Now Gooney Bird says that he is thinking about someone who grows up to be a woman. Which picture is he thinking about? (girl) Prove it.

Gooney Bird says, "I am thinking about something that rhymes with *toast*. You might dress up like on of these on Halloween." Guess what he is thinking about. (ghost) Prove it.

Note: Record #5, side A, band #3 may be used to play the Prove It Game.

TALKING ABOUT WORDS WITH G IN THE INITIAL POSITION

You were good guessers for Gooney Bird. Mr. G wants you to be good guessers for him too. Mr. G doesn't have pictures to show us. He will just tell us what he is thinking about.

Guessing Words From
Context Clues

First, Mr. G is thinking about something that starts the same way as Gooey Gum. You put it in the tank of a car. Without this, the car won't go. Guess what it is. (gas)

Mr. G is thinking about something that starts with his Gooey Gum sound. It rhymes with the word *class*. He drinks water, milk and soda from it. Guess what he is thinking about. (glass)

Mr. G is thinking about a musical instrument that starts with his Gooey Gum sound. It makes music when he moves his hands over the strings. Guess what he is thinking about. (guitar)

Mr. G is thinking about an animal that starts with his Gooey Gum sound. The name of this animal rhymes with the word *coat*. Guess what he is thinking about. (goat)

Mr. G is thinking about something that starts with his Gooey Gum sound. It is a place where he plants flowers and vegetables. Guess what he is thinking about. (garden)

Tell Mr. G some things that you know that start the same way as Gooey Gum. If you give him a clue, Mr. G will guess what you are thinking about.

Making Up Definitions

Encourage children to give their own definitions of words.

Mr. G wants us to make or find some things to put into his bag. Remember, we have to prove each thing to him before we can put it in his bag.

Making Things For Mr. G's Bag

Encourage the children to use many different materials to give their pictures dimension. (e.g., pipe cleaners or yarn can make the strings for a guitar; pipe cleaners can be planted in clay to make a garden) Have the children share the things they find and make with Mr. G and each other.

TYING IT TOGETHER

Distribute copies of Alpha Time Master #122.

Have children name the pictures (i.e., glasses ghost, girl, gloves) and prove that they begin with Mr. G's Gooey Gum sound. Children may draw lines from the pictures to Mr. G's Gooey Gum.

ON THEIR OWN

Children may choose from the following activities:

Sound Discrimination

Using Picture Card 8. Children may name some of the things that begin with Mr. G's sound.

Story Telling

Telling the story of Gooney Bird to Mr. G.

Art

Drawing a picture of Gooney Bird looking for a sound for Mr. G.

2G₂

PLANNING AND PREPARATION: Huggables, Mr. G, Mr. T and Mr. L; sheets of drawing paper for each child; art materials; Alpha Time Master #123.

READING COMPREHENSION

Listening To A Story

Gather the children around Mr. G and Mr. T.

Mr. G likes to give gifts. What is another word for *gift*? (present)

Why does Mr. G like the word *gift* better than the word present? (It begins with his sound.)

Mr. G gave a gift to Mr. T. He gave Mr. T some of the gooiest gum he had ever made.

Mr. T used his Tall Teeth to chew the gum. The gum was so gooey that it got stuck all over Mr. T's Tall Teeth.

Mr. T wasn't worried. He just called his tall toothbrush. The tall toothbrush started brushing—but it could not brush for very long! The tall toothbrush got stuck in the Gooey Gum.

Poor Mr. T had to walk around with a tall toothbrush stuck to his Tall Teeth. It took him a long time to get it loose.

Mr. G sent gifts to Mr. H and to Mr. M. He sent them Gooey Gum too. Can you guess what happened? Let's look at a picture story and see.

"Reading" Pictures

Give each child a copy of Alpha Time Master #123. Discuss each picture with them:

Frame #1

Looking For Detail Predicting Outcomes

Look at the first picture.

What *gift* did Mr. M get? (Gooey Gum)

What is Mr. M going to do with his Gooey Gum? (put it in his mouth)

What do you think will happen?

Let's look at the next picture and find out.

Frame #2

Making Inferences

What has happened to Mr. M? (His mouth is full of gum.)

Why can't he open his mouth? (It's stuck together.)

How do you think Mr. M feels?

What do you think Mr. M will do now?

Frame #3

Recognizing Cause And Effect Relationships

Let's look at the next picture and see who gets a Gooey Gum gift this time.

Who has the Gooey Gum gift this time? (Mr. H)

How can Gooey Gum be a problem for Mr. H?

288

Frame #4

Let's look at the next picture and find out what happened.

What happened with the Gooey Gum gift this time? (It is stuck to Mr. H's hair.)

How do you think Mr. H will get the Gooey Gum out of his hair?

What would you do if you were Mr. H?

TALKING ABOUT FEELINGS

*Discussing
Gift Giving*

Mr. G is getting more and more Gooey Gum gifts ready for the other Letter People. Why do you think Mr. G gives everyone Gooey Gum? (because he likes it best)

Mr. G loves Gooey Gum and so he thinks that everyone should love Gooey Gum.

Tell us about a gift that you have decided to give someone. How did you decide what to give to the person?

Lead the children to the conclusion that gifts should be chosen to please the people who get them.

Mr. L said that he has a gift that is the best gift of all.

Mr. G said, "Really Mr. L! I don't like Lemon Lollipops best of all!"

Mr. L smiled and said, "I don't mean Lemon Lollipops. The gift I am talking about is something that is not sold anywhere, but the people who have it know that it is better than any other gift in the whole world."

Mr. G cannot guess what Mr. L is talking about. Who can guess?

*Talking
About Love*

Lead the children to the conclusion that Mr. L is talking about love.

The gift of love is the most wonderful gift in the world.

Mr. L says that when you love someone, you want to share things with that person. The gift of love means sharing. . . not only sharing candy or toys, but sharing what you think and feel.

*Talking About
Sharing*

What are some feelings we can share with our friends, parents, family?

What are some feelings we can share with our classmates, teachers?

Mr. G said, "That sounds good. How do I get this gift of love, Mr. L?"

Mr. L laughed and said that the gift of love is one you can get only if you can give it.

"That sounds like a riddle," said Mr. G.

Help the children think and talk about the idea of showing or giving love and friendship and so getting love and friendship in return. Questions such as the following might start further discussion:

How do we give the gift of love?

How can we show our parents, brothers, and sisters that we love them?

Why does Mr. L think that the gift of love is better than getting a new bicycle?

Why is the gift of love a gift that is good for everyone no matter how old he is?

Mr. G agrees that the gift of love is something everyone wants. Then he thought of another gift that everyone would like. He giggled and giggled when he thought of it. It is the gift of laughter. People often laugh when they are happy. Tell us about a time you laughed.

Mr. L likes to make people laugh.

Mr. G likes to make people giggle.

Let's help Mr. G give the gift of laughter by making a giggle book.

Distribute sheets of paper each of which will become a page in Mr. G's giggle book. Help each child decide what kind of picture will make people giggle.

TYING IT TOGETHER

Using their copies of Alpha Time Master #123 children may take turns choosing one frame, and telling about it. They may tell which picture makes them giggle most, and why.

ON THEIR OWN

Children may choose from the following activities:

Crafts

Using gift wrapping paper, ribbons, boxes and decorations for wrapping gifts.

Making gifts for a grab bag.

Developing A Sense Of Humor

Making giggle gifts such as a necktie for a giraffe, shoes for a centipede, flower duster for a bee, a pin cushion for a darning needle, toast for a butterfly, earmuffs for a rabbit.

Sound Association

Including Mr. G's Picture Squares, puzzle, and playing cards in games listed in the *Games* section.

2G₃

EACHER OBJECTIVES:

To reinforce the characteristic and sound of Mr. G.

To lead children in classroom games.

PERFORMANCE OBJECTIVES:

The child will say words with the *g* (hard sound) in the initial position.

The child will become aware of the names and basic descriptions of different games.

DEVELOPMENT

Mr. G is very worried.
He's afraid he might have gotten gooey gum on the "All About Us" booklets he made.
When Mr. G gives you a booklet, check it carefully to see that it is not sticky.

Distribute the booklets to the children.

Ask the children to find the words "All About Us" at the top of the booklet and say them for Mr. G.

Which Letter Person's picture is on the booklet? (Mr. G)
Whose picture is next to Mr. G? (his friend's)
Touch the sentence at the bottom of the booklet.
It says, "Mr. G has a friend."

What is special about Mr. G? (his gooey gum)
Where does Mr. G carry all his gooey gum? (in a pack on his back)
Look at the picture of Mr. G's friend.
What is on his friend's back? (a knapsack)
What do you think Mr. G would like his friend to carry in his knapsack? (gooey gum)
Let's fill the knapsack with gooey gum.

Give the children the opportunity to draw the gooey gum.
Suggest they finish the picture of Mr. G's friend to look like themselves or anyone else.

Have the children open their booklets.
Ask them to find the first sentence on the left-hand side.

What picture did Mr. G put in the first sentence? (gooey gum)

Read aloud, "Mr. G likes gooey gum."
Let the children pretend to reread the sentence with you.

Mr. G told us he likes gooey gum.
He also wants to tell us his favorite game.
He wants us to look at the picture at the bottom of the page.
The picture will show us Mr. G's favorite game.

Discuss the picture with the children.
Many of them may not be familiar with the game of golf.
You may wish to explain the game.
Draw their attention to the golf club and the golf ball.
Read aloud, "Mr. G's favorite game is golf."
Why does Mr. G like games?
Why does he like golf? (*Games* and *golf* start like *gooey gum*.)

Mr. G used this whole page to tell us about himself.
What two things did he tell us? (He likes gooey gum. His favorite game is golf.)
Mr. G wants us to use the next page.

Have the children touch the first dotted line.
Explain that Mr. G wants each of them to write his/her name on it.
After the children have had an opportunity to do this, select and read a booklet. (*e.g.,* Frances likes   .)
Mr. G says the sentence is not finished.
Mr. G's sentence tells that he likes gooey gum.
Frances' sentence does not tell what Frances likes.
How can Frances finish the sentence? (by drawing a picture of anything Frances likes to chew, by cutting out a picture from a magazine or by dictating a word.)

Explain that Mr. G wants them to look at the picture he drew on the back of the booklet.
The picture will show different games.

Have the children turn to the back page of the booklet.
Read aloud, "Let's talk about games."
Discuss the illustration with the children.
Have them discover and name the different games being played.

In addition to games that the children may or may not be familiar with, such as games of low organization (tag, *it* games, line games, circle games), you may wish to play those games with youngsters that require language arts skills (Simple Simon) or those utilizing manual dexterity (Tic-Tac-Toe, pencil-and-paper games).
Children can describe games they have at home. Tell what the goal of the game is, then have the children open their booklets.
Draw their attention to the second sentence on the right-hand side.
Explain that Mr. G wants them to use the sentence to tell him the name of their favorite game.
First have the children write their names on the dotted lines.
Select and read an incomplete sentence. (*e.g.,* Sharon's favorite game is   .)
Elicit from the children why the sentence is not finished.

Help the children complete their sentences.
Read several completed sentences aloud.
Have the children tell Mr. G what their sentences say.
Encourage the children to take their booklets home.
Have them ask members of their family to tell Mr. G what their favorite games are.

2C₁

PLANNING AND PREPARATION: Huggable, Mr. C; Record #2; Mr. C's Picture Squares; a bag for Mr. C; magazines, art materials, construction paper, pipe cleaners, small boxes; Alpha Time Master #124.

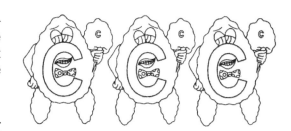

A "Clicking Camera" will be needed during the lesson. A real camera without film is ideal, or, make one by cutting a round hole in each end of a shoe box so the children can see through it. Attach a pipe cleaner or string to one side as the camera's "clicker."

Mr. C's music, (record #2, side A, band #4) may be played to set the mood.

DISCOVERING THAT MR. C WILL GET HIS SOUND FROM "COTTON CANDY"

Put your arm around Mr. C and tell the children what happened to him.

Listening To
A Story

Mr. C was very excited this morning. He had put a big red circle on his calendar to make sure that he would not forget the day. Today was the day! It had finally come. Today was the day that Mr. C's sound would come to him.

Mr. C kept looking at the door waiting for his bell to ring.

At last the bell rang!

Mr. C was so excited he almost jumped right out of his Cotton Candy!

Mr. C opened the door and—what a disappointment. It wasn't his sound at all. It was a delivery of Cotton Candy.

The Cotton Candy delivery man said, "Mr. C, aren't you glad to see me? I thought you would be waiting for me to come."

"Oh, I'm glad to see you," said Mr. C, "I was really waiting for my sound. You only have Cotton Candy for me."

The delivery man laughed. He said, "Mr. C, I'm giving you Cotton Candy. And you can stop waiting for your sound to be delivered. It has already arrived."

"How can that be?" asked Mr. C. "I've been waiting at home all day. No one else has been here. No one else has brought anything. How could my sound have arrived?"

The delivery man smiled again. "No one else has been here, that's true. I have brought your sound to you."

Mr. C said, "The only thing you've given me is Cotton Candy. There's no sound that I can see."

The delivery man answered, "Cotton Candy is the clue. Figure it out— it's up to you!"

Mr. C kept repeating: "Cotton Candy is the clue. Cotton Candy is the clue. I'll figure it out. That's what I'll do."

291

Mr. C needs our help. Let's help him figure out why Cotton Candy came when he was waiting to get his sound.

Help the children discover that Mr. C will get his sound from Cotton Candy.

Mr. C likes his sound. He says, "Cotton Candy is the best place for me to find my sound."

AUDITORY RECOGNITION OF WORDS WITH C IN THE INITIAL POSITION

Mr. C has been thinking of words that start the same way as Cotton Candy. He would like us to prove some of his words for him. Let's listen to some of Mr. C's words.

Guessing Words
From Given Clues

Give the children the clues below and have them identify each word and "prove it."

Mr. C says, "I am thinking of a word that starts the same way as Cotton Candy. It is the name of an animal that says 'meow.' My word rhymes with the word *hat.*"

What word is Mr. C thinking about? (cat)

Prove it to Mr. C.

Mr. C says, "I am thinking of a word that starts the same way as Cotton Candy. It is the name of a vegetable that I like to eat. My word rhymes with *parrot.*"

What word is Mr. C thinking about? (carrot)

Mr. C says, "I am thinking of a word that starts with my Cotton Candy sound. It is something that you wear. My word rhymes with the word *goat.*" (coat)

Mr. C says, "I am thinking of a word that starts the same way as Cotton Candy. It is something that you may drive when you are older. My word rhymes with the word *star.*" (car)

Mr. C says, "I am thinking of a word that starts with my Cotton Candy sound. It is something you blow out on a birthday cake. My word rhymes with the word *handle.*" (candle)

Mr. C says, "I am thinking of a word that starts the same way as Cotton Candy. It is a vegetable that is yellow. My word rhymes with the word *horn.*" (corn)

Mr. C says, "I am thinking of a word that starts with my Cotton Candy sound. It is something that a baby sleeps in when you take him for a walk. My word rhymes with the word *marriage.*" (carriage)

Mr. C says, "I am thinking of a word that starts the same way as Cotton Candy. It stands on a plate that is called a saucer. My word rhymes with the word *up.*" (cup)

Mr. C says, "I am thinking of a word that starts with my Cotton Candy sound. It is the part of a shirt that goes around your neck. My word rhymes with *dollar.*" (collar)

292

Show the children the camera (see planning and preparation) and put it next to Mr. C.

Mr. C loves to take pictures. He takes pictures with his camera. Everytime he takes a picture his camera makes a noise. Mr. C calls that noise a *click*. Mr. C says, "My camera is a clicking camera." Mr. C wants to show us some pictures that he took with his clicking camera.

Identifying Picture Words

Show the children Mr. C's Picture Squares (i.e., cookies, comb, cat, car, cow). Have them name each picture. Ask them why they think Mr. C's clicking camera took these pictures.

Following Game Directions

Explain the "Camera Clicks For A Clue" game to the children:

Place Mr. C's Picture Squares face down on a table. Let one child be the Cameraman. He closes his eyes and selects one of the pictures. Keeping his eyes closed, he shows the picture to the class. He then gives it to another child who will hold it for Mr. C. The Cameraman opens his eyes, takes the clicking camera, and says: "Click, click—the camera clicks for a clue. Give me a clue that tells me which picture I took." The children give clues to the cameraman.

The camera keeps clicking for clues until the Cameraman guesses the name of the picture he took.

The games continues this way until several children have had a chance to click for clues.

Making And Finding Things For Mr. C's Bag

Using magazines and a variety of art materials have the children look for pictures of things that start with Mr. C's Cotton Candy sound. They may then take a picture of each thing. They may put these pictures in Mr. C's bag after they have "proven" them to him.

Children may make their own cameras out of small boxes, construction paper and pipe cleaners.

TYING IT TOGETHER

Distribute copies of Alpha Time Master #124 to the children. After they have identified Mr. C's pictures (i.e., cow, car, cookies, cat) they may draw other things that Mr. C can photograph with his clicking camera. Some of Mr. C's pictures may be attached to his Cotton Candy characteristic.

ON THEIR OWN

Children may choose from the following activities:

Sorting And Matching

Including Mr. C's puzzle, Picture Squares, playing cards in any of the games described in the *Games* section.

Auditory Discrimination

Playing Mr. C's song (record #2) and listening for words that begin with Mr. C's Cotton Candy sound.

Looking at Mr. C's Picture Card (9) and finding things that begin with Mr. C's sound.

Crafts

Making clicking cameras out of boxes.

Photography

Using a camera to take real pictures.

2C 2

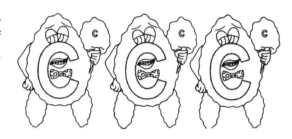

RECOGNIZING VARIOUS SOUNDS

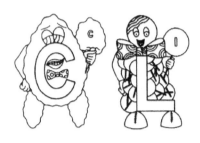

Put Mr. C and Mr. D in front of the classroom so they look as if they are talking.

Mr. C says that last night he could not sleep because he kept hearing sounds.

Mr. D asked Mr. C what made the sounds.

Mr. C said, "You are very silly, Mr. D. It was late at night. It was very dark. I could not see anything. When you can't see, you can't tell what makes the sounds."

Mr. D said that isn't true. He said that you don't always have to see what is making the sound to know what makes the sound. How can you tell what is making a sound without seeing it?

Encourage the children to give examples of how they can tell what makes a sound without seeing it.

If you heard a meowing, how would you know what was making the sound even if you couldn't see it?

If you heard a tick tock, how would you know what was making the sound even if you couldn't see it?

Let the children give examples of sounds which are equally familiar to them.

Mr. C is going to tell us some sounds that start the same way as Cotton Candy. If we do what each word says, we will be making sounds.

Making Sounds

Mr. C's first word is *clap.* Let's clap. Close your eyes and *clap.* Listen to the clapping sound.

Mr. C's next word is *cough.* Let's cough. Close your eyes and cough. Listen to the coughing sound.

Follow this same procedure for the words cry, creep, cut, crumple, crash. To illustrate "cut," have one child cut a piece of paper. For "crumple," give each child a piece of paper to crumple. For "crash," let one child drop several blocks.

Mr. C wants to find out how many sounds he remembers. He is going to play a game with us.

Following
Game Directions

In order to play the game, let one child stand with Mr. C, his back to the class. Another child whispers a direction to the class (e.g., clap). The class claps. The child standing near Mr. C tells what Mr. C thinks the class is doing. (Sometimes Mr. C tricks the class with an unexpected guess.) The game continues until all the words and sounds have been identified by Mr. C. (One child may have to demonstrate the words "cut" and "crash" rather than the whole class.)

VISUAL DISCRIMINATION OF VARIOUS LINES

Mr. L and Mr. C are having an argument. They are arguing about something that is drawn on a piece of paper. Mr. L says that anyone who looks at the paper can see that what is on the paper is a word that begins the same way as Lemon Lollipops. Mr. C says that he can prove that what is on the paper begins with his Cotton Candy sound.

Let's look at the paper and decide to whom it belongs. We will think before we make a decision.

Distribute copies of Alpha Time Master #125 and let the children look at the lines that are drawn.

What do you see drawn all over this paper? (lines)

Why does Mr. L think that the paper belongs to him? (The word *Lines* starts with his Lemon Lollipop sound.)

Mr. C says that it is true that there are lines all over the paper but the paper still belongs to him and not to Mr. L. Mr. C explains that these are not just lines. Each line is drawn a special way. The words that tell what is special about the lines start with Mr. C's Cotton Candy sound.

Look at the lines in the first box. What word could you use to tell us something about the kind of lines they are?

Use your hands to show us how the lines look. When your hands are moving they are making *curves*. These lines are not straight. They are *curved*.

Why does Mr. C want us to use the word *curve* to tell about these lines? (*Curve* begins with Mr. C's sound.)

Let's look at the next group of lines.

These lines are straight. Why doesn't Mr. C want us to use the word *straight* to tell about these lines? (*Straight* doesn't begin with his sound.)

Mr. C says that these lines do something to each other. If we think about what the lines are doing to each other, we will find a word that starts the same way as Cotton Candy. Show us with your fingers what the lines are doing to each other.

What word is Mr. C thinking about? (crossing lines) These straight lines are crossing each other. *Crossing* starts with Mr. C's Cotton Candy sound.

Look at the next group of lines.

Mr. C says that another word that starts the same way as Cotton Candy tells something about these lines.

What word is Mr. C thinking about? (curly)

Mr. L says no matter what kind of lines they are, they are still *lines,* and lines begin with Mr. L's sound. He says the paper belongs to him.

Mr. C says they are not just lines, they are curved, crossing and curly and all those words begin with the Cotton Candy sound. The paper should belong to him.

Making Judgments Based On Given Facts

Mr. C and Mr. L want us to make a decision about to whom this paper belongs. Think of the facts. To whom does the paper belong?

Let the children decide to whom they think the paper belongs. . . to Mr. L, to Mr. C, or to both of them. Any answer is acceptable and the more discussion the better.

TYING IT TOGETHER

Mr. C wants us to do some things with the lines on this paper. He will give us directions. Listen to Mr. C's first direction:

Use a crayon to color the lines that are curves.

Now, Mr. C says that some crossing lines would like to touch some curved lines.

Mr. C says to connect crossing lines with curved lines. Draw a line connecting crossing lines with curved lines.

Mr. C's next direction has two parts. He says, "Count 1, 2, 3 and then color the curly lines."

Count and color the curly lines. Those are Mr. C's directions.

Here is Mr. C's last direction. He wants us to turn the page over and cover the back of the paper with lines that we think he would like. Cover the back of the paper with lines.

Children may want to draw lines that make corners (angles); lines that are cut (broken lines); lines that make a cube.

ON THEIR OWN

Children may choose from the following activities:

Art

Drawing or painting a design made from a variety of lines (e.g. thin, thick, slanted, parallel, curved, zigzag).

Cutting out "lines" of varying kinds.

Sewing or embroidering a variety of lines.

Making lines for Mr. L (i.e., long, looping, little, lumpy lines).

Observing

Looking for different lines at school, in the street, at home (e.g., *straight* —doors, windows, books, paper; *curved*—clock, glass, dome, door handle, trees, cup; *angle*—roof, desk).

Sound Discrimination

Trying to identify as many sounds as possible with eyes closed.

2C₃

TEACHER OBJECTIVES:

To reinforce the characteristic and sound of Mr. C.

To help children recognize and identify the numerals 1–5.

To help children write the numerals 1–5.

To help children understand what the numerals 1–5 represent.

PERFORMANCE OBJECTIVES:

The child will say words with the *c* in the initial position.

The child will identify the numerals 1–5, show what symbolizes the numerals and count from 1–5.

The child will demonstrate knowledge of numerals 1–5 by connecting sequential dots to form a picture.

DEVELOPMENT

Mr. C's telephone keeps ringing.
All the Letter People are calling to tell him puffs of cotton candy are everywhere.
He has been so busy making "All About Us" booklets that he forgot to turn off the cotton candy machine.

Distribute the Mr. C. "All About Us" booklets to the children.

Ask the children to find and say the words "All About Us."

Which Letter Person's picture is on the booklet? (Mr. C)
Whose picture is next to Mr. C? (his friend's)
Touch the sentence at the bottom of the booklet.
It says, "Mr. C has a friend."

What is special about Mr. C? (his cotton candy)
What did Mr. C give his friend? (a cotton candy cone)
What did he forget to put in the cone? (cotton candy)
Let's fill the cone with cotton candy.

Give the children the opportunity to draw the cotton candy.
Suggest they finish the picture to look like themselves or anyone else they wish.
Encourage them to add the lower part of the body to the figure.

Have the children open their booklets.
Ask them to touch the first sentence on the left-hand side.

What picture did Mr. C put in the first sentence? (cotton candy)
Read aloud, "Mr. C eats cotton candy."
Let the children pretend to reread the sentence with you.

Mr. C told us he eats cotton candy.
He likes to know how many he eats.
He learned how to count.
Read aloud, "Mr. C can count: 1 2 3 4 5."
Be sure to pause after each numeral so the children can repeat it.

Have the children find the cotton candy cones at the bottom of the page.

Show Mr. C one cotton candy cone between your hands.

Have the children frame one cotton candy cone between their hands.

Now show Mr. C two cotton candy cones between your hands.

Have the children frame two cotton cones between their hands.

Follow the same procedure until the children have framed five cotton candy cones between their hands.

Mr. C took this whole page to tell us about himself.

What two things did he tell us? (He eats cotton candy. He can count.)

Mr. C wants us to use the next page.

Have the children put their fingers on the first dotted line on the right-hand page.

Explain that Mr. C wants each of them to write his/her name on the dotted line.

After the children have had an opportunity to do this, select and read a booklet. (*e.g.*, Dudley eats   .)

Mr. C says the sentence is not finished.

Mr. C's sentence tells that he eats cotton candy.

Dudley's sentence does not tell what Dudley eats.

How can Dudley finish the sentence? (draw a picture of something he eats or cut out and paste a picture or dictate a word)

Help the children complete their sentences.

Read several completed sentences aloud.

Draw the children's attention to the second sentence.

Explain that Mr. C wants them each to count to 5.

He wants them to write the numerals as they say them.

Help the children complete their sentences by writing their names and the numerals from 1—5.

Select and read several completed sentences.

Encourage the children to tell their sentences to Mr. C.

Have the children turn to the back of the booklet.

Read aloud, "Let's talk about counting."

Explain that Mr. C wants them to finish the picture by connecting the dots.

Have the children touch the dot near numeral 1.

Have them put another finger on the dot near the numeral 2.

Show them how to draw a line between the two dots.

Continue this procedure, connecting the dots in numerical order.

When the dots have been connected, the children will see a picture of a cat.

Ask them why Mr. C would like a picture of a cat. (*Cat* starts like *cotton candy*.)

Encourage the children to take their booklets home.

Have them ask members of their family to count for Mr. C.

2 I₁ **PLANNING AND PREPARATION:** Huggables, Miss I and Mr. C; Miss I's initial sound Picture Squares; drawing paper and crayons; Alpha Time Master #126.

Miss I's music (record #2) may be played to set the mood.

DISCOVERING THAT MISS I'S SOUND COMES FROM ITCHING

Remind the children of Miss I's Itch and of how the ĭ ran away from the Itch.

The ĭ wants to know if Miss I really needs it.

"Of course," said Miss I. If there is no ĭ, you can not say Itch. "Try it." The ĭ tried. All it could say was "tch."

Let the children try to say the word "Itch" without the ĭ sound.

Miss I had been trying to decide what she wanted her sound to be. Seeing the ĭ gave her a wonderful idea.

Now she knew what her sound would be.

What idea do you think the ĭ gave Miss I? What sound will Miss I choose?

Help the children decide that Miss I will take ĭ as her sound.

When Miss I told the Itch that ĭ would be her sound, the Itch was very happy. Miss I was also happy because she won't have any trouble remembering her sound. The ĭ is always around, saying ĭ- ĭ- ĭ.

NAMING WORDS WITH I IN THE INITIAL POSITION

Give several children a chance to repeat the short vowel sound of "ĭ".

The ĭ and Little Miss I have been busy practicing saying ĭ. Now Miss I wants to hear how the ĭ sounds at the beginning of a word. She asked Mr. C to come and listen.

Mr. C says it is not easy to think of words that start with ĭ.

Miss I said, "Mr. C, I will show you some pictures. You guess what word goes with each picture. All the words start with ĭ from the word *Itch*. I know one picture you will never guess."

"Impossible, impossible, impossible," said Mr. C. "I can guess anything you show me. Didn't I think of the word *impossible? Impossible* starts with ĭ. So there!"

Miss I just said, "Let's start to play, Mr. C, and see what happens."

Identifying Miss I's Picture Squares

Show the children Miss I's initial sound Picture Squares (i.e., Indian; igloo; inch; ill; one blank picture for the word "invisible." Tell the children that Miss I will give Mr. C clues to help him think of words for the

297

pictures that begin with ĭ). Remind them that when Mr. C tells them a word, he will have to "prove it."

NOTE: Miss I's word-pictures are quite difficult, therefore Mr. C is the one who comes up with an answer. In this way it is Mr. C, not the child who is wrong. When a child identifies a picture, he is only repeating what Mr. C tells him. If the answer is incorrect, Mr. C is teasing.

Here is the first picture clue.

Miss I says: "I am thinking of a picture that starts with the ĭ from Itch. It is a picture of someone who wears a feather headdress. He was one of the first Americans. He hunted with a bow and arrow."

Tell the children to ask Mr. C which picture he thinks it is. (Indian)

Another picture starts with the ĭ from Itch. This word rhymes with *pinch.* It is measured with a ruler. (inch)

Remind the children to prove each word for Miss I.

Another picture starts with the ĭ from Itch. An Eskimo lives in this kind of house. He makes this house out of ice and snow. (igloo)

This picture is another word for *sick.* The word rhymes with *pill.* (ill)

Miss I says that Mr. C may not be able to figure out the last picture. Let's look at it before Mr. C does. Let's try to figure it out before we have any clues.

Show the children the blank Picture Square.

What picture do you see? (nothing)

Do you think Miss I forgot to put a picture on this card?

Ask Miss I.

Miss I says that it is not a mistake. This picture starts with the ĭ sound from Itch.

Give the children a chance to guess what the ĭ can possibly mean.

Mr. C says that Miss I must give him clues.

Miss I says, "Mr. C, you think I showed you a blank card to trick you. You can't see anything on the card, that's true, but not being able to see anything is the very best clue." What word can Miss I mean?

When something is there and we cannot see it, what word do we use?

Let Mr. C tell us what he thinks the word may be.

It may take many guesses before the children think of the word "invisible." If no one is able to guess the word, pretend that Mr. C has finally thought of the answer and tell it to the children for him.

TYING IT TOGETHER

Distribute copies of Alpha Time Master #126 to the children. Have them prove that each of the pictures start with Miss I's ĭ sound.

Miss I says that she would like her pictures that start with the ĭ from Itch (Indian, ill, igloo, inch, invisible) to touch her "Itch." Connect Miss I's Itch to her pictures.

ON THEIR OWN

Children may choose from the following activities:

Art
Drawing any of Miss I's word-pictures, then giving clues for each picture so that the rest of the class may guess.

Dramatic Play
Enacting a play with an invisible character such as a dog, a friend or a ghost. (Ideas may come from popular TV shows.)

Sound Discrimination
Listening for words that begin with ĭ in Miss I's song. (record #2)

Sorting And Matching
Using Miss I's Picture Squares, playing cards, and puzzle in any of the activities suggested in the *Games* section.

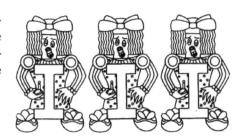

PLANNING AND PREPARATION: Huggable, Miss I; Miss I's Picture Book, one for each child; drawing paper and crayons; Miss I's "In the Middle" Picture Squares; Alpha Time Master #127.

READING COMPREHENSION

Miss I asked the Letter People to help her fill her bag. The Letter People wanted to help Miss I. Miss I wants to tell us about the strange thing that happened when the Letter People said they would fill her bag. She has a picture-book for us to read.

Reading A Picture Book

Give each of the children a copy of Miss I's Picture Book. Discuss each picture with them.

Cover

NAME _ _ _ _ _ _ _ _ _ _ _ _

Miss I's Picture Book

Predicting outcomes

Let's look at the cover.

Who is there? (Miss I)

What does she have with her? (a bag)

Why do you think she has the bag?

What do you think this story will be about?

Let's look at the first page of the story.

Page #1

Which Letter People are here? (Miss I, Mr. H, Mr. M, Miss E)

What is Little Miss I showing to the Letter People? (her bag)

Why do you think she is showing them her bag? (She wants them to fill it.)

How can they help Miss I? (make things for her bag)

What do you think the Letter People will do?

Numeration

Page #2

Let's turn the page and see how they help her.

What are the Letter People doing? (starting to make things)

What is Mr. H doing? (cutting something out)

Let's look at the next page and see what the Letter People are making.

Looking for detail

Page #3

What is Miss E making? (an Indian)

What did she use to make the Indian? (clay, feather)

What has Mr. H cut out? (an igloo)

Let's turn the page and see what Mr. M is doing.

Relating experiences

300

Page #4

Making inferences

Page #5

Recognizing emotions

Page #6

Making inferences
Recognizing humor

What can Mr. M be making?

What does his face look like?

Let's look at the next page and watch the Letter People fill Miss I's bag.

Look at Miss I's face. How does she look? (She is happy.)

Who is putting things in Miss I's bag? (Miss E, Mr. H)

Let's turn the page.

Who is bringing something for Miss I now? (Mr. M)

What is Mr. M carrying?

Help the children realize that Mr. M is carrying nothing!

Look at the expression on Miss E's face. How does she look?

How does Mr. H look?

Why are they puzzled?

One of Miss I's words is the clue to the mystery.

Remind the children of the blank card that Miss I used when Mr. C was trying to guess her words. Have them recall the word "invisible."

Did Mr. M play a trick on Miss I?

Did he want to make Miss I unhappy?

Why is Mr. M's gift a good one for Miss I?

Thinking Of A Title
For The Story

Tell the children that Miss I needs a title for her story. Encourage them to think of titles that include the idea of things being invisible. The children may want to tell Miss I the following rhyme:

> When something is there that we cannot see,
> There's a word to think of — what can it be?
> *Invisible* — that is the word to know.
> It means something is there but it does not show.

IDENTIFYING THE SHORT I SOUND IN THE MEDIAL POSITION IN WORDS

Miss I says she likes to hear her ĭ sound in big words like *invisible, impossible, important*. Now she would like to hear her ĭ sound in some little words, too.

Miss I has thought and thought but she could not find many little words that started with her ĭ sound. Miss A and Miss E have a wonderful idea. They say that Miss I can hear her ĭ sound in little words if her ĭ sound is in the middle of a word.

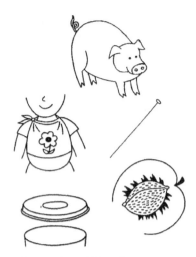

Miss I says that she doesn't understand what that means.

Tell Miss I what it means to have a sound "in the middle."

Help the children explain that it means to hear her sound between other sounds instead of at the beginning of a word. Then show them Miss I's "in the middle" Picture Squares (i.e., pig, pin, bib, lid, pit).

If Miss I says the word that goes with each of these pictures she will hear her sound in the middle of the word.

She wants us to listen to clues about each of her pictures. Miss I will turn her back. Let's help Miss I. After we figure out the name of the picture and hear her ĭ sound, we may turn Miss I around to face us.

**Guessing Words
From Given Clues**

Read the following clues to the children and have them identify each picture from its clue.

I am a farm animal. I give people ham.
If I were invisible, my *oink, oink* would tell you who I am. (pig)

Turn Miss I around if you hear her ĭ sound.

I have a head and am very thin.
If you touch my point you'll prick your skin. (pin)

Turn Miss I around if you hear her ĭ sound.

When baby eats, I'm under his chin.
His clothes stay clean—but what a mess I'm in. (bib)

Turn Miss I around if you hear her ĭ sound.

Inside every peach I will surely be.
You can eat the peach but don't eat me! (pit)

Turn Miss I around if you hear her ĭ sound.

I am the top of a can, that is true.

But I have another name too. (lid)

Turn Miss I around if you hear her ĭ sound.

TALKING ABOUT MISS I'S "DOING WORDS"

Miss I has thought of some "doing words" in which her ĭ sound is "in the middle." She will whisper her "doing words" to someone. He will pretend to be doing the "doing word" without talking.

Whisper one of the following words to a child. The child pantomimes the actions for the word while the rest of the class tries to guess each word. The words are: sit, dig, hit, sip, zip, lick, skip.

Miss I wants to play the "In The Middle Game." Miss A and Miss E have told her how much fun it is. Let's play it with Miss I.

Adapt the "In The Middle" Game, for Miss I as explained in lesson 2A4.

302

TYING IT TOGETHER

Distribute drawing paper and crayons and other art materials. Children may draw "invisible doing" pictures for Miss I. (e.g., *dig:* someone digging with an invisible shovel; *sit:* someone sitting on an invisible chair; *hit:* someone hitting a ball with an invisible bat; *sip:* someone sipping an invisible soda through a straw)

NOTE: Alpha Time Master #127 is a letter to parents explaining the progress the children have made thus far with ALPHA TIME. This letter may be sent home with the children at this time.

ON THEIR OWN

Children may choose from the following activities:

Playing "Invisible" with Miss I.

Auditory Discrimination

> Rules: One child at a time will pretend to be something invisible that makes a sound (e.g., a tiger, fire engine, wind) the other players must guess what the invisible object is.

Sequence Skills

Separating the pages of Miss I's Picture Book and putting them in order again.

Game Skills

Including Miss I's Picture Squares, playing cards and puzzle in the games described in the *Games* section.

Drawing Original Picture-Stories

Drawing or telling a story about a time when a Letter Person was invisible. *Child selects one Letter Person as the hero of his story and tells a story or draws pictures that show that would happen if that Letter Person were invisible. (e.g., Mr. M might take bites out of things, Mr. F might leave footprints behind him, Mr. N might blow in people's ears.)*

21₃

TEACHER OBJECTIVES:

To reinforce the characteristic and sound of Miss I.

To have children pronounce words with initial *i*.

To have children write the letter i.

To teach the concept of initialing.

To have children write their own initials.

PERFORMANCE OBJECTIVES:

The child will say words with the short *i* sound in the initial position.

The child will write the initials of his or her own name.

DEVELOPMENT

Miss I has an impossible itch.

That impossible itch makes her so itchy that sometimes when Miss I writes, the letters are all wiggly.

When she gives us a booklet, she wants us to check the letters to be sure they are not wiggly.

Distribute the Miss I "All About Us" booklets to the children.

Ask the children to find the words that tell the name of the booklet and say them for Miss I.

Which Letter Person's picture do you see? (Miss I)

Whose picture is next to Miss I? (her friend's)

Touch the sentence at the bottom of the booklet.

It says, "Miss I has a friend."

Look at Miss I.

How does she feel all the time? (itchy)

What makes Miss I itchy? (her impossible itch)

Look at the picture of Miss I's friend.

How can you tell the impossible itch is visiting her friend? (The friend looks itchy.)

Miss I could not finish the picture because her friend couldn't stand still for a minute.

Miss I wants us to finish the picture.

Let's make each thing we add look itchy so everyone knows the impossible itch is visiting.

Suggest that the children use wiggly lines.

Give the children the opportunity to finish the picture.

Remind them that the picture may be made to look like themselves or anyone else.

Have the children open the booklet.

Point to the full-page picture on the left-hand side.

Explain that Miss I used this whole page to show what happens when the impossible itch keeps making her itchy. (Miss I wiggle hops.)

Have the children role-play.

One child is the impossible itch, another is Miss I.

The impossible itch says, "I am looking for Miss I. I will make her itch."

The impossible itch touches Miss I.

Miss I says, "The impossible itch found me. I am so itchy. I must wiggle hop."

The child taking the role of Miss I shows how she wiggle hops.

Have the children look at the right-hand side of the booklet.

Explain that Miss I has been noticing that people have letters on things that they wear.

Some people wear a letter on a chain around their neck.

Miss I asked them what the letter meant.

They told her it was the first letter in their name.

The letter that starts their name is called their initial.

Why do you think Miss I loves the word "initial"? (Initial starts like her impossible itch.)

Miss I decided to write her initial in the first sentence on this page.

Read aloud, "Miss I writes her initial."

What letter did Miss I use to write her initial? (I)

Touch Miss I's initial.

Now Miss I wants us to write our initials.

We each have more initials than Miss I has.

Our first initial is the letter that starts our first name.

Demonstrate this by asking a child to say her first name. (*e.g.,* Carol)

Ask Carol the letter that starts her name. (C)

Write the capital C on the blackboard.

Explain that this is her first initial.

At this grade level it is not necessary to discuss the punctuation that comes after an initial.

Follow the procedure with several of the youngsters.

Then adapt the procedure to show the children how they find the initial of their last name.

Help the children complete their sentences.

Select and read several completed sentences aloud.

Encourage the children to tell Miss I their initials.

Have the children turn to the back of the booklet.

Explain that Miss I drew a picture showing initials in different places.

Read aloud, "Let's talk about initials."

Have the children find the different initials in the picture.

They may want to write their own initials on things in the picture.

Discuss actual articles on which they would write their initials to indicate ownership. (boots, mittens, baseball mitt, bat)

Suggest the children take their booklets home.

Have them ask the members of their family to tell Miss I their initials.

10₁

PLANNING AND PREPARATION: Huggables, Misses A, E, I, O, Mr. C, Mr. D, Mr. B; envelope containing note paper; Record #3; small pieces of aluminum foil about 5" square, art materials; Alpha Time Master #128.

Keep Miss O concealed until after the children have heard the recorded dramatization.

MEETING MISS O

Listening For Enjoyment And Information

Tape the envelope to Mr. C's hand and gather the other Letter People around him. Tell the children that Mr. C has received a message from Letter People Land and that the Letter People want to know all about it.

What do you think the message from Letter People Land says? Let's listen to the story.

Play Miss O's Story (record #3, side B, band #1). When the recording is over, reveal Miss O.

Talking About Miss O

What is the new Letter Girl's name? (Miss O)

What is the meaning of *Obstinate?* (stubborn)

How was Miss O Obstinate in the story? (e.g., She wouldn't come out of the pool.)

Why do you think Miss O's mouth is open so wide? (She is saying ŏ, ŏ, ŏ.)

What is Miss O holding in her hand? (a mirror)

Why does she need a mirror? (to be sure her mouth is open wide when she says ŏ ŏ ŏ)

PRACTICING THE SHORT O SOUND

Obstinate Miss O would like us all to practice saying ŏ ŏ ŏ with her. We will need mirrors.

Making Mirrors

Distribute the squares of aluminum foil, and let several children at a time hold up their "mirror" and say ŏ ŏ ŏ.

IDENTIFYING THE UPPER AND LOWER CASE LETTER O

Have the children gather around Miss O. Tell them that Miss O would like to see her capital and lower case letters.

Let's show Miss O her capital O. Then let's find the lower case o.

Finding The Letter O on Miss O

Where is the lower case o? (on Miss O's mirror)

How is the capital O the same as the lower case o? (same shape)

How are the two letters different? (different size)

What kind of line is used to make the O? (curved)

304

TYING IT TOGETHER

Distribute Alpha Time Master #128 and discuss it with the children.

Look at the top picture.

Where is Miss O? (in the pool)

Who else is there? (Mr. C, Mr. D and Miss E)

What do you think they are saying to Miss O?

What book do you think Mr. D is carrying? (dictionary)

Look at the picture on the bottom.

Where is Miss O? (at the doctor's office)

What do you think the doctor is saying?

ON THEIR OWN

Children may choose from the following activities:

Drawing A Picture Story	Drawing several scenes from Miss O's story and stapling the pages together to make a book.
Dramatic Play	Taking the parts of each of the Letter People in Miss O's story and making it an extemporaneous play.
Listening	Listening to Miss O's story (record #3).
Story Re-telling	Re-telling Miss O's story to one of the Letter People who was not there. (This may be recorded if a tape recorder is available.)
Coloring	Using crayons to color Miss O in the pool on the Alpha Time Master.
Letter Tracing	Using Alpha Time Master #69 to trace the upper and lower case letter O.

10 O₂ PLANNING AND PREPARATION: Huggable, Miss O; Record #2; Alpha Time Master #129.

REMEMBERING OBSTINATE MISS O

Listening To
Miss O's Song

Tell the children that Miss O hopes they have not forgotten about her. She would like them to hear her song to remind them.

Play Miss O's song (record #2, side A, band #6) and discuss it with the children.

What are some things Miss O tells us?

Show Miss O how the music makes you want to move.

PREDICTING OUTCOMES

Pretend that Miss O is talking to you and telling you a story. Then tell the children the following short stories, each of which shows how Miss O is Obstinate.

Miss O is trying to remember a word. It is the word that tells she is stubborn. What word do you think Miss O means? (Obstinate)

Miss O wants to tell us what happened to her yesterday. She wants to know if we think she was being Obstinate.

Listening To
"Obstinate" Stories

Early in the morning Miss O went out to wait for the school bus. Some of the other Letter People were waiting too. Miss O said, "I will sit in the seat behind the bus driver. I do not like any other seat." When they got on the bus, the seat behind the driver was taken. The Letter People said that Miss O could choose any other seat on the bus. Miss O would not sit on any other seat. She just kept saying, "No, no, no."

What do you think happened?

Let several children tell what they think happened when Miss O insisted she sit behind the bus driver. Have several small groups act out the situation.

Tell Miss O why you think she was Obstinate.

Miss O wants to tell you about another time when she was called Obstinate. The Letter Girls wanted to play a game. They needed four girls. Miss A, Miss E and Miss I wanted to play, but Miss O said that she didn't like that game. If Miss O didn't play, the other girls couldn't play either because there would not be enough people for the game. Miss O said, "No, no, no, I won't play."

What do you think happened?

Follow the procedure used above for this story and the two stories following, encouraging as many points of view as possible.

Miss O has another story to tell us. Let us see why she was called Obstinate this time. When Miss O came to school, Miss A showed her where to hang her hat and coat. She showed her where to put her boots. Everyone put their hats, coats, and boots away; everyone except Miss O. Miss O just sat there in her hat and coat and boots, wiping her face with a tissue. She was very warm all bundled up like that, but she said, "No, no, no I won't take off my coat."

How was Miss O Obstinate?

What do you think happened?

Something else happened to Miss O and once again she was called Obstinate. Miss O came to school wearing a beautiful party dress. She was going to a party after school. Miss O decided she wanted to paint. "That is not a good idea," the Letter People said. "It is not good to paint while you are wearing your party dress!" You know Obstinate Miss O! She just took a brush and started to paint.

What do you think happened?

PRACTICING THE SHORT VOWEL SOUND Ŏ

When people want to know where a kitten or a puppy is, they sometimes put a bell around its neck. When they hear the bell they know where to find the puppy or the kitten. The Letter People did not put a bell around Miss O's neck, but they can tell where she is by something they hear.

Remember what sound Miss O makes all the time. (ŏ, ŏ, ŏ)

What do you think the Letter People hear wherever Miss O is?

Help the children decide that the Letter People can hear Miss O saying ŏ, ŏ, ŏ. Then introduce the "Where Is Miss O?" game.

The Letter People say if we close our eyes and listen for the ŏ, ŏ, ŏ, we can tell where Miss O is.

Let's try it.

(Sara), you stand at the classroom door with Miss O. Miss O will practice ŏ, ŏ, ŏ as she stands there.

Let's listen to her say ŏ, ŏ, ŏ with our eyes open.

Now let's close our eyes and listen to her say ŏ, ŏ, ŏ.

Remember how the ŏ, ŏ, ŏ sounds when Miss O is standing at the classroom door.

Repeat, placing Miss O in different parts of the room (e.g., near the window, the block corner, the supply shelves). Then start the game.

Playing A Game

Directions: One child pretends to be Miss O and stands in one of the four places where the class heard Miss O saying ŏ, ŏ, ŏ. The other children close their eyes and listen to Miss O saying ŏ, ŏ, ŏ. Miss O calls on a child, saying: "Where am I practicing my ŏ, ŏ, ŏ:" The child answers: "You are practicing your ŏ, ŏ, ŏ in the—(block corner)." If the guess is not correct, another child is called. The game continues with other children taking the part of Miss O.

307

Make sure that the children include ŏ, ō, ȯ in their questions and answers as often as possible.

TYING IT TOGETHER

Recalling Miss O's Stories

Miss O has been telling everyone that she is never Obstinate. The Letter People keep saying, "Remember how Obstinate you were on the bus and in school!" Miss O just says, "I don't remember."

The Letter People want us to show Miss O pictures that will remind Miss O when she was obstinate. They want us to tell her what happened in each of the pictures.

Distribute Alpha Time Master #129 and have the children remind Miss O what happened in each picture.

ON THEIR OWN

Children may choose from the following activities:

Making A Picture Book

Cutting out the pictures on Alpha Time Master #129, coloring the pictures, mounting each on a separate sheet of paper, and stapling the sheets together to make an Obstinate book.

Dramatic Play

Enacting parts of Miss O's Obstinate stories.

Music And Dance

Playing Miss O's music (record #2) and dancing to it, or learning the words to the song.

1K₁

Hide Mr. K where he cannot be seen, but where he may be easily produced at the appropriate moment.

MEETING MR. K

Tell the children that a new Letter Person is ready to come to class.

Talking About The New Letter Person

The new Letter Person keeps doing one thing all the time. He would like us to guess what he does. It is very hard to guess what someone does when you don't have any clues. The new Letter Person said that he will help us guess.

Show the children a ball. (A football is ideal, but any ball will do.)

The new Letter Person said that we should do something to this ball. Show us what we can do to a ball (e.g., throw, slap, kick, punch, catch, bounce).

The new Letter Person says he does only one of these things. He says that he does what you can do to a ball if you use only your feet.

Help the children conclude that what they would have to do is to kick.

The new Letter Person says that he kicks all the time but he never ever kicks anything but a ball. The new Letter Person is very anxious to meet us. He wants to see how we kick. If you close your eyes, and kick three times, the new Letter Person will come.

While the children have their eyes closed, reveal Mr. K.

The Letter Person has a song for us. Let's listen and find out what his name is.

Listening To Mr. K's Music

Play Mr. K's song (record #2, side A, band #7). As the children listen they may kick to the music or move in any way they like.

The new Letter Person wants to know if anyone remembers his name. (Mr. K)

Mr. K is happy that he came to work with us and the other Letter People. He is eager to start making a sound. Mr. K says that before he left Letter People Land, they told him where he would get his sound. That's the only sound that he will use.

Discovering That Mr. K's Sound Comes From Kicking

From where do you think Mr. K will get his sound? (Kicking)

Mr. K says that he is Kicking all the time. He will get his sound from Kicking. Most of the Letter People think this is a good idea.

Miss E does not think so. Miss E says, "Mr. K, if you get your sound from Kicking, there will be a terrible problem with another Letter Person."

"Why will there be a problem if I get my sound from Kicking?" asked Mr. K.

Why do you suppose there might be a problem?

Which Letter Person might not want Mr. K to get his sound from Kicking?

Let the children discuss why they think Mr. K's Kicking might lead to a problem with another Letter Person.

Miss E explained that the sound Mr. K wanted had already been given to another Letter Person.

"Oh, that's funny," said Mr. C. "What other Letter Person has the Kicking sound?"

Miss E laughed and laughed. Then Miss I started to laugh and laugh. Then Mr. L and then Mr. M—and soon all the Letter People were laughing and laughing, but not Mr. C.

"What is so funny?" shouted Mr. C.

"You are," said Miss E.

What do you think Miss E means?

What is it that Mr. C does not realize?

Discovering That C And K Have The Same Sound

Lead the children to the conclusion that "C" and "K" have the same initial sound.

"Mr. C, just listen," said all the Letter People. "Cotton Candy-Kicking."

"That's good," said Mr. C. "Kicking can go in my bag."

"Oh no," said Mr. K. "Kicking belongs to me. I kick, kick, kick, all the time. Kicking must be mine. Kicking is my game."

"Wait a minute!" said Mr. C. "You can't have the same sound I have!"

Miss E was right. This was a problem. Mr. C did not want to share his sound. There was nothing the Letter People could do.

Mr. K was told he would get his sound from Kicking. The Letter People could not change what was decided in Letter People Land. Mr. C was very upset. He sat in a corner and frowned. Poor Mr. K! He felt bad. He felt so bad he started to cry. The Letter People said, "Please don't cry Mr. K. We'll help you find things that start the same way as Kicking. We may not be able to find too many things because Mr. C had the sound first and he has taken many of the things, but we are sure that we can find some things for you."

That made Mr. K happy, he started to kick a ball again and again.

IDENTIFYING WORDS WITH K IN THE INITIAL POSITION

Show the children Mr. K's Picture Squares (i.e. king, kitchen, kite, kitten, key).

The Letter People showed Mr. K some of his picture words. They will give Mr. K a clue and we will find the picture.

The first picture starts the same way as Kicking. It is something we use for unlocking doors. The word rhymes with *me.* What is the word that Mr. K will have? (key)

Show Mr. K how you would use a key to unlock a door.

Let's listen to the next clue to find out what the next thing is that starts the same way as Kicking.

This picture shows something that you hold by a string as it flies in the air. It rhymes with the word *flight.* What is the word that Mr. K will have? (kite)

Show Mr. K how you would fly a kite in the air.

Let's listen to the next clue to find out what starts with Mr. K's Kicking sound.

This is the name of a baby cat. It rhymes with the word *mitten.* What is the word that Mr. K will have? (kitten)

Be a kitten. Show Mr. K how you creep around and meow.

Let's listen to another clue.

This is the name of a man who lives in a castle and wears a crown. It rhymes with the word *ring.* What is the word that Mr. K will have? (king)

Be a king. Show Mr. K how you wear a crown.

Mr. K has one more word. It is a room in your house. It is where you find the stove and the refrigerator and it is where people do the cooking. What is the word that begins with Mr. K's sound? (kitchen)

Make believe you are in a kitchen. Tell us something that you are doing. (e.g., cooking, opening the refrigerator, washing the dishes)

IDENTIFYING THE CAPITAL AND LOWER CASE LETTER "K"

Analyzing The Shape Of "K"

Mr. K wants us to show him his capital letter.

Show Mr. K his capital letter K with your hand.

How many parts are there in the capital letter K? (three)

How many children will we need to make the capital K? (three)

Look at each part. What kind of lines are there? (slanted, and straight lines)

311

Have three children form the capital K with their bodies. Have all the children form groups of three and make several K's. Then have the children show Mr. K his lower case letter. Have them discuss its shape and compare it with the capital letter K.

TYING IT TOGETHER

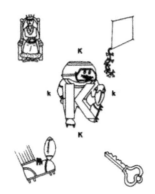

Give the children a copy of Alpha Time Master #130. Encourage them to identify each of Mr. K's pictures (i.e., king, kite, kick, key). Some children may want to connect the letter K to some of Mr. K's pictures.

ON THEIR OWN

Children may choose from the following activities:

Auditory Discrimination

Including Mr. K's puzzle, playing cards, Picture Squares in any of the games suggested in the *Games* section.

Letter Tracing

Using Alpha Time Master #65 to trace the upper and lower case K.

Letter Recognition Color Discrimination

Marking the upper case K on Alpha Time Master #130 with green and lower case k with black.

Motor Coordination

Playing kick ball.

Discrimination Between Left And Right; Counting

Kicking with Mr. K. Mr. K gives directions such as kick with right foot, left foot, kick two times, kick three times, etc.

Music And Dance

Listening to Mr. K's music and kicking to the rhythm.

1K₂

PLANNING AND PREPARATION: Huggables, Mr. K and Mr. T; a bag for Mr. K; Mr. K's Picture Squares; Alpha Time Master #131; paper, scissors, crayons, paste, materials for making keys, keychains, keyrings, and keycases; a keyring, a keycase; Record #2.

AUDITORY RECOGNITION OF WORDS THAT HAVE K IN THE INITIAL POSITION

Mr. K says no one has proven his pictures for him.

"Proving" Mr. K's Words For Him

Show the children and Mr. K his Picture Squares (i.e., king, kite, kitchen, kitten, key). Have the children name and prove each picture and then put into Mr. K's bag.

Each time you prove a picture for Mr. K, he would like to see how you kick. Remember Mr. K never never kicks a person. He would be very unhappy if you kicked anything you could hurt.

After several children have had a chance to name, prove, and kick for Mr. K, play a kicking game with the children. Give them these directions.

Following Directions By Playing A Game

First, Mr. K says we must take off our shoes (so we don't hurt anyone when we kick)

We will put Mr. K's word pictures on the chalkboard.

Then we will play Mr. K's music (record #2, side A, band #7). As the music plays, we will move in a circle showing Mr. K how we kick with our right foot and then with our left foot.

When the music stops we will stop. Then we will close our eyes. Mr. K will ask someone to take away one of his pictures. When we open our eyes, we will have to guess which picture was taken away.

We will say, "Mr. K, did you take away the (key)?"

The child who is helping Mr. K by removing a picture will answer for him. He may say, "No, the (key) is still here." "Guess again." or, "Yes, you're right, the (key) is gone."

As the game continues different children may be called to remove a picture for Mr. K. After a while the procedure can be varied and two pictures may be removed at the same time, then three and then four.

PUTTING TWO WORDS TOGETHER TO MAKE A NEW WORD (COMPOUND WORDS)

Mr. K says that he doesn't care about Mr. C having more words than he has. He has figured out a way to get some more words of his own.

Mr. K likes *keys*. He likes the word *key*. He told the Letter People that he could make lots of words with the word key.

The Letter People said, "Mr. K, *key* is only one word. How can you make many words with one word?"

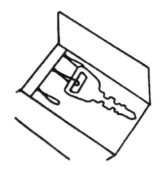

**Making Keys
And Keyrings**

**Analyzing
Compound Words**

Mr. K said, "Listen, sometimes I carry many keys. I don't want to keep them loose in my pocket because I'm afraid I'll lose them. I put them all on a ring. It is not an ordinary ring. It is a ring for keys, it is a. . . (key-ring)."

If available, show the children a keyring.

"*Keyring* is a new word. The first part of the word is *key*. The second part of the word is. . . (ring). When I put the two words together I have the word *keyring*."

The Letter People all clapped their hands. They said, "Mr. K, do it again. Make another new word!"

Mr. K said, "Some people do not like to keep keys on a keyring. They like to keep their keys inside of something. They keep their keys in a case."

Show the children a keycase.
"It is called a. . . (keycase)."

Keycase is another word. The first part of the word is *key*. The second part of the word is *case*. When the two parts of the word are put together we have the word *keycase*.

Mr. K says, "I can think of another one. Sometimes people like to keep their keys on a *chain*. What can we call a chain that holds keys?" (key-chain)

Let the children decide that Mr. K can put together the words "key" and "chain" to make the word "keychain."

What is the first part of the word? (key) What is the second part of the word? (chain) When you put together the two words, which new word do you have? (keychain)

Repeat procedure for *key* and *hole* to make *keyhole*.

Gather the children around the arts and crafts center.

Mr. K would like us to make keys, keys and more keys. Then we can make a keycase for some of the keys, a keyring for some of the other keys and a keychain for the rest of the keys.

What are some materials we can use to make these things for Mr. K?

Let each child talk about the art materials he would like to use.

Mr. K has thought of a way to make more big words out of little words. All of the Letter People want to try to take one of their words and make more words with it.

Gather the children around Mr. T.

Mr. T has something that is made of two words. He uses it to brush each tooth. What is the word? (toothbrush) What two words did Mr. T put together to make the word toothbrush? (*tooth* and *brush*)

Mr. T uses another word that has tooth in it. It looks like paste. You squeeze it onto your toothbrush when you brush your teeth. What is it? (*toothpaste*)

What two words did Mr. T put together to make the word toothpaste? (*tooth* and *paste)*

Follow the same procedure for the words toothache and toothpick. Describe what the new word means, tell the children what the new word is, then let them decide what two words have been combined. Try to include as many Letter People's characteristics as possible.
(e.g. Foot: football, footprint, footstep; Button: buttonhole, buttonhook; Gum: gumdrop, gumball)

TYING IT TOGETHER

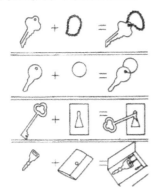

Give each child a copy of Alpha Time Master #131. Have the children identify the two pictures that combine to form a new word (i.e., key plus chain: keychain; key plus ring; keyring; key plus hole: keyhole; key plus case: keycase.

ON THEIR OWN

Children may choose from the following activities:

Word Study

Making a picture list of compound words (e.g., *foot* + *ball*=football).

Art

Drawing or painting pictures of compound words.

Sorting And Classifying

Making a list of different types of cases (e.g., violin case), chains (e.g., bicycle chain) and rings (e.g., curtain ring).

1K₃

PLANNING AND PREPARATION: Huggables, Mr. K and Miss A; Picture Card 10; Alpha Time Master #132; paper, crayons, scissors, paste and other art materials; pots, cans and boxes of food, blocks, paint brushes, musical instruments or other classroom items that can be mixed-up and then sorted for Mr. K; oaktag, mural or chart paper with outlines of kitchen cabinets and drawers.

PICTURE READING FOR COMPREHENSION

*Discussing A
Picture Card*

Frame #1

Finding Detail

Frame #2

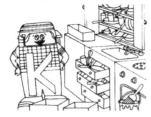

*Drawing Conclusions
From Given Facts*

Frame #3

*Describing And
Projecting*

Mr. K loves his kitchen better than any other room. Why do you think he likes his kitchen? (*Kitchen* starts with his Kicking sound.)

Mr. K had his kitchen painted. Now he has boxes and boxes of things that he must put into the cabinets and drawers.

Mr. K wants to show us how he is going to put everything away.

Show Picture Card 10 to the children. Give each child a matching copy of Alpha Time Master #132.

Let's look at the first picture and see what Mr. K is doing.

Where is Mr. K? (in his kitchen)

What does he have in the boxes? (knives, forks, dishes, pots, pans)

Look at the cabinets. Look at the drawers. Why are they empty? (They were painted.)

If you were unpacking for Mr. K, tell us what you would put in the cabinets and in the drawers.

Tell us what things are in the cabinets and drawers in your kitchen at home.

Let's look at the next picture and see how Mr. K unpacks.

Look at the way Mr. K has started to put his kitchen things away. What do you see in the cabinets? drawers? shelves?

What is wrong with the way Mr. K is arranging his cabinets and shelves and drawers? (They are not neat and all the things are mixed up.)

Why will it be hard for Mr. K to find things if he puts them away like this?

What would you have put in the cabinet? In the drawer?

Mr. K wants to invite some of the Letter People for lunch. Miss A has come to help him set the table. What do you think will happen when Miss A tries to find things to use to set the table?

Why does Miss A look worried?

What are the things Miss A will need to set the table? (knives, forks, plates)

What do you think Miss A will do?

316

Frame #4

Describing, Sorting And Classifying

Let's look at the last picture.

What is Miss A doing with all the things Mr. K had in the cabinets and drawers? (taking them out and arranging them neatly)

Why has Miss A made piles on the table? How do you think she will re-arrange the cabinets and drawers so that things are easy to find?

How should **Mr. K** put things away in his cabinets and drawers?

Lead the children to the conclusion that in one cabinet we put the big plates, next to it we put the smaller plates. Knives and forks may be put into one of the drawers etc.

SORTING AND CLASSIFYING

Making Things For Mr. K's Kitchen

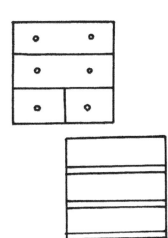

Outline several cabinets and several drawers on large oaktag, mural, or chart paper. Tell the children that they may make things for these cabinets and drawers. They may make dishes, pots, silverware, cans and boxes of food.

Tell them that Mr. K has learned that it is easiest to put all the things that are the same in one place. The children may show Mr. K how they can do this.

First have the children decide what they want to store in each of the cabinet and drawer outlines. They may then use a variety of art materials to make any of the things mentioned.

As the children make each item, they may paste or tape it on the cabinet or drawer they have designated for it. Have them check to make sure that things that are the same are being stored together. (e.g., all the knives in one place, all the forks in another place)

Mr. K has watched us put things in his kitchen so that all the things that are the same are in one place. He says that the kitchen looks better but he is not sure that it really will work better!

The Letter People have thought of a good way for us to prove it to him. The Letter People will keep talking to Mr. K so that he doesn't see what is happening in the classroom. While they talk to Mr. K we will make the classroom look the way Mr. K thought the cabinets and drawers should be.

Mixing Up Blocks, Musical Instruments, Paints And Crayons

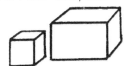

We won't have all the blocks together the way we usually keep them. We'll put some blocks here, some over there and some blocks in another place. We'll do the same thing with the musical instruments, the paints, the crayons. Then we'll ask Mr. K to build a house. He will see how hard it is to find all the blocks he needs when they are not together in one place.

TYING IT TOGETHER

Have one child work with Mr. K collecting the scattered blocks to build the block house.

Then tell the children that Mr. K wants to have a rhythm band. He needs all the rhythm instruments. Again, let one child work with Mr. K and see how difficult it is to find the rhythm instruments when they are not kept together.

317

Repeat this procedure with the other things that have been mixed-up. Help the children to conclude that keeping things together makes them much easier to find and use.

ON THEIR OWN

Children may choose from the following activities:

Sequence

Cutting apart the frames of Alpha Time Master #132 and putting them back in order. Order may be checked against Picture Card 10.

Storytelling— Dramatic Play

Using Picture Card 10 to retell Mr. K's story or as a background for a stick puppet play.

Sorting And And Classifying

Arranging a pile of mixed up materials according to size, color, use or fabric. (This activity may be part of playing store or house.)

1K₄

PLANNING AND PREPARATION: Huggables, Mr. K and Mr. L; Mr. K's Picture Squares; Alpha Time Master #133.

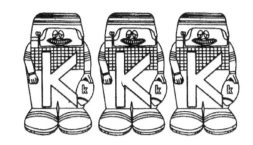

TALKING ABOUT MR. K's KICK

Remember what Mr. L said about love? Mr. L thinks that love and loving people is very important. He loves all the Letter People. He loves Mr. K and so he doesn't understand why Mr. K kicked him.

Tell the children this story:

*Listening To
A Story*

It all happened early this morning. Mr. L was putting sticks on some lollies. He was making them into lollipops. All of a sudden Mr. L jumped up and the lollies crashed to the ground.

Someone had kicked him! He said, "Leaping Lollies! I must have made a mistake. It couldn't have happened." Mr. L went back to work and it happened again. He knew that the only Letter Person who kicks is Mr. K.

Mr. L loved Mr. K. He thought that Mr. K loved him too. Why did Mr. K kick him?

The other Letter People heard Mr. L crying. They were very upset. Everybody loved Mr. L. Mr. L told them what had happened. All the other Letter People were angry at Mr. K.

Mr. K had promised that he would never kick anything but a ball. Now he had kicked Mr. L. The Letter People marched right over to Mr. K's house and banged on Mr. K's kitchen door. When Mr. K opened the door, he knew that something was wrong. He could tell by the angry faces of the Letter People.

They said, "Mr. K, why did you kick Mr. L?"

"I would never kick Mr. L. It must be a mistake," said Mr. K.

"It's no mistake," cried the Letter People. "Mr. L was kicked two times and no one else kicks but you, Kicking K. Don't you do that again!" Poor Mr. K scratched his head. He couldn't understand what had happened. He would never kick anyone!

Mr. K wants to be as nice to everyone as Mr. L is. In fact, Mr. K had spent the night looking through a dictionary. Mr. K was looking for one of his words that means the same thing as loving. He found the word *kind*.

The dictionary said that when you are kind to people you are good and gentle to them. Mr. K had planned to call Mr. L first thing this morning to tell him that *loving* and *kind* meant almost the same thing.

Now Mr. L and all the Letter People were angry at him. Mr. K could not understand it.

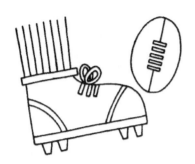

Suddenly Mr. K heard something giggling and giggling and giggling. "Who is giggling?" he asked.

"It's your Kick," said the Kick.

"What's so funny?" asked Mr. K.

"You should have seen Mr. L leap in the air when I kicked him. It was so funny," said the Kick.

"You kicked him?" said Mr. K.

"Oh, sure," said the Kick. "While you were sleeping, I went to have some fun. I love to kick people."

"Oh dear," said Mr. K. "You can't kick people. That's mean. Kicking a ball—that's fun. To kick people is terrible! I want you to be a kind Kick."

"What does *kind* mean?" asked the Kick.

Kind Means Loving

"*Kind* means something like loving," said Mr. K.

"I do not want to be a kind Kick," said the Kick.

"Well," said Mr. K. "Then you cannot be my Kick."

"Without me you can't be called Kicking K. Without me you won't have a sound," said the Kick.

"That's true," said Mr. K. "Even so I do not want anything but a kind Kick."

Talking About Kindness

"Well, I'm packing and leaving home," said the Kick. The Kick packed his suitcase and left. Mr. K was no longer Kicking K.

Without his Kick, Mr. K did not have a sound.

When the Letter People found out what had really happened, they felt sorry for having blamed Mr. K. They should have known that kind Mr. K would never kick anyone.

That naughty Kick turned up in the strangest places, kicking everyone.

The Letter People made big signs that said, "Watch Out For the Kick Who Won't be Kind."

None of the Letter People would talk to the Kick. When they saw him, they chased him away.

Soon the Kick was very unhappy. Wherever he went he heard people singing about him.

Sing the following song with the children to the tune of "Farmer In The Dell."

320

*Dramatizing The
Kick Song*

The children may dramatize by having one child be Mr. K and the other,
the Kick. They may then follow the actions described in the song, as it
is sung.

The Kick won't be kind.
The Kick won't be kind.
Hi Ho, the kick-kio,
The Kick won't be kind.

Chase the bad Kick away.
Chase the bad Kick away.
Hi Ho, the kick-kio,
Chase the bad Kick away.

K sent the Kick away.
K sent the Kick away.
Hi Ho, the kick-kio,
K sent the Kick away.

The Kick has decided that he does not want to be bad anymore. He will
try to be a kind Kick.

The Kick wants to go back to Mr. K but the Kick is worried. He thinks
that Mr. K doesn't love him anymore and will not forgive him. The Kick
wants us to talk to Mr. K and find out how he feels.

*Let the children talk to Mr. K. Then have them tell the Kick how Mr. K
feels about him. Have them ask Mr. K if he will take the Kick back. Then
pretend to talk to Mr. K yourself and tell the children the following:*

*Talking About
Forgiveness*

Mr. K says that he has always loved his Kick. He says that sometimes
people we love do things that we don't like. We may not like what they do
but we don't stop loving them. We forgive them and try to help them do
the things they should.

Mr. K says that he does not want his Kick to kick people. He wants his
Kick to be a kind Kick. He did not stop loving the Kick. He hoped that the
Kick would find out that it is best to be a kind Kick. Mr. K will be happy if
the Kick comes back and becomes Mr. K's kind Kick.

The Kick is happy too. He will be glad to get back to Mr. K and start kicking balls again.

*Sing the following words, again to the tune of "Farmer In The Dell."
Have the children join in, dramatizing the words of the song.*

The Kick is back with K.
The Kick is back with K.
Hi Ho, the kick kio,
The Kick is back with K!

Let's kick and kick away.
Let's kick and kick away.
Hi Ho, the kick kio,
The Kick is back with K!

Mr. K has visited each of the Letter People. He does not want them to
chase his Kick anymore. He wants them to know that now he has a kind
Kick. He rings the doorbell at each house. The Letter Person says, "Who
is there?" Mr. K answers, "It is Mr. K and his kind Kick."

All the Letter People are happy that the Kick has decided to be kind. They think that that was a good decision for the Kick to make.

Now when we prove things for Mr. K, we don't have to say only Kick, anymore. "What may we say instead?" (*Help the children decide that now they may say "Kind Kick" when they name things for Mr. K.*)

Mr. K says that this makes him happy. When you prove things for all the other Letter People you use two words, such as Funny Feet. Now Mr. K may have two words too — Kind Kick.

Show the children Mr. K's Picture Squares (i.e., king, kitten, kite, key, kitchen) and have them prove each for Mr. K using the term "Kind Kick."

TYING IT TOGETHER

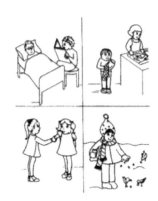

Distribute copies of Alpha Time Master #133. Have the children name and talk about each "kindness" in the picture. (i.e., someone reading to an elderly or sick person; child helping to dry the dishes; child sharing an ice cream cone; someone feeding the birds on a cold day)

ON THEIR OWN

Demonstrating Feelings

Classifying

Record Keeping

Children may choose from the following activities:

Being kind to at least one person in the class each day.

Making a list of kind things that may be done at home.

Keeping a kindness record.

1K₅

TEACHER OBJECTIVES:

To reinforce the characteristic and sound of Mr. K.

To have children discuss objects found in the kitchen.

PERFORMANCE OBJECTIVES:

The child will say words with the voiced ⧸ in the initial position.

The child will identify objects found in th kitchen.

DEVELOPMENT

The Letter People showed Mr. K the "All About Us" booklets they made. Mr. K was so excited that he stopped kicking until he finished making booklets.

Distribute the Mr. K "All About Us" booklets.
Have the children find and say the title of the booklet for Mr. K.

Which Letter Person's picture is on the booklet? (Mr. K)
Whose picture is next to Mr. K? (his friend's)
Touch the sentence at the bottom of the booklet.
It says, "Mr. K has a friend."
What is special about Mr. K? (his kind kick)
What is the only thing Mr. K kicks? (a football)
With what does Mr. K kick the ball? (his foot)
Look at the picture Mr. K drew of his friend.
What did Mr. K forget to draw? (the foot that kicked the ball)
What must we draw to finish the picture? (the foot)
Give the children the opportunity to draw the missing foot.
Then suggest they finish the picture of Mr. K's friend to look like themselves or anyone else.

Have the children open their booklets.
Ask them to touch the first sentence on the left-hand side.
What picture did Mr. K put in the first sentence? (his kick)
Read aloud, "Mr. K likes to kick."

Mr. K says there's one room in his house he likes more than any other room.
Look at the picture at the bottom and find out which room he likes. (kitchen)

Why do you think Mr. K likes the kitchen? (*Kitchen* starts like *kind kick*)
Tell Mr. K all the things you see in his kitchen.
Touch the sentence Mr. K wrote.
It says, "Mr. K's kitchen has a
Mr. K. says the sentence isn't finished.
It doesn't tell what his kitchen has.
He drew a picture to show us the things in his kitchen.
Say the name of something in Mr. K's kitchen. (e.g., refrigerator)
Let's use that word to finish the sentence.
I'll read the sentence Mr. K wrote.
When I stop, everyone will say the word "refrigerator."
That will finish the sentence.

322A

The incompleted sentence may be read many times.
The children may finish the sentence by supplying a different word each time.
The word they choose can be anything that is pictured in Mr. K's kitchen.
They may enjoy finishing the sentence with a series of words said in rapid succession. (*e.g.*, stove, sink, table, pot)

Mr. K took this whole page to tell us about himself.
What two things did he tell us? (He likes to kick. His kitchen has a *e.g.*, refrigerator.)
Mr. K wants us to use the next page.
Have the children touch the first dotted line.
Explain that Mr. K wants each of them to write his or her name.
After the children have had an opportunity to do this, select and read a booklet. (*e.g.*, Lorenzo likes to   .)

Mr. K says the sentence is not finished.
Mr. K's sentence tells he likes to kick.
Lorenzo's sentence does not tell what Lorenzo likes to do.
Mr. K drew pictures under the sentence.
If Lorenzo likes to do one of the things in the picture, Lorenzo can circle the picture.
The picture will finish his sentence. (*e.g.*, Lorenzo likes to jump.)

If the children do not want to circle one of the pictures, they may draw or cut out and paste a picture of something they like to do.
Read several completed sentences aloud.

Explain that Mr. K drew a picture on the back of the booklet.

Have the children turn to the back of the booklet.
Read aloud, "Let's talk about things in a kitchen."
Have the children find and name all the different objects in the picture. You may want them to tell the purpose of each object.

Ask the children to open their booklets.

Draw the children's attention to the second sentence on the right-hand page.
Explain that Mr. K wants them to tell him what is in their kitchens.
Help the children complete their sentences with pictures of dictated words.

Read several sentences aloud.
Encourage the children to tell Mr. K the names of the objects in their kitchens.

Encourage the children to take their booklets home.
Have them ask members of their families to tell Mr. K the different things that are in their kitchens.

1W₁

PLANNING AND PREPARATION: Huggables, Mr. K and Mr. W; a bag for Mr. W; Record #2; Mr. W's Picture Squares; drawing paper; crayons (including several red, green and black ones); scissors; paste; magazines; other art materials; Alpha Time Master #134.

Place Mr. K near you. Conceal Mr. W where he will be easily available.

MEETING MR. W AND HIS WONDERFUL WINK

Tell the children that Mr. K knows something about the next Letter Person who is coming to class.

Mr. K received a message from Letter People Land. The message said that the next Letter Person keeps doing something with one of his eyes.

What could he do with one of his eyes?

Lead the children to the conclusion that the next Letter Person winks.

Tell the children to turn to the back of the room and to wink their eyes. Place Mr. W in front of the class.

Our new Letter Person says his name is Mr. W and he has a Wonderful Wink.

Show Mr. W how you wink.

Show us Mr. W's Wonderful Winking eye.

Let's listen to Mr. W with his Wonderful Wink as he sings his song for us.

Listening And Moving To Mr. W's Music

Play Mr. W's song (record #2, side B, band #1) and discuss it with the children. Then replay the song and let the children participate.

What are some things Mr. W said?

Show Mr. W how his music makes you want to move.

What does Mr. W think is the most wonderful thing in the world? (his Wonderful Wink)

Let's play the song again and wink with Mr. W.

IDENTIFYING THE UPPER AND LOWER CASE LETTER W

Forming The Capital W With Their Bodies

Have the children find Mr. W's capital and lower case letter. After they have traced the capital letter W with their fingers and counted four slanted lines in the letter, they may form groups of four and make the W with their bodies.

DISCOVERING THAT MR. W WILL GET HIS SOUND FROM WONDERFUL WINK

Now that Mr. W knows which letter will work in words for him, he would like you to think about where he will get his sound.

From where do you think Mr. W will get his sound? Think of what Mr. W likes best of all.

Lead the children to the conclusion that Mr. W's sound will come from the beginning sound of Wonderful Wink. Tell the children that Mr. W has brought some pictures with him that begin the same way as Wonderful Wink. Mr. W would like to give clues to the children so that they may guess which pictures he is talking about.

AUDITORY DISCRIMINATION OF WORDS WITH "W" IN THE INITIAL POSITION

Identifying Mr. W's Pictures

Show the children Mr. W's Picture Squares, (i.e., wig, watch, wallet, window, worm). They will listen to Mr. W's clue, pick the picture that goes with it, prove it, and put it into Mr. W's bag.

Mr. W says that all the things he is thinking about start the same way as Wonderful Wink. Let's listen to the first riddle:

It says tick tock.
It is not a clock.
You wear it on your wrist,
It has a knob you wind and twist.

Find the picture Mr. W is thinking about. (watch)

Listen to the next riddle.

This is something to wear.
It looks like your hair.
It goes right on your head.
It can be black, brown, blond or red. (wig)

Fold this in half or open it wide.
You'll find pictures and money and cards inside.
Women put it in handbags, it will easily fit.
Men think that a pocket is the best place for it. (wallet)

It is made of glass so you can look outside.
Fresh air comes in when you open it wide.
It can have covers of different kinds,
Curtains, shades, or pull-up blinds. (window)

I wiggle and squirm and live in the ground.
Sometimes in an apple I am found.
You need to have me when you wish,
To go to the river to catch some fish. (worm)

Mr. W has another game he wants to play with us. In this game, Mr. W needs some children to be artists who will draw for him. He needs some children to be "Wonderful Winkers." The winkers watch the artists.

Choose children to be artists, the rest will be winkers. Give each artist a sheet of drawing paper and a few crayons. Make sure each has a red, green and black crayon. Each artist has his own group of winkers around him. Whisper to each artist the name of the picture Mr. W wants him to draw (i.e., a witch, a worm, a watermelon, a wagon, a woodpecker). As the artist draws, read the clue to the winkers. As soon as a winker knows what the artist is drawing, he starts to wink. The winkers wink until the picture is finished.

324

Illustrating
Mr. W's Words

Remember winkers, start to wink when you know what Mr. W is thinking about. When you think you know the answer, prove it to yourself to make sure it starts the same way as Wonderful Wink.

Give the children clues for the first picture the artists are drawing (i.e., witch).

The artists are drawing a picture. They will use their *black* crayons.

The person they are drawing is dressed all in black.

She wears a big black pointed hat.

She has a broom.

Sometimes she has a black cat. (witch)

Select different children to be artists for each of the following sets of clues.

I creep and crawl on the ground.

Sometimes people put me on a fishing hook to try to catch fish.

I rhyme with the word *squirm*. (worm)

I am something to eat.

I grow on the ground.

I am all green on the outside.

When you cut me open the part that you eat is red.

I have black pits. (watermelon)

I have four wheels. My wheels are round.

I have a handle so a little girl or boy can pull me.

Sometimes children like to sit inside of me and take a ride. (wagon)

I am a bird.

I am very good at climbing tree trunks.

I have a long bill. I peck and get the bugs from the bark of the tree trunks.

When I drill to get the bugs, I make a lot of noise. (woodpecker)

Making Things For
Mr. W's Bag

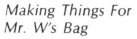

Mr. W would like to see all the things you make and find for his bag.

Let the children make or cut out objects for Mr. W's bag. They may use art materials and a variety of magazines.

Singing A
Winking Song

Let the children practice winking for Mr. W. Then they may form a circle around Mr. W and sing this winking song to the tune of "Frère Jacques:"

We are winking.
We are winking.
Wink with us.
Wink with us.
We welcome you with winking.
We welcome you with winking.
Wink, wink, wink,
Wink, wink, wink.

TYING IT TOGETHER

Distribute copies of Alpha Time Master #134 to the children. They may draw lines to connect the picture of the "window" to the "wallet", the "wig" to the "wallet", the "wig" to the "worm", the "watch" to the "worm", thereby forming a capital W. Before the lines are connected, each picture must be "proven" to Mr. W.

ON THEIR OWN

Children may choose from the following activities:

Music And Dance

Dancing to Mr. W's music (record #2).

Auditory
Discrimination

Listening for words in Mr. W's song (record #2) that begin with his sound.

Including Mr. W's Picture Squares, puzzle, playing cards in the games listed in the *Games* section.

Letter Tracing

Using Alpha Time Master #77 to trace the upper and lower case letter W.

Oral Communication

Introducing Mr. W to the other Letter People, telling each one that Mr. W has a Wonderful Wink.

1W₂

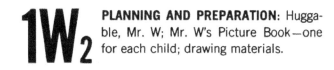

PLANNING AND PREPARATION: Huggable, Mr. W; Mr. W's Picture Book—one for each child; drawing materials.

READING COMPREHENSION

Reading A
Picture Book
Cover

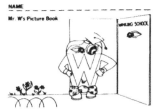

*Making inferences
looking for detail*

Page 1

Auditory discrimination

Talking About
"Doing Words"

Extending vocabulary

Everyone has heard about Mr. W's Wonderful Wink, and now everyone and everything wants to learn how to wink.

Mr. W has decided to start a Winking School. Anyone or anything may have winking lessons at his school.

Mr. W has books for us that will tell us what happened one day at Mr. W's Winking School.

Give each child a copy of Mr. W's Picture Book.

Let's look at the cover of Mr. W's book. What is Mr. W doing? (standing in front of his school)

What is Mr. W looking at? (his watch)

Why do you think he is looking at his watch?

Why is Mr. W standing at the door? (waiting for people to come to his school)

Who is coming to Mr. W's Winking School? (duck, dog, worm)

Why do you think the duck, the dog and the worm are coming to the school? (They want to learn to wink.)

The duck says, "Winking is a Mr. W 'doing word.' I want to learn to wink."

The duck says, "I know a Mr. W 'doing word' that I do all the time."

What does a duck do that starts the same way as Wonderful Wink? (waddle)

Be a duck. Show Mr. W how you waddle.

Ducks are good at waddling, but what will Mr. W have to teach this duck to do? (wink)

The dog who came to Winking School knows a Mr. W "doing word." He does it with his tail.

What "doing word" is the dog thinking about that starts the same way as Wonderful Wink. (wag)

Be a dog. Show Mr. W how your tail wags.

Dogs are good at wagging but what will Mr. W have to teach him? (how to wink)

The worm who came to Winking School knows a Mr. W "doing word." He does it as he moves along the ground.

What does the worm do that starts with Mr. W's Wonderful Wink sound? (wiggle)

Be a worm. Show Mr. W how you wiggle along the ground.

Worms are good at wiggling but what will Mr. W have to teach this worm? (how to wink)

Let's turn the page and look at the next part of the story and see what happens.

Page 2

Predicting outcomes

Where are the dog, the duck and the worm? (in the classroom)

What is happening? (Mr. W is teaching them to wink.)

Why do you think Mr. W will be a good teacher?

What kind of pupils do you think they will be?

Let's look at the next page and see if they learned to wink at the Winking School.

Page 3

Relating experiences
Making judgments

Who has learned to wink? (the worm and the duck)

How can you tell that the worm and duck have learned to wink? (They are wearing a badge around their necks.)

Why is Mr. W still working with the dog? (The dog needs more help.)

How do you think the dog feels?

Tell Mr. W how you felt when you couldn't learn something as fast as someone else.

What things might the dog learn to do faster than the duck or the worm?

Why doesn't everyone learn the same way as everyone else?

Help the children realize that people learn at different speeds.

Let's turn the page and see what happens in the next part of the story.

Page 4

Interpreting feelings

Why do you think Mr. W is holding the dog on his lap?

Be Mr. W. Tell us what you are whispering to the dog.

If you were the dog and were having so much trouble learning to wink what would you do?

Let's look at the next part of the story.

Page 5

Solving problems

What is the dog doing? (talking to the duck and the worm)

Who else is at the Winking School? (witch, watermellon)

What is Mr. W doing? (teaching them to wink)

The duck and the worm know how to wink. The dog wants to learn but he is having trouble learning. How can the duck and the worm help?

Be the dog and tell us what you are saying to the duck and the worm.

Be the duck or the worm and tell us what you are saying to the dog.

Tell the duck and the worm about a time when you helped someone in our class.

Tell the dog about a time when you asked someone in our class to help you.

Why can't Mr. W stay with the dog all the time until he learns to wink? (Mr. W must help others to learn.)

Page 6

Predicting outcomes
Main idea

Mr. W didn't have time to finish the story. Let's finish it for him.

The children may tell their ending to the class or they may draw it on the last page (p. 6) of the book.

Show the children how the different endings can affect the title of the story. (e.g., If one child ends the story with the dog learning to wink, the child might call the story "The Dog, Duck and Worm Learn to Wink." Another child might end the story by having the dog try and try but be unable to learn to wink. Ask the child why the first title could not be used with this ending.)

TALKING ABOUT "DOING WORDS"

Everyone has a good time at Winking School. After they have learned to wink they like to try to do two things at the same time.

The duck *winks* and *waddles*. Try it.

Dramatizing Words

The worm *winks* and *wiggles*. Try it.

The dog *winks* and *wags* his tail. Try it.

A mop came to Winking School. What does a mop do that starts the same way as Wonderful Wink? (wash)

Now the mop can *wash* and *wink*. Try it.

A dust cloth spends its time wiping the furniture. After it came to Winking School the dust cloth could *wink* and *wipe*. Try it.

Follow the same procedure for the words wave, wax and weed. (e.g., Try waving and winking. Try waxing and winking. Try weeding and winking.)

TYING IT TOGETHER

Play the "Winking and Doing" game with the children. One child decides what to do while he is winking and the class dramatizes it with him to the tune of "Did You Ever See A Lassie?"

Did you ever see me winking, me winking, me winking?
Did you ever see me winking and waving as well?

     Go winking and waving,
     Go winking and waving.
     Did you ever see me winking and waving as well?

Auditory
Discrimination

Draw large outlines of windows on the chalk board. Divide each window into several panes. Give a child who is at the chalkboard a damp sponge to wash a part of Mr. W's "window." Before they wash the window the children must tell Mr. W something that starts the same way as Wonderful Wink. If the children have difficulty recalling a word they may look for something in Mr. W's bag.

ON THEIR OWN

Children may choose from the following activities:

Sequence Skills

Separating the pages of Mr. W's Picture Book, mixing them up, and then putting them back in order.

Storytelling

Telling the story about Mr. W's Wonderful Winking School to one of the Letter People.

Dramatic Play

Taking a part in the dramatization of Mr. W's story.

Arts And Crafts

Drawing windows and pasting pictures of things that start the same way as Wonderful Wink on each pane. Children may make sponges out of paper and pretend they are washing the window panes as they name each picture.

1W₃

TEACHER OBJECTIVES:

To reinforce the characteristic and sound of Mr. W.

To make children aware of the concept of weight.

PERFORMANCE OBJECTIVES:

The child will say words with the *w* in the initial position.

The child will show, with the movement of hands, that some things weigh more than others.

The child will show, by using a balance scale, that some things weigh more than others.

DEVELOPMENT

Mr. W said if Mr. K could stop kicking long enough to make "All About Us" booklets, he would stop winking.
Mr. W stopped winking for a week and made the booklets.

Distribute the booklets.

Ask the children to find the words "All About Us" and say them for Mr. W.

Which Letter Person's picture is on the booklet? (Mr. W)
Whose picture is next to Mr. W? (his friend's)
Touch the sentence at the bottom of the booklet.

It says, "Mr. W has a friend."
What is special about Mr. W? (his wonderful wink)
Look at the picture of Mr. W's friend.
What is missing on the face? (an eye)
What special thing do you think Mr. W wants his friend to do? (wink)
Let's make the picture look as if Mr. W's friend is winking.

Then suggest they finish the picture to make it look like anyone they wish.

Have the children open their booklets.
Ask them to touch the first sentence on the left-hand side.
What picture did Mr. W put in the first sentence? (his wink)
Read aloud, "Mr. W likes to wink."
Mr. W says the next sentence will tell us there's something else he likes to do.

Read aloud, "Mr. W likes to weigh things."
He uses a special scale to discover which things weigh more than other things.
He puts one thing on each side.
The thing that weighs more makes that side of the scale go down.
What two things is Mr. W weighing at the bottom of the page?
Which side of the scale has been forced down? (the side holding the wagon)
How do we know the wagon weighs more than the watch?

Mr. W wants us to use the next page.

Have the children touch the first dotted line.
Explain that Mr. W wants them each to write their name on it.

After the children have had an opportunity to do this, select and read a booklet. (*e.g.*, Mary Ellen likes to   .)
Mr. W says the sentence is not finished.
Mary Ellen's sentence does not tell what Mary Ellen likes to do.
Lead the children to conclude that the sentence can be finished with a picture that is drawn or cut out and pasted, or by dictating a word that tells what Mary Ellen likes to do.
After the children complete their sentences, select and read several aloud.

Draw the children's attention to the second sentence and have them each write his or her name on the dotted line.
Select booklets and read the sentences aloud. (*e.g.*, Anne weighs things.)

Mr. W says the scale at the bottom of the page is weighing two things.
We cannot see the two things because he made them invisible.
Touch the side of the scale holding the invisible thing that weighs more.
Prove to Mr. W that you are right. (The side that is lower holds the heavier object.)
Mr. W wants us to make the invisible things appear by pasting a picture on each side of the scale.
The thing that weighs more must be pasted on the side that is down.

First Mr. W wants us to look at the pictures he drew on the back of the booklet.
Let's turn to the back.

Read aloud, "Let's talk about weighing things."
Have the children find the scale that is comparing the weight of the whale to the weight of the airplane.
Ask them to touch the side that has been forced down.
Remind them that the side holding the thing that weighs more is down.
Ask them which weighs more, the airplane or the whale.

Follow the same procedure with the other two scales.
Draw their attention to the fact that the scale comparing the weight of the carton of eggs to the weight of the chicken does not have one side forced down very much.
Explain that this means both things weigh almost the same.
In direct contrast, draw their attention to the scale comparing the weight of the worm to the weight of the elephant.
Ask them why the side holding the elephant is as far down as it can go. (The elephant weighs much more than the worm.)

Give the children the opportunity to compare the weights of different objects in the room.

If a balance scale is not available, show the children how to use their hands to represent the two sides of the balance scale.

Initially, it will be easier for them to make judgments if there is an extreme difference between the weights of the objects. (*e.g.*, a heavy wooden block held in one hand, a piece of chalk held in the other hand)

After they have had experiences comparing weights, suggest that they turn to the inside of the booklet.

Have them place a picture on either side of the scale that is supposedly holding the invisible objects.

Placing the pictures before they paste them enables you to check and see if the pictures have been properly placed.

Encourage the children to tell Mr. W about the objects they weighed.

Suggest the children take their booklets home.

Have them ask members of their family to help them compare the weight of two objects.

Be sure they understand that their hands can be used to represent the sides of the balance scale.

1Y₁

PLANNING AND PREPARATION: Huggables, Mr. Y, Miss O, Mr. S, Mr. H, Mr. T; Alpha Time Master #135; Record #2; paper; crayons; tape; The words *why, what, when,* written on separate sheets of paper.

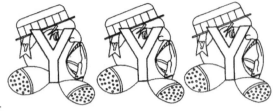

Group the Letter People where they can be seen. Hide Mr. Y where he is easily available but not visible.

MEETING MR. Y

Gather the children around the Letter People.

The Letter People are confused. They received a message from Letter People Land. A new Letter Person is coming.

The Letter People think that there is a mistake in the message. The message says that the new Letter Person's name is "Y."

Miss O asks, "How can Y be a name?" She says that *why* is a word that asks a question.

She asks, "Why do I have to get up? Why do I have to go to sleep?"

*Listening To
A Story*

Mr. S says, "I also ask, Why. Why should I eat spinach? Why should I wear a hat?"

Mr. H wants us to tell him when we use the word *why.*

Tell him about some of the times you have asked "Why?"

Mr. T is sure there is some mistake. He says that no one can have the name "Y."

We will have to wait until the new Letter Person comes. Then we will ask him. If you close your eyes I think that he will come.

While the children's eyes are closed, reveal Mr. Y. Let the children discuss him, talk to him and talk about him.

Look at Mr. Y. What do you think he is doing? (yawning)

When do people yawn? (when they are tired)

I wonder why Mr. Y is yawning. What can be making him so tired?

Let's ask Mr. Y how he got his name and why he is Yawning.

TALKING ABOUT QUESTION WORDS

Tell the children the following story:

Mr. Y says that when he was in Letter People Land he was always asking questions.

There are some words that are called "question words."

Whenever you want to ask a question you start by using one of those words.

331

If you want to know what you are going to have for lunch, you would ask, "What am I having for lunch?"

Tell us the word that started your question. *(what)*

The word *what* is a question word.

Ask another question beginnning with the word *what*.

If you wanted to know where you were going to play after school, you would ask, "Where am I going to play after school?"

Tell us the word that started your question. *(where)*

The word *where* is a question word.

Ask another question starting with *where*.

If you wanted to know when you were going shopping, you would ask, "When am I going shopping?"

Tell us which word started your question. *(when)*

When is a question word.

Ask another question starting with the word *when*.

Mr. Y would never use any of those words. If he wanted to know what he was eating for lunch he would ask, "*Why* am I eating for lunch?"

"Why are you eating for lunch?," said someone. Would you rather sleep for lunch?"

Mr. Y could not understand why people gave him funny answers when he asked a question.

One day Mr. Y wanted to know where he was playing after school. Instead of saying, "Where am I going to play?" Guess what he said!

He said, "*Why* am I playing after school?"

One of his friends was surprised. He said, "If you don't want to play, don't play."

Again Mr. Y could not understand why his friend was angry at him for asking a question.

Another time someone promised to take Mr. Y shopping.

Instead of saying, "When am I going shopping?" Guess what he said!

He said, "*Why* am I going shopping?"

"Why?" shouted the person who was going shopping with Mr. Y. "You have been asking me to take you shopping and now you ask me why you are going! Now I won't take you."

Poor Mr. Y! Everytime he asked a question people were angry at him. Other people asked questions and they got answers.

Mr. Y knew that something was wrong. Soon, when anyone in Letter People Land saw him they would say, "There goes Mr. Y. All he ever says is why, why, why?"

Soon it was time for Mr. Y to leave Letter People Land and come to us. Before he came, the people in Letter People Land had to give him a name. It usually took a long time to decide on a name. Not this time. A decision was made very quickly. His name was Mr. Y.

Mr. Y says that he gets tired of asking why, why all the time. He just Yawns and Yawns.

Listening To
Mr. Y's Music

Let's listen to Mr. Y's music.

Play Mr. Y's song (record #2, side B, band #2). discuss the song with the children. Encourage them to move (and Yawn) along with the music the second time it is played.

USING QUESTION WORDS

Mr. Y is new in our class. He wants to ask many questions. What word will he use every time he asks a question? (Why)

Mr. Y still does not understand about "question words."

We have to show Mr. Y that he must use the other question words.

One of us will make believe he is new in the class. He will ask a question.

Mr. Y will ask the same question but he will ask it the Mr. Y way.

Playing A
Question Game

Let one child talk for Mr. Y. Let another child pretend to be a new young-ster in the class. Help them to phrase questions such as the following:

(Johnny) wants to know whether he comes to school in the morning or in the afternoon. He wants to know when he comes to school.

(Johnny), use the question word *when,* and ask the question. (When do I come to school?)

Let's answer (Johnny's) question.

Mr. Y wants to know the same thing, but Mr. Y will not use the question word *when.*

He will not ask, "When do I come to school?"

Let's listen to Mr. Y ask the question the "Y" way. ("Why do I come to school?")

Let's answer Mr. Y's question.

Have the children tell Mr. Y why he comes to school.

Why doesn't Mr. Y know *when* to come to school? (He used a different question word and so got a different answer.)

Let's try another question.

Select two different children for the two roles.

(Mary) is hungry. She wants to know when we will have our snack.

(Mary), use the question word *when* and ask the question. (When do we have snacks?)

Let's answer (Mary's) question. (E.g., At ten o'clock.)

Mr. Y wants to know the same thing, but Mr. Y will not use the question word *when.*

He will not ask, "When do we have snacks?"

How will Mr. Y ask the question? (Why do we have snacks?)

Let's listen to Mr. Y ask the question. (Why do we have snacks?)

Answer Mr. Y's question.

Have the children explain to Mr. Y why they have snacks.

Why did Mary and Mr. Y get different answers? (They used different question words.)

Let's try another question.

Select two different children for each question asked. Follow the same procedure as outlined above for each of the following situations.

(Sue) wants to paint. She wants to know where we keep the paints.

(Sue), ask the question using the question word *where.*

Continue as above with Mr. Y asking the question the Mr. Y way.

(Tom) wants to play with clay. He wants to know where we keep the clay.

(Tom), ask the question using the question word *where.*

(Follow with Mr. Y.)

(Bob) wants to know what we sing in school.

(Bob), ask the question using the question word *what.*

(Follow with Mr. Y.)

(Patty), wants to know what we learn in school. (Patty) ask the question using the question word *what.*

Mr. Y still won't use any of the other question words. Mr. Y just keeps saying "why, why."

Maybe if we draw pictures for the "question words" Mr. Y will see that other question words are as important as "why."

*Drawing Pictures
For The
Question Words*

Write the words "what?""where?" "when?" on separate pieces of paper. Tape each word somewhere in the room. Tell the children that they may draw a picture to answer any or all of the question words. Give them the following examples:

If you were drawing a picture to answer the "question word" *where*, it might be a picture that shows where you went, (e.g., movies, school, bowling alley).

If you were drawing a picture to answer the "question word" *what*, it might be a picture that shows what you eat (e.g., meat, bread, ice cream, cake).

If you were drawing a picture to answer the "question word" *when*, it might show when you are happy or sad.

Have the children decide under which "question words" they want to put their pictures. Read the "question words" for them. Encourage the children to ask questions about the pictures. Remind them that their questions must start with the "question word" under which the picture has been placed.

TYING IT TOGETHER

Give each child a copy of Alpha Time Master #135. Explain to the children that the marks around Mr. Y are called "question marks." Demonstrate how a question mark is used by writing a question the children dictate on the board, and then placing a question mark at the end of the sentence.

The children may dictate a question which may be filled in at the bottom of their pictures.

ON THEIR OWN

Children may choose from the following activities:

Music And Dance

Listening and dancing to Mr. Y's music.

Word Usage

Asking a *why, when, where* and *what* question and answering in complete sentences.

Psychology

Experiment—Have some children watch as one person yawns. See how soon they start to yawn themselves.

1Y₂

PLANNING AND PREPARATION: Huggable, Mr. Y; Mr. Y's Picture Squares; Picture Card 11; Alpha Time Master #136; paper, crayons, (some yellow), scissors, paste and other art materials; a yo yo, if available.

DECIDING THAT MR. Y WILL GET HIS SOUND FROM "YAWNING"

Gather the children around Mr. Y.

Mr. Y keeps asking "why, why, why." The Letter People try to answer him but as soon as they say anything, he asks "why, why" again and again.

Mr. Y gets tired of asking questions and never finding out what he wants to know. He gets very, very tired. All he does is yawn and yawn. When he finishes yawning he starts asking "why, why" again.

The Letter People don't know what to do with him. In fact, when they watch Mr. Y yawn they all start yawning themselves.

Finally, Mr. H had a good idea. Mr. H said, "Let's give Mr. Y a sound. He'll be so busy looking for things that start with his sound that he won't have time to ask "why, why."

The Letter People ran to tell Mr. Y about Mr. H's idea. Mr. Y wanted to ask, "Where will I get my sound?"

Instead of using the question word *where,* what word did he use? (why)

Let several children ask the question as Mr. Y would ask it. (i.e., Why do I get my sound?)

"How can you ask why," yelled the Letter People. "Every Letter Person wants a sound more than anything in the whole world."

Let the children decide that Mr. Y really means "Where will I get my sound?"

Mr. Y kept asking the same question. The Letter People got angrier and angrier. Mr. Y just yawned. He could not understand why people gave him funny answers and then became angry at him.

Finally, Mr. H said, "Mr. Y, you are going to have a sound and that's that—and please don't ask why." Mr. Y was afraid to say anything so he just yawned and yawned.

RECOGNIZING THE SOUND FOR Y IN THE INITIAL POSITION IN WORDS

The Letter People said, "Mr. Y always yawns. Let him get his sound from Yawning."

"Yes, Yes," said Mr. Y, and then he yawned and yawned and yawned.

Mr. Y is always tired, said the Letter People, we are not going to give him many words. We will only let a few words start with his Yawning sound.

Then he won't have to work too hard. Mr. Y won't even have to fill a bag. Mr. Y was about to say "why?" but he just yawned instead.

Show the children Mr. Y's Picture Squares (i.e., yo-yo, yelling).

The Letter People have two pictures for Mr. Y.

Mr. Y can't figure out a name to give each picture. He just yawns and yawns.

One picture shows something with which we play. One picture shows a "doing word."

Each word starts the same way as Mr. Y's Yawn.

Let's try to help Mr. Y.

Discuss the pictures with the children.

Select the picture that shows a boy doing something. Think of a "doing word" that starts the same way as Yawning and that tells about this picture.

What is the boy doing? (yelling)

Prove to Mr. Y that yelling begins with the same sound as Yawning.

Mr. Y wants to know why the boy is yelling. Tell Mr. Y why the boy is yelling.

Let several children tell Mr. Y why they think the boy is yelling.

The second picture shows a toy. Its name starts the same way as Yawning.

If a yo-yo is available, show it to the children.

Tell Mr. Y the name of this toy. (yo-yo)

Prove it for him.

Mr. Y says that he doesn't know anything about a yo-yo. Since yo-yo starts with his sound he wants to know all about it.

Show Mr. Y how you play with a yo-yo.

Identifying Mr. Y's Words

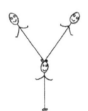

IDENTIFYING THE UPPER AND LOWER CASE LETTER "Y"

Let's show Mr. Y his capital letter Y.

Let the children outline the capital "Y" on Mr. Y's body. Let them outline the lower case "y". Have them discuss the parts of the capital letter and then form the letter using their bodies.

TYING IT TOGETHER

Show the children Picture Card 11 and distribute matching Alpha Time Master #136. Discuss some of the aspects of this busy city street scene.

What are some things you see in this picture?

Show Mr. Y the traffic light. Which light do you think he likes best? (the yellow light in the middle)

What other yellow things do you see? (e.g., sun, street lamp, shirt)

Mr. Y says there are other things in this picture that start with his sound.

Show Mr. Y someone who is very young. (e.g., baby)
Prove to Mr. Y that *young* begins with his Yawning sound.

Show Mr. Y someone who is saying "you."
How can you tell he is saying "you." (He is pointing at the lady.)

Show us someone yelling; playing with a yo-yo.

Show us a yard.
What do you see in the yard? (boy, grass)

Why does Mr. Y like yards? (The word begins with his sound.)

Use your yellow crayon to color all the things that begin with Mr. Y's sound.

ON THEIR OWN

Children may choose from the following activities:

Auditory Discrimination

Including Mr. Y's puzzle, Picture Squares, playing cards in games listed in the *Games* section.

Art

Painting a yellow picture.

Letter Tracing

Using Alpha Time Master #79 to trace the capital and lower case Y.

Classifying And Counting

Using Alpha Time Master #136 to count various objects such as people, men, women, children, cars, windows, etc.

Shape Discrimination

Marking all the circles, squares, rectangles in different colors on Alpha Time Master #136.

Grammar

Point to all the things people are *doing* on Picture Card 11 and saying the "doing word" that describes the action.

Dramatic Play

Using Picture Card 11 and puppets to dramatize what happens on a busy street and what noises are heard.

1Y₃

TEACHER OBJECTIVES:

To reinforce the characteristic and sound of Mr. Y.

To familiarize children with the color yellow.

PERFORMANCE OBJECTIVES:

The child will say words with the *y* in the initial position.

The child will recognize the letter Y.

The child will identify objects colored yellow.

DEVELOPMENT

Mr. Y said if Mr. W could stop winking and Mr. K could stop kicking long enough to make "All About Us" booklets, he would stop yawning.

Now he's yawning again because the booklets are finished.

Distribute the Mr. Y "All About Us" booklets.
Have them say the title for Mr. Y.

Which Letter Person's picture is on the booklet? (Mr. Y)
Whose picture is next to Mr. Y? (his friend's)
Put your finger on the sentence at the bottom of the booklet.
It says, "Mr. Y has a friend."

What is special about Mr. Y? (his yawn)
Look at the picture Mr. Y drew of his friend.
What do you think Mr. Y wants his friend to do? (yawn)
What is missing on the face? (a mouth)
How can we finish the picture to make it look as if Mr. Y's friend is yawning?

Give the children the opportunity to finish the picture.
Have the children open their booklets.
Ask them to touch the first sentence on the left-hand side.
What picture did Mr. Y put in the first sentence? (his yawn)
Read aloud, "Mr. Y likes to yawn."
Let them pretend to reread the sentence with you.

Mr. Y says the next sentence will tell something he uses all the time.

Read aloud, "Mr. Y uses yellow yarn."
Show the children some yellow yarn.
Ask them to look at the picture and tell how Mr. Y uses yellow yarn.

Mr. Y took this whole page to tell us about himself.
What two things did he tell us? (He likes to yawn. He uses yellow yarn.)

Mr. Y wants us to use the next page.

Have the children touch the first dotted line.
Explain that Mr. Y wants them each to write their name.

After the children have had an opportunity to do this, select and read a booklet. (*e.g.*, Dick likes to   .)
Mr. Y says the sentence is not finished.
Mr. Y's sentence tells'us he likes to yawn.
Dick's sentence does not tell what Dick likes to do.
How can Dick finish the sentence?
Lead the children to conclude that the sentence can be finished with a picture that is drawn, or cut out and pasted, or by dictating a word.

Help the children complete their sentences.
Select and read several completed sentences aloud.
Encourage the children to tell Mr. Y what their sentence says.

Explain that Mr. Y drew a picture on the back of the booklet showing animals using yellow yarn.
Have the children turn to the back of the booklet.

Read aloud, "Let's talk about yellow."

Give the children the opportunity to enjoy the picture.
Have them tell how each animal uses the yellow yarn.
Be sure to draw their attention to the bird carrying a piece of yellow yarn in its beak.

Have the children open their booklets.
Draw their attention to the second sentence on the right-hand side.
Explain that Mr. Y wants them to use yellow yarn.

Distribute some yellow yarn to each child.
If yellow yarn is not accessible, have the children use a yellow crayon.
After each child writes his/her name on the dotted line, the yarn may be pasted on the booklet.
The children may make any shape or shapes they wish.

Encourage the children to take the booklets home.
Have them ask members of their family to make yellow yarn pictures for Mr. Y.

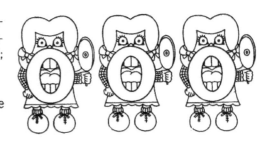

201

PLANNING AND PREPARATION: Huggable, Miss O; Miss O's initial sound Picture Squares; Alpha Time Master #137; optional: jar of olives.

Miss O's song (record #2, side A, band #6) may be played to set the mood for the lesson.

MISS O GETS A SOUND

Gather the children around Miss O.

Obstinate Miss O has been so busy saying ŏ, ŏ, ŏ, that she forgot to think about a sound that she can make in words. What would be a good sound for Miss O?

Thinking Of A Sound For Miss O

Lead the children to the conclusion that Miss O's sound may be ŏ, the sound that she practices and the sound that begins Obstinate.

Obstinate Miss O says that she wants to pick her own pictures. She knows that each picture must be something that starts with her ŏ sound. Miss O went to look for things that could be her pictures.

HEARING WORDS WITH SHORT O IN THE INITIAL POSITION

First Miss O met a strange looking bird.

Hold up the Picture Square of the ostrich.

Miss O went to meet the strange looking bird. Miss O asked, "What kind of bird are you?"

The bird said, "I am the biggest bird in the whole world."

"Do you start with my ŏ sound?" asked Miss O.

"Yes, I do," answered the bird. "Try to guess my name."

Dramatizing Words

"Are you an oppity-poppity? Oppity-poppity starts with my ŏ sound," said Miss O.

"I am not an oppity-poppity," said the bird. "Try again."

"Are you an ollylolly? Ollylolly starts with my ŏ sound," said Miss O.

"I am not an ollylolly," said the bird. "Try again."

"Are you an oggledyboggledy? Oggledyboggledy starts with my ŏ sound," said Miss O.

"I am not an oggledyboggledy," said the bird.

"I can not guess your name," said Miss O. "The Letter People have to help me."

Some of the Letter People want to guess the name of this great big bird. See if one of them will whisper to you what they think the name of the bird is.

Talking About Ostriches

Give the children a chance to have one of the Letter People whisper a name for the bird to them. Have them remind the Letter People that the bird's name must start with Miss O's ŏ sound. Give several children a chance to try to guess the bird's name.

The bird says he is an ostrich. *Ostrich* starts the same way as Obstinate. It begins with Miss O's ŏ sound.

The ostrich said, "I am obstinate like you, Miss O. I am the most obstinate bird you ever met. Think of all the birds you know. What can they do? (They fly.) I am so Obstinate that I do not fly.

> "I say, no, no, no, an Obstinate ostrich am I.
> I will not fly.
> I can run as fast as can be,
> But no one can make a flying bird out of me."

How is the ostrich Obstinate? (He won't fly.)

Be the ostrich. Be another bird and try to make the Obstinate ostrich fly.

Dramatizing Words

Let the children take the roles of the ostrich and some flying birds. The birds try to convince the Obstinate ostrich to fly, while the ostrich repeats the rhyme above.

After Miss O left the ostrich, she went to the ocean. She heard that there was something in the ocean that started with her sound. Miss O spoke to the fish that were swimming. They told her about something that crawled along at the very bottom of the ocean. They said it started with her ŏ sound.

Show the children the Picture Square of the octopus.

Look at the picture, and see what it is. This animal has eight arms, lives at the bottom of the ocean, and starts with Miss O's ŏ sound.

Let's help Miss O figure out what its name is.

Let the children think of names. They may enjoy using nonsense names that begin with the ŏ sound.

If no one guesses, tell the children that it is an octopus. Have them share with each other any knowledge they have of an octopus.

The octopus said, "Miss O, I am as Obstinate as you. I don't swim with the other fish. I like to crawl along the bottom of the ocean. I am an Obstinate octopus.

Miss O let the octopus be one of her pictures.

Be the octopus. Tell us what you are saying to the fish. Be the fish. Tell us what you are saying to the Obstinate octopus.

Miss O is very happy. She has two things for her pictures. She has an ostrich and an octopus.

Then Miss O went to a farm to find an animal that starts with her ŏ sound.

Let's look at the next picture and see what animal Miss O found at the farm.

Show the children the Picture Square of the ox. Let the children try to guess as before.

Which animal starts with her ŏ sound? (ox)

The ox told Miss O that he was Obstinate too. Many of the other farm animals want to play, but the ox only wants to work. Miss O wanted the ox to be one of her pictures.

Be the Obstinate ox. Tell us what you say to the farm animals when they ask you to play. Be one of the farm animals. Tell us what you say to the Obstinate ox as you try to get him to play with you.

Miss O decided to go to the Munching Monday Market to buy some things. In the Munching Monday Market she found something on the shelf that started with her ŏ sound and was very Obstinate.

Let's look at the next picture and see what Miss O found on the shelf.

Show the children the Picture Square of the olives. Some children may not know what olives are. If possible, show them a jar of tightly packed olives, let them try to take one out of the jar and taste it.

Miss O likes to shop at the Munching Monday Market because she can taste things as she shops. Miss O was having a very good time tasting things until she tried to taste the olives.

Miss O tried and tried but she could not get even one olive out of a jar. The olives said to Miss O, "We won't come out. We are Obstinate olives." Miss O said, "Obstinate olives, that's just what I need for one of my pictures."

Be Miss O and try to get an Obstinate olive out of the jar. Be an Obstinate olive. Tell us what you say as Miss O tries to get you out of the jar.

Miss O found one more Obstinate thing while she was preparing her lunch. Let's look at the next picture and see.

Show the children the Picture Square of the omelet.

Miss O loves to eat omelets. Omelet begins with Miss O's ŏ sound.

The omelet wanted to be one of Miss O's pictures. The omelet said, "I am an Obstinate omelet. I insist on having a filling. I am not like other eggs. Sometimes I like to have jelly. Sometimes I like to have meat or cheese."

Be the omelet. Tell us what you say to the meat or the jelly or the cheese.

Be the meat or the jelly or the cheese. Tell us what you say to the Obstinate omelet.

TYING IT TOGETHER

Distribute copies of Alpha Time Master #137 to the children. Have them prove that each picture begins with Miss O's ŏ's sound. Some children may tell how each picture is Obstinate.

ON THEIR OWN

Children may choose from the following activities:

Dramatic Play

Playing the parts of the Obstinate ostrich, ox, olive, octopus.

Visual Memory
Sound Discrimination

Using Miss O's Picture Squares in any of the activities listed in the Games section.

Music And Dance

Singing Miss O's song (record #2).

Cooking

Making a jelly, meat or cheese omelet.

20 2

PLANNING AND PREPARATION: Huggable, Miss O; Miss O's Initial Sound Picture Squares; a bag for Miss O; a variety of art materials; Record #5; Alpha Time Master #138.

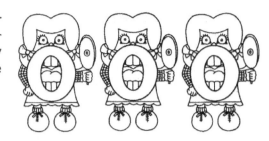

USING WORDS WITH SHORT O IN THE INITIAL POSITION

Show the children Miss O's initial sound Picture Squares and tell them that Miss O wants to play a guessing game with her pictures.

We will form five groups. Each group will take one of Miss O's pictures. Each group will act out a story to help Miss O guess which picture it is. Instead of talking we will show what is happening with our hands, our feet, and our body. Then Miss O will whisper to someone in another group which of her pictures she thinks is being described.

Pantomiming

Have the children form five groups, each group taking one of Miss O's Picture Squares (i.e., ox, octopus, omelet, olive, ostrich). Let each group of children decide how they will show how Obstinate their object is. Let each group practice their pantomime for Miss O and the other groups. After Miss O guesses which Obstinate object is being pantomimed, the Obstinate object may be placed in her bag.

Miss O likes her pictures. She would like us to make more pictures for her bag. She wants us to draw or make one of her Obstinate pictures. Then we must tell her how the object we made is Obstinate.

Play the Prove It Song (record #5, side A, band 3). After a child proves his drawing he may place the picture in Miss O's bag.

TYING IT TOGETHER

Distribute copies of Alpha Time Master #138 to the children and discuss the pictures.

Sorting And Classifying

Look at the pictures in the boxes. What do you see? (a zoo, an ocean, a shelf, a frying pan, a farm)

What pictures do you see in the center of the paper? (ostrich, omelet, olive, octopus, ox)

Where does the omelet belong? (frying pan)

Draw a line from the omelet to the frying pan.

Continue in this manner until the children have connected all five objects to the places where they belong.

ON THEIR OWN

Children may choose from the following activities:

Sound Discrimination

Playing Miss O's song (record #2) and listening for words that begin with her sound.

Motor Coordination

Playing with Miss O's puzzle.

Matching And Sorting

Using Miss O's playing cards or Picture Squares in any of the games described in the *Games* section of the manual.

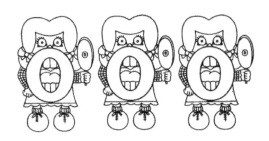

20₃ **PLANNING AND PREPARATION:** Huggable, Miss O; Miss O's "In The Middle" Picture Squares, Alpha Time Masters #139 and #140.

IDENTIFYING THE SHORT Ŏ SOUND IN THE MEDIAL POSITION IN WORDS

The other Letter Girls have been telling Miss O how much fun it is to hear their sounds "in the middle."

Now Miss O wants to hear her ŏ sound between two of the boys' sounds. She wants her sound to be "in the middle."

Miss O will say a word. Then she wants us to tell her if we hear her ŏ sound in it.

Remember, her ŏ sound is not going to be the first thing we hear. It is going to be "in the middle" of the word.

Hearing And Saying Words With ŏ "In The Middle"

Introduce each of the following words separately, stressing the ŏ sound as you say it: hop, cot, log, pop, not, got, dot. After the word has been repeated by the children encourage them to talk about the position of the sound.

What sound did Miss O make when she said (hop)? (ŏ)

Where is Miss O's sound in the word (hop)? (in the middle)

IDENTIFYING PICTURE WORDS

Show the children Miss O's "in the middle" pictures (i.e., pot, hot, log, top, mop). Have Miss O's back turned to the children.

Miss O likes to hear her ŏ sound when it is in the middle of a word. She has pictures of words in which she is in the middle.

Let's play the "Turn Me Around Game" with Miss O. She will give us clues and we will guess which "in the middle" word Miss O is thinking about. Then Miss O will say, "Turn me around if you hear my ŏ sound."

Before we turn her around, we must tell her where we hear her ŏ sound. She only wants to hear words in which her ŏ sound is in the middle.

Miss O is ready to begin. Look at the pictures and then listen to her clues.

Your mother uses me when it is time to cook.
What's inside me? Raise my lid and look.
Here's another clue—I rhyme with *dot*.
What am I? I am a. . . (pot).
Turn me around if you hear my ŏ sound.

Which picture is Miss O thinking about? Say the word *pot* so that she can hear her ŏ sound. Remember, before you turn Miss O around, you must tell her where you hear her ŏ sound. (in the middle of *pot*)

Follow this same procedure for each of the following rhyming clues:

I stand together with the brooms.
I wash the floors in many rooms.
Another clue—I rhyme with *pop*.
What am I? I am a. . . (mop).

I am a toy that spins around
When I slow up I fall to the ground.
Another clue—I rhyme with *hop*.
What am I? I am a. . . (top).

A fireplace is the place for me,
I used to be part of a tree.
Another clue— I rhyme with *fog*.
What am I? I am a. . . (log).

I'm what you feel, when the temperature's high.
In the middle of summer when the sun's in the sky.
Another clue—I rhyme with *cot*.
What am I? I am. . . (hot).

Playing The "In The Middle" Game With Miss O

Have the children recall the "In The Middle" game and play it with Miss O. (Adapt the game as described in lesson 2A3.)

TYING IT TOGETHER

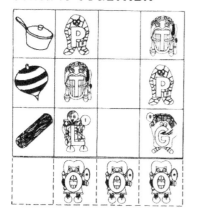

Give each child a copy of Alpha Time Master #139. Discuss the pictures. Help the children to name each picture (i.e., pot, top, log) and decide where in the word they hear Miss O's ŏ sound. Some children may cut out Miss O and paste her "in the middle."

Which Letter People do you see? (e.g., Mr. P, Mr. T)

Where will we put Miss O? (in the middle)

NOTE: Alpha Time Master #140 is a letter to parents explaining the progress the children have made thus far with ALPHA TIME. This letter may be sent home with the children at this time.

ON THEIR OWN

Children may choose from the following activities:

Sound Discrimination

Listening for the sounds that *begin* each word on Miss O's "in the middle" Picture Squares. (e.g., Mr. P begins the word *pot*)
   NOTE: Some children may be able to determine the end sounds.

Art

Drawing or painting a picture of Miss O standing between two Letter People.

Vocabulary Building

Making words by adding a beginning sound to *ot, op, og, ock.*

20₄

TEACHER OBJECTIVES:

To reinforce the characteristic and sound of Miss O.

To teach the concept of opposites through the letter O.

PERFORMANCE OBJECTIVES:

The child will say words with the ŏ sound in the initial position.

The child will identify two words, pictures or objects as opposites.

DEVELOPMENT

The Letter People can never get Miss O out of the pool.
They pretended she was the only Letter Person that had not made "All About Us" booklets.
That did it!
She jumped out of the pool and started working at once.
The booklets are ready for us to see.

Distribute the Miss O "All About Us" booklets to the children.

Read aloud, "All About Us."

Which Letter Person's picture do you see? (Miss O)
Whose picture is next to Miss O? (her friend's)
Touch the sentence at the bottom of the booklet.
It says, "Miss O has a friend."

Look at Miss O.
What must Miss O practice saying all the time? (her ŏ ŏ ŏ sound)
"How does the mirror help Miss O?" (She looks into it to be sure she is practicing her sound the right way.)
Look at the picture of Miss O's friend.
Miss O's friend wants to practice saying ŏ ŏ ŏ.
What does Miss O's friend need? (a mirror)
Miss O wants us to draw a mirror for her friend to hold.

Give the children the opportunity to finish the picture.
Remind them that the picture may be made to look like themselves or anyone else.

Have the children open the booklet.
Point to the full-page picture on the left-hand side.
Explain that Miss O used this whole page to show where she likes to practice her ŏ ŏ sound.
Have the children find clues that prove it is very cold.
Recall with them what happened when Miss O will not come out of the pool.
Children may enjoy pretending to be Miss O.
It is an excellent opportunity for them to practice saying the short o sound.

Explain that Miss O has discovered something special.
She says that sometimes words are as different as different can be.

Miss O thought of the word "sit."
She says the word "stand" is as different as different can be.
Miss O says "sit" and "stand" are opposite.
Miss O thought of other words that are as different as different can be.
She says "up" and "down" are as different as different can be.
They are opposite.

Follow the same procedure with: *in* and *out, run* and *walk, cry* and *laugh.*

Then draw the children's attention to the right-hand side of the page.

Explain that Miss O drew a picture to put in the first sentence.

The picture tells an opposite.

Miss O wants us to figure out the opposite.
She says to look at the cover of the peanut jar in the top picture.
Then look at the cover of the peanut jar below it.

After the children have discovered that the opposite is *on* and *off,* read aloud, "Miss O finds an opposite: *on* and *off.*"

Now Miss O wants us each to find an opposite.
When we find two pictures that tell an opposite, we can paste them at the end of the second sentence.
Before we look for pictures, let's talk about the opposites Miss O drew on the back of the booklet.

Have the children turn to the back of the booklet.

Read aloud, "Let's talk about opposites."

Draw the children's attention to the first set of pictures.

Have them look at the expression on the girl's face on the left.

Ask them to tell a word that describes how this girl feels. (*e.g.,* happy)

Then refer them to the picture to the right.

Explain that this is a picture of the same girl.

Ask the children how they think she feels in this picture. (*e.g.,* sad)

Have the children say the two words that describe how the girl feels. (*e.g.,* happy-sad)

Explain that *happy* and *sad* are as different as different can be. They are opposite.

Follow the same procedure with the other two pairs of opposites. (*i.e.,* fat-thin, sun-rain)

Have the children look in magazines for pictures that can represent an opposite.

Help them complete their sentences on the inside of the booklet.

Select and read aloud several completed sentences.

Encourage the children to tell the opposite they've found to Miss O.

Suggest they take their booklets home.

Have them ask members of their family to tell Miss O an opposite.

1R₁

PLANNING AND PREPARATION: Huggables, Mr. R and Mr. K; Record #2; Alpha Time Master #141; popsicle sticks or straws; rubberbands; (there should be enough rubberbands for each child to make his own puppet); Mr. R's Picture Squares; a bag for Mr. R.

Prepare several rubberband puppets to be used at the beginning of the lesson. To make the puppets, paste or staple rubberband legs and arms onto popsicle sticks or straws. Faces can be drawn on pieces of paper and pasted on as well.

Keep Mr. R concealed until Mr. K introduces him.

INTRODUCING RIPPING RUBBERBANDS

The Letter People have some visitors.

Show the children the rubberband puppets and make them move.

Let's ask them who they are, and how they came here.

After several children have had a chance to talk to the rubberband puppets, tell the class the following:

Our visitors say they are Ripping Rubberbands who have run away. They belong to the next Letter Person who is coming to our class, but they have run away from him.

Do you remember when the ĭ ran away from the Itch? Tell the rubberbands what happened.

Do you remember when the Kick ran away from Mr. K? Tell the rubberbands what happened.

Why do you think these Ripping Rubberbands ran away? Let's ask them.

The Ripping Rubberbands are saying that the Letter Person to whom they belong made them do something bad, that's why they ran away.

Listening To The Rubberband's Story

Manipulate one or two of the puppets as you tell the following story:

Here is what the Rubberbands say:

We rubberbands can do many good things.

We can keep papers or cards together.

We can keep hair braided.

We are used on braces.

We can keep packages wrapped.

What other good things have you done with us?

Let the children talk about ways in which they have used rubberbands.

347

DISCOVERING MR. R

All rubberbands belong to the new Letter Person. He calls us Ripping Rubberbands because he is always making us rip around the room. We go so fast that we can't see where we're landing. Sometimes we land right on someone. Many times we hurt people. We say that we are sorry but the person is still hurt.

We talked to this Letter Person. We told him that we don't like doing bad things. He just keeps right on shooting us around the room. We decided that we had to run away. We won't go back to him until he promises to stop shooting us at people.

How can we help the Ripping Rubberbands?

Let the children discuss how they might be of help.

Mr. K will bring the new Letter Person. If we all close our eyes he will come.

Reveal Mr. R. Let the children gather around him, greet him, talk to him.

Listening To Mr. R's Song

Let's find out what the new Letter Person's name is.

Play Mr. R's song (record #2, side B, band #3) and discuss it with the children. Encourage them to move along with the music the second time it is played.

What does Mr. R tell us about the kind of person he is?

Ask one of the other Letter People what he thinks about Mr. R shooting Ripping Rubberbands.

Show us how the music makes you want to rip around the room.

Do you think that Mr. R will ever stop shooting Ripping Rubberbands?

What do you think Mr. K thinks about hurting people?

Ask some children to be Mr. K and to tell Mr. R about kindness. Some children may compare Mr. K's Kick and Mr. R's Rubberbands.

Finding A Sound For Mr. R

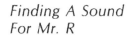

Mr. K says that we should give Mr. R a sound. Then he might not shoot so many Ripping Rubberbands. Then he and his Ripping Rubberbands can find pictures to put into his bag.

Mr. K says that finding pictures is a good thing to do. Maybe if we show Mr. R lots of good things he can do, he will stop doing bad things.

Mr. K has had a long talk with the runaway Ripping Rubberbands. They will go back to Mr. R because he needs every rubberband to help him with his sound.

From what do you think Mr. R will take his sound?

Help the children decide that Mr. R will get his sound from Ripping Rubberbands.

USING WORDS WITH R IN THE INITIAL POSITION

*Answering Riddles
By Using
Context Clues*

The Letter People have pictures for Mr. R.

We'll listen to a rhyming riddle and try to find the picture that fits each riddle.

Place Mr. R's Picture Squares (i.e., rope, robot, ring, rabbit, racket) where the children can easily reach them. Then tell the children the following riddles:

People can jump with me, tug me or tie me.
I'm as long as long can be.
You'll find I rhyme with the word *soap*.
You must know that I'm a. . . (rope).

Find the picture of a rope. Show it to Mr. R. Prove to him that it starts the same way as Ripping Rubberbands. Mr. R will put the picture into his bag.

Follow the same procedure for each of the following riddles:

My shape is round.
On your finger I'm found.
I rhyme with *sing*,
You must know that I'm a. . . (ring).

I'm an animal who hops around.
You'll see my cotton tail when I leave the ground.
I rhyme with *habit*,
You must know that I'm a. . . (rabbit).

Mr. R says that you are so good at guessing his words that he won't give us a rhyming word anymore. Do you think we will be able to guess his words? Let's see.

For playing tennis, you must get
Me, a tennis ball, and a net.
You must know that I'm a. . . (racket).

I look and act like a man you know.
But it's a machine that makes me go.
You must know that I'm a. . . (robot).

Mr. R is happy with his pictures. He would like us to make more pictures for him. He would like us to think of more words that start the same way as Ripping Rubberbands.

*Making Things For
Mr. R's Bag*

Give the children clues to help them think of words such as radio, rocket, rag, reindeer, rock, roof, room, ruler.

Have the children use the art materials laid out for them to make objects for Mr. R's bag. Some children may make their own Ripping Rubberband puppets.

TYING IT TOGETHER

Give each child a copy of Alpha Time Master #141.

Whom do you see in the picture? (Mr. R, children)

How do these children feel? (angry, unhappy, upset)

What is each person doing about being hit? (crying, scolding, hitting back, running away)

Who is right?

What would you do if you were hit by Mr. R's Ripping Rubberbands?

Making Value Judgments

Why do you think Mr. R keeps on shooting rubberbands?

Do we ever do things we know are wrong, but can't seem to keep from doing?

ON THEIR OWN

Children may choose from the following activities:

Crafts

Making a variety of rubberband puppets.

Dramatic Play

Using the puppets to enact the story of the runaway Ripping Rubberbands.

Music And Dance

Listening and dancing to Mr. R's song (record #2).

Auditory Discrimination

Listening for words in Mr. R's song (record #2) that begin with his Ripping Rubberband sound.

Playing any of the games involving Mr. R's Picture Squares in the *Games* section.

Measuring

Comparing the length of a rubberband when it is stretched and unstretched.

Classifying

Making a list of things that are made out of rubber (e.g., tires, balloons, balls, boots, erasers).

Physics

Making a list of things rubber can do (e.g., bounce, stretch, resist water, melt).

Music And Crafts

Making a harp by stretching rubberbands across nails in a wooden frame and plucking the strings.

1R₂

PLANNING AND PREPARATION: Huggables, Mr. R, Mr. F, Mr. L and Mr. D; Mr. R's Picture Squares; Picture Card 12; Alpha Time Master #142; paper; rubberbands; crayons.

Gather the children around Mr. R.

IDENTIFYING THE CAPITAL AND LOWER CASE LETTER "R"

Forming The Capital R With Their Bodies

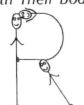

Let's show Mr. R his capital letter R and his lower case letter. How many parts are there in the capital "R"? (three)

What is the shape of each part? (a straight line, a curve, a slanted line)

Let's use our bodies to make the capital R.

TALKING ABOUT MR. R's "DOING WORDS"

Hold your arm around Mr. F and Mr. R.

Mr. F says that no one follows Funny Feet Road anymore. He can't understand why. Someone told him that it was Mr. R's fault.

When Mr. R saw Mr. F's Funny Feet Road, he said that he was going to make his own road.

What do you think we will find on Mr. R's road instead of Funny Feet? (Ripping Rubberbands)

What did we do when we followed Funny Feet Road?

Help the children recall that they had to name a word for Mr. F before they could step on the footprints on Funny Feet Road.

Mr. R says that we must do something different to move along Ripping Rubberband Road.

He says that we can't walk on Ripping Rubberband Road at all.

Walking starts with Mr. W's Wonderful Wink sound, not with Mr. R's Ripping Rubberbands sound.

Mr. R would like us to do something that starts with his sound.

Dramatizing Mr. R's Doing Words

We have to think of some Mr. R "doing words."

Help the children think of some Mr. R "doing words." If this is difficult for them, give them clues to help them discover words (e.g., run, race, rock, roll, ride, read, roar, row, rake, rub). They may ride a rocking horse, along Ripping Rubberband Road. They may roller skate along the road. Have the children demonstrate each Mr. R "doing word" before they decide what they want to do on Ripping Rubberband Road.

Mr. R says that we know many of his "doing words," and so we are ready to make Ripping Rubberband Road. How shall we make the road?

| Making Plans For | Have the children recall how they made Funny Feet Road (i.e., Cutouts |
| "Rubberband Road" | of feet were laid end to end). Let them discuss various ways in which |

Making Plans For
"Rubberband Road"

Have the children recall how they made Funny Feet Road (i.e., Cutouts of feet were laid end to end). Let them discuss various ways in which they might make Ripping Rubberband Road. For example, they may attach rubberbands on sheets of paper, (one band to a she⌐t). The sheets of paper may then be laid down to become the road.

Several roads may be set up so that the children do not have to wait too long for their turn. As each child moves along the road, the class may give a description of what he is doing. (e.g., He is "running" on Ripping Rubberband Road; He is "resting" on Ripping Rubberband Road.)

READING COMPREHENSION

Mr. F says that he is angry with all the Letter People. Mr. F says that they are "flat leavers." What does Mr. F mean by a "flat leaver?"

Encourage one of the children to explain that "flat leaver" describes a child who leaves one child to play with another child.

Tell Mr. F about a time, someone left you flat.

Tell Mr. F how you felt about it.

Ask Mr. F how he feels about it.

Mr. F wants to tell us what happened but he is so upset that he can't talk about it. He has a picture story for us.

Hold up Picture Card 12 and give each child a copy of matching Alpha Time Master #142. Discuss each picture.

Let's look at the first picture in the story.

Frame #1

Where are Mr. F and the Letter People? (Funny Feet Road)

How does Mr. F look? (happy)

Why are the Letter People following Funny Feet Road? (They like the game.)

Why is Mr. F happy? (It's fun to play with his friends.)

Numeration

Mr. F invited all the Letter People to come and play with him on his road. They all came except Mr. R. Mr. R said that it's a baby game and he won't play.

Frame #2

Who has come to Funny Feet Road? (Mr. R)

How can you tell that Mr. F is happy to see Mr. R? (He is smiling and waving at Mr. R.)

Mr. F thinks that Mr. R has changed his mind and has come to play.

Why do you think Mr. R has come?

What do you think he is telling the Letter People?

Making inferences
Predicting

Be Mr. R. Tell us what you are whispering to the Letter People.

352

Why doesn't Mr. R want Mr. F to hear what he is saying?

Be Mr. F. Tell us how you feel about what is happening.

What do you think the Letter People will do?

Let's look at the next part of the story and find out.

What have the Letter People decided to do? (go with Mr. R)

How do you feel about the decision they have made?

Frame #3

Interpreting feelings

What is Mr. F doing? (crying)

Mr. F thinks that the Letter People were mean to him.

Why does Mr. F feel that the Letter People were mean to him?

How could they have been nicer to Mr. F?

Where do you think the Letter People are going?

Let's look at the next part of the story.

Where did Mr. R take the Letter People? (Rubberband Road)

Frame #4

How did Mr. R get the idea of making Ripping Rubberband Road? (from Mr. F)

How is playing on Ripping Rubberband Road different from playing on Funny Feet Road? (Ripping Rubberbands instead of Funny Feet)

How do you know that Mr. L is thinking about something? (by looking at his face)

Mr. L told us all about love.

What should he have remembered before leaving Mr. F?

Be Mr. L. Tell us what you are thinking.

How do you know that Mr. R doesn't feel sorry about making the Letter People leave Mr. F? (He is laughing.)

Making judgments

Is it all Mr. R's fault or are the other Letter People also to blame?

What could the Letter People have told Mr. R when he asked them to leave Mr. F and go with him?

PREDICTING OUTCOMES

Deciding How The Story Should End

Help the children decide how the story should end.

Mr. F wants us to talk with the Letter People and then we must make a decision.

We must decide how the story ends.

Tell the children that they may dictate one ending for the story, or each child may dictate his own ending so that there are many different endings for the story. Some children may draw a picture that shows how the story ends.

Naming The Story

A story should have a name. We could not give the story a name until we knew how it ended. (If the endings are different, the names will be different.)

What name will you give your story?

Getting The Main Idea

Show the children how the ending they decide upon will affect the title of their story. i.e., If one child ends his story with the Letter People asking Mr. F to join them, the title selected might be "Mr. F Plays Too." Show the children how this title would be unsuitable for an ending in which the Letter People keep playing on Ripping Rubberband Road.

Tell the children that Mr. D found a word in his dictionary that tells about Mr. R. The word is jealous.

Talking About Jealousy

What does it mean to be jealous?

How does it feel to be jealous?

Let the children discuss their definitions of jealousy. Lead them to the conclusion that when a person is jealous he is afraid of losing someone's love. He thinks that someone else is loved more than he is.

Mr. R knows that everyone loves Mr. F.

Mr. R knows that everyone likes to play on Funny Feet Road.

Mr. R thinks that people love Mr. F because he has Funny Feet Road.

Mr. R thought that everyone would love him when he made Ripping Rubberband Road.

Do the Letter People love Mr. F just because of Funny Feet Road?

Will they love Mr. R just because he made Ripping Rubberband Road?

Have the children recall what Mr. L has told them about love.

Mr. R thinks that if the Letter People love Mr. F they can't love him too. Mr. R is jealous of Mr. F. He doesn't understand that the Letter People can love Mr. F and Mr. R.

Let's help Mr. R. He wants to know if we were ever jealous.

Let the children talk about times when they had feelings of jealousy. Often children feel jealous toward a new baby in the family.

Tell Mr. R how you felt when a new baby came to your home.

Did you think that people would stop loving you because they loved the new baby?

Tell Mr. R how you felt when you were jealous.

Mr. R wants the Letter People to love him too. He wants to know what he can do to make the Letter People love him.

Give several children a chance to tell their ideas about how Mr. R can make the Letter People love him.

Mr. R has been listening and thinking. He is sorry for some of the mean things he has done.

How can we help him?

Do you think that Mr. R will ever do bad things again?

Mr. R wants to change the way he behaves. He will try to do what is right but it is not always easy.

He may forget and do things he should not do. We will have to understand and give him time to change.

Tell Mr. R about the times that you forgot and did things you should not have done.

Let the children talk about times when they have done things they should not have done.

Sometimes Mr. R gets very angry. When he is angry he may do things he should not do. Tell him about things you do when you are angry.

Miss A says Mr. R should not feel bad. Miss A has been jealous too. She thinks that most of the Letter People have been jealous at some time.

TYING IT TOGETHER

*Dramatizing
The Story*

Help the children enact the story of Mr. R and Rubberband Road. They may dramatize several different endings for the story.

ON THEIR OWN

Children may choose from the following activities:

Motor Coordination

Using Mr. R's puzzle, playing cards, Picture Squares, in any of the games described in the *Games* section.

*Oral/Aural
Discrimination*

Playing the Rubberband Road Game with the following variation: Mr. R will put some of his pictures on a few of the papers on the road. The children may only step on the papers that have pictures. The children must tell Mr. R the name of each picture as they step on it.

Letter Tracing

Using Duplicating Master #72 to trace the upper and lower case R.

Storytelling

Using Picture Card 12 to retell or record Mr. R's story.

Making Inferences

Using Alpha Master #142 to tell about the different emotions shown by the Letter People (e.g.,Mr. R—mean, laughing; Mr. F—happy, sad; Mr. L—doubting).

1R₃

PLANNING AND PREPARATION: Huggables, Mr. R, Mr. K, Mr. B, Mr. W, Mr. T, and Mr. P; colored papers or pieces of chalk for each of the following colors: violet, indigo, blue, green, yellow, orange, red; a prism (if available); several wooden blocks; Alpha Time Master #143.

MAKING COMPOUND WORDS

Gather the children around Mr. R.

The Letter People have been trying to keep Mr. R out of trouble. They keep thinking of ways to keep him busy so that he won't shoot his rubberbands. Each Letter Person takes a turn keeping Mr. R busy.

Remembering Mr. K's Compound Words

Today it is Mr. K's turn.

Mr. K told Mr. R how he used the word *key* and made more words with it.

Tell Mr. R some of the words that Mr. K made with the word *key*. (keychain, keycase, keyring)

Mr. K told Mr. R that he could take one of his words and do the same thing.

Mr. R got so excited that he stopped shooting his Ripping Rubberbands.

Mr. R thought of the word *rain*. He wants to make more words using the word *rain*.

Answering Riddles

Mr. R likes riddles. He also likes to rhyme his words. He will give us a rhyming riddle and we will figure out the words that he has made using the word *rain*.

Tell the children the following rhyming riddles and have them identify the compound word for each:

> The rain falls on your window,
> With a pitter, patter, plop.
> It runs down the pane —
> It is a rain (. . . drop).

Raindrop is a word that Mr. R made out of the word *rain* and the word *drop*.

Dramatizing Compound Words

Mr. R put them together and made a new word which is *raindrop*.

Be a raindrop. Do a raindrop dance for Mr. R.

Mr. R says that he is ready for another rhyming riddle.

> When it is raining, and you are
> The fisherman out in his boat,
> You won't get your clothes wet
> If you wear a rain (. . . coat).

Raincoat is a word that Mr. R made out of the word *rain* and the word *coat*.

Mr. R put them together and made a new word which is *raincoat*.

It is still raining. The raindrops are falling. You are a fisherman in a boat. You don't want your clothes to get wet while you fish, you are wearing a raincoat.

Be the fisherman. Show us how you put on your raincoat.

> The fisherman sees black clouds
> Starting to form.
> Hurry back—don't get caught
> In the big rain (. . . storm).

Rainstorm is a word that Mr. R made out of the word *rain* and the word *storm*.

He put them together and made a new word which is *rainstorm*.

What is a rainstorm? How is a rainstorm different from a rainy day?

Be a rainstorm. Let's hear your thunder. Let's hear your lightning.

> After it has rained,
> You must know,
> The arc in the sky—
> It is called a rain (. . . bow).

Rainbow is a word that Mr. R made out of the word *rain* and the word *bow*.

He put them together and made a new word which is *rainbow*.

What colors are in a rainbow?

Have colored pieces of paper or chalk available to show each of the colors in a rainbow. (violet, indigo, blue, green, yellow, orange, red)

Select groups of seven children. Let each child within a group hold one color (or use it on the chalkboard) of the rainbow. By overlapping the seven sheets of paper, the groups can form rainbows to show Mr. R. Perhaps you can use a prism to show the children a real rainbow.

MAKING NEW WORDS BY ADDING PREFIXES

Mr. R says that he knows another way to make words that start with his Ripping Rubberbands sound.

He won't tell any of the Letter People how he is going to do it. He says, "Just watch me and you'll find out!"

Mr. R says, "Let's go to the block corner with Mr. B." Mr. B says, "Build a house."

Have several of the children build a house out of blocks. After the house has been built, have Mr. R knock it down. Pretend to question Mr. R.

Mr. R, why did you knock down the house?

Mr. R said that he wanted to show us how he can make a new word with the word *build.*

The new word will start the same way as his Ripping Rubberbands.

Mr. R says that the new word means we have to build the house again.

The new word is *rebuild.*

Mr. R wants us to rebuild the house.

Mr. R says that *build* is Mr. B's word.

When he puts *re* in front of *build,* the new word, *rebuild,* is a Mr. R word.

Let's *rebuild* the house for Mr. R.

Now Mr. R wants to change one of Mr. W's words. Mr. R wants us to go to the sink with Mr. W. Mr. W says that he wants us to wash our hands.

We will wash our hands.

Now, Mr. R wants us to wash our hands again!

Let's wash our hands again for Mr. R.

Mr. R says that he will put *re* in front of *wash* and make a new word.

What word did Mr. R make that tells us to wash our hands again? (*rewash*)

Now Mr. T wants someone to tell a story.

Tell Mr. T a story.

Mr. R says that he wants us to tell the story again.

What will he put in front of the word *tell*? (*re*)

What new word will he make? (*retell*)

What does *retell* mean? (tell again)

Let's retell the story for Mr. R.

Call on a child to retell the story that was told.

Mr. P wants us to paint a paper purple. Paint a paper purple for Mr. P.

Mr. R says he wants us to paint the paper again.

How will Mr. R make a new word that means to paint the paper again?

Let's *repaint* the paper for Mr. R.

This time we can use red paint for Mr. R.

Dramatizing The Word "Retell"

358

Follow the above procedure for any of the following words: rebutton, reroll, refold, retie, restack, regroup, refill, recount.

TYING IT TOGETHER

Give each child a copy of Alpha Time Master #143 and red and blue crayons.

What do you see in the picture? (a rainstorm, people wearing raincoats and rainhats, people running, raindrops)

Have the children use a red crayon to mark all the things that are compound words. Then they may use a blue crayon and remark those things.

What will you do when you remark? (mark again) Now let's use the red crayon to mark the capital letter R wherever we see it.

Remark the capital letter R in blue.

Repeat with lower case letter r. Children may also count and recount the letters.

ON THEIR OWN

Children may choose from the following activities:

Making Compound Words

Using other weather words such as snow and sun to make compound words (e.g., snowsuit; snowtires; snowflakes; sunglasses; sunsuit; sunburn).

Mixing Colors

Using red, yellow and blue chalk or paint to make rainbow colors (i.e., red and blue = violet, yellow and red = orange, blue and yellow = green).

1R₄

TEACHER OBJECTIVES:

To reinforce the characteristics and sound of Mr. R.

To have children discover rhyme.

PERFORMANCE OBJECTIVES:

The child will say words with the *r* in the initial position.

The child will identify words that rhyme.

The child will become aware of rhyming words.

DEVELOPMENT

Mr. R wanted to put a rubberband around each "All About Us" booklet.
He didn't have enough.
He put one rubberband around all the booklets.
Let's take it off and look at the booklets.

Distribute the Mr. R booklets.
Read aloud, "All About Us."

Which Letter Person's picture is on the booklet? (Mr. R)
Whose picture is next to Mr. R? (his friend's)
Touch the sentence at the bottom of the booklet.
It says, "Mr. R has a friend."

What is special about Mr. R? (his rubberbands)
Look at the picture Mr. R drew of his friend.
What is his friend holding? (pencils)
Mr. R did not have a rubberband to give his friend to put around the pencils.
He is waiting for a delivery from Letter People Land.
Mr. R wants us to draw a rubberband around the pencils.

Give the children the opportunity to draw a rubberband around the pencils.
If rubberbands are accessible, the children may enjoy winding a rubberband around the pencils.
Suggest they add to the picture making it look like themselves or anyone else.

Have the children open their booklets.
Ask them to touch the first sentence on the left-hand side.
What picture did Mr. R put in the sentence? (his rubberbands)
Read aloud, "Mr. R has rubberbands."

Explain that Mr. R discovered something about words.
He said these words out loud. (e.g., rat, hat, fat, cat)
Mr. R says part of each word is the same.
Each word has "at" in it.
Let's listen and see if he is right.
The first word is "rat."
Do you hear "at" in "rat"?
Mr. R is right.
There's an "at" in "rat."
Let's try the next word.
Follow the same procedure with each of the words.
Explain that Mr. R says these words rhyme.
Mr. R likes to find words that rhyme.
That's what the next sentence tell us.

359A

Read aloud, "Mr. R finds a rhyme."
Look at the picture Mr. R drew.
Touch the boat.
Say the word "boat."
What is on the boat? (a goat)
Say the word "boat."
Say the word "goat."
Mr. R says "boat" and "goat" rhyme.
We hear "oat" in "boat."
We hear "oat" in "goat."
What is the goat wearing? (a coat)
Say the words "boat," "goat," "coat."
What can we tell Mr. R about the words? (they rhyme)

Mr. R took this whole page to tell us about himself.
What two things did he tell us? (He has rubberbands. He found a rhyme.)

Mr. R wants us to use the next page.

Have the children touch the first dotted line.
Explain that Mr. R wants them each to write their name on it.

After the children have had an opportunity to do this, select and read a booklet. (e.g., Charlie has   .)
Mr. R says the sentence is not finished.
Mr. R's sentence tells us he has rubberbands.
Charlie's sentence does not tell what Charlie has.
How can Charlie finish his sentence?

After you have helped the children complete their sentences, select and read several aloud.

Have the children turn to the back of the booklet.
Read aloud, "Let's talk about rhymes."

Have the children name each thing in the picture. (e.g., moon, star, hat, cat, spoon, car)
Explain that each word has a word with which it rhymes.
Have a child say one of the words. (e.g., cat)
Another child finds the picture of the rhyming word. (e.g., hat)
She calls out the word.
All the children say the rhyming words in unison. (e.g., cat — hat)
Follow the same procedure with each pair of rhyming words.

Have the children open their booklets.
Draw their attention to the second sentence on the right-hand side.

Explain that Mr. R wants them to use the sentence to tell him about a rhyme they find.

Discuss different pictures the children can look for to complete their sentences.
Help them find, draw pictures of, or dictate two rhyming words.

Encourage them to tell Mr. R the rhyme they found.

Suggest they take their booklets home.
Have them ask members of their family to tell Mr. R words that rhyme.

1J₁

PLANNING AND PREPARATION: Huggables, Mr. R and Mr. J; Record #2; Mr. J's Picture Squares; paper and crayons; Alpha Time Master #144.

Place Mr. R where he can be seen by the children. Hide Mr. J where he will be easily available.

MEETING MR. J AND HIS "JUMBLED JUNK"

Gather the children around Mr. R.

Mr. R is being a rascal again. He told everyone that he has met the next Letter Person and that this Letter Person does the silliest thing. Mr. R just laughed and laughed at him.

Mr. R told the new Letter Person that everyone else would laugh at him too.

Now the new Letter Person is worried about meeting us. He is afraid we will laugh at him. Let's ask Mr. R what this new Letter Person does that makes Mr. R laugh at him.

Discovering Mr. J

Give several children a chance to talk to Mr. R and to tell the class what he says to them. Then tell the children the following story.

Mr. R says that the new Letter Person collects Junk, and he jumbles it all up over his body. This Letter Person keeps things that everyone else would throw away.

Is it right for Mr. R to laugh at this new Letter Person? Tell Mr. R how you would feel if you were the new Letter Person.

Let the children discuss how they feel when people laugh at them.

Let's meet the new Letter Person and find out how he feels.

Have the children close their eyes. Reveal Mr. J. Let them meet Mr. J, greet him, and talk about the Jumbled Junk that covers him.

*Listening To And
Moving To
Mr. J's Music*

The new Letter Person says he has a song for us. We will hear his name in the song.

Play record #2, side B, band #4. Encourage the children to move along with the music the second time it is played. Discuss the song with the children making sure they know the Letter Person's name is Mr. J and that his special feature is Jumbled Junk.

DISCOVERING THAT MR. J WILL GET HIS SOUND FROM "JUMBLED JUNK"

Discuss the kinds of junk Mr. J has on his body (e.g., broken bird cage, watch, cracked fish bowl). Talk to the children about how junk may be made useful again (e.g., cans, paper, bottles may be recycled). Some children may know about pollution prevention. Perhaps a committee may be set up to start a neighborhood clean-up campaign. Some children may make posters to remind people not to litter. Talk about how some people's junk may be useful to others, such as old furniture, out grown clothing, old books and records. Talk about how certain items that are junk may be repaired (e.g., painted, mended, new parts added).

Mr. J likes to collect Jumbled Junk for many reasons. Sometimes he fixes the junk and gives it to people who can use it.

Sometimes he collects cans or papers or bottles and takes them to be recycled or used again in factories. Sometimes he collects junk to keep the streets or park clean; then he puts the Jumbled Junk into trash cans.

Mr. J has been so busy he has not had time to think of a sound he could make. Finally the Letter People had a meeting. They said that it was time for Mr. J to have a sound.

Where will Mr. J get his sound?

Lead the children to the conclusion that Mr. J will get his sound from "Jumbled Junk."

AUDITORY DISCRIMINATION OF WORDS WITH J IN THE INITIAL POSITION

The Letter People want Mr. J to listen to some words that start the same way as his Jumbled Junk. They will give him riddle clues and he will have to guess each word.

Answering Rhyming Riddles

Show the children Mr. J's Picture Squares (i.e., jar, jam, jump, juice, jog). Then tell them the following riddles:

> We're thinking of something,
> In which foods are packed.
> On supermarket shelves,
> You'll see them stacked.
> This word rhymes with the word car.
> We are thinking of a. . . (jar).

Find the picture of the jar and show it to Mr. J.

Prove to him that jar starts with the same sound as Jumbled Junk.

> Squeeze cut oranges and quick as a wink!
> You made something good to drink.
> This word rhymes with the word *loose.*
> The word we're thinking of is. . . (juice).

Find the picture of the juice.

Prove to Mr. J that juice starts the same way as Jumbled Junk.

> This makes fingers sticky,
> But it's good to eat.
> Spread it on toast,
> And the toast will taste sweet.
> This word rhymes with *ham.*
> The word we're thinking of is. . . (jam).

Tell the children that the next two pictures show a Mr. J "doing word."

> This Mr. J "doing word" rhymes with *bump.*
> What is this "doing word?"
> It is. . . (jump).

Show Mr. J how you jump.

Prove to Mr. J that *jump* starts the same way as his Jumbled Junk.

> We move like this for health or fun.
> It is something like a skip or run.
> This "doing word" will rhyme with *fog*.
> The word we're thinking of is. . . (jog).

Let's all jog around the room.

Filling A Bag
For Mr. J

Mr. J likes the words that start with his Jumbled Junk sound. He wants to know if we can think of any more.

Mr. J would like us to fill his bag for him.

Have the children make things for Mr. J's bag using a variety of art materials.

TYING IT TOGETHER

Distribute copies of Alpha Time Master #144. The children may prove that each picture begins with the same sound as Jumbled Junk.

ON THEIR OWN

Children may choose from the following activities:

Music And Dance

Dancing to Mr. J's music, possibly with Mr. J.

Counting

Counting some of the pieces of Jumbled Junk on Mr. J's body.

Measuring

Making orange juice by squeezing cut oranges or mixing frozen canned juice with measured water.

Art

Making a Jumbled Junk table arrangement or sculpture using discarded objects found, or brought from home.

Exploring The
Community

Taking a trip to the local "junk" or used article shop and talking about some interesting items for sale there.

Citizenship

Starting a school or neighborhood clean up campaign.

Collecting good used articles to be donated to the Salvation Army or other civic groups.

Science

Finding out more about pollution.

1J₂

PLANNING AND PREPARATION: Huggables, Mr. J, Miss I and Miss A; Mr. J's Picture Book—one for each child; art materials (for making jewelry and jewelry trays).

READING COMPREHENSION

Gather the children around Mr. J.

Mr. J keeps getting Jumbled Junk from everyone. He has gotten jumbles and jumbles of rings, watches, bracelets, necklaces, pins, and cuff links.

Why do you think rings and cuff links and necklaces and bracelets are Mr. J's favorites?

Help the children to decide that all of these things are jewelry, and jewelry starts with Mr. J's sound.

Mr. J decided to open a Jumbled Junk Jewelry Shop. Everyone was anxious to shop in Mr. J's Jumbled Junk Jewelry Shop.

However, after Miss I visited the shop she told the other Letter People not to go. She said, "It is just a mess. You will never be able to find anything."

Miss A said, "It must look like Mr. K's kitchen before I helped him. I will have to help Mr. J."

Tell Mr. J what was wrong with Mr. K's kitchen.

Let the children recall the picture story about Mr. K's kitchen and how his kitchen things had to be neatly arranged.

Reading A Picture Book

Distribute copies of Mr. J's Picture Book to the children and discuss each page with them.

Cover

Let's look at the cover.

Whom do you see? (Mr. J)

What is Mr. J doing? (collecting junk)

What do you think this story will be about?

Let's turn to the first page.

Page 1

What is Mr. J doing in this picture? (carrying junk jewelry into his shop)

Where did he get all this jewelry? (collected junk)

What are the different kinds of jewelry that you see? (e.g., bracelet, necklace, rings)

Have you ever been in a shop that sells jewelry? Tell us how it looks.

How do you think Mr. J's Jumbled Junk Jewelry Shop will look?

Let's turn the page and read the next part of the story to find out.

Page 2

How is Mr. J putting the jewelry into the showcases? (throwing it in a jumble)

How is this the same as what Mr. K did in his kitchen? (Mr. K also did not arrange things neatly.)

Why will it be very hard to find anything when Mr. J's jewelry is all jumbled up?

How would you feel about shopping in Mr. J's store?

How should Mr. J put the jewelry into the showcases? (Things that belong together should be put in the same place.)

Let's read the next page and see how Miss A feels.

Page 3

How does Miss A feel about the way Mr. J has arranged his Jumbled Junk Jewelry? (She does not like it.)

How did Miss A help Mr. K? (She helped him put things back the way they belong.)

How can she help Mr. J? (by doing the same thing)

Let's turn the page and look at the next part of the story and see how Miss A helps Mr. J.

Page 4

What has Miss A done to the tray on the counter? (arranged it neatly)

What is on the tray now? (rings)

Are all the rings alike? (no)

Why did Miss A put all the rings together? (They will be easier to find.)

Let's look at the next page and see what Miss A will do.

Page 5

Which tray is Miss A working with now? (bracelets)

How can you tell that the only things Miss A wants on this tray are bracelets? (That's all she has put there.)

What other kinds of trays will Miss A arrange?

Why will it be easier to shop in the Jumbled Junk Jewelry Shop when Miss A is finished? (People will find what they want.)

How will it be easier for Mr. J to work in the shop? (He will know where everything is.)

How is Miss A kind to Mr. J? (She helped him.)

Let's turn the page and look at the last part of the story and find out how the Letter People like the Jumbled Junk Jewelry Shop.

How do the Letter People feel about shopping in Mr. J's store? (They like it.)

How can you tell they like it? (expression on their faces)

Be one of the Letter People and tell us how you feel about Mr. J's Junk Jewelry Shop.

Be Mr. J and help a Letter Person find the piece of jewelry he wants.

IDENTIFYING THE UPPER AND LOWER CASE LETTER J

Forming The Letter J

Let's show Mr. J his capital letter and his lower case letter. Then we will make the capital J with our bodies.

Help the children form the capital J. Some children may be able to make it alone while others will need two children per letter.

TYING IT TOGETHER

Mr. J is very happy with the way Miss A helped him. He can hardly remember how his store looked before Miss A fixed it. He wants us to make some pictures for him.

In one picture we will show how the store looked when he put the jewelry in the showcase.

In another picture we will show how it looked after Miss A arranged it for him.

When both pictures are finished we will compare them.

ON THEIR OWN

Children may choose from the following activities:

Auditory Discrimination And Sound Association

Including Mr. J's Picture Squares, puzzle and playing cards in any of the activities listed in the *Games* section of the manual.

Letter Tracing

Tracing the letter J on Alpha Time Master #64.

Junk Exchange

Having a Junk Jamboree at which each child brings a piece of junk and exchanges it with another member of the class. (This may also be a junk sale, with proceeds going to the school fund.)

Playing Store

Dramatizing Mr. J's story.

Art

Making a junk collage.

Crafts And Sorting

Making different pieces of jewelry and putting them onto jewelry trays. (The tops of shoeboxes make good trays.) Jewelry may be made of pipe cleaners, clay, buttons, beads and other materials. When they have finished, the children can sort one another's trays. They can set up a jewelry shop and try shopping with jumbled jewelry trays first, and then with sorted jewelry trays.

1J₃

PERFORMANCE OBJECTIVES:

The child will say words with the *j* in the initial position.
The child will draw inferences from pictures.
The child will discuss any job with which he or she is familiar.
The child will write his or her name.

TEACHER OBJECTIVES:

To reinforce the characteristic and sound of Mr. J.
To encourage children to talk about jobs.

DEVELOPMENT

The "All About Us" booklets Mr. J made got mixed up with his jumbled junk.
The Letter People had to help him separate the booklets from the jumbled junk.

Distribute the Mr. J booklets.
Have them say the title for Mr. J.

Which Letter Person's picture is on the booklet? (Mr. J)
Whose picture is next to Mr. J? (his friend's)
Touch the sentence at the bottom of the booklet.
It says, "Mr. J has a friend."

What is all over Mr. J's body? (jumbled junk)
Mr. J collects jumbled junk from everyone.
Look at the picture Mr. J drew of his friend.
His friend will collect jumbled junk.
In what will his friend keep the jumbled junk? (a large container)
Mr. J wants us to put pictures of jumbled junk in the container.

Give the children the opportunity to find pictures in magazines.
They may wish to draw their own pictures.
The pictures may be pasted on the container.
Then suggest they add to the picture of Mr. J's friend, making it look like themselves or anyone else.

Have the children open their booklets.
Ask them to touch the first sentence on the left-hand side.
What picture did Mr. J put in the sentence? (his jumbled junk)

Read aloud, "Mr. J has jumbled junk."
Let them pretend to reread the sentence with you.

Mr. J likes to talk about jobs.
He says each Letter Person has a very important job.
They each work in words.
Mr. J likes working in words.
But he dreams about another job.
Mr. J says if we look at the picture at the bottom of the page, we will know what he wants to be.

What is Mr. J doing in the picture? (throwing three balls in the air)
What do you call a person who can keep three balls in the air at the same time, without letting any of them drop? (juggler) .

365A

What do you think Mr. J wants to be? (a juggler)
Mr. J's sentence says, "Mr. J wants to be a juggler."

Mr. J took this whole page to tell us about himself.
What two things did he tell us? (He has jumbled junk. He wants to be a juggler.)

Mr. J wants us to use the next page.

Have the children touch the first dotted line.
Explain that Mr. J wants them each to write his or her name.

After the children have had an opportunity to do this, select and read a booklet. (*e.g.*, John has jumbled junk.)
Have John name all the jumbled junk pictured at the end of the sentence.
John may want to circle his favorite piece of junk.
Follow the same procedure with several booklets.

Explain that Mr. J drew a picture on the back of the booklet.
Have the children turn to the back of the booklet.

Read aloud, "Let's talk about jobs."
Have them discuss each illustration and name the job that is pictured. (*e.g.*, painter, policewoman, baker, bus driver)
Give the children the opportunity to discuss jobs that are not pictured.

This is an excellent opportunity for you to begin teaching about career awareness. After the children have discussed job titles, you may wish to discuss with them not only job descriptions but the roles particular jobs play. Let them talk about the importance of jobs to them. Why is it important that people hold certain jobs? Why do we need policemen, firemen, doctors, teachers, farmers, factory workers, etc? Make sure treatment is equal for men and women in jobs. The best way is for children to tell what they want to be. Watch for self-stereotyping. Point out that a boy may want to be a nurse; a girl may want to drive a truck.

Have the children open their booklets.

Draw their attention to the second sentence on the right-hand side.
Explain that Mr. J told them he wants to be a juggler.
Mr. J wants each child to tell him what he or she wants to be.

They may draw or find a picture representing a job or complete their sentences by dictating the name of their favorite job.

Encourage the children to tell Mr. J what their sentences say.
Suggest that they take their booklets home.
Have them ask members of their family to tell Mr. J about different jobs.

1U₁

PLANNING AND PREPARATION: Huggables, Miss A, E, I, O, U; an umbrella, sunglasses, sunhat; Record #3; Alpha Time Master #145.

MEETING MISS U

Listening To A Recorded Dramatization

Group the five Letter Girls together.

After the children have had a chance to look at Miss U tell them that the Letter Girls had a funny experience, and play Meet Miss U (record #3, side B, band 2) and discuss with the children questions such as the following to stimulate discussion.

Why was Miss U worried about meeting the Letter People? (e.g., She was afraid they wouldn't like her because she was different.)

Who tried to comfort Miss U? (her umbrella)

What did the Letter Girls want to give Miss U? (sunglasses, sunhat)

Why did they want to give the glasses and hat to her? (They wanted her to put the umbrella away.)

How did the umbrella feel? (jealous)

Why do you think the umbrella kept taking Miss U ŭ ŭ upsy-daisy?

Why didn't it want Miss U to stay with the girls? (It was afraid she wouldn't want it anymore.)

Encourage the children to talk about similar feelings they have had such as fear of losing a friend.

What made the umbrella happy in the end? (Miss U decided to stay with it.)

Tell Miss U what you think about her decision to stay with the umbrella.

Using the umbrella, sunglasses, and sunhat as props, the children may dramatize the story of Miss U. (Children may make the props as a craft activity.)

IDENTIFYING THE UPPER AND LOWER CASE U

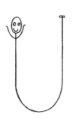

Miss U would like us to show the umbrella her letter.

Where is Miss U's capital letter?

Have several children trace the upper case U.

What kind of line do we use to make the capital U? (curved)

How many children will we need to make the U?

When the children have formed the capital U with their bodies, they may find the lower case u.

TYING IT TOGETHER

Distribute copies of Alpha Time Master #145. The children may draw lines from the umbrellas to Miss U, then they may mark the upper case letter U with one color, and the lower case u with another color.

ON THEIR OWN

Children may choose from the following activities:

Dramatic Play

Using the Letter Girls to reenact Miss U's story.

Storytelling

Retelling the story of Miss U. If a tape recorder is available, the stories may be recorded.

Letter Tracing

Using Alpha Time Master #75 to trace the upper and lower case U.

1U₂

REMEMBERING MISS U

Listening To And Dancing To Miss U's Song

Gather the children around Miss U.

Miss U would like to sing her song for us today.

Play Miss U's song (record #2, side B, band #5). Encourage the children to sing and move along with it the second time you play it. Then discuss the song with the children.

Recalling A Story By Using Picture Clues

Mr. R, Mr. F, and Mr. J were not here when we heard the story of how Miss U arrived. Miss U drew some pictures for us so that we can tell the Letter Boys the story as it happened.

Give each child a copy of Alpha Time Master #146. Let several children retell the "Upsy-Daisy Story" to the Letter Boys as they show them each picture on the Alpha Time Master.

Frame 1

What are Miss U and the umbrella doing? (flying)

How did Miss U come here from Letter People Land? (She flew with her Umbrella.)

What does the Umbrella say when it flies with Miss U? (ŭ ŭ upsy-daisy)

Frame 2

What is Miss E doing? (giving Miss U sunglasses)

How does the umbrella look? (unhappy)

Why was the umbrella upset when Miss E gave Miss U the sunglasses? (It was afraid Miss U wouldn't need it.)

What do you think Miss E is saying?

What do you think Miss U is saying?

Frame 3

Who is in this picture? (Miss I, Miss U, Umbrella)

What is happening here? (Miss I gave Miss U a sunhat)

How does the Umbrella feel? (worried)

What do you think it is thinking?

Frame 4

How does the Umbrella look? (happy)

What is making it happy? (Miss U loves it.)

What do you think Miss U is saying?

What do you think the Umbrella is saying?

Miss U wants to make the girls understand that she does not want something else to take the Umbrella's place.

Tell the Letter girls how Miss U feels about her Umbrella.

Tell the girls how the Umbrella feels.

DISCOVERING THAT MISS U WILL GET HER SOUND FROM UMBRELLA

Miss U loves her Umbrella. She wants to get her sound from Umbrella. She will take the ŭ from Umbrella.

She wants to get her sound from Umbrella. She will take the ŭ from Umbrella.

Let's all say ŭ ŭ ŭ.

Singing A Song

Sing the following song with the children to the tune of "Old MacDonald."

Little Miss U has a sound,
ŭ ŭ ŭ ŭ ŭ.
In Umbrella it was found,
ŭ ŭ ŭ ŭ ŭ.
With an ŭ ŭ here,
And an ŭ ŭ there,
Here an ŭ,
There an ŭ,
Everywhere an ŭ ŭ.
Little Miss U has a sound,
ŭ ŭ ŭ ŭ ŭ.

IDENTIFYING WORDS WITH "U" IN THE INITIAL POSITION

Miss U likes her ŭ sound. She has been waiting for her Umbrella to tell her words that start with her ŭ sound. All of a sudden Miss U's Umbrella started to cry. It said, "I have been looking and looking for words that start with ŭ. I cannot find very many. I finally found some words but I don't know what they mean."

Miss U said, "Don't worry, tell me the words you found and together we will try to understand what they mean."

"Well," said the Umbrella," I found a word in a baseball book. The word starts with ŭ." The word is *umpire*. What does it mean?

Show the children the Picture Square of the umpire and discuss the meaning of the word with them.

The Umbrella said it found another word in a book about a family. One person in the family was an *uncle*. Uncle starts the same way as Umbrella. You can hear the ŭ sound in *uncle*.

Show the children the Picture Square of "uncle" (i.e., man and boy). Have the children tell Miss U about their uncle. Help them to understand that an uncle is a relative.

The Umbrella said it found another word that starts with Miss U's ŭ sound. The word is *under*. Let's show Miss U what the word *under* means.

369

Help the children show what the word "under" means. Show them the Picture Square of a book under the table. Let them put a book under a table; discover that the floor is under their feet; hold one piece of paper under another.

The next word the Umbrella found is a kind of clothing.

Show the children the Picture Square of "underwear." Some children may realize that this is a big word made of two little words.

Then the Umbrella said that the last word he had for Miss U was not difficult, it was easy to remember.

Show the children the Picture Square of the "umbrella."

What word is the Umbrella thinking of? (umbrella)

AUDITORY DISCRIMINATION OF WORDS WITH U IN INITIAL POSITION

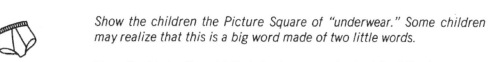

Let's play a guessing game with Miss U's ŭ words.

Display Miss U's initial Picture Squares where they are easily reached by the children. Explain that Miss U will tell some riddles and the children will try to find the correct picture for each riddle. Remind them to prove each picture for Miss U.

When I'm with Miss U she won't complain.
I shield her from the sun and rain.
Guess which picture I can be.
Help Miss U find me.(umbrella)

At baseball games no matter how you shout,
When I say a player is out—he's out!
Guess which picture I can be.
Help Miss U find me. (umpire)

I am a man who is part of a family.
Your father is my brother, who can I be?
Guess which picture I can be.
Help Miss U find me. (uncle)

I'm a word that rhymes with *thunder*.
I am the opposite of over.
Guess which picture I can be.
Help Miss U find me. (under)

I am a kind of clothes.
But not for your head or toes.
Guess which picture I can be.
Help Miss U find me. (underwear)

TYING IT TOGETHER

Distribute drawing paper and have the children draw as many of Miss U's pictures as they like.

ON THEIR OWN

Music And Dance

*Using Words Of
Location*

Art

Crafts

*Matching And
Sorting*

Children may choose from the following activities:

Dancing to Miss U's song (record #2).

Making a list of things around the room that are "under" others (e.g., table is under the plant).

Drawing a picture of a favorite uncle.

Making an umbrella out of construction or tissue paper and an ice cream stick.

Using Miss U's playing cards, Picture Squares, puzzle, in any of the activities described in the *Games* section.

PLANNING AND PREPARATION: Huggables, Miss U and Mr. R; Alpha Time Master #148.

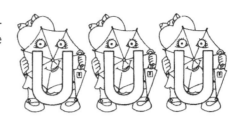

MAKING COMPOUND WORDS

Gather the children around Miss U and Mr. R.

Miss U would like to have more words that start with her ŭ sound.

Mr. R told Miss U that he made more words for himself by putting *re* in front of other Letter People's words.

Miss U said, "If I put *re* in front of words, the words will still not start with my ŭ sound."

Mr. R said, "That's right—you can't use *re*. You must find a little part that starts with ŭ."

Miss U could not think of a part to put in front of words. Suddenly the strangest things were happening to Miss U.

Miss U put on her coat and buttoned all the buttons. All of a sudden, the buttons were not buttoned anymore. Miss U's coat was *un*buttoned.

Miss U took off her coat and put on her jacket. She zipped her jacket. All of a sudden, the zipper was not zipped anymore. Her jacket was *un*zipped.

Then Miss U wanted to get a present that she had wrapped. Miss U had wrapped the present with beautiful red paper. Guess what! The present was not wrapped anymore. The present was *un*wrapped.

Miss U had tied the package with beautiful red ribbon. Guess what! The ribbon was not tied. The ribbon was *un*tied.

Miss U could not understand why her coat was unbuttoned, her jacket unzipped, her present unwrapped, her ribbon untied. Suddenly, Miss U saw Mr. R smiling. She said, "Mr. R, you are mean! You have been doing all these tricks."

Mr. R said, "Miss U, I was not being mean. I did all these things to help you. I unbuttoned, unzipped, unwrapped and untied for you. Think how each of those words starts. Ask your Umbrella how the first part of each of those words can help you."

Talking About The Prefix 'Un'

Help the children realize that putting "un" before a word will turn it into a Miss U word.

The Umbrella told Miss U that if she let *un* be the first part of some words, she would be able to have many more words that start with her ŭ sound.

Miss U wants to know how *un* changes a word.

Have the children show Miss U the difference between button and unbutton, zip and unzip, wrap and unwrap, tie and untie.

Help the children to discover that putting "un" in front of a word gives that new word the opposite meaning. Other examples you can use are happy/unhappy, lock/unlock, curl/uncurl, fold/unfold.

TYING IT TOGETHER

Distribute Alpha Time Master #147. Discuss the pairs of pictures, letting the children mark the "un" pictures in each set (i.e., unbutton, unzip, unwrap, untie).

ON THEIR OWN

Word Study

Children may choose from the following activities:

Demonstrating a word and asking another child to demonstrate it after *un* has become its first part.

Illustrating pairs of words showing what happens when *un* becomes the first part of a word.

Art

Painting a picture of how Miss U looks while Mr. R is playing tricks on her.

1U₄

PLANNING AND PREPARATION: Huggables, Miss U, Miss A, Miss E, Miss I, Miss O; Miss U's "In the Middle" Picture Squares; Alpha Time Master #148.

READING COMPREHENSION

Miss U's Umbrella made friends with the other Letter Girls.

Miss U drew a picture story for us so that we may see how the Umbrella helped the other Letter Girls.

Give each child a copy of Alpha Time Master #148. Discuss each picture with the children. Have them dramatize portions of the story as they go along.

Frame 1

Numeration

Let's look at the first part of the story.

Which Letter Girl is in this story? (Miss A)

What is happening to Miss A? (dog is chasing her)

How do you think Miss A feels?

How do you think the dog feels?

Be Miss A. Be the dog. Show us how they would act.

Let's look at the next part of Miss A's story and see who helps her.

Frame 2

Drawing conclusions

Who helped Miss A? (the Umbrella)

How did the Umbrella help Miss A? (carried her up)

What do you think the Umbrella said to Miss A? (ŭ ŭ upsy-daisy)

Be Miss A. Tell us how you feel when the Umbrella helps you.

Why is it nice of the Umbrella to help Miss A?

Let's look at the next part of the story and see what happened to Miss E.

Frame 3

Making inferences

Predicting outcomes

Where is Miss E? (on a slide)

Why won't she slide down? (She is afraid.)

Tell Miss E about a time when you climbed up a slide and then were afraid to slide down.

Why can't Miss E walk down the steps she has climbed up? (The children are on steps behind her.)

How do you think Miss E will get help?

Let's look at the next part of Miss E's story and see how she gets help.

Frame 4

Dramatizing

Who has come to help Miss E? (the Umbrella)

How do you think Miss E feels about the Umbrella now that it has helped her?

Have several children take turns playing the roles of Miss E and the Umbrella.

Let's look at the next part of the story and see who needs help next.

Frame 5

Who is in this picture? (Miss I)

Where is Miss I? (in the street)

What else is in the street? (cars)

What did Miss I forget to do before she crossed the street? (look in both directions, look at the light)

Why does Miss I need help?

How can the Umbrella help Miss I?

Have several children play the roles of Miss I and the Umbrella.

Let's look at the last picture.

Miss O is very Obstinate. The Letter People told her not to dive into the pool. They had a good reason, but Miss O ran away before they could tell her what it was. Let's see if we can figure out why Miss O should not dive into the pool.

Why didn't the Letter People want Miss O to dive into the pool? (The pool is empty.)

Why doesn't Miss O know that there isn't any water in the pool? (She is not facing the pool.)

What might happen to Miss O if she dives into an empty pool?

Frame 6

Predicting outcomes

How can Miss O be helped?

Let's draw a picture of how the Umbrella helps Miss O.

Have several children dramatize the roles of Miss O and the Umbrella.

IDENTIFYING WORDS WITH U IN THE MEDIAL POSITION

The Letter Girls told Miss U how their sounds may be in the middle of a word. They said that they would help find words in which Miss U's ŭ sound is "in the middle."

Show the children Miss U's "In the Middle" Picture Squares (i.e., bus, sun, cup, bug, gum). Explain that the Umbrella will give them clues to Miss U's words. The pictures will help them guess the words. When the children figure out a word in which Miss U's sound is "in the middle," they can tell Miss U where they hear her sound, hold her up high, and maker her go ŭ ŭ upsy-daisy.

Listen to the clue and decide which of the pictures Miss U is thinking about.

375

Taking children to school is one thing I do.
I ride in the city and in the country too.
You'll find that I rhyme with the word *us*.
What am I? I am a. . . (bus).

Which picture is Miss U thinking about? (bus)

Say the word *bus* so that Miss U can hear her ŭ sound before you pick
her up high and say ŭ ŭ upsy-daisy.

Miss U is ready for the next word.

I shine in the sky warm and bright as can be.
When there are no clouds I am easy to see.
You'll find that I rhyme with the word *fun*.
What am I? I am the. . . (sun).

I stand in a saucer whenever I'm able.
Because a saucer keeps me from staining the table.
You'll find that I rhyme with the word *pup*.
What am I? I am a. . . (cup).

I have six legs that help me crawl.
Compared to you, I'm very small.
You'll find I rhyme with the word *rug*.
What am I? I am a. . . (bug).

I'm bad for your teeth, that's very true.
I am something Mr. G likes to chew.
You'll find I rhyme with the word *hum*.
What am I? I am. . . (gum).

*Continue the game with words such as bun, run, fun, cut, rug, tug, tub,
rub, mud, bud, cub. The clues do not have to be in rhyme.*

TYING IT TOGETHER

*Children may enjoy playing "In the Middle" with Miss U as described in
Lesson 2A3.*

*Help the children draw or make umbrellas decorated with Miss U's "in
the middle" pictures.*

ON THEIR OWN

Children may choose from the following activities:

Word Study   Making words by putting beginning sounds on *ut, um, us, ug, un*.

Art   Drawing pictures of other ways an umbrella is helpful.

1U₅

To reinforce the characteristic and sound of
Miss U.
To demonstrate the short *u* sound.
To identify objects that go up.

PERFORMANCE OBJECTIVES:

The child will say words with the short *u*
sound in the initial position.
The child will recognize the short *u* sound in
words.
The child will locate examples of objects
that go up.

DEVELOPMENT

*Miss U wanted to show the Letter People the "All About Us"
booklets she made.*
She could not find them anywhere.
*Miss U remembered that her upsy daisy umbrella always makes
things go upsy daisy.*
Miss U asked the umbrella to bring all the booklets back for us.

Distribute the Miss U "All About Us" booklets to the children.

Read aloud, "All About Us."

Which Letter Person's picture do you see? (Miss U)
Whose picture is next to Miss U? (her friend's)
Touch the sentence at the bottom of the booklet.
It says, "Miss U has a friend."

Look at Miss U.
What special thing does Miss U have? (her upsy daisy umbrella)
Look at the picture of Miss U's friend.
Miss U's friend wants an upsy daisy umbrella, too.
What part of the umbrella did Miss U give to her friend? (the
handle)
Miss U wants us to finish the picture of the umbrella.

Give the children the opportunity to complete the picture of the
umbrella.
Remind them that they may make Miss U's friend look like
themselves or anyone else.

Have the children open the booklet.
Point to the full-page picture on the left-hand side.
Explain that Miss U used this whole page to show how she goes
upsy daisy.

Have the children pretend to be Miss U and go upsy daisy with the
upsy daisy umbrella.
They may each tell where they land. (*e.g.*, a rooftop, a bird's nest,
a flagpole)
The children should say, "I am Miss U. I am going u u upsy daisy.
Guess where I will land."
This will enable the children to have practice repeating the short *u*
sound.

Have the children look at the right-hand side of the booklet.
Explain that Miss U has discovered that many things go up without an upsy daisy umbrella.
Read aloud, "Miss U finds things that go up."

Have the children name each thing that Miss U found. (airplane, satellite, balloon, bird)
You may want to discuss how each object goes up.

Miss U wants us each to draw or paste pictures at the bottom of the page of things that go up.
Before we do that, let's look at the back of the booklet.

Read aloud, "Let's talk about things that go up."

Have the children find and talk about all the things in the picture that go up. Ask them to try to think of other things that go up.

Have them look in magazines for pictures of things that go up.
Help them complete their sentences on the inside of the booklet.

Select and read aloud several completed sentences.
Encourage the children to tell Miss U all the things they found that go up.

Suggest they take their booklets home.
Have them ask members of their family to tell Miss U all the things they can think of that go up.

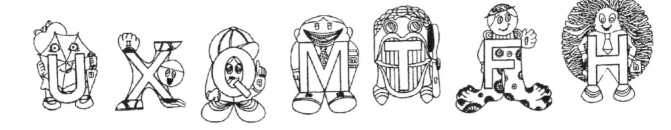

376B

1X₁

PLANNING AND PREPARATION: Huggables, Mr. H, Mr. L, Mr. G, Mr. D, Mr. J and Mr. X; Record #2; Alpha Time Master #150; a sheet of letter paper in an envelope, mirrors, if available; blue and green crayons.

NOTE: In these lessons the children will not learn the sound for x as there are no words that have the x sound in the initial position. They will, however be able to recognize and to identify the letter X.

Display Mr. H, Mr. L, Mr. G, Mr. D, Mr. J. Hide Mr. X where he can be easily revealed.

TALKING ABOUT FEELINGS

Gather the children around you and tell them the following:

Mr. H has received a message from Letter People Land. The next Letter Person is worried about coming to see us.

He says, "No, they won't want me. I won't go. The Letter People will not like me."

Mr. H wants each Letter Person to tell him why he thinks the new Letter Person is afraid to come.

Talking About Love

Mr. L says, "I guess he thinks I won't like him because he doesn't know what love is. We can write him a letter and tell him all about love."

Have the children discuss what their letter about love might say.

What will we say in the letter? (e.g., Love is caring about someone.)

Mr. G says, "Maybe he wants to bring all of us gifts and he doesn't know what to bring us. He doesn't know about the greatest gift of all! We can write him a letter and tell him about the greatest gift of all."

What will this letter say? (e.g., The greatest gift of all is love.)

Talking About Making Decisions

Mr. D says, "I think the new Letter Person doesn't know about *decisions*. He doesn't know how to make a *decision*. We can write him a letter and tell him how to make a decision."

What will this letter say? (e.g., We must think before we make decisions.)

Help the children discuss what they might write about decisions.

Talking About Jealousy

Mr. J says, "Maybe the new Letter Person gets jealous. He may not know that all of us get jealous sometimes. We try to understand why we are jealous. Let's write him a letter and tell him about the time Miss U's Umbrella was jealous."

What will our letter say? (We are jealous when we are not sure someone loves us.)

Help the children discuss their letter about jealousy.

377

Mr. H thinks it is a wonderful idea to send these letters to the new Letter Person.

Dictating Letters To The New Letter Person

Have the children decide which of the letters they would like to write. The letters may be dictated by the children. The children may wish to illustrate their letters. The letters can then be "mailed" to the new Letter Person.

Note: Continue the rest of the lesson the following day to allow time for a reply to the children's letters.

Show the children a stamped envelope containing a piece of paper and tell them that Mr. H received a letter from Letter People Land.

The new Letter Person read all of our letters. They helped him to understand about love, decisions and jealousy but he is still afraid to come to us. He says that he looks so different from the other Letter People that he is sure you won't love him. He says he is put together all wrong.

Why isn't the way a person looks the most important thing?

How does each one of us look different from the other?

MEETING MR. X

Have the children discuss looking different. If you have a mirror available the children will enjoy looking at themselves and at each other's reflections. They may also draw pictures of themselves to show to the new Letter Person.

Let's give Mr. H the pictures we drew of ourselves. He will show them to the new Letter Person. The Letter Person will see that we all look different from each other. Then maybe he'll understand that we will love him no matter how he looks.

Mr. H wants us to close our eyes and he'll try to bring the new Letter Person to class.

While the children have their eyes closed, place Mr. X in front of the classroom next to Mr. H.

Mr. H wants to introduce us to the new Letter Person. Mr. H says his name is Mr. X.

Mr. X says that you have made him understand that it doesn't matter if he looks different from the other Letter People. In fact, he says being put together all wrong can be fun. He wants you to look at him and tell him how he is different from each of us.

Discovering That Mr. X Is All Mixed Up

How is he different from each of the other Letter People? (His body parts are all mixed up.)

Listening To
Mr. X's Song

Mr. X has a song for us. Let's listen to what he tells us about himself.

Play Mr. X's song (record #2, side B, band #6) and discuss the words and music with the children. The children may enjoy moving to Mr. X's song.

After listening to Mr. X's "all wrong" sentences, the children may want to scramble other sentences and let some of the Letter People unscramble them. (e.g., do How do, Mr. you X. —How do you do, Mr. X.)

IDENTIFYING THE UPPER AND LOWER CASE X

Call on several children to trace their finger over Mr. X's upper and lower case letter. (Some children may recognize that it is similar to the mark some teachers put on work that is wrong.) They may then form the letter X with their bodies in groups of two.

TYING IT TOGETHER

Distribute Alpha Time Master #150. Have the children say what each of the Letter People in the picture is thinking. Then they may put a blue mark on the upper case X and a green mark on the lower case x.

ON THEIR OWN

Children may choose from the following activities:

Music And Dance Listening to and moving to Mr. X's music (record #2).

Letter Tracing Tracing the upper and lower case X on Alpha Time Master #78.

Humor Cutting pictures of animals or people out of magazines, mixing up their body parts, and pasting them together all wrong.

Unscrambling the following sentences:

Logical Thinking
Mr. X all wrong is. (Mr. X is all wrong.)
Mr. M a Munching has Mouth. (Mr. M has a Munching Mouth.)
Miss U an has Umbrella. (Miss U has an Umbrella.)

1X₂

PLANNING AND PREPARATION: Huggable, Mr. X; Picture Card 13; Alpha Time Master #151; drawing paper.

DISCOVERING THAT MR. X WILL NOT HAVE A SOUND

Mr. X is very happy that he came but he wants to ask us for a favor.

He says, "Please, is it all right if I don't have a sound right away? Some day I will want a sound. Soon I will also work in words, but right now I just want to get used to everyone."

Tell Mr. X how you feel about the favor he is asking.

Discuss with the children the fact that Mr. X will not have a sound. Lead them to the conclusion that Mr. X does not need his sound right now if he is not ready for it.

TYING IT TOGETHER

Mr. X is so happy that you are patient with him. He would like to tell you about the mixed up neighborhood he comes from. He says there are many things there that are all wrong just as he is.

Show the children Picture Card 13 and distribute matching Alpha Time Master #151 and a sheet of drawing paper.

Let's look at this picture.

What are some things that are all wrong? (e.g., square wheel, dog with shoes, horse with five legs)

How could the wheel be made right? (make it round)

How could the horse be made right? (remove a leg)

NOTE: The children may enjoy finding the following additional "all wrong" things: apples growing instead of flowers; duck walking backwards; boat on land; boy wearing boots and scarf; sun and stars out at the same time; door and window on house reversed; propeller in wrong place.

Put an x on all the things in your picture that are wrong. Then, on the drawing paper show how one of the wrong things in the picture should look.

ON THEIR OWN

Children may choose from the following activities:

Motor Coordination   Using Mr. X's puzzle.

Art   Drawing more "all wrong" pictures.

Map Making   Drawing a map of the school or neighborhood and mark the room or the school with an X.

1X₃

TEACHER OBJECTIVES:

To reinforce the characteristic of Mr. X.
To have children recognize, identify and write X.

PERFORMANCE OBJECTIVES:

The child will recognize and write the le
X.

DEVELOPMENT

Mr. X made "All About Us" booklets all wrong.
The Letter People had to help him.
They love Mr. X and always help him.

Distribute the Mr. X booklets.

Have them say the name "All About Us" for Mr. X
Which Letter Person's picture is on the booklet? (Mr. X)
Whose picture is next to Mr. X? (his friend's)
Touch the sentence at the bottom of the booklet.
It says, "Mr. X has a friend."

What do we know about Mr. X? (He is all wrong.)
Look at the picture Mr. X drew of his friend.
What is wrong in the picture?

Give the children the opportunity to enjoy the picture.
The children may color and add to the picture in any way they
wish.

Have the children open their booklets.
Ask them to touch the first sentence on the left-hand side.
Explain that Mr. X put two pictures in the first sentence to help
him remember what the sentence says.

Read aloud, "Mr. X writes x's."
Draw the children's attention to the second sentence.
Read aloud, "Mr. X uses x's."
Ask the children how Mr. X is using x's. (He's playing a game
called Tic Tac Toe.)

Mr. X took this whole page to tell us about himself.
What two things did he tell us? (He writes x's. He uses x's.)

Mr. X wants us to use the next page.

Have the children touch the first dotted line.
Explain that Mr. X wants each of them to write his or her name
on it.

After the children have had an opportunity to do this, select and read a booklet. (*e.g.*, Laurie writes   .)
Mr. X says the sentence is not finished.
Mr. X's sentence tells us he writes x's.
Laurie's sentence does not tell what Laurie writes.
How can Laurie finish her sentence?

Lead the children to conclude that Mr. X would like Laurie to finish the sentence by writing x's.
He will understand if she prefers writing a different letter.

Help the children complete their sentences.
Select and read several completed sentences aloud.

Draw the children's attention to the second sentence.
Explain that Mr. X wants each of them to write his or her name on the dotted line.
Then he wants them to use x's in the "Tic Tac Toe."
Encourage them to show Mr. X how they used x's.

Explain that Mr. X wants them to turn to the back of the booklet and look at the picture.
Read aloud, "Let's talk about x's."
Have them find and tell Mr. X the things that are wrong. They then mark an x on each wrong thing.
Some children may be able to tell him what is wrong with each thing.

Encourage the children to take their booklets home.
Have them tell members of their family all about Mr. X.

After the children have finished this booklet, continue the language arts skills of observing. You may wish to draw or cut out some pictures for the children to look at. Be certain that each picture contains something wrong. Have the children discover what is wrong in each picture. Have them place an x on the incorrect thing.

10Q₁

PLANNING AND PREPARATION: Huggables, Mr. X, Mr. H and Mr. Q; Record #2; Picture Card 14; Alpha Time Master #152; crayons; a blank sheet of letter paper.

Display Mr. X in the classroom. Place Mr. Q where he cannot be seen but where he can be easily revealed.

MEETING MR. Q

Gather the children around Mr. X.

The Letter People love Mr. X. They have decided that they would like another Letter Person who is not ready to work in words.

They wrote to Letter People Land and here is the answer they received.

"Read" the following letter to the children:

Dear Letter People:

We will send you one more Letter Person. He will be the last letter Person we will send. This Letter Person cannot work in words by himself because he cannot speak. We call him Quiet Mr. Q. We'll be glad to send him to you.

Why do you think the people in Letter People Land call this new Letter Person Quiet Mr. Q?

Why do you think Quiet Mr. Q can't speak?

Let's close our eyes, put our fingers over our mouth, says *shh* and Mr. X will bring Quiet Mr. Q.

Discovering Mr. Q

While the children have their eyes closed place Mr. Q in front of the classroom and have the children introduce themselves and the Letter People to him.

Let's tell our names to Quiet Mr. Q.

Now let's introduce the Letter People to Quiet Mr. Q.

How can we tell by looking at Mr. Q that he is Quiet? (His finger is over his mouth.)

Mr. H says that the Letter People will tell us about Mr. Q because Mr. Q doesn't speak.

Listening To Mr. Q's Music

Play Mr. Q's song (record #2, side B, band #7). Discuss the song with the children.

What do the Letter People tell us about Quiet Mr. Q? (e.g., He doesn't make a sound.)

What are some of the things mentioned on the record that do make a sound? (ducks, cow, horns, bells)

What do you think Quiet Mr. Q is thinking?

TALKING ABOUT MR. Q

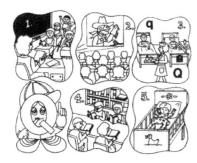

Picture Reading

Show Picture Card 14 to the children.

What are some things you see in this picture? (classroom, movies, hospital, library, sleeping baby)

Why do you think Mr. Q likes these pictures? (They are quiet places.)

Discuss the importance of being quiet in certain circumstances.

How should people act while a teacher is speaking or reading to them? (listen quietly)

Why should they be quiet? (so they can hear what the teacher says)

Why should people be quiet at the movies or theater or in the auditorium? (so everyone can hear and see what is on the stage)

Why should people be quiet in a hospital? (Sick people need rest and peace.)

How should people act when they are in the library? (quietly)

Why is it important to be quiet in the library? (People are reading and don't want to be disturbed.)

Why should people be quiet while someone is sleeping? (not to waken them)

When else is it important to be quiet?

Mr. Q may be Quiet but that doesn't mean he doesn't want to do things with us. Let's listen to some of the things Quiet Q can do with us.

Read the following rhyme to the children:

> Quiet Q can not talk,
> But we can take him for a walk.
> Quiet Q has nothing to say,
> But we can show him games to play.
> Quiet Q can not speak,
> But he can exercise—he's not too weak!
> Quiet Q can not make a sound,
> It's our job to show him around!

Dramatizing Things To Do With Quiet Q

Give several children a chance to do something with Quiet Mr. Q. Remind them to be sure to tell Mr. Q what they are going to do with him. (e.g., Mr. Q, let's take a walk.)

IDENTIFYING THE UPPER AND LOWER CASE LETTER Q

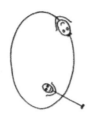

Have the children trace with their fingers the upper and lower case Q. Then they may form groups to make the capital Q with their bodies.

TYING IT TOGETHER

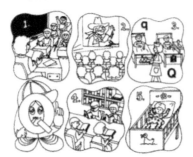

Distribute copies of Alpha Time Master #152. Have the children explain why Mr. Q belongs with the illustrations in the picture. (They are all quiet pictures).

Some children may write an upper or lower case Q next to each quiet picture.

ON THEIR OWN

Children may choose from the following activities:

Letter Tracing	Using Alpha Time Master #71 to trace the upper and lower case Q.
Motor Coordination	Working with Mr. Q's puzzle.
Matching	Including Mr. Q's playing cards in any game described in the *Games* section.
Music And Dance	Singing along with Mr. Q's song.
	Dancing to Mr. Q's music.
Classifying	Making a list of quiet things (e.g., snow, feathers, marshmallows, cat paws).

1Q₂

TEACHER OBJECTIVES:

To reinforce the characteristic and sound of Mr. Q.

To have children become familiar with the use of the question mark.

PERFORMANCE OBJECTIVES:

The child will identify the symbol representing the question mark.

The child will state a reason for using question marks in sentences.

DEVELOPMENT

Mr. Q cannot tell us about "All About Us" booklets he made because he's called Quiet Mr. Q.
We'll find out about them ourselves.

Distribute the booklets.
Read aloud, "All About Us."

Which Letter Person's picture is on the booklet? (Mr. Q)
Whose picture is next to Mr. Q? (his friend's)
Touch the sentence at the bottom of the booklet.
It says, "Mr. Q has a friend."

Look at the picture of Mr. Q.
How can you tell he is quiet? (His finger is placed over his mouth.)
Mr. Q's friend wants to look quiet.
How can we make his friend look quiet?

Give the children the opportunity to complete the picture.

Have the children open their booklets.
Ask them to touch the first sentence on the left-hand side.
What picture did Mr. Q put in the first sentence? (a picture to show he's quiet)
Read aloud, "Mr. Q is always quiet."

Explain that since Mr. Q doesn't have a sound to practice, he keeps himself busy by looking for things.
Draw a question mark on the board.

This is what Mr. Q found.
It is called a question mark.

Mr. Q drew a picture to show us where he found the question mark.
Look at the picture and find the question mark.

After the children find the question mark in the tree, read aloud, "Mr. Q finds a question mark."

Mr. Q took this whole page to write about himself.
What two things did we discover about him? (He is always quiet. He found a question mark.)
Mr. Q wants us to use the next page.

Have the children touch the first dotted line.
Explain that Mr. Q wants each of them to write his or her name on the line.

After the children have had an opportunity to do this, select and read a booklet. (e.g., Steven is   .)
Mr. Q knows the sentence is not finished because it does not tell what Steven is.

Discuss with the children the different words that could complete the sentence. (e.g., happy, excited, noisy, sad)
The children may find or draw a picture to finish the sentence. They may dictate a word.

Help the children complete their sentences.
Select and read several aloud.

Draw the children's attention to the second sentence and the picture.
Explain that Mr. Q wants them to find a question mark in the picture he drew.
Have them circle each question mark.

Have the children turn to the back page of the booklet.
Read aloud, "Let's read a question."

The Letter People don't know what to do with the question marks Mr. Q found.
Mr. Y had an idea.
He said whenever a sentence asks something, a question mark will be put at the end of it.
Mr. Y wrote a sentence.
It said, "Do you like to yawn?"
What did Mr. Y ask?
If a sentence asks something, what will be put at the end? (a question mark)
Follow the same procedure with the sentences. (*i.e.*, Can you wink? Did you go upsy daisy?)

Some sentences ask things.
Each sentence Mr. Q wrote on this page asks something.
Let's listen to the first sentence and find out what it asks.
Read aloud, "Can a flower sing?"
What does the sentence ask?
What did Mr. Q put at the end of the sentence? (a question mark)
When do we put a question mark at the end of a sentence? (when it asks something)
Let the children say the sentence with you.
Have a child answer the question.
Follow the same procedure with the other two sentences on the page. (*i.e.*, Can a fish swing? Can a bird fly?)

Encourage the children to take their booklets home.
Ask them to have members of their family read Mr. Q's sentences.

REVIEW

PLANNING AND PREPARATION: Huggables, M, T, F, H, N, A, B, Z, P, S, V, E; Record #5, Filmstrip—Memories of the Letter People, Part 1; paste and scissors; Duplicating Masters #154, 155 and 156A.

NOTE: This lesson may be done in two parts, reviewing M, T, F, H, N, A one day, and B, Z, P, S, V, E on the next.

REMEMBERING THE LETTER PEOPLE

Gather the children around the letter people and help them remember some of the things that happened when they first arrived. Questions such as the following will stimulate discussion.

Let's look at all these Letter People.

Which one was the first Letter Person to arrive? (Mr. M)

Who can tell us what happened at the Munching Monday Market?

Which of the Letter People was the first girl to arrive? (Miss A)

Who can show us the Letter Person who had trouble with popping Pointy Patches?

Mr. S talked to us about words that mean the same thing.

Tell Mr. S what he called his bag. It was a word that meant the same thing as *bag* but started with his sound. (sack)

What are some other things you remember about any of these Letter People?

Using Visual And Context Clues

Predicting Outcomes

Show the children the Filmstrip "Memories of the Letter People" which is coordinated with record #5, side B, band 1. A frame change is indicated by a beep on the record.

There are two frames devoted to each Letter Person. The first frame gives clues to who the Letter Person is, and the second frame actually tells the name of the Letter Person.

The children should be encouraged to say the name of the Letter Person before it is given.

TYING IT TOGETHER

Distribute Alpha Time Master #154. Scissors and paste should be available.

What Letter People do you see on the page? (Mr. M, Mr. T, Mr. F, Mr. H)

Look at the box under Mr. M, Mr. T, Mr. F and Mr. H.

What do you see there? (They each have a bag.)

What do you see on Mr. M's bag? (a Munching Mouth)

384

What do you see on Mr. T's bag? (Tall Teeth)

What is on Mr. F's bag? (Funny Feet)

What does Mr. H's bag have? (Horrible Hair)

Look at the boxes on the bottom.

What picture do you see in the first box? (tent)

Which Letter Person's sound begins the same way as *tent?* (Mr. T)

Prove it to Mr. T. (Tall Teeth — tent)

In whose bag does *tent* belong? (Mr. T's bag)

Please cut out the picture of the tent and paste it on Mr. T's bag.

Proceed as above for the rest of the pictures on the page. If the children can continue on their own, they may complete Alpha Time Masters #155 and #156A on their own.

Distribute Alpha Time Master #155.

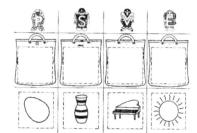

What Letter People do you see on this page? (Mr. N, Miss A, Mr. B, Mr. Z)

Look in the boxes underneath the pictures of the Letter People.

What picture do you see on the bag that belongs to Mr. N, Miss A, Mr. B, Mr. Z?

Look at the pictures at the bottom of the page.

Cut out the pictures and paste them onto the bag of the Letter Person whose sound is the same as the Letter Person.

Tell each Letter Person why you gave them the picture.

Children can also name other things that begin with each Letter Person.

Distribute copies of Alpha Time Master #156A.

Name each Letter Person you see.

What sound does Mr. P make? What sound does Mr. S, Mr. V, and Miss E make?

Where do you see their characteristics? Name the characteristic for each Letter Person.

Now look at the pictures on the bottom of the page.

Paste each picture onto the bag they belong to.

Prove to each Letter Person why you gave them the picture you did.

Children can name other things they might paste onto the bags. (e.g., Mr. P might also have a pipe for his bag.)

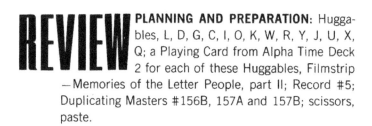

REVIEW PLANNING AND PREPARATION: Huggables, L, D, G, C, I, O, K, W, R, Y, J, U, X, Q; a Playing Card from Alpha Time Deck 2 for each of these Huggables, Filmstrip —Memories of the Letter People, part II; Record #5; Duplicating Masters #156B, 157A and 157B; scissors, paste.

NOTE: This lesson, as the previous one, may be done in two parts (i.e., discussing letters L, D, G, C, I, O, K and W one day and R, Y, J, U, X and Q on the next day).

REMEMBERING MORE LETTER PEOPLE

Have all the children form a circle. The Letter People, L, D, G, C, I and O should be part of the circle. Give six of the children the playing cards from Deck 2 which have the characteristics of the Letter People in the game (e.g., lollipop, doughnut, gum).

The Letter People thought of a new way of playing Farmer in the Dell.

Have the children decide which characteristic will start the game.

That characteristic steps into the center of the circle and all the children sing to the tune of Farmer in the Dell. For example, if the child holding the lollipop is the first in the circle, the children will sing:
Lollipop is in the dell.
Lollipop is in the dell.
Hi! Ho! the Letter-O,
Lollipop is in the dell.

The child holding the lollipop tells the children which characteristic he is going to pick and the children sing accordingly, e.g.:

Lollipop picks the itch.
Lollipop picks the itch.
Hi! Ho! the letter-O,
Lollipop picks the itch.

The game continues until all the characteristics have been picked. Then the characteristic runs back to its owner, starting with the first (lollipop).

Lollipop runs to Mr. L.
Lollipop runs to Mr. L.
Hi! Ho! the Letter-O,
Lollipop runs to Mr. L.

The child who holds the card with the lollipop on it, stands behind the Letter Person whose characteristic he is holding (Mr. L). The game continues until all characteristics are standing behind the correct Letter Person.

Show the children the filmstrip, "Memories of the Letter People, Part II" and play record #5, side B, band 2, turning the picture frame at each beep. This filmstrip recalls some of the events that revolved around the events of the Letter People.

Distribute copies of Alpha Time Master #156B.

What are the names of the Letter People you see on this page?

What are the characteristics for each Letter Person? Name them and tell where you found them.

Paste the picture that begins with the sound of the Letter Person onto his bag.

TYING IT TOGETHER

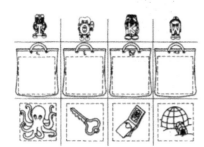

Distribute copies of Alpha Time Master #157A.

What are the names of these Letter People?

Name their characteristics and tell where you found them.

Find the picture on the bottom of the page that belongs to each Letter Person and paste it onto his bag.

Children can also draw additional objects that have the same beginning sound as the Letter People. Paste the new objects onto the bag of the Letter Person who makes the same sound.